FROM BEIRUT TO JERUSALEM

FROM BEIRUT
TO JERUSALEM

With a New Introduction
on the
40TH
ANNIVERSARY

SABRA-SHATILA
MASSACRE
September 1982

ANG SWEE CHAI

TOP
The Other Press
Kuala Lumpur

First published 1989
Grafton Books & Times Books International

This updated edition 2023
The Other Press Sdn. Bhd.
607 Mutiara Majestic, Jalan Othman
46000 Petaling Jaya, Selangor, Malaysia
www.ibtbooks.com

The Other Press is affiliated with Islamic Book Trust.

Perpustakaan Negara Malaysia   Cataloguing-in-Publication Data

Ang, Swee Chai
   From Beirut to Jerusalem / Ang Swee Chai.
   ISBN 978-967-0957-54-8
   1. Ang Swee Chai.
   2. Volunteer workers in medical care--Lebanon.
   3. Palestinian Arabs--Lebanon--Beirut.
   4. Massacres--Lebanon--Beirut.
   5. Lebanon--History--Israeli intervention,
      1982-1984--Personal narratives.
   6. Shatila (Lebanon : Refugee camp).
   7. Sabra (Lebanon : Refugee camp).
   I. Title.
   956.92044

Printed by
SS Graphic Printers (M) Sdn Bhd
Lot 7 & 8, Jalan TIB 3, Taman Industri Bolton
68100 Batu Caves, Selangor

*To the Palestinians
and their friends...*

CONTENTS

FORTY YEARS AFTER THE SABRA-SHATILA MASSACRE:
A Journey From Death To Life

The COVID pandemic had made it difficult, if not impossible, for many of us to visit our Palestinian friends living under occupation in West Bank and Gaza, or in exile in the refugee camps outside Palestine. As 2022 began, the COVID restrictions seemed to be relaxed as the number of cases decreased, and many of us from abroad were planning to participate in the Commemoration of the Fortieth Anniversary of the Sabra-Shatila Massacre in Lebanon.

Each year, on every anniversary, we congregate in Martyrs Square, the mass grave where the bodies of 1,000 to 1,700 Palestinians and Lebanese murdered during the Sabra-Shatila Massacre in 1982 were initially dumped. It was at the end of the main road of Shatila camp, Rue Sabra, where it joins the outside world. The mutilated bodies, often bullet riddled, with body parts amputated, were covered with earth and white lime, and later on with garbage. It was only after the end of the Civil War, in the nineties, that this mass grave was converted into a memorial by the Ghobeiry Municipal, Palestinian and Lebanese organizations and committees, supported by many foreign solidarity groups and governments. The garbage was cleared, trees and rose bushes planted, a proper gate built around it, and the mass grave became a dignified memorial to the bodies it

TOP LEFT: Picture of the mass grave of 1982. Homes were bulldozed and an area dug out. About 1,000 to 1,700 bodies were thrown in and earth brought in to cover the bodies. You can see the bulldozer tracks. White lime was sprinkled over the earth to dissolve the flesh and also to disinfect the area.

When I return to the mass grave in 2002, twenty years after the Massacre, it had become Martyrs Square (see text).

BOTTOM: Picture of the gate of Martyrs Square opened for the commemoration of the twenty fifth anniversary of the massacre. I was waiting with the families of the martyrs for the arrival of Palestinians from all over Lebanon as well as international delegation to come in.

17 SEP 2010

16 SEP 2008

19 SEP 2014

TOP: Palestinian kids and adults at the memorial in Martyrs Square paying their respect and solidarity.

TOP LEFT: Wreaths on memorial in Martyrs Square.

BOTTOM LEFT: Palestinian woman with pictures of her children killed in the Massacre.

Posters inside Martyr Square.

With young Palestinian children born a generation after the Massacre.

Pictures of women, solidarity groups,
brass band marching into Martyrs Square.

TOP: Marching into Martyrs Square.
BOTTOM: Palestinian women sitting under
the trees in Martyrs Square.

held—and properly named the Martyrs Square. The survivors, friends and families of those murdered—whose memories were scarred by the horrific massacre and the preceding incessant bombing of Lebanon by land, air and sea, and the siege of its capitol Beirut since the Israeli Invasion of June 1982—would meet us there each year on the anniversary of the massacre. Many of us have become part of their extended Palestinian family.

For me, it was always an extremely moving experience to stand at the camp entrance and watch Palestinian refugees from all the twelve refugee camps of Lebanon marched in procession into Martyrs square to pay homage to the dead and lay flowers every year. They carried photographs of family members killed, Palestine flags and large banners, maps of Palestine, Keffiyehs, wreaths and posters. Bands of Palestinian youngsters played the Lebanese and Palestinian national anthems as they marched into Martyrs Square. The survivors of the Tel-a-Zaatar Massacre in 1976, during which several thousand residents of the camp were murdered, had fled to live in Sabra-Shatila. Many of them were slaughtered during the Sabra-Shatila Massacre too. They were also remembered on the anniversaries of the Sabra-Shatila Massacre along with many Lebanese killed in Cana, Marwahine, Chiah and subsequent wars in Lebanon.

After the laying of wreaths and paying our respect to the dead, many of us would then leave Martyrs Square and walk into the camp along its main road, Rue Sabra, into Shatila camp to meet with the families living there. At the end of this road was Gaza Hospital. This was the reverse of the journey we, the international volunteer doctors and nurses to Gaza Hospital, took when we were forced marched out of Gaza Hospital on 18 September 1982, the last day of the massacre, by gunmen with machineguns.

Gaza Hospital was a tall building—eleven floors, with the twelfth floor still under construction in 1982. It was a majestic building and from afar looked like a solid fortress. It was the only hospital of the Palestine Red Crescent Society in Lebanon left standing while the other 8 hospitals were flattened by bombs. It provided state of the art medical and surgical treatment to everyone in need, free of charge.

But the Gaza Hospital of today is no longer a hospital. When the siege of Shatila camp started in 1985, it was invaded by hostile Lebanese militia who used the higher floors to snipe and shell into the camp, and the lower floors to torture Palestinians. The pharmacy and stores were burnt; doctors and nurses killed. At the end of the siege in 1988, when the militia withdrew, all the equipments and furnishings of the hospital were looted and stripped, leaving an empty shell into which dozens of impoverished and destitute Palestinian families fled to seek shelter after their homes in the camps were flattened. With each passing year, the structure of the building deteriorated. Yet people survived there, children were born and grew up there, despite the squalor and the deprivation. With time, the demography also changed as some Palestinian families managed to move to other refugee camps, and others such as the recently arrived Syrian refugees, and migrant workers from Bangladesh and other third world countries, moved in to occupy the space left by the Palestinians.

I was invited to a photo exhibition by a French Lebanese lady. She had juxtaposed pictures of the old Gaza Hospital with bright white patient wards, and specialist clinics with the current Gaza Hospital Buildings which had become a tall vertical squat for dozens of families. She was highly educated and lived in an up-market area in East Beirut where Lebanese Christian elites lived. She accidentally passed Rue Sabra on business one day and her curiosity drew her to "explore" what was in this tall dilapidated building. She was shocked and scandalised to discover the story of Gaza Hospital and the massacre. She made friends with the people living in it and listened to them.

She got to know a Palestinian family whose son was about to graduate as an engineer. She brought her own son of about the same age to visit them. He was about to graduate as an engineer too. Her son reacted so badly on entering the building as he was

1

PHOTOS:

1. Gaza Hospital under ICRC protection in 1982.
2. Gaza Hospital shelled in 1982, doctor's residence on sixth floor destroyed.
3. Top floors of Gaza Hospital bombed by war planes 1982.
4. Gaza Hospital attacked and occupied, photo during a short ceasefire in 1985.

2
3 4

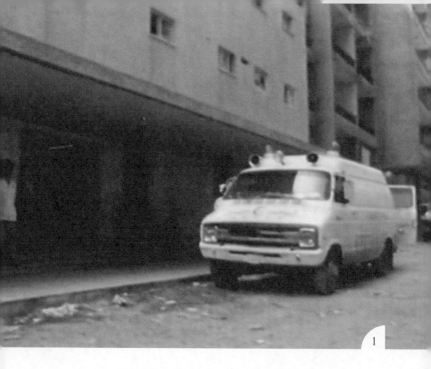

1

Photos of Gaza Hospital courtesy
of Suttvuess film "*Gaza Hospital*".

2

3

PHOTOS:
1. Gaza Hospital before the Israeli Invasion of 1982.
2. Gaza Hospital hit by multiple shells during the Camp War 1985-88.
3. Gaza Hospital as a vertical refugee centre 2004.
3. Gaza Hospital as a refugee centre view from the courtyard.

4

Gaza Hospital, a dilapidated building
coming into view at the end of Rue Sabra 2004.

Photo courtesy of Suttvuess film "*Gaza Hospital*".

overwhelmed by the stale air, heat and smell that she was forced to tell him to pull himself together. She told him that no matter what he thought of the state of the building, it was the home of many human beings and he got to be respectful. After meeting the Palestinian family she told her son that they both would soon be engineers. But he being Lebanese would be able to find a job in Lebanon, and also choose to work abroad. But for the Palestinian young man, the laws of Lebanon forbade him to work as an engineer and being a refugee he would have no passport to work abroad.

She asked me what I thought of the current state of Gaza Hospital—or Gaza Buildings. I swallowed hard and told her that I thought of Gaza Hospital as a mother. She spent her youth saving lives and treating diseases. She was beautiful and strong. But she was so badly wounded that she was no longer able to carry out that role. But even in her wounded state, she continued to protect and shelter the poorest of the poor with what was left of her body. Just as she told her son—I also do not look at the squalor and the stench—but how it is still home to so many in need.

Every anniversary is a painful occasion. Some will not join as they could not bear to re-open the old wounds. Others weep at Martyrs Square for their loved ones as they did when they first learnt of their death in 1982. But the presence of young Palestinians and children always brought me to tears. They have an extremely difficult life journey ahead. Yet their presence affirms that Palestine is very much alive. They have grown up in the dark and long shadow of wars, massacres, deprivation and squalor but had carried Palestine in their heart and soul with such dignity. The anniversary of the Sabra-Shatila Massacre is a rendezvous I have kept annually. We must honour the martyrs and renew our commitment to justice and our support for the Palestinians. We must not forget.

For me, who have been imprisoned in, and deported multiple times from Israel, the passionate longing for "Next Year in

Jerusalem" has become a cry from the depth of my heart, but it can only be fulfilled in a free Palestine.

I remember being under arrest with my colleague Dr Asif Chaudry in 2014, waiting to be taken to an Israeli detention centre sarcastically called "the hotel" by the Israeli guards. We were en route to Gaza answering a call for help from doctors at the height of Operation Protective Edge. That Israeli military operation had killed more than 2,022 civilians and wounded at least 12,000 of which 5,000 were children. More than a thousand of those children were disabled permanently. While waiting, we met a Palestinian man who had become a Dutch national, sobbing loudly. He had flown in from Amsterdam to see his eldest brother who was dying in a hospital in Jerusalem. His father died when he was very young, and this brother was a de facto father to him. He had lived in the Netherlands for a long time and this was his first return to the Jerusalem of his ancestral family, childhood and birth. But the immigration officers insisted on deporting him since as a Palestinian he was not entitled to enter Israel through Tel Aviv Airport. He was only allowed to visit Jerusalem making his way from Jordan across the bridge over the River Jordan. He was pleading with them just to let him in for only one evening to see his brother in hospital and he would leave the following day. Jerusalem is 66 kilometers from Tel Aviv and roughly an hour drive from the airport. To be deported out from Tel Aviv and to return via Jordan across the bridge over River Jordan would take at least a couple of days and he would not be able to bid farewell to his dying brother. They deported him nevertheless.

In 2018, while serving as a volunteer doctor on the Freedom Flotilla, Al-Awda, heading for Gaza, with much needed medicines and dressings for the hundreds of unarmed demonstrators shot by Israeli snipers, we were captured by the Israeli Navy in international waters. Our boat, medicines, and all personnel on board were forcibly taken to Ashdod, a port in Israel. From Ashdod, the crew and all on board were taken overland to Givon Prison. The boat was indefinitely detained in

Ashdod; medicines and our personal belongings looted. We were released from prison and deported, thanks to the intervention of our embassies, but only after they had stripped us of our possessions which had never been returned.

With successive imprisonments and deportations, I am forced to accept that my fate has become like the 6 million Palestinian exiles in the refugee camps outside Palestine. Like them, I am not able to set foot on Palestine, but Palestine lives in my heart. So next year in Martyrs Square Shatila becomes a yearly homage, till we meet in Jerusalem.

This year, I would not be able to make our rendezvous in Shatila, having been diagnosed with an aggressive and malignant cancer. But I have kept the Palestinians in my heart for the last forty years and if I fail to survive this illness, I will continue loving them—in death as in life.

As we approach the 40th anniversary of the Sabra-Shatila Massacre, the situation in the West Bank and Gaza and for the Palestinians living in refugee camps in countries neighboring Israel could not be more dark and grim. The constant arrests, house demolitions and killing of unarmed Palestinians in the West Bank and the regular bombing of blockaded Gaza are rarely reported in the mainstream media anymore. Funding for Palestinian refugees is also in jeopardy. The Gulf's normalization with Israel resulted in severe funding cuts to UNRWA. Fourteen U.S. Republican senators are also trying to erase Palestinian refugees by redefining who is a refugee and conditioning aid to UNRWA. Many people will not understand that for the Palestinians, their refugee status is their only claim to humanity. They are a stateless people the world tries to forget. But their refugee status gives them their right of return, and its removal will rob them of this sacrosanct right.

The six million refugees living outside historic Palestine (now called Israel) are all but forgotten. Many of us have allowed them to fade in our consciousness. Yet every Palestinian killed—be they the recent 256 Palestinians, including 66 children, killed by Israeli bombardment of Gaza in

2021; or the 2,022 killed, including 526 children, in Operation Protective Edge in 2014; the 1,400 deaths, including 300 children, in Operation Cast Lead in 2008-9; or those in the Great March of Return—cannot be forgotten. Likewise the daily death toll of Palestinians killed by settlers and Israeli soldiers continue to hurt us deeply.

These deaths wrench out the hearts of their family and those who love them, leaving large gaping wounds which have not healed. There is no healing as the violence against the Palestinians is ongoing. There is no post-traumatic stress syndrome; there is only ongoing traumatic onslaughts and repeated wounding of their bodies and souls. Every child born in Gaza after 2008 has experienced four major military assaults with intensive bombardment, deaths and injuries. Two million Palestinians are held under blockade in Gaza since 2007 converting Gaza into a large prison whose "inmates" are bombed and not allowed to escape.

This year also marks the 74th anniversary of the *Nakba*— and the 105th anniversary of the Balfour Declaration, drafted with support of U.S. Justice Louis Brandeis and two other Americans who were part of the then-nascent Zionist movement. In his very short letter to Rothschild, on 2nd November 1917, Lord Arthur Balfour had spelt out the British Government's position of "favouring the establishment of a national homeland for the Jewish people in Palestine." The Declaration was only 67 words in length, but an effective death warrant to Palestine! Britain was on its ascent in colonial power, and this Declaration usher in the giving away of the homes of 1.5 million Palestinians and wiping Palestine off the world map.

�����

SABRA AND SHATILA MASSACRE

This year marks the 40th anniversary of the invasion of Lebanon and the Sabra-Shatila massacre of 1982. Many readers of this chapter were not born then. Some will want to bury these events;

others simply to forget. But I want to remember the Palestinians who taught me profound lessons about justice and struggle. I will honor their memories and share them with you.

Forty years ago, I arrived as a volunteer surgeon with the British Christian Aid team to war-torn Lebanon, ravaged by Israel's invasion. I was a Zionist Christian then who believed that the Palestine Liberation Organisation (PLO) was a bunch of terrorists who were using Lebanon as a base for destroying Israel, and that Israel had no choice but to invade Lebanon to flush out the PLO. I had supported Israel and never knew Palestinians existed as a people. My views had changed since.

I was posted to the Palestine Red Crescent Society (PRCS) and worked in its Gaza Hospital in Sabra-Shatila. Eight of the nine hospitals run by the PRCS and thirteen clinics were flattened by bombs. That invasion killed thousands and destroyed homes, livelihoods, hospitals, libraries, factories, schools and offices. It also split 14,000 Palestinian families through the deportation of their beloved husbands and sons and brothers, euphemistically called the "evacuation of the PLO" in exchange for a ceasefire. The U.S. Habib Peace Plan guaranteed the protection of the non-PLO civilians left behind. But the evacuation only paved the way for the land invasion of Lebanon in September by hundreds of Israeli tanks.

A contingent of tanks proceeded to seal all the escape routes from Sabra-Shatila refugee camp so that the brutal and infamous Sabra-Shatila massacre could be conducted over the days of Sept. 15-18, 1982. At least 3,000 unarmed and defenseless Palestinians and their Lebanese neighbors were murdered by Israel's ally, the Lebanese Christian militia, trained and armed by Israel. Many more were abducted and disappeared. No one came to defend the helpless children, women and old people from being slaughtered. The Multinational Peace Keeping Force had deserted them. Many were tortured and women raped before being killed in those three dark days and nights.

When the photographs of the heaps of dead bodies in the camp alleys were published, there was worldwide outrage and condemnation. But international attention was short-lived. The victims' families and survivors were soon left alone to plod on with their lives and to relive the memories of the tragedies of the massacre, the preceding ten weeks of intensive land, air and sea bombardment, the blockade of Beirut during the invasion, and the breaking up of their families through the forced deportation of 14,000 bread-winners and leaders of their Palestinian society. Every family had lost loved ones through the invasion, the evacuation and the massacre. Many of them were also wounded. The survivors were left to rebuild their shattered lives and homes, bring up their children while burying the dead in mass graves. The world moved on and they were forgotten—dead to the consciousness of the international community.

Since then, the everyday downward spiral of hopelessness, poverty and despair, made worse by the sense of being forgotten and abandoned, worsens. They just do not excite the headlines of mainstream media anymore. As someone close to the Palestinians in Lebanon I would ask   where is solidarity and where is hope for them?

Yet, when I talk to Palestinians in Lebanon directly, they rarely complain about being forgotten. Their first concern is about occupied Palestine. They live for Palestine. They know that Lebanon will make sure they cannot settle and has progressively made it more and more difficult for them to live in dignity in Lebanon. It is like a punishment for having been expelled from Palestine into a country that had enough of them, and therefore would want to get rid of them by making life unbearable and unlivable. Their only option is to go back to Palestine, but their enshrined right of return has never been honored.

Twelve official United Nations Relief and Works Agency for Palestine Refugees in the Near East (UNRWA) refugee camps in Lebanon were established to host the initial 110,000 persons who fled to Lebanon— they were some of the 750,000 refugees from Palestine expelled to make way for Israel in 1948. Since then, four generations have lived and died in those refugee camps. Children were born refugees, grew up refugees and died refugees on those little plots of Lebanese soil which make the finite, rigid borders of the official camps. The same plots for the 110,000 refugees from 1948 now have to accommodate a population grown to half a million just by natural increase, together with the influx of Palestinian refugees from Syria. Simple arithmetic will conclude that the camps' population density has increased fivefold!

Their situation is dire—no right to work, no right to own a home, hungry, despised, a typical refugee camp squashing 100,000 persons into 1.7 square kilometers (0.657 sq miles) to live, die and be buried. Their survival as dignified human beings is at stake and must be supported and safeguarded by all of us.

I remember vividly the morning of 18 September, 1982, when Ellen Siegel and I, as part of our 22-member team of international medical volunteers, were forced out of Gaza Hospital at machine-gun point, leaving behind 30 critically wounded patients, many of them children.

We had struggled non-stop for three days and nights to save the many dozens of wounded brought to Gaza hospital. Some died while awaiting treatment, and filled the mortuary. We ran out of blood, medicine and food. About 2,000 terrified camp residents fled into our hospital hoping to escape being slaughtered by militia breaking into homes and shooting everyone. Our Hospital Director received news that our hospital was no longer safe as the militia had invaded a neighbouring hospital killing doctors, nurses and patients. She told the people seeking safety to leave immediately. She told us to discharge patients who could leave the night before as we got news that our hospital would be invaded anytime, but the critically wounded on life-support could not leave. As we were forced to leave at gunpoint that morning, I was desperate and thought our patients would be killed once we left them. At that point, Louise Norman, a Swedish nurse, and a German medical student insisted on staying with the patients. It was their selfless courage which saved the lives of this group of patients.

The children of Shatila.
"We are not afraid".

I looked for them on every subsequent trip to Lebanon,
but never found them. I think they must have perished,
but I will always re-visit their picture for inspiration
when the going is tough. Their beauty and courage as
they confront destruction and death always live in me.

With guns pointing at us we walked along the main road of the camp. Dozens, perhaps hundreds of unarmed camp people—women, old men and children—were rounded up by militia. I remember the terror in their eyes. A desperate young mother passed me her baby—so warm and cuddly. At gunpoint she was forced to take him back. Both were killed, together with those rounded up, after we were taken away. Homes were bulldozed by large military bulldozers.

Those who sought to annihilate Palestinians thought—surely this will put an end to them! We have solved the "Palestinian problem" in Lebanon, and they will never raise their heads again.

A couple of days later, I returned to visit Sabra and Shatila. There were mass graves, decaying bodies, broken homes and grieving relatives. There was despair, desolation, piercing screams and a vale of tears.

But it was not over. Among the children who made it, including many homeless orphans, the spirit of defiance was very much alive. As they lined up for me to take their photograph, they raised their hands in the victory sign saying, "We are not afraid. Let the Israelis come." Behind them were their homes bombed and shelled to rubble, in the foreground decaying bodies yet to be identified. The air was filled with the stench of decaying human flesh. But between death and destruction were the destitute Palestinian children defiantly staking their right to be part of humanity.

They were my first green shoots of life!

This year I was unable to join the commemoration of the fortieth anniversary of the massacre in Beirut because of my cancer. I fought my isolation and ill health by writing, speaking online and sending what I wrote for publication. Only three articles were published. What I wrote are just very short pieces limited by publishers to around a thousand words each, but that was better than nothing. The justice sought by the Palestinians has not been found. But the first step to justice is to give voice to the victims, and all of us must do this. We will speak up.

From Death to Life: Forty years after the Sabra Shatila Massacrehttps://www.wrmea.org/kar8q

https://www.counterpunch.org/2022/09/02/remembering-the-sabra-shatila-massacre-forty-years-later/

https://www.middleeasteye.net/opinion/lebanon-sabra-shatila-massacre-terror-defiance

What happened forty years ago is now replaced by the reality of a whole younger generation born after the massacre. They are courageous and steadfast and meeting them gives me hope that they will and can bring a Palestine of freedom and justice to fruition in their generation.

Maybe next year I can be there at the entrance of the Martyrs Square like years bygone, and watch them march into the Square with banners, flowers, musical bands, Palestine flags in lengthy procession to pay their respects to the martyrs. The young children who survived the massacre would now be in their fifth and sixth decades of life. They are now parents and even grandparents. They had brought their children to the Commemoration every year. It has been a very difficult journey for them. May their children be the generation that will be refugees no more. They know their roots, where they came from, and where they are going, and no matter what happen, I know they will get there. As I approach the end of my own life, I must record for them my own witness in gratitude for being able to be part of their family. Even if I might not be there when they return to Palestine, right now in my heart, and my minds' eye I have already seen them reclaiming their full rights in their homeland. Only then can the wounds begin to heal, and true rejoicing take place in a land of justice, peace, freedom, dignity, security and love. And there will be endless celebration! And the laughter of their children and their bright future will be the reward for all their sacrifice.

Dr Ang Swee Chai
September 2022

ACKNOWLEDGEMENTS

Writing this book has been no easy task: it has involved my going back over the past six years, reliving certain very painful memories and reopening old wounds. I want to thank Steve Savage for his patience, support and encouragement; as well as his editorial advice, without which this book would be totally unreadable. My thanks also to everyone else at Grafton Books.

As well as the MAP volunteers, supporters and staff who are mentioned in the book, I want to thank those whose names are not in, either for reasons of personal safety, or by their own choice, or just from lack of space. It is they who are the true friends of the Palestinians. It is they who slave away so that the medical programme can continue.

My fellow MAP board members, who have had to put up with me ever since we were formed, especially Major Derek Cooper, our President, and his wife Lady Pamela, David Wolton, our Chairman, and Dr Riyad Kreishi, the acting Director of MAP during Dr Rafiq Husseini's absence – I thank them for their enormous contributions to my understanding and their much-valued guidance.

The Palestinians always try to thank their friends. Now I want to thank them for being so strong, for being a constant source of inspiration to me, especially in the depths of despair. Above all, I thank the Palestine Red Crescent Society, for all it has taught me, and for making me, I hope, a better doctor and human being.

I also thank my Jewish friends who encourage me to speak up and not be fearful.

My parents and family in Singapore, whom I have postponed seeing for years, I am grateful for their patience and forgiveness. Francis Khoo, related to me incidentally by marriage, I have to thank thrice. First, for his untiring efforts in bringing MAP to birth. Second, for his advice and criticism during the writing of this book. Third, for not putting me out even though I caused him many anxious and sleepless nights while I was out in Beirut.

Professor Jack Stevens, Alan Apley, J. M. Walker, R. C. Buchanan, Fred Heatley, Tom Wadsworth, Ian Pinder, Jo Pooley, Peter Robson, Ron Sutton, Kevin Walsh and the rest of my senior orthopaedic colleagues and teachers who not only trained me, but fought the prejudice of the surgical establishment against small coloured women becoming surgeons, making it possible for me to pursue a career in orthopaedic surgery.

Lastly, thanks to many people from all over the world who continue to live in faith, hope and love. Without them, this journey from Beirut to Jerusalem would not have taken place.

INTRODUCTION

My parents first met in a Japanese internment camp during the
Second World War. My mother was only 19 years old when
she was taken prisoner. She was a school teacher who gave up
her work to become a community organiser for the 'Oppose
the Japanese Invasion' campaign. My father was a young
Chinese language editor of a paper which took a similar
position.

Mother acquired her strong views at an early age. Her
father was extremely conservative and never believed women
should have schooling, claiming it made them bad housewives.
Indeed, he had three, none of whom could read or write.
Mother would have none of this and at the early age of seven,
decided to register herself with the headmaster of the
neighbourhood school. It was a *fait accompli* by the time
grandfather discovered this and he was flabbergasted.

When grandfather reached the age of 60, he decided to
take a fourth wife. Mother was furious and was even more
livid when her own mother supported the decision. She decided
to have none of this and packed her bags and left home.
Grandfather, who always held a soft spot for his independent

young daughter, could not dissuade her. His flood of tears and pleadings went unheeded.

But being a woman in a man's world had some advantages, though for the wrong reasons. When the Japanese invaded, informers said mother was an important member of the resistance. She was taken in, badly tortured and never confessed. Her life was spared because the Japanese interrogators could not believe a woman could have held such a key role.

When her chidlren were grown-up, mother would tell us, 'It's not as bad as it sounds. The first time, you're scared you'll give away your friends. But there comes a point when you pass out. Once that happens, you cannot feel pain anymore. Once you have learnt that, you can beat your torturers.'

After her torture sessions, mother was locked up in the Outram Road prison in Singapore. Conditions there were atrocious and many prisoners died from torture, starvation and disease. There appeared not to have been segregation, and at Outram, she met Ang Peng Liat, my father.

Father had also run away from home. But unlike mother, he was a first generation Chinese and fled southern China to escape an arranged marriage with a girl he had never met. His father ran his home with iron discipline and would not accept 'no' for an answer.

Father found his feet quickly and, by the time he was 20, edited a Chinese daily paper. War broke out and he mobilised his paper and public opinion against the invasion. His paper was soon shut down and he found himself in Outram Road prison.

When peace finally came following Japan's surrender, the prison gates were opened. People flooded in to meet the internees and greeted them with flowers. My parents, four years older, settled down to have a family.

The immediate postwar years in Singapore and the rest of what was then Malaya, were marked by economic depression.

poverty, hunger and sickness for all except the wealthy. My two elder brothers died in their infancy from malnutrition and infectious diseases. Four decades later, mother still weeps when she thinks of them.

Fortunately, mother soon found herself pregnant again. This time, she returned to her hometown of Penang Island, to have her baby. It was a long and difficult labour. When the midwife held out an eight-and-a half pound girl to an exhausted young woman, everyone was relieved. A baby girl was of less value than a boy in traditional Chinese families, but a tough little granddaughter was still definitely better than no grandchild at all. So grandfather immediately offered me as a godchild to the Chinese Goddess of Mercy, *Kuan Yin*, and asked her blessing and protection to ensure I would escape the fate of my two elder brothers.

My early childhood was spent in my grandfather's house at Penang's district of Ayer Itam. Mother wanted me to be nursed in his spacious rural house surrounded by lush tropical plants. Mother's mother was then the only wife of his left alive and she felt Penang's natural beauty was probably the best place to escape the effects of the trauma of the war's aftermath.

Grandfather had sobered in his old age and greeted the arrival of my brother Lee Cyn, a year later, with equal delight. Boys may have been more valuable than girls for others, but his granddaughter was different. So Lee Cyn and I were treated equally and had a very happy childhood in Penang, surrounded by trees and flowers, grown-ups doting on us, doves, a black-and-white dog and a large ginger cat.

I can still remember the large ginger cat. It had a very large head and plenty of affection. I seem to be surrounded by cats and even in our current little flat in London, we have a 12-year-old *'ang moh'* tabby with a very Chinese name, 'Meowee'. But that ginger cat was the only one I have ever met in my life who could sit patiently while I stole its dinner. My grandmother nearly fainted when she found me on all fours eating Ginger's food and in his little wooden hut built for him by grandfather. There was just room for the two of us and Ginger just watched and purred.

Father's work soon took mother, Lee Cyn and I to Singapore a few years later. We left Penang and our doting grandparents to move into a two-bedroom, first floor flat just off a busy trunk-road at Upper Serangoon. Cars and lorries stirred up dust and fumes day and night and we all got our loud voices trying to talk through the din.

Father worked long and hard to feed his growing family. Mother made sure her little kids were subjected to a strict routine. We were given a timetable which covered our every waking moment, copies of which were posted by our bedside, in the sitting room and in the kitchen. Story hour meant that mother would read us novels and short stories by Guy de Maupassant, Oscar Wilde and Edmondo de Amicis. Soon we graduated to Tolstoy, Gogol and Turgenev. She read them to us in Chinese and I never realised until much later that the writers wrote them in different European languages. Comics were absolutley forbidden and so were Enid Blyton adventures and pop music.

During playtime, Lee Cyn and I found ourselves making paper boats and wishing all the time we could sail away in them to visit our grandparents in Penang. But our strict upbringing paid off in schooling terms and enabled us to top school examinations collecting prizes and medals.

Swee Kim and Swee Hua, my sisters, soon arrived and both Lee Cyn and I had to stop making our paper boats. Suddenly I became 'Big Sis' and he, 'Second Brother'. The two younger sisters made us a real family and the flat a real home.

Lee Cyn and I soon went to a primary school nearby. Going to the Kwong Avenue Primary School and coming back was a pleasant walk each day. After mother's rigorous timetable, school became fun and easy-going. Those school years were great years. I made friends, read new books, acted in school concerts and plays and, of course, received prizes each year.

I can still remember many of my primary school classmates. Hatifah was the fastest sprinter. She caught up with me recently when I received a letter from her in February 1989, following the launch of my British edition of this book. She currently lives in West Germany and had read an article I wrote which appeared in the German weekly magazine *Der Spiegel*, about my work for the Palestinians in the occupied territories of Gaza. She reminded me how thrilled I was when Sputnik went into orbit in 1957 and how I vowed to be a scientist one day when Yuri Gargarin became the first cosmonaut a few years later.

In primary school, I saw the world an exciting place and science was my passion. But I was also aware many important things were happening in the then Malaya and Singapore. The British were ending their rule in Singapore and I remember how we elected our very own government in 1959 for the first time. As a 10-year-old, party politics made very little sense, but the thought that Singaporeans were having their own rule and their own national anthem was simply grand. Everyone was a Singaporean or a Malaysian, whether their ancestors came from India, China or Indonesia.

After the entrance examination I found myself at Raffles Girls' School. Life was less idyllic and I was soon put in my place. My classmates were all extremely bright and for the very first time, I found I had to study hard to keep myself among the top in class. So I had to allow no time for socials, parties and dating. Music and reading were my passions but I also foolishly fell in love with the game of chess. Chess was extremely time-consuming – what with tournaments and practising, I found I had to cut down on my music lessons and reading if I wanted to be good at the game.

At secondary school, my interest in science grew. But it took a new turn. I still found the world fascinating and the various scientific disciplines stimulating. Soon I realised science was not neutral and had a role to serve the needs of society. I cannot remember how this came about but it must have come from the career guidance programme given by the Ministry of Education. We were told at school that 'science, to be meaningful, must be channelled to alleviating suffering and poverty. I took that message seriously and began to ask how science could help and soon found myself asking questions about poverty itself, about hunger, bad housing, disease and illiteracy. Some of my close friends soon began to worry about my very eccentric 'philosophical' questions.

After my 'O' and 'A' Levels, I chose to study medicine at the University of Singapore. I thought medical science could do a great deal. Lee Cyn followed in my footsteps and father had to work day and night to pay our tuition fees.

I proceeded to do a masters' degree in public health and community health medicine and then an FRCS (England) to become an orthopaedic surgeon. Academic degrees and gold medals merely gave me the chance to apply medical technology. Surgery also combined my three passions: medicine, kitchen work (using knives and cutting up meat) and sewing. These were skills women were equally adept at as their male colleagues.

At medical school, I was also converted into Christianity. My parents, having gone through much suffering and seen much death, chose to remain 'areligious' but always insisted their children had the right to choose their own faiths.

My Christianity made me ask more questions about my role as a doctor. The skills we possess and the knowledge we hold, allow us to make plenty of money. They also gave us prestige. But doctors live in society and must serve its members.

On 29 January 1977, I married Francis Khoo, a Catholic lawyer, who was also asking many questions about his role in society. As a Baba of many generations in Singapore and more comfortable in Malay than in Mandarin, he was fiercely proud about his country and region. He told me, and still does, that we must never adopt the footloose mentality of the migrant. 'We must set roots wherever we are, otherwise there would be no Singapore and no Malaysia. Otherwise we become neither here nor there; we should be both here and there.'

Ang Swee Chai
February, 1989

PART I
Journey to Beirut
Summer 1982

===============

CHAPTER 1

The summer of 1982 was our sixth summer in Britain. My husband, Francis, had left our home country of Singapore, and I joined him in London. It took us some time to get settled, but by 1982 we were living in a small flat in the city centre.

Night after night, the television news bulletins featured the Israeli invasion of Lebanon. What was particularly horrifying was the way Beirut was being attacked from the air. Francis and I sat and watched Israeli planes dropping bombs on to blocks of flats: they were bombing densely populated, civilian areas in the capital of Lebanon. News programmes showed pictures of high-rise blocks along the Beirut sea-front: they reminded us uncannily of our old flat in Marine Vista, back home in Singapore. There were horrible scenes of wounded and dead people, many of whom were children. Then came the news of the Israeli blockade of Beirut. Medical aid was denied to the wounded; the city was denied water, electricity and food.

Lebanon and Beirut were unfamiliar names to me, but Israel was not: my church had taught me that the children of Israel were the chosen people of God. Many of my Christian friends held that the gathering of the Jews from all over the world into the State of Israel was the fulfilment of scriptural prophecies.

1

Israel had my support for other reasons. In London, I had spent hours watching television programmes which showed how appallingly the Jewish people had suffered under the Nazis. Both of my parents had suffered at the hands of the Nazis' allies, the Japanese Imperial Army. As a refugee in a foreign country, I understood what it meant to be stateless. The creation of the State of Israel, giving all Jews a home free from persecution, seemed to me to be an act of justice – even one of divine justice.

The newspapers said that the Israeli invasion of Lebanon had made a hundred thousand people homeless and had killed fourteen thousand people, and this upset me terribly. I could not understand why Israel had done this. There had to be a good reason for it.

Most of the news stories in Britain depicted the invasion as an attempt by Israel to flush out the Palestine Liberation Organisation – or PLO – from its bases in Lebanon. All I knew about the PLO was that it was an Arab group which hijacked passenger jets, planted bombs and hated Jews.

Some of my Christian elders told me that the Palestinians were the descendants of the Philistines of the Old Testament, and everyone knew that the giant Goliath was a conquering Philistine who terrorised his opponents. The tale of David and Goliath had been one of my favourites when I was a Sunday School teacher: I loved telling my kids how little David brought down the mighty Goliath. (I am a couple of inches under five foot tall myself.)

From the news coverage, however, it looked as though Israel had turned into Goliath: a swaggering giant bringing destruction, terror and death to neighbouring Lebanon. An Israeli leader told the press that much as he regretted the casualties, to make an omelette one first had to crack eggs.

Crack eggs? That remark shocked me. What kind of 'omelette' was Israel trying to make, and were the people in Lebanon eggs to be cracked? It was clear from the news reports that nearly all of the people who had been killed, wounded or made homeless were civilians, many of them women and children. Bombing civilians is a disgraceful way to make war. The bombs fell for days: on playgrounds, cemeteries, houses, hospitals, schools and factories. Even International Red Cross ships bringing food and medical supplies to Beirut were targets.

From what I heard, I concluded that nobody cared, and that God had turned away from Lebanon. Seeing the wounds of the people in Lebanon hurt me, firstly because they had been inflicted by Israel, secondly because I am a Christian and thirdly because I am a doctor. I could not understand how Israeli planes could drop phosphorus bombs on to civilians in such a crowded city. I asked God for an explanation, asked Him to grant me understanding.

Then one day in August 1982 I heard from a colleague – Bryan Mayou – that an international S.O.S. had been sent out for an orthopaedic surgeon to treat war victims in Beirut. God had answered my prayers: as an orthopaedic surgeon, I knew what I had to do. For the first time that summer since the war had broken out, I felt at peace.

CHAPTER 2

When I had been unsure about what to do with my life, my brother had nudged me towards medicine. When I had been shocked by the gruesome reality of medical school, my parents had persuaded me to stick to it. When community medicine had got me into hot water for being too outspoken for Singapore, orthopaedic surgery had provided me with a bolthole. When Francis and I had to leave Singapore, I wanted to work as a surgeon in Britain, but found plenty of white male prejudice in the British medical establishment. I got my way, and became a Fellow of the Royal College of Surgeons. Now I was officially an orthopaedic surgeon, it was time to put my skills to good use.

When I first applied to go to Beirut, the Christian charity in Britain which organised the volunteers did not want to send me, because I did not have a passport. All I had was a 'British Travel Document'. The charity was afraid that I would not be able to enter Lebanon without a passport. Francis spoke to the British Foreign Office, and they assured us that although my travel document would not normally entitle me to the protection of British diplomatic or consular representatives abroad, they would be as helpful as possible if I ran into trouble and needed help

4

from the British Ambassador in Beirut. Armed with this verbal assurance, I managed to persuade the Christian charity to take me on. Francis next spoke to Colonel Gray of the British Red Cross to make sure that I was experienced enough for the job. Colonel Gray was delighted by the news, and wished Francis the best of luck in his venture. It was a while before he realised that it was not Francis who was planning to go to Beirut.

It did not take long to get ready to travel. I resigned from my hospital in Britain, packed my bags and set off for the airport. Because the Israelis had closed down Beirut International Airport, we had to fly to Larnaca in Cyprus and then take a ferryboat from there. A number of us flew out at the same time – I was by no means the only doctor to volunteer to go to Beirut. Altogether, there were about a hundred medics from all over the world. We had different colours of skin and practised various religions – Christianity, Islam, Judaism and others. We had all left our homes in the hope of being able to help the wounded people of Lebanon. In the ensuing months, some of us were to become very close friends.

August was peak holiday time, and the jet took off from London's Heathrow Airport packed with carefree tourists bound for sunny Cyprus and its beaches. After a few hours sharing the plane with these rather strange fellow-travellers, I stepped out of the plane at Larnaca Airport.

In some ways Cyprus reminded me of South East Asia, and I soon found myself thinking of home. When I decided to become a doctor back in Singapore, this caused a difference of opinion between my parents. My mother was thrilled to bits at the thought of her daughter becoming a doctor, but my father was in favour of a musical career. I got my way, and resolutely set off for my first day at medical school.

What nobody told me was that I would be spending my first day there dissecting human cadavers preserved in formalin. The anatomy dissection room looked like the set of a horror movie, and the smell of formalin was so pungent I nearly suffocated: it went up my nose, burning the lining, and made my eyes water.

There were twenty-two women in our year, and ninety-eight men: we were put into groups of six, and each group was allotted one dead body to dissect. The poor cadaver was going to be cut up bit by bit over the academic year. Pieces of mutilated limbs and sliced-up lungs, brains and hearts, which had been left by our predecessors, were lying about on dissection tables, in basins and even on the floor.

On dissecting table number one was my group's cadaver. I had a look at it. The label said, 'Male, unknown identity, unclaimed.' Then the Professor of Anatomy came in: he was loud and lively, and wielded a human thighbone, which he was using as a pointer.

'Hello, small miss!' said the professor. With a grin on his face, he lightly tapped me on the top of my head with the thighbone. Startled, I nearly let out a scream, for I had never been touched by a bit of a dead human being before. Fortunately for me, there was a loud bang and the whole class turned round to look. Two of the male students had collapsed on to the floor. That saved the day, and the class was adjourned while my two classmates were lugged outside to the field for some fresh air and a drink of water.

What with all the commotion, I got away. When I reached home, I told my mother that I was through with medicine. However much I wanted to devote my life to the relief of disease and suffering, my disposition was too delicate for me to confront death and decay every day.

My poor mother was terribly upset to hear this. She reminded me of the progress made by women in the twentieth century: only fifty years earlier, Chinese villagers had drowned baby girls quite regularly in rivers. 'You have so much to give others if only you seize the opportunity,' she said. 'Here you are wanting to throw it all away just because you refuse to overcome your fear of dead bodies! Since when have I brought you up to be such a weakling?

You disappoint me!' Mother could not go on: she was crying.

In that moment, I realised how hard things had been for her. She had given up her career as a teacher and writer twice. The first time was to organise resistance against the Japanese military occupation, and she ended up in an internment camp as a result; the second time was to bring us up. She had sacrificed a great deal for us children, and she had given us a lot as well. Where my schooling had taught me to read and write, my mother had educated me. Through her, I learnt about the poverty and suffering of ordinary people and the degradation and abuse of women. From her, I received a vision of life as it ought to be. I owed her a lot. But she did not manage to change my mind about giving up medicine.

Father took it differently. When he was told that I would not have anything further to do with medical school, he contented himself with calmly informing me that I had broken my agreement with him, and asking me if I would like to consider giving him back the year's fees which he had just paid. I was back in that awful dissection room the next day.

After a few weeks I really liked the Professor of Anatomy, and soon I was so at home in the dissection room that I would be eating sandwiches and drinking coffee while at the same time examining bits of the cadaver.

As a 'houseman' or 'intern', I soon realised there was nothing special about being a doctor. Medicine is just the application of technology so as to mitigate disease and pain. A doctor is a technician trained to deal with certain problems. Noble thoughts about saving lives soon go out the window: we apply 'know-how' and 'training' to medical emergencies and difficult diseases, and try to find solutions. Other people fix broken-down cars, or unblock sinks. They are technicians too.

I thoroughly enjoyed both my medical studies and working in the Singapore General Hospital. I was fully occupied throughout my waking hours. Life revolved around the wards, the out-patient clinics, clinical conferences, operating theatres and the library. My social circle consisted of colleagues and patients, and occasionally members of my family. The hospital became my place of work and play, of joy and sorrow, of success and failure – it was where I lived, and it became my whole world. That is how any young doctor working a hundred-hour week manages to stay alive.

On those rare days when I was free and not 'on call', I ventured out of the innards of the hospital. Sunlight, clouds, open air, then the pavement beneath my feet: they all felt unreal at first. Large shopping centres with brilliantly-coloured window displays in department stores, ladies with fashionable clothes and classy make-up, busy traffic and crowded buses, flashing lights, pop music blaring out of shops: it was a strange world to step into.

Singapore is an extremely hectic city – urban, modern, commercialised, industrialised and often electronic. People are always in a great hurry. Delicious meals are gulped down in eating places. That might be the right way to treat hospital food, but out in the city where our local food is so varied and rich, not to spend a moment or two savouring it is a crime.

To stop the place becoming a concrete jungle, the Government has embarked on an extensive tree-planting campaign to turn Singapore into a 'garden city', as the tourist promotion board puts it. There are large parks and gardens, which make the whole place very pleasant.

For the first time in ages, I became violently homesick for Singapore. In Cyprus I was walking about in the heat of the sun, and the red hibiscus made me think of South East Asia and home.

Because we arrived during a thirty-six hour air.raid on Beirut, we had to spend a few days in Cyprus. A United Nations official on the island told us that twenty thousand families in Lebanon had lost their homes because of

Israel's invasion, but that an accurate count of the dead was impossible, partly because many of the bodies were buried under rubble and partly because many people had been taken away by the Israelis and there was no way of telling if they were dead or alive.

While we were waiting in Cyprus, news came that the Israelis had bombed yet another International Red Cross ship. Being a doctor seemed to confer no immunity where these Israelis were concerned. If they could do that to the International Red Cross, which was protected by the Geneva Convention, what would they do to me, a volunteer doctor protected only by a refugee's travel document? What would they do to the other volunteers? I thought to myself, well, all right, at least if I happen to be blown up the people in Lebanon will have had one Singapore friend who did try.

Then I thought about Francis. Leaving Singapore had cost him his career as a lawyer, his home, his family and his friends. All he had left was me – his wife – and yet he supported my decision to go to Lebanon. Back in London, he had said to me, 'Look, Swee Chai, if I were a doctor, I'd have gone myself. But I'm not a doctor, so the least I can do is support you in going.' And he put on a brave front and helped me pack my bags. He probably did not think I realised that his whole being was crumbling inside him at the prospect of having to receive my dead body if the Israelis saw fit to drop a bomb on my hospital. The night before I left, I made him take a sleeping pill and asked him to resign himself to the fact that I might come home in a big, black, plastic bag.

As I was stepping out of a lift, a voice interrupted my thoughts: 'Doctor, are you going to Lebanon to help my people? Thank you very much, and welcome.'

Wearing white trousers with a tan belt, and a pale cotton shirt, the speaker was tall, dark-skinned and middle-aged.

'Are you Lebanese, then?' I asked.

'No, I am Palestinian,' he said.

This was the first Palestinian I had met. The word
'Palestinian' had an unpleasant ring to it, despite this man's
perfect English and very polite manners. I really did not
like the idea of talking to a Palestinian. 'You mean you are
PLO?' I asked, furtively looking to see if he was hiding a
gun or a grenade somewhere on his body.

The man explained that he was not a member of the PLO
but a university lecturer. His subject was Arabic Literature. Loudly breathing a sigh of relief, I agreed to have
lunch with him. He then started to tell me about himself,
and I was quite bewildered by what he had to say.

My new acquaintance's family came from a town called
Jaffa. 'You will have heard of the famous Jaffa oranges,' he
said. 'The Israelis say that they made the desert bloom, but
I was born in an orange grove: my ancestors had grown
oranges for centuries. They drove us out. We lost our home
and our oranges, and we became refugees. My family was
split up. My mother and my sisters fled to Jordan. One of
my brothers is now in Saudi Arabia, another is in Yemen,
and the last one is in Kuwait. My father stayed in the West
Bank, and kept me with him. Unfortunately, the West
Bank became harder and harder to live in, and when I was
thirteen I ran away from home because I couldn't stand it
any more. I reached Beirut and got into the university
there. So my family is all scattered now. I just wish that one
day I could see all of them again.'

This was the first time I had heard such a story. 'What do
you think of the PLO?' I asked.

He had a very straightforward relationship with the
PLO: he gave it five percent of his income and saw it as his
government. No one had ever described the PLO to me as
a government before. I must have looked surprised,
because he asked for some paper. When I gave him a large
piece of white paper, he started drawing a diagram of the
PLO's organisation: there was the National Council, his
parliament; the Trade Union Federation, his Ministry of
Labour; the General Union of Palestinian Women; the

Palestine Red Crescent Society, his Ministry of Health; and so on. The paper filled up with more and more organisations. Suddenly he stopped writing, and said, 'You know, we're always called "terrorists". There are five million of us. If we were all terrorists, we would have destroyed the whole world in one day!'

It did not convince me a hundred percent. Looking at his sheet of paper, now completely filled up with boxes, lines and words, I had to admit that the diagram did look like the sort of structure you might expect of a government representing five million people. But it did not square up with my image of the PLO. Was this a band of Arab terrorists or what? Were these hijackers, bombers, Jew-haters?

The other thing that did not square up was 'Palestine'. Incredible though it may seem, I just had no idea where this 'Palestine' was. From my handbag, I took out a map of the Middle East. There was no 'Palestine' on it. When I asked him to show me where his Palestine was, he put his finger on Israel, and said that that was 'occupied Palestine'.

'The occupiers drove nearly one million Palestinians out of my country in 1948,' he said. 'Not only did they take over all the land and property of those who were driven out, but they changed the name of my country to Israel. Those of my people who refused to leave were badly persecuted, and still are, even today.'

After a two-hour discussion over lunch, I finally realised – for the first time in my life – that the Palestinians were exiles. What my Palestinian acquaintance was telling me was that the PLO was their government in exile. Although I wanted to ask him about how the PLO was connected to the Israeli invasion of Lebanon, I was late for a briefing session for the medical volunteers, and had to hurry off. As I was leaving, he came after me, and said very seriously, 'Doctor, you must see Palestine. If you get there, please see if my father's house is still there, and send me a picture if it is.' He told me where his father's house was, and gave me his own address.

The briefing session was not very useful, at least as far as I was concerned, because I did not really concentrate on it. My mind kept wandering off, thinking of the things I had just heard about the Palestinians. If what I had been told was true, I could not understand why I had never heard this about the Palestinians before. If I had not volunteered to go to Lebanon, I might never have found out about them. But on the other hand, the man might have been a PLO agent feeding me misinformation. Why should I believe his story at all? If the PLO were not terrorists, why did everybody say they were? I had no way of knowing what the truth of the matter was, but it seemed likely that I would discover it in Lebanon soon enough.

The next day, we boarded a boat for Beirut. The voyage was uneventful – apart from being stopped once by an Israeli gunboat. The boat itself was a typical Mediterranean ferryboat, with people sitting around on the decks, and gambling at the casino inside. But there was a strange air of uneasiness. No one wanted to talk about the war, but each time a moving object was spotted on the horizon, everyone murmured, 'Israelis'. The restaurant was closed for the day, but drinks were available.

Most of my colleagues sat on the top deck, on long wooden benches, and stared long and hard at the sea. We had been warned not to talk too freely to strangers, no matter how friendly they seemed. A young man came up to me, and asked if our party was going to look after war victims. I answered, 'Yes'. He then started expressing his admiration for medical workers who volunteered their services to others who were suffering, but told me in no uncertain terms that the Palestinians and Muslim Lebanese in West Beirut were troublemakers and deserved no help. His comments led me to believe that he must either be Israeli or an Israeli sympathiser, and I quickly excused myself from his company to avoid being dragged into further controversies.

CHAPTER 3

The boat pulled into Jounieh, the harbour to East Beirut, at dusk. I could see how this small harbour might have been an idyllic holiday resort, were it not for the presence of so many uniformed soldiers with machine guns. Brightly-dressed women with typical Mediterranean features, wearing fancy hats, helped me to forget for a moment that I had come into a country at war. Beyond the heavy military presence were rich green mountains and a clear blue sky, and in the foreground was the sparkling Mediterranean Sea, with numerous sailing boats, even then.

We were met by the Lebanese organisation which was going to look after us and act as our employers, and they put us up in the first floor of a hospital in East Beirut. The city was divided by the 'Green Line of Peace' into a Christian East and a Muslim West: why it was called the Green Line of Peace I do not know, because over the years more battles were fought across the Green Line than anywhere else. Possibly it was from an old ceasefire between the Christians and the Muslims. If so, the ceasefire had clearly broken down. Several roads linked East and West Beirut, and those roads formed the 'crossings'. The Christian end of a crossing was usually guarded by Christian soldiers, and the Muslim end by Muslim soldiers, both of which were usually part of the official Lebanese Army, which was divided into brigades along religious lines. Thus the Sixth Brigade was composed mainly of Shi'ite Muslims, the Eighteenth Brigade was Sunni Muslim and the Fifth Brigade was Christian.

As well as the official Lebanese army, there were many non-official militias, both Christian and Muslim, each connected with a political or religious group, and there were also the private militias of the prominent and wealthy.

Next morning we found that the Green Line crossing we planned to use was closed, and so we had the day free to wander round East Beirut. As a total stranger, I was warned that until I knew the local groupings and their allegiances I had better use my eyes and my ears and keep quiet, especially in front of soldiers and militia members. Any slip of the tongue might endanger both me and my colleagues. For instance, expressing anti-Israeli sentiments could spark off a hostile reaction from certain Christian militias or sections of the Army, because at that time the Christians and the Israelis were allies.

East Beirut was a large, busy city. There were shops, banks, cars, traffic lights, people going about their business. The Lebanese are good-looking people on the whole, with healthy tanned skin and typically Southern European features. The women are especially attractive, with the warmth and vivacity of daughters of sunny climes. The main reminder that there was a war on came from the many soldiers, military vehicles and tanks. The soldiers' uniforms were very interesting: some wore dark green, some light green and some khaki. Certain soldiers had special insignia, while others had large coloured patches on their uniforms. I quickly learnt to recognise the colours and insignia of the Israeli soldiers, and was surprised when I saw groups of young Lebanese girls going up to them to present them with flowers.

After a while, I found a large, crowded post office, where I paid a hundred Lebanese lira – £30 sterling – to make a three-minute call to London. I spoke to Francis, assured him that I was in good hands and told him that I would probably cross from East to West Beirut the next day if the crossing was open.

Once I had made my phone call, I found a bookshop and bought a dictionary, an English-French one, because most of the Lebanese I had met spoke French. Then I got hold of some sweet, fragrant Lebanese pastry, found a place to sit on the stairs going into a large office, and started to devour both food and dictionary. The former was absolutely delicious, but trying to learn French gave me the most awful indigestion!

After wandering around the city all day, I returned to the hospital, went to bed and fell asleep almost immediately.

The next day we all rose early to cross the Green Line into West Beirut. We were driven along a dusty, winding road, punctuated every fifty or a hundred metres by sandbags and soldiers. These checkpoints were all controlled by different groups of militia members. Apart from the nuisance of being stopped at them to have our papers and luggage checked, we were not given a hard time. The nearer we got to West Beirut, the dustier the road became. Suddenly we were past the Green Line into West Beirut, which looked just like it did on television, except that now it was life-sized and three-dimensional.

By the time I arrived in West Beirut, the worst of the air raids were over. Although it was a relief that bombs and shells were not falling out of the sky, I was shocked at the destruction of the city. Bombed-out buildings, piles of rubble, collapsing walls, large potholes dug in the road by bombs and shells – the whole place looked an utter mess to the uninitiated, and was a ghastly nightmare for her inhabitants. Those pockets of Beirut which had escaped destruction were still very beautiful. In my mind's eye, I could see what this city must have been like before the wars began. The 'Pearl of the Middle East', set against the mountains and washed by the waves of the Mediterranean, must have been a paradise planted with cedar trees, orange trees, roses and jasmine flowers, which were nourished by the rivers and blessed by the sun.

But most of the lovely buildings of polished stone and marble had been turned into hideous bombsites. War had tarnished this beautiful pearl, leaving deep, dark wounds which might never heal. Our Lebanese driver pointed out that not all the destroyed buildings had been blown up by Israeli bombs. Some had been destroyed as far back as the 'First Civil War' of the mid-1970s. Lebanon had not seen peace for years and years. Like most Lebanese, our driver was sick of wars.

Some of the latest weapons had been tested on this city. The implosion bomb, also known as the 'vacuum bomb', was capable of 'sucking' a ten-storey block of flats to the ground in a matter of seconds – reducing it to a mighty heap of concrete and rubble, burying all its occupants alive. It was all over in an instant, unlike what happened with the phosphorus bombs: the phosphorus stuck to the skin, lungs and guts of the victims for ages, continuing to burn and smoulder, and causing prolonged agony. Phosphorus is a metal many people will remember from chemistry lessons at school: it is quiet under water, but take it out and it starts to burn spontaneously. Victims of phosphorus bombs who had taken phosphorus into their lungs were doomed – they exhaled phosphorus fumes to their last breath. Burns on the skin often penetrated deep into the muscles and bones.

Then there were the anti-personnel bombs – the fragmentation or cluster bombs. These exploded and scattered small pieces over a large area. The pieces lay dormant till accidentally picked up, often by curious toddlers, and then they exploded into countless bits of shrapnel. People wounded by such shrapnel often suffered multiple injuries to the face, eyes, bones and viscera. Fragmentation bombs with delayed trigger mechanisms, dropped on densely populated areas, were clearly aimed at civilians, and especially children. As well as all these sophisticated and cruel inventions, there were of course conventional high explosive bombs and shells.

So was this the 'omelette', then? Or was it just 'cracking eggs'?

The offices of my Lebanese employers were located in Hamra – the fashionable district of West Beirut which contained the American University Hospital, offices, hotels, posh apartments, banks and department stores, and which had escaped the worst of the bombing. The luxury hotels were packed with journalists: the Beirut war was a hot story for them, and hotel prices soared as a result. Steak and wine, salmon and champagne, music and guest artists – within hotels such as the Commodore these were freely available to those who could afford them. But while the hotels filled their swimming pools for the enjoyment of their guests, the rest of the city was queuing up at water points.

Hamra contained two worlds: the highly-paid foreign correspondents in the large, sophisticated hotels and the refugees with no home to call their own. Most of the offices and flats had been deserted by their wealthy owners, who had fled to Switzerland, France or just up to the mountains behind East Beirut. Wealthy Lebanese often owned three or four homes in three or four different countries. The buildings they had left were now occupied by thousands of squatters from the southern suburbs of Beirut and from south Lebanon, where the bulk of the bombs and shells had landed, destroying their homes.

Refugees were huddled in temporary shelters in empty buildings, garages and stairways. Relief centres for displaced and homeless families had been set up, where water, food and bedding were handed out by relief agencies and by the United Nations.

The plight of these destitute people made our own problems look trivial. So what if there was no tissue paper, no Danish cheese, no running water, no electricity? All of us knew we had a home to go back to. We were only doing a few months or a year in Beirut, but there was no light at the end of the tunnel for the refugees.

In fact, when I revisited Beirut nearly six years later, I found that many of the refugees were still living in the same temporary shelters – in garages and abandoned buildings, just as crowded and dimly-lit as before. I heard the same cries of hungry children and anxious mothers. But there was one difference. In 1982 I assumed that their problems would be sorted out once the invasion was over. In 1988 I knew that they were homeless Palestinians and Lebanese who would remain homeless for many years.

In the evening, the foreign medical volunteers returned from a tiresome day-long briefing session to our temporary quarters, which were at the nurses' hostel at the American University. This was within walking distance of the American University Hospital. The whole complex was pretty empty, since most of the students had fled from the war. Most of the hospital's nurses had gone too, except for a lot of Filipino nurses.

Naturally we got to talking with them. 'It really is so good of you to stay behind to look after all these war casualties,' I said. 'Aren't you afraid?'

'Of course we are,' replied one of the Filipinos, 'but our passports have been kept, so we couldn't leave even if we wanted to!'

This upset the three newly-arrived volunteer nurses from the USA: they thought it was wrong to keep the Filipinos' passports.

The American University Hospital had saved countless lives. It always had excellent standards and was comparable to any large British teaching hospital, with well-trained staff and the latest laboratory and technical facilities. The medical and surgical staff were good by international standards.

Unfortunately the hospital was entirely private. At that

time a patient had to put down a deposit of ten thousand Lebanese lira (about £3,000 sterling) before even being admitted to the hospital. People who did not have enough money were turned away. For someone like me, who had spent years working in Britain's National Health Service, this kind of 'cash on the nail' medicine was almost impossible to accept – especially if we were going to be dealing with wounded people.

Nearly all Lebanon's hospitals were private. The American University Hospital, being the finest one, charged the highest rates, and less prestigious ones charged less. So you got what you paid for – there was a kind of sliding scale. Even that system had been disrupted by the Israeli invasion: most of the other hospitals had been destroyed. The Lebanese told me that any building flying the red cross had been a target for Israeli bombardment. The Makassad, Babir, Akka and Gaza hospitals were all attacked and put out of action. In the south, hospitals in Nabatieh and Saida were also hit. But they did not dare to attack the American University Hospital. So, although it was expensive, there was still a fine, functioning hospital left for the desperate people of Lebanon.

But I had not come all the way to Beirut to work in a private hospital. I wanted to help those in need, and those who were most in need were poor, and could not pay for treatment. The next morning we arrived at the office of our Lebanese hosts, and there we were introduced to Dr Rio Spirugi. He was a wiry Italian Swiss, who had once worked for the International Red Cross, but had given it up to be the co-ordinator for the Palestine Red Crescent Society (PRCS). He had come up to the office looking for surgeons, anaesthetists and theatre nurses – in short, a surgical team – to work in Gaza Hospital, which was run by the Palestine Red Crescent Society. Dr Spirugi explained that Gaza Hospital offered free medical care to all those in need, and I was absolutely delighted to hear this. I remembered that the Palestinian man I had met in Cyprus had told me about the medical services of the Palestine Red Crescent Society. At that time, of course, the last thing in my mind was any idea that I might end up working with the PRCS.

Six of us volunteered to work with Dr Spirugi. Mr Bryan Mayou, a brilliant consultant plastic surgeon from St Thomas's Hospital in London, who had taught me nearly all my reconstructive surgery and microsurgery, would be the head of the team. Besides having been my teacher, Bryan was also a friend of mine. It was Bryan who had brought to my attention the appeal for volunteers to go to Lebanon. The others in the team were Dr David Gray, an anaesthetist from Liverpool, Dr Egon, an anaesthetist from Germany, two theatre nurses – Ruth, from Denmark, and Sheila – and myself. Dr Spirugi seemed reasonably happy with the little flock he had gathered. He packed us into his blue Peugeot estate car, on which was painted the insignia of the PRCS, and set off with us for Gaza Hospital.

'You know,' he said to me, 'I worked in South Vietnam as part of the International Red Cross during the US war. But unfortunately Thieu threw me out.' He chuckled.

I guessed that he took me for a Vietnamese, so I explained that I was a Singaporean.

'Most of you have probably worked in other countries outside Europe,' he said as we drove along. 'What you must understand is that the Red Crescent had no shortage of medical staff before the invasion. But during the first week of the invasion they arrested a hundred and fifty doctors and nurses. Many others are still missing, and those who worked throughout the war are finished – they're too tired. Some of them are shell-shocked.'

We passed a television crew. 'Tourists,' said Dr Spirugi. 'These journalists are simply tourists. They treat the war as one big spectacle. Always on the look-out for couleur locale, they have no commitment to anything. And they don't feel anything for the people here.'

The journalists receded behind us. Dr Spirugi obviously

did not like them, but I could not help wondering how the rest of the world would know anything about the Israeli invasion if it were not for these 'tourists'.

'Guess what!' said Dr Spirugi. 'I had some trouble with that crazy lot in the offices this morning. When I asked if I could take some of you to work in Gaza, all they wanted to know was whether you would be able to join the rest of the volunteers for weekend trips up into the mountains. We're in the middle of a bloody war, for God's sake, and all they care about is holidays and excursions. It's madness.'

He laughed out loud. I did not see what was so mad about it. The war was not being fought everywhere: we had just come through East Beirut, where there was no war. Our Lebanese hosts obviously wanted us to see more of Lebanon than just piles of rubble in West Beirut. But we said to Dr Spirugi that we would be happy to forgo the weekend trips if we were needed at the hospital, and that cheered him up a lot.

This was the first time I had been taken round West Beirut. Except for the odd vehicle, there was no traffic on the roads, and Dr Spirugi drove very fast. Luckily he was worried about overturning a large barrel of concentrated chlorine in the back of the car, or he would probably have driven even faster. 'Mind the chlorine, it is for disinfecting the whole of West Beirut,' he repeated a few times, as he went sharply round the bends.

He chose a route to take us past the Babir and the Makassad hospitals, to show us the destruction visited upon two major Lebanese hospitals. 'The evacuation of the PLO will start soon,' he said, as we drove past Makassad Hospital, 'and once that is over, we'll move the casualties from the field hospitals back to Gaza and Akka hospitals.'

Eventually we arrived at what Dr Spirugi said was Akka Hospital. What greeted our eyes was a huge pile of concrete waste – tons of rubble in what looked like a demolition site. There was no hospital left. Once he had parked the car, Dr Spirugi did not even give us time to take a second look: he marched us straight on into the rubble. We stumbled over torn-up cables and debris, and found a staircase going down beneath the partially collapsed walls.

For a moment, I felt a little lost. The concrete steps were uneven, and it soon became so dark that I could not even see my own fingers. My eyes got used to the darkness, however, and Dr Egon found a torch from one of his eight pockets. We stumbled on down. Were we going into a dungeon? Then I realised that we were in the basement of Akka Hospital. The tons of rubble up above must have prevented the basement from being totally destroyed.

Rio Spirugi started calling, presumably in Arabic – I knew it was not Chinese, French or Malay. Some people came out of a room to greet him. They were some of the staff of the Palestine Red Crescent Society. Five or six men and women, they all looked haggard and traumatised. I wondered if they were suffering from shell-shock. We were introduced, and then they showed us round.

Normally I would have asked a lot of questions. I am not known for keeping quiet. But how could I ask the Red Crescent staff, who had obviously been through hell, what had happened to their hospital?

It was at Akka Hospital that I learnt my first word in Arabic: 'halas' – 'finished'. The school of nursing and the Arab centre for research and specialist treatment of injuries were both 'halas'. And the PRCS had not lost just one hospital: thirteen clinics and nine hospitals all over Lebanon had been destroyed in this way. Only Gaza Hospital, for a reason I was to discover three years later, was still standing. At the height of the air raids, when the Palestinians found out that every single PRCS hospital and clinic was a bomb target, they put three Israeli soldiers captured in south Lebanon on the upper floors of Gaza Hospital, and radioed a message to the Israeli Army saying that any further military action on Gaza Hospital would result in Israeli lives being lost. That saved Gaza Hospital from further destruction.

One of the staff who spoke English told us that Akka Hospital had been a five-storey building before the Israeli air raids.

'The floor for cardiac bypass operations had just been opened,' he said. 'Now there is nothing left.' Then, as if he suddenly remembered something, he gestured to us to follow him. We went back up the steps: as we came out from the dark basement into the open air we were momentarily blinded by the glare of the sun. We followed him through a maze of half-demolished walls. They had started to clear a large pile of rubble from the twisted remains of what had obviously been a patient's bed. Next to it was a drip stand, holding half a packet of stale blood. From the label, I could see that once it had fed into the vein of a nine-year-old girl. One of the raids had abruptly ended her treatment, and her life.

'My patient,' said the man quietly.

We returned to the basement in silence. The Red Crescent staff wanted to give us coffee, but Rio Spirugi firmly refused on our behalf. 'We have to get going,' he said, picking up a box used for transporting blood. 'If we stopped everywhere to drink coffee, we would never get anything done.' As we were walking up the steps again, he suddenly turned and went back down, to check that all the taps were off. This was very important, because if the municipal water supply came on again litres of precious water could be wasted through sheer carelessness. After he had checked the taps, he made a point of reminding the staff to keep the taps switched off.

Our next port of call was Gaza Hospital. I liked it at once: it was a majestic eleven-storey building. The top two floors had been severely damaged by bombs, and the ceiling of the ninth floor was full of holes made by bombs and rockets, but there the damage stopped, for the reason I explained earlier. As at Akka Hospital, there was neither running water nor electricity.

As well as in-patient accommodation, Gaza Hospital had three large operating theatres, a six-bed intensive care unit, a modern blood bank and laboratory, an X-ray department, a large casualty department and an out-patient department. Each floor of the hospital served a different function: Floor One was for intensive care and operating theatres, with attached recovery rooms, Floor Two housed the wards for orthopaedic in-patients, Floor Three was for general medical wards, Floor Four was for general surgical in-patients, and so on.

Attached to Gaza Hospital was an obstetric and gynae-cological hospital, the Ramallah. But apart from a handful of staff, Gaza Hospital was empty. We were told that the patients had been evacuated to temporary hospitals, and that was where most of the staff were working. Apparently Gaza Hospital was in one of the most heavily bombarded areas, and most of the time it was impossible to reach or to leave the hospital. For the past three months the hospital administrator and staff had not left the hospital.

Immediately before the 1982 invasion, the PRCS in Lebanon was handling an annual turnover of one million clinic attendances and in-patient treatments. All this was entirely free and available to all in need, regardless of race, religion or wealth. Many poor Lebanese people were treated free by the PRCS. Being an entirely humanitarian organisation, and an observer member of the International Committee of the Red Cross, the PRCS would never have expected the Israelis to pick on its hospitals and clinics for bombing raids. When the invasion happened and the PRCS hospitals and clinics were destroyed, the victims of the war lost a valuable medical service just when they most needed it.

The PRCS evacuated the bulk of their patients and services to temporary hospitals. These were often called field hospitals, but in the Beirut of 1982 no hospital would survive long out in the open. The temporary hospitals were in the basements of buildings, such as the Near East School of Theology, or the Lahut, as it was known locally. Dr Spirugi was very keen for us all to get into action straight away, and he suggested that we start work in Lahut Hospital the following day.

So off we went to the Lahut, where we found an entire hospital extending for three floors underground, complete with operating theatres, wards and emergency, resuscitation and X-ray facilities. Here, away from the refugee camps and the southern suburbs, right in the middle of Hamra, the Red Crescent continued its work of looking after the sick and wounded. The entire pharmacy of Akka Hospital had been evacuated to the Lahut. Rio introduced us to the staff and asked them to put us to work when we returned in the morning.

'You can work here until Gaza Hospital reopens,' he said, and explained that when that happened he would expect us to provide an initial service until things got sorted out. 'Don't forget,' he added, 'that most of these people have been through absolute hell for the last three months. They could do with a bit of support. Dr Habib, for example, almost died, and he is still suffering from shell-shock. It's probably best for him to go on working: if he keeps busy it might take a few things off his mind. But he can't be pushed. Most of these people have lost homes and members of their families. It's going to take time for them to recover. You lot are fresh and energetic. Don't forget that they need your help.'

Actually I was not particularly fresh and energetic. The fresh and energetic one was Dr Rio Spirugi: he was tireless. I had watched him in action the whole day. He always did three tasks at once, spoke to five or six people simultaneously and was probably thinking through half a dozen projects at the same time. His fiery temper forced everyone into action – and given the chaos and despondency at the time this was a huge achievement. I owe it to Dr Spirugi that I was given the honour and opportunity of working with the Palestinians. It was Rio's single-mindedness that set me to work almost straight away, first in the Lahut and later in Gaza Hospital. Many of the volunteers who flew out with us never got to work with the war victims, but were sent to north and east Lebanon, where it was relatively calm.

We got into trouble at the end of the day. Bryan Mayou, the British plastic surgeon, was staying in a Hamra block of flats called the Mayfair Residence. It looked posh, but it had no running water. The nurses' hostel at the American University, where the women volunteers were staying, did have running water. Although male visitors were strictly forbidden in our hostel, we thought we would be able to conceal Bryan under a large towel and smuggle him into the shower room to have a wash.

Bryan succeeded in getting to the shower, only to be hauled out minutes later by a very irate warden. Although the sight of a half-clothed, six-foot Englishman being ordered out of the women's showers made all of us break down into fits of giggles, the incident was regarded as a serious misdemeanour, and it caused considerable embarrassment to our Lebanese hosts. We were reminded that we had to respect local custom: it was not considered at all polite for men to invade women's showers.

After this little escapade, we had supper in the Relief Centre, a large cafeteria which now functioned as a kind of soup kitchen. In the circumstances, we volunteers were really taken care of very well. I dined on okra, green beans, even a small piece of meat, rice, yoghurt and pitta bread. As I ate my first mouthful, I suddenly realised that I had eaten six meals since arriving in West Beirut without treating one single patient. 'How awful!' I said to myself. 'I shouldn't be just an extra mouth to feed like this. Tomorrow I must work, and earn my keep.'

The sun was setting as I walked back with a young Lebanese friend towards the American University. The street lights, presumably working three months before, failed to light up. Through the silhouettes of buildings and rubble, I could still see the beauty of Beirut: the Mediterranean coastline itself, the Flame-of-the-Forest trees, the bougainvilleas coloured purple, white, pink and red, and the large hibiscus flowers. The war had failed to destroy these. The cedars made me think of a verse in Psalm 92: 'The righteous shall flourish like the palm-tree: he shall grow like a cedar in Lebanon.' Soon the deep red sun sank into the sea, and thousands of stars appeared in the dark blue sky.

Outside the university I could hear, somewhere across the streets, a low, soft singing – in Arabic. My Lebanese friend told me the singers were Palestinian fighters who were going to be evacuated in the morning. I asked him what the words meant, but there were tears in his eyes as he listened to the singing and he could not bring himself to translate for me. He was only a boy, still in his teens perhaps, and the last ten weeks must have been too much for him. I remembered the destruction in Beirut, the hospitals, the wounded and the homeless, and I stopped asking. Maybe I would understand the words of the songs one day – in God's own good time. Meanwhile it was early to bed for me, so that I would be ready, useful and working in the morning.

CHAPTER 4

═══════════

Early in the morning I was awakened by the sound of continuous machine-gun fire in the distance. It reminded me of waking to the sound of firecrackers at the Chinese New Year in Singapore. I went to sleep once more. Then Jill, one of the nurses from America, woke me up. It was only 6.30 AM. Most of the volunteer medical workers were already up, washed and dressed. They were all planning to go to the harbour to watch the day's great event – the evacuation of the PLO fighters from Beirut. Looking out of the window, I could see two large patrol boats on the horizon in the distance. My friends told me that one was French and the other was Italian, and that they had been assigned to oversee the evacuation. The international peace-keeping force was moving into Beirut, to protect the civilian population and to prevent the Israelis from taking advantage of the evacuation and the chaos to move into the city.

'Are you coming or not, Swee?' shouted Mary impatiently. She was another of my American nurse colleagues. Should I go with Mary and Jill?

'No, I'd better not,' I replied after a moment's hesitation. The evacuation of the PLO was clearly going to be a highly political affair, and I did not think I ought to be seen mixed up with a whole lot of PLO fighters. Partly I was scared, maybe, and partly I still saw the PLO as terrorists. At any rate, I had come here to treat wounded people, not to be seen with the PLO. Imagine if the Singapore Government heard I had been messing around with the PLO! What would my Christian friends say? What would my parents think of me? What would my medical colleagues in Britain think of me? The more I thought about it, the more reasons I came up with for not being seen anywhere near those Palestinian fighters. But none of them were reasons I felt like giving to Mary and Jill, so I ended up lying to them.

'I'd love to come, Mary,' I added, 'but I promised to see some patients in the Lahut. I'll rely on you to tell me all about it tonight. Have a good day.'

The two American nurses left without me, and I got ready to go to the Lahut.

As I walked out of the American University, large red posters greeted my eyes. Bearing slogans in French, Arabic and English, they were hanging from trees, lamp posts and buildings. Many of them said, 'Goodbye, Beirut, we love you'. Presumably the departing PLO had put them up. The word 'love' struck me forcibly: it seemed a strange word for terrorists to use. I hurried on towards Lahut Hospital.

On the way I stopped to talk to a grief-stricken woman with her young kids in a shelter. Her husband and two sons were to be evacuated, and their home in the south had been destroyed by the Israelis. She showed me photographs of the three who were being evacuated: the younger boy was just fourteen.

'But without your husband and your two elder sons, how on earth are you going to manage?' I asked. 'How are you going to be able to rebuild your home in the south and bring up your family single-handed?'

She had not thought that far. She was overwhelmed by the awful thought that once her loved ones embarked on that boat she might never see them again. Her family came from the Gaza Strip: since leaving home in Palestine, they had moved house seven times. This woman had grown used to poverty, war and harassment but now she was weeping because not only was she homeless but her family was being split up. Because I knew I could not console her in her grief, I just shut up and listened. Suddenly she dried her tears and invited me for coffee. How hospitable these people were, despite all the cruel treatment they had suffered!

This was the first time I realised that PLO fighters were people who had homes and families in Lebanon. They were leaving behind them wives, children, sisters, brothers and parents. The evacuation was forcing the men and women to separate: it was effectively destroying the family structure.

At Lahut Hospital, I arrived just in time to join the ward round. I was introduced to two doctors who worked for the PRCS, and a British volunteer doctor, Paul Morris. We went round all the patients, and I was introduced as 'the Singapore orthopaedic specialist sent by Britain'. The fifty or so in-patients were all civilian war casualties, and many of them were children. The main victims of this invasion had been the civilians, unaware that they were going to be the targets of attack.

There were many sorts of war wounds. Large pieces of shrapnel, sometimes the size of a concrete slab, could easily amputate a limb, or kill someone instantly. There were simple flash burns, and there were deep burns penetrating down to the muscles. By the time I saw them, most of the wounds had been infected for weeks. The most pitiful were the victims of what the American nurses called the 'Reagan-Begin Syndrome': typically they were shell-shocked kids, thin and frightened, struck dumb, and refusing food and water. Often all their relatives had been killed in the bombardment. From the medical point of view, the Reagan-Begin Syndrome meant an amputated limb or two, a large chest wound through which the child might well have lost a lung, and a long abdominal wound which had removed parts of the liver, kidney or spleen. There was often an infected open fracture as well. As I treated these kids, the Israeli leader's words kept ringing in my ears: much as he regretted the casualties, to make an omelette one first had to crack eggs.

Since I was the only orthopaedic surgeon around, I was asked to take over the management of all the broken bones. Compound fractures, where the broken bones had come through the skin, were very common. I was not entirely happy with the way most of these had been treated. The doctors had tended to go straight for 'internal fixation', that is to say they had tried to go in through the wound to fix the bones directly with plates, screws or nails. Then they had generally opted for 'primary closure', that is to say, they had stitched up the wound at once. This was a modern approach which undervalued tried and tested traditional methods.

If they had been treating civilian injuries in well-equipped, clean operating theatres, in Europe or America, immediate internal fixation and primary closure would probably have given acceptable results. But they had been working on blast injuries and gunshot wounds in septic theatres, and internal fixation was a total disaster: just about every case treated that way in a war zone like Beirut developed gangrene, requiring amputation, or chronic bone infection, which was very hard to cure. Under the circumstances, open fractures were best treated by traditional methods: thorough cleansing – cutting away all the dead and contaminated tissues – and lightly covering the wound with a dressing. If an external fracture fixator was available, it could be used to treat the fracture, if not, then splints or traction could be used.

The wound had to be attended to daily. Once it was healthy, it could be closed with a skin flap or a simple skin graft. Only later, when all the infection had settled, might it be a good idea to do a bone graft or to do internal fixation. It might seem a roundabout approach, but I saw too many injuries go gangrenous through primary closure. The age-old method of leaving all the injuries open initially was still the best.

If a fracture had to be stabilised so that a patient could be evacuated or transported, and if an external fixator was not available, then a splint, such as the Thomas splint designed by Hugh Owen Thomas of Liverpool, which again was tried and tested, was just as good, or even simply a plaster of Paris cast.

In the chaos of air raids, with dozens of volunteers from all over the world, all of whom insisted in doing things the way they thought best, I found it difficult to ensure that these very basic but also very safe principles of fracture care were implemented.

Once the Palestinian fighters had been evacuated, peace did return to West Beirut. The air raids stopped altogether. There was no shelling, and people came out from their shelters and hiding places, and headed for home again. I left the nurses' hostel in the American University as the nurses started to return to work, and moved in with the rest of the volunteers in the Mayfair Residence. But it became inconvenient for us to commute to Gaza Hospital daily, so our volunteer surgical team moved into the hospital, where we were allotted a large, empty suite on the ninth floor. The windows were broken, but otherwise the bomb damage at our end of the building was minimal. It was great to be so high up: the mosquitoes could not get us, and it was cool at night.

Moving into Gaza Hospital made me realise what a hopeless home-maker I had always been. My colleagues worked diligently setting up the 'foreign doctors' quarters'. First they swept the floor clean of concrete debris; then they bought domestic items such as a gas cooker, a kettle, pots and pans, and groceries, and bit by bit made the empty deserted suite a homely place.

Meanwhile the patients were gradually moved back from the temporary treatment centres – the Lahut, the Protestant College, and so on – and started filling the wards of Gaza Hospital. As the patients were still in more than one place, I was doing rounds in the Lahut as well as Gaza Hospital. There was not much by way of surgery that I could do then, since our limited resources had to be husbanded for emergencies, and so my job was limited to debriding wounds (that is to say, trimming and cleaning them by removing damaged tissue), changing plaster casts and sorting out antibiotics. Some of the patients were on eight different antibiotics and quickly becoming resistant to all eight. Working out some sort of antibiotic policy was important. It was also not very easy.

One day I was waiting for the jeep to take me from Gaza Hospital to the Lahut, and I fell into conversation with a PRCS nurse. I asked her if it was possible for me to visit the 'camps'. After all, everyone was always talking about the refugee camps, and I felt as if I was the only one who had never visited them. This was a few days after we had started working at Gaza.

'Camps?' asked the nurse. Then she smiled, took me by the hand and led me through the door of the hospital. A narrow lane separated the hospital from a long row of multistorey buildings – a mixture of shops and flats. We turned right, and walked a few metres down the road to the market which I passed every day, where Dr Egon bought oranges, tomatoes and vegetables for our apartment. There was a mosque by the market, and more blocks of flats and shops. Women with white, black and many-coloured scarves around their hair were hurrying to and fro with their shopping. Kids were pushing wheelbarrows laden with bricks and building materials towards destroyed buildings. Everywhere people were repairing their homes.

The nurse from Gaza Hospital put her arms around me. 'Doctora Swee,' she said, 'welcome to Sabra and Shatila!'

This bustling market with its vegetable and fruit stalls,

and its livestock, was Sabra market. The buildings all around it were Shatila Camp. The buildings around Gaza Hospital were Sabra Camp.

For the last few days I had been eagerly watching families returning to rebuild the bombed-out buildings. Every morning I had looked out of the window on the ninth floor of Gaza Hospital and had seen new arrivals coming with their scanty belongings – cases, mattresses, pillows – to occupy broken buildings. One day they would move in somewhere covered with dirt and dust, with shattered windows, and holes in the walls. The next morning I would look again: the same building would be transformed. Freshly-laid bricks would have patched the holes in the walls, new windows would have been put in, laundry would be hanging out to dry, and the laughter of children could be heard. I had thought this was just part of West Beirut getting back to some kind of normality, and all the time I had been right bang in the middle of the camps!

My mental image of a refugee camp is something like a large field covered with rows of tents. 'So where are the tents?' I asked the nurse. 'It's supposed to be a camp, isn't it?'

She explained that when the Palestinians in northern Galilee had been uprooted in 1948, many of them had walked across the northern border into Lebanon. The Galileans became refugees in Lebanon; other communities from the rest of Palestine fled to Jordan, Egypt, Syria, Iraq and all over the Arab world. Atlases no longer had maps of Palestine, but that did not stop the 750,000 exiles from remembering their homeland.

It was hoped then that the refugees would be 'absorbed' into the neighbouring Arab countries, and thus join the countless communities which have been erased from history. The UN, together with several humanitarian and relief organisations, supplied tents and set up refugee camps for the newly homeless Palestinians. The Galileans found themselves in some of these 'temporary' camps –

Sabra, Shatila and Bourj el-Brajneh in the southern suburbs of Beirut.

The nurse from Gaza Hospital explained to me that the refugees had not been 'absorbed', because they were not truly refugees. They were exiles, and there was a difference. As exiles, they always wanted to return home. The tents had soon been demolished – by the Galileans themselves. In exile, from their memories, from bits of pictures of their homes, they had begun to rebuild their own community. Many of the houses were carefully built to look like their beloved homeland. As the tents made way for brick houses and flats, so the camps became exile towns, with kindergartens, schools, workshops, clinics and hospitals. They named their hospitals Gaza, Haifa and Akka after towns in Palestine so that they would never forget their roots.

Apart from the lack of tents, and the fact that the refugees were exiles, there was another popular misconception about the 'Palestinian refugee camps': the word 'Palestinian'. It was true that the camps had originally been set up for the refugees from Palestine. However, the Palestinians had transformed their deprivation into a principle of non-discrimination which pervaded all their institutions, and so the camps had never been for the Palestinians alone.

The hospitals run by the Palestine Red Crescent Society gave free treatment to all in need. They did not quibble about country of origin, or race, or religion, the nurse reminded me. The Palestinian schools provided free education for all. Their vocational institutions and their women's organisations ran an open-door policy. As a result, over a third of the people in Sabra and Shatila were not Palestinians, but Lebanese who identified with the Palestinians through bonds of poverty and deprivation.

Most surprising of all, said the nurse, were the Jewish families living in the middle of the camps: not many, but these were Jewish families who had left in protest along with the Galilean exiles, and had stayed with the folks in the camp. A fifth of the Palestinians were Christians.

My nurse laughed, for my face was a picture of bewilderment caused by ignorance. She invited me to her home for coffee, but I turned down the invitation as I had to catch the hospital jeep to the Lahut.

'Bokra,' I said, flaunting the second Arabic word I had learnt, which meant 'tomorrow'.

The next day, when I returned to the camps, the place was even busier: the rebuilding of the camps was in full swing. More families had returned. The hospitals were bustling and full of life, and those hospital staff who had escaped imprisonment or death were back in full force. They were clearing rubble, scrubbing the hospital floors, taking stock of medical supplies and transporting beds and equipment up and down the floors so as to get the wards ready for the patients. Akka Hospital, which had been merely a mess of rubble when we had visited it the week before, was now swept clean and the ground floor had been refurbished. Heaps of bricks and steel pipes had been brought in, presumably to rebuild the hospital.

This was a very exciting time: for once, I felt part of the vibrant force of creation. How I wished Francis could have been there, so that he could share this wonderful spirit! Israel's military might had failed to destroy this. I wished I had taught him first aid. I could have brought Francis along as an ambulance driver! We two were refugees, but we had to learn from these camp folks – from their will to survive and to turn the existing nightmare of a wartorn camp into proper homes. Suddenly I burned with the instincts of home-making and longed to decorate our tiny flat in crowded central London with hundreds and hundreds of bunches of flowers. Here in Sabra and Shatila, in the midst of poverty and persecution, life, abundant life, had returned, and no one and nothing could take that away from the camp folks – not the bombs, not the shells, not even the pain of evacuation.

Every morning from then on, I would run to the sixth floor of Gaza Hospital to share breakfast with the PRCS doctors and nurses. I would make them talk to me about the camp, about themselves, while I looked out of the window, eager to study the changes in the camp homes: new doors, new windows, freshly-painted walls, holes patched up overnight. I admired the diligence of these people.

The official reopening of Gaza Hospital was set for 29 August 1982, but people were visiting the hospital days before that for all sorts of treatment. They came because of coughs and colds, and to get treatment for war wounds which were two or three months old. The people in the camps referred to Gaza as their hospital: they loved to tell me the story of how the head of the PLO, Yasser Arafat, whom they called Abu Amar, had refused treatment from the sophisticated American University Hospital when he had been taken ill, and had chosen Gaza Hospital instead.

The staff of Gaza Hospital, all employees of the PRCS, were very courageous people. There was never the slightest murmur of complaint from any of them, and their extreme stoicism made it easy for us foreign volunteers to forget that, like everyone else in the camps, they too had lost homes or loved ones. In particular, I remember a young Palestinian orthopaedic surgeon from south Lebanon: he was a devout Muslim, and rose early each day to pray. During the Israeli invasion of Lebanon, he had refused to leave his hospital in the south until all the patients and staff had left and he had been ordered out. The war had cost him nineteen kilograms in weight, his home and his hospital in the south. Far from being bitter or resentful, however, the young orthopaedic surgeon plunged into the task of rebuilding Gaza Hospital.

The medical director of Gaza Hospital was Amir Hamawi, a young Lebanese surgeon. His cheerful, sunny disposition, his diligence and his warm enthusiasm certainly made life much more bearable for many others. Lebanese and Palestinian doctors and nurses worked side by side in Gaza in complete harmony. The professor of general surgery was one of Beirut's top specialists, but he was a very quiet, modest and unassuming man. I learnt a lot from him, and I also tried to learn from his opposite number, the co-ordinator of medical staff, a disciplinarian who did his ward round in the style of a commander-in-chief inspecting his troops. I thought this a very useful tactic, but try as I might to copy his style, I never succeeded in marshalling that much respect.

We, the foreign medical volunteers, were of diverse backgrounds, and that sometimes created problems. The PRCS medical staff were always courteous and friendly towards us. However, some of my colleagues from the West were rude and loud, and some tried to conceal their inexperience and incompetence under a cloak of blustering immodesty. This problem was not peculiar to volunteer health and relief workers in Lebanon: it was generally the case where volunteers from 'developed' countries thought that they ought to be one up on the 'natives'. Some of my more ignorant and patronising colleagues could not bring themselves to acknowledge the fact that Gaza's professor of surgery was a specialist of international standing long before they had even entered medical school.

Moreover, doctors from western countries did not always find it easy to appreciate that Lebanese and Palestinian doctors had stacked up many years of practical experience in dealing with war wounds. The western doctors had no such experience unless they had been in a war zone like Korea or Vietnam.

Although Gaza was functioning again, there was still no water or electricity from the mains. Electricity came from the hospital generator, which ran on rationed diesel oil. There was usually enough fuel for three hours a day.

As soon as the generator started running, there would be a sudden burst of activity. Water was pumped up to the tanks on the higher floors. Toilets were flushed and

washed. Laboratory equipment started working: investi-
gations and X-rays were carried out. The lifts started
moving: patients and equipment were transported from
floor to floor. The operating theatres lit up: operations
were carried out. All too soon, the three hours would be
up, it would be black-out time once more and candles
would be lit. Any transporting of patients from one floor to
another would have to be done by hand, as the lifts were
dead again.

One day a patient was brought in during a black-out. He
had returned, like many others, to live in the camps, but he
had found his home and family wiped out by an air raid. In
his despair, he had tried to take his own life by drinking a
bottle of organophosphorus. This is an insecticide, a
powerful poison which attacks a vital body enzyme called
cholinesterase. Convulsions, severe colic, respiratory
arrest and cardiac arrest then result. Atropine in high doses
is the antidote, but even in the best of circumstances the
victims of organophosphorus poisoning usually go under
and die. He needed help in breathing, and was artificially
ventilated for a week. Because there was no electricity,
ventilation had to be carried out by hand. We all took turns
squeezing the bag, and in the end the poison wore off and
he recovered consciousness. He did some thinking, and
became more positive and glad to be alive. It was a credit to
the anaesthetics department that this young man – against
all the odds – survived.

Throughout the entire Israeli invasion, the siege of
Beirut and its aftermath, the administrator of Gaza
Hospital was Azziza Khalidi, a fine young Lebanese-
Palestinian. She was extremely bright, with a PhD from the
American University of Beirut at the age of twenty-six.

Behind the fair complexion and the bright, beautiful and
apparently permanent smile was an extremely competent
administrator. Azziza's was a difficult task during a chaotic
time. Everything was difficult. There were staff shortages
and shortages of equipment. There were political pres-

sures. On top of everything else there were impatient and bad-tempered foreign volunteers who seemed unable to grasp that after three months of air raids and shelling Beirut was not like London or New York where a hospital administrator simply had to pick up the phone to order supplies. Some of them also found it hard to accept that operating theatres with large shell holes in the walls which lacked electricity and running water should only be used for the most urgent, life-saving operations.

Although we were not all aware of it, Azziza also had to deal with the personal and social lives of her staff, who might be homeless, or might have lost their loved ones through evacuation or because of death. In addition, Gaza Hospital was not just a hospital, but was also a welfare centre where the camp folks brought all their financial and domestic problems. What could you say to the mother of six young children who between them had lost five limbs, when she had neither husband nor grown-up son to be the family breadwinner? Many of the problems were insoluble.

Community medicine was very nearly my chosen specialisation. Realising I knew little of my own society in Singapore, I left the hothouse hospital atmosphere and spent two years at Singapore University's faculty of community medicine. While based there, I visited factories and learnt about lead poisoning, noise-induced deafness and industrial accidents. I also studied maternal and child health. There were clear links, in my view, between disease and poverty and ignorance. A doctor could act as a technician trying to put right the effects of a whole series of causes, but a doctor could also try to eliminate the basic causes of illness.

Trying to hit at the root causes of illness is not easy: as well as using medical technology, it involves educating the public and trying to influence the powerful. It was all too much for me: I did get a gold medal for my community medicine studies, but I also had to leave the department, because I had upset too many bureaucrats and academics.

I returned to hospital practice. Tucked away in the wards and operating theatres, doing a hundred hours a week, I could not make trouble by preaching that unequal distribution of wealth resulted in unequal distribution of health. It was better to treat streptococcal infections in young people than to treat late complications of these infections with heart and kidney transplants – but stating such obvious truths was now off-limits. I became a skilled technician once more, and I chose to train as a surgeon, since surgery combined aspects of three subjects I loved: medicine, cookery and sewing. (Work it out.) I concentrated on minding my own business and doing a competent job once more.

Although I was now a surgeon, I was well aware of the way Azziza and her team extended the hospital's role so that it tried to meet the social needs of the community as well. People would come to Azziza for food – usually bread – or building materials for their homes, or jobs. In the middle of all these demands on her, our young hospital administrator never lost her cool.

Of course, she also had some extremely good and loyal staff, most of whom were women. They had refused to abandon the hospital during the war, even at the height of the bombing, when they would have been safer elsewhere. They simply refused to jump ship! Those Arab women with their gentle and graceful ways really restored my faith in the strength of women.

CHAPTER 5

═══════════

A week after the official reopening of the hospital, we had sixty in-patients and a waiting list of twice as many again. Three quarters of the in-patients were orthopaedic patients, but the hospital's senior orthopaedic surgeon had been evacuated, and so I was put in charge of the Orthopaedic Department. Although I knew I was too inexperienced for this job, there was no one else around, and I had to accept the responsibility. What I lacked in experience, I tried to make up for with hard work, because I soon came to love and respect these people deeply. I just wished I was stronger, and could make do with less sleep. The need was pressing: I could have worked continuously, resting only when there was no electricity or no water. Even then it was often possible to do smaller operations using local anaesthetic, with a nurse holding a torch.

In the evening, I used to take walks around Sabra and Shatila. These are now among my fondest memories of those early days. Feeling completely at home, I would enjoy the hospitality of the families in the camps. No matter what misfortunes had befallen them, I was always greeted kindly and welcomed into their homes. Sometimes a home might have been reduced to broken walls, but it did not matter. The floor would always have been swept extremely clean, and I would invariably be offered Arabic coffee. I had not encountered such hospitality for a long time – not since leaving South East Asia, where rural Malays and Chinese fisher folk always welcomed strangers into their homes with open arms. The people in the camps would share their family pictures with a stranger like me, pictures of their loved ones, of weddings, of births and of their Palestine. They would often try to give me some of their few precious belongings.

The girls would frequently remove their earrings, their bracelets or other bits of jewellery and force them on me. The really poor people would try to make me accept their family pictures, or pieces of cloth such as tea towels. I soon learnt never to make a complimentary remark about any household item in a Palestinian home, because it would certainly be offered to me as a gift. Their generosity often made me deeply ashamed of my own selfishness. I was a Christian on a 'mercy' mission; I had been hailed as a 'Lady of Mercy' by Singapore's press, but I had so little to give these folks, and in fact received from them the best humanity had to offer a thousand times over. In the camps, in Gaza Hospital, with people who enlightened me through their attitudes and their actions, I felt closer to God than ever before.

Gaza Hospital went from strength to strength. We got busier and busier by the day: the wards filled up, and more and more operations could be carried out as the water and electricity supplies improved. Many nurses emerged from hiding and came back to the hospital. Among them were the very skilled and experienced ones. They became among my best friends during my time in the camps. Autoclaves, X-ray machines and laboratory facilities were gradually brought back into action. A fortnight after the official opening, Gaza Hospital was in full swing.

The hospital routine consisted of morning ward rounds and clinical case conferences, followed by out-patient and specialist clinics, operating sessions and then, for the medical staff who were on call that day, work in the emergency room. My own work had started to expand into the area of non-trauma or 'cold' orthopaedics. This included looking after patients with congenital orthopaedic problems such as club feet or hip dislocations, and patients with degenerative conditions like osteoarthritis and backache. People started to turn up with the sort of injuries I associated with civilian life, such as domestic fractures, cuts and burns.

The hospital received visits from outside groups, prominent among them being journalists and television crews. Although I found the television visits fairly distracting, I did appreciate the importance of the media. They helped to remind the outside world of the camps and their people. Up till then the media had focused on the war and destruction: now we hoped it would capture the optimistic mood in the camps as their people plunged wholeheartedly into the work of reconstruction. Perhaps just this once, I hoped, the will of the people to survive and put their broken lives together would strike a chord in the hearts of people in the west.

Our patients were eager to talk to the journalists about the war. At first they were camera-shy, but after a while they would pour their hearts out and recount the horrible events of the war. They would show their anger at those injustices, but many of them obviously felt triumphant, and were proud that nothing could break their spirit.

The children in my orthopaedic ward were incredible. Little Essau, a Christian Palestinian boy with short, curly, black hair, had been wounded by the same cluster bomb which killed his mother. Both his legs had been broken in many places by the explosion. Many of Essau's wounds were septic, and he needed an orthopaedic operation to remove the dead and septic bones. After the operation, his fractures needed to be set straight so his legs would not be crooked. Whenever reporters came to his ward, Essau would usually start by telling them that when he grew up he was going to be a 'fighter', so as to defend his people and his camp. Before he could be labelled a 'terrorist' by the reporters, a nurse would pull back his sheets to reveal a pair of scarred and crooked legs riddled with large, festering wounds. Seven-year-old Essau would look down, and fall silent. None of us were sure if he would even walk again, let alone become a 'fighter' when he grew up.

Milad Faroukh was an eight-year-old Lebanese boy whose father once had a farm in south Lebanon. The farm had been destroyed by Israeli bombs, and one of the bombs had fallen on to the field where Milad was playing frisbee with his little brother. His brother was killed outright, and Milad's heel was blown off. My British colleague Dr Paul Morris spent hours and hours patiently trying to talk him out of his withdrawn state and persuading him to eat. At last he succeeded, and Milad started to eat something. He had been reduced to skin and bones, but now he made a steady recovery. The first time Milad smiled, we all thought an angel was smiling in wartorn Lebanon, so beautiful was his face.

Although he remained shy and reserved, Milad became very brave, and soon started learning how to change his own dressings. As he peeled off the bandages from his heel, a large, raw crater was revealed. It must have been agony, but he gritted his teeth and bravely washed his wound with hydrogen peroxide before dressing it.

There was also Leila. When we changed the dressings on her large, raw burns, her mother and the nurses all knew that she was in agony. Such large wounds on a three-year-old really ought to have been dressed under a general anaesthetic, but there was a shortage of drugs. We had to make do with what we called a 'vocal anaesthetic': Leila's mother and the nurses talking or shouting the little child into co-operation.

From all over the place came more children – children with war wounds, children with pieces of shrapnel: very, very brave children on whose bodies the advanced technology of modern warfare cruelly left its indelible marks.

Many of the kids were now orphaned and homeless, and had found temporary shelter with neighbours or distant relatives.

Many times I quietly prayed for strength, prayed to God to help me cope. The most straightforward operation could be turned into a complicated nightmare by a sudden power cut. Sometimes the nurses were down to dressing wounds with nothing more than soap and water. This was the aftermath of war, but at least there was a ceasefire. The camp folks were glad the bombs and shells had stopped falling. Occasionally an unexploded bomb or a landmine would go off and claim its unwary victims, but as the days passed such incidents became less frequent. Outside the camps, major political events were unfolding.

Various 'peace plans' were being discussed. Events which attracted our attention on the BBC news, such as the restoration of the Lebanese Parliament, became the talk of the markets, the streets and the taxi drivers. Multinational peacekeeping forces were stationed in many places, and were well-accepted by the local people. We were told that the peacekeeping forces would remain till the President-elect of Lebanon, Bashir Gemayel, had been sworn into office and the Lebanese Army had been able to regain control of the country.

After nearly a decade of civil war, Lebanon had become a place full of armed militias. Many private individuals owned a machine gun or at least a pistol. Private organisations owned rocket-launchers and even tanks. Now a major disarmament exercise took place: this war-weary country was prepared to have a real go at peace. Throughout Beirut the people gave up their guns, and units of the Lebanese Army toured the cities and the camps calling on people to turn in their weapons. Arms depots were emptied by the army.

Everyone thought that this time they would see an end to war. The price of a Kalashnikov plummeted to seven Lebanese lira (about £2.50 sterling). I saw women going up to surrender their sons' weapons. People trusted the peace proposals, and they were prepared to show that they wanted peace. Sandbags, roadblocks and landmines were gradually cleared. Roads which had been blocked by large heaps of sand were cleared so that large vehicles could use them. Bulldozers were kept extremely busy clearing roads and war debris. Shops reopened. Piped water returned and the 'electricity of the government' became available once more.

Hamra came back to life, and various luxury items were available again. I acquired a taste for croissants, a French delicacy which was totally alien to the Singaporean tongue.

There was a postwar euphoria: the local population was both enthusiastic and united. When asked if they were Lebanese or Palestinian, people often answered, 'Both,' and said that there was no difference between the two communities. Far from dividing the two peoples, the invasion had obviously united them in their common hatred of the Israelis. People would drag me along to see the bombed-out buildings.

'Look, doctora,' they would say. 'Shops, hotels – Israeli rockets and bombs make "whoosh", and now no more shops, houses and hotels.' The wreckage spoke for itself.

Tuesday, 14 September 1982, was a good day. The roads were entirely cleared of road blocks. The hospital's water supply had been restored, as had the electricity. It was so good to have electric lighting and to be able to wash my hands under a running tap. Dr Phil McKenna, my anaesthetist colleague from Ireland – a wonderful friend – decided to reorganise the whole emergency room. 'Now that the war is over,' she said, 'we can establish some sort of system.'

She went downstairs, asked for a towel, and wiped the tables and trolleys in the emergency room. Then she sat down to sort out the resuscitation equipment: all the endotracheal tubes she arranged by size, the laryngoscopes were checked, as were the anaesthetic gases, the machine connections and even the gauze and bandages.

As I had finished operating, I came down to help the nurses prepare surgical dressings. We cut large pieces of gauze into smaller pieces, and then folded them into little squares. We prepared abdominal packs by stitching the edges of large pieces of folded gauze. Cotton wool balls were rolled and packed for the newly-functioning autoclave. Then everything was laid out ready for use the next day. Helping make the dressings was wonderfully relaxing – it was my favourite job of the day. I got to know the nurses, and picked up some more bits of Arabic.

Abu Ali, the operating theatre superintendent, was in his early middle age, and spoke good English. He was an especially proud and happy man that day, because he was celebrating the successful wiring of the autoclave. From then on, it was going to be possible to 'autoclave' all surgical instruments. Abu Ali started to explain to the student nurses the differences between sterilising surgical instruments using the autoclave, which he called 'steam heat', and sterilising them using boiling water, which he called 'water heat'. The autoclave was more effective for a number of reasons, which he explained, and I nodded in approval.

Abu Ali had a very stabilising influence on me, because somehow he managed to produce all the surgical instruments required for my operations. This was more than many theatre nurses in British hospitals could do. Often I held back from asking for sophisticated orthopaedic instruments, because I did not want the Gaza theatre staff to feel inadequate. Frequently, to my absolute delight and amazement, one of the instruments I needed to use, but dared not ask for, would be put into my hands by one of the scrub nurses. Time and time again I was told by this excellent theatre superintendent that there was no need to compromise good surgical standards for expediency.

The PRCS theatre staff were obviously very proud of their own work, and tried to keep standards up. Sometimes Abu Ali would shake his head ruefully and tell me, 'Before the invasion we had a good working system, but unfortunately our system was destroyed by the war. However, we are now beginning to re-establish our standards.'

That night I went to bed early, feeling very satisfied and looking forward to the next day's work. We had scheduled some fairly major orthopaedic reconstructive cases for the next day – three cases with infected fractures of the lower limbs which had not united, one burn case with about ten per cent area to skingraft, and a few smaller operations.

I was woken up at eleven o'clock that night by a loud bang. It sounded like an explosion far away, but the whole building was vibrating from it. None of us knew what it could be. The midnight news confirmed that a large bomb had gone off in East Beirut, and that the President-elect of Lebanon, Bashir Gemayel, had been among those assassinated. We were all shocked by this news. Could it mean that there was going to be trouble again?

PART II

The Sabra–Shatila Massacre

Autumn 1982

CHAPTER 6

All our worst fears started to come true the next day. It was
the morning of 15 September. I was sound asleep in the
foreign medical volunteer apartment in Hamra when I was
rudely woken by the planes screaming overhead. They
were coming in from the Mediterranean and heading south
towards the area of West Beirut where the refugee camps
of Sabra and Shatila were located. Beirut International
Airport had been closed ever since I arrived. These planes
were flying low, breaking the sound barrier. They were not
airliners. It was about 5.30 AM. My first reaction was it must
be another Israeli air raid, and I immediately thought of
Gaza Hospital and the camps. I jumped out of bed,
grabbed my toothbrush and towel, cleaned myself up,
hastily put on some clothes and, leaving my volunteer
colleagues behind in their beds, ran downstairs to catch a
taxi to the camps. There was no time to waste. Once an air
raid started, my chance of making it to the camps from
Hamra would be nil, and I would not be able to treat the
wounded.

'Hurry, please hurry,' I pleaded to the taxi-driver,
desperate to get to the camps. The bumpy roads were
deserted – no cars and no pedestrians. There was not even
anybody at the checkpoints. Where on earth had everybody gone? We drove straight to Gaza Hospital without

stopping, arriving at around 6.30 AM. I cannot remember how much money I had to pay him – loads, since all the other taxis refused to drive anywhere near the camps. He made a sharp U-turn once I got out, and drove away at high speed. It was already bright by then.

I dashed into the Accidents and Emergency – but there were no patients. All the PRCS medics were up and having a discussion. The atmosphere was tense. Strangely, the planes had stopped flying, and no bombs had fallen yet. The news bulletin announced that Israel was invading West Beirut 'to flush out two thousand "terrorists" left there by the PLO'. That could only mean trouble for the camps, we knew, but we wondered why no bombs had been dropped.

The medics started the morning by discharging all in-patients well enough to go home, to make room for expected casualties. All elective operations were cancelled, and everyone was put on standby, waiting for the wounded to be brought in. I went up to the orthopaedic wards and explained to all my patients that I could not do their operations now, as we needed to reserve the operating facilities for new casualties.

One of my patients said, 'Never mind, Doctora, we understand that you did not cancel our operations. Sharon did.' Ariel Sharon was the Israeli Government Minister in charge of the armed forces.

It was not until 8 AM that we heard the first explosions. They sounded like shelling from tanks, not bombs from the sky. I went up to the top of the hospital – to the tenth floor – and watched the shells exploding on the houses of West Beirut. With hindsight, the top of a tall building was perhaps not the safest place to be while the shells were exploding, but none landed on me. I was soon joined by other foreign volunteers, who also wanted to know where the explosions were happening. To begin with we saw shells landing in one direction from us. By midday, shells were landing around Gaza Hospital in a circle ten kilometres in diameter. I thought of all the roads being cleared of heaps of sand and roadblocks over the past few days. I could not help wondering whether it was in preparation for tanks to advance into the streets of West Beirut. Soon, Gaza Hospital was surrounded by a circle of smoke from burning buildings.

Only walking wounded came to the hospital that morning, as the roads leading to the hospital were closed to ambulances. These were patients wounded by shrapnel from exploding shells. Later, people who were more severely wounded were carried into the accident room by their relatives. The patients told us that Israeli tanks were coming into West Beirut from different directions and were firing shells in all directions as they advanced. Two PRCS ambulances had been sent out on a rescue mission earlier. They never returned.

The shelling came nearer and nearer. By roughly a quarter to four in the afternoon, we reckoned that the zone of shelling and explosives had closed in to about three quarters of a kilometre away from the hospital. People who tried to leave the camp returned and said that all roads leading out of the camps were blocked by Israeli tanks.

At 4.30 PM news arrived at the Gaza Hospital that Israeli troops had invaded Akka Hospital, and shot dead nurses, doctors and patients. They had begun to surround Sabra and Shatila camp. People fled into the camp, with news that tanks were following them. At 5 PM we were told that Israeli commandos were on the main roads of the camps. I had not seen an Israeli soldier since coming across the Green Line from East Beirut. They had always attacked West Beirut by air or sea, or from across the mountains. Why did they want to make it on land this time? Perhaps they dared to come in now that the PLO fighters had left. Perhaps they wanted to check if the camps were holding terrorists or not. If their mission was the latter, I thought to myself, I could easily have told them that the PLO fighters had actually left.

By nightfall, it was clear that we were entirely surrounded.

The shelling stopped, but the rattle of machine-gun fire continued throughout the night. The skies above Sabra and Shatila were lit with military flares. I must have dozed off to sleep some time after 4 AM, since that was the last time I remembered looking at my watch.

An hour later, I was again woken up by aircraft screaming over us at a low altitude. It was the morning of Thursday, 16 September 1982. We heard shelling and explosions continuing after that, and could distinctly hear machine-gun fire. The fact that the shooting was still going on made me wonder if there were some PLO men around after all.

Frightened people began to come into the hospital. In the middle of the morning, casualties poured in. The first of them was a woman shot in the elbow. Her entire elbow joint was missing – and out through the disorganised mess of bleeding flesh jutted the ends of the humerus, radius and ulnar bones. She lived in the camp, and had been shot as soon as she stepped out of the door of her house. Following her came a stream of women, shot in the jaw, the head, the chest, the abdomen. Most of them had been shot in the streets of the camp while going out to buy food, or on their way to the water points to fetch water for their families. Their injuries were high-velocity gunshot wounds consistent with sniper fire. They kept being brought in, and with only two functioning operating theatres, Gaza Hospital could not cope. Some of them were then transferred by PRCS ambulances to a neighbouring Lebanese hospital, the Makassad. We only transferred those whom we thought might survive: moribund patients just had a drip put up, and were given some painkillers. The rest we operated on ourselves in the basement theatres of Gaza.

Very soon, the pattern changed. The wounds were still being caused by bullets, but by around noon it was evident from the casualties being brought in that gunmen had gone into homes in Sabra and Shatila and had started shooting people there. We were told that these were not Israelis, but gunmen with a Ba'albek accent. I made a mental note of that, but had no time to ask any questions – I just kept seeing patients and operating. Mercifully, there was water and electricity - they had been fixed up two days before.

The medical team – we were two surgeons, two anaesthetists and five residents – worked non-stop. In less than twenty-four hours, about thirty very seriously wounded people were brought in and died while still receiving first aid treatment. About another thirty were fit enough to be operated upon. About ninety wounded were treated in the Casualty Department. Another thirty or so patients were transferred to the Makassad Hospital.

After only twenty-four hours, the hospital's supply of food ran out. We had nothing like enough provisions to feed the hundreds of people who sought refuge in the hospital. No one could leave the hospital to buy more food because of the continuous shooting and shelling outside. I was too busy to eat anything, but at one point Azziza Khalidi, the hospital administrator, insisted that I stopped operating so that I could eat a slice of pitta bread and some olives she had brought down to the theatre for me. It was only much later that I found out she had given me the last food in Gaza Hospital. How many times did I take for granted the kindness and consideration which the Palestinians extended to me!

By nightfall, we estimated that over two thousand of the camp people had flocked into the hospital seeking refuge, and were sleeping all over the hospital staircase and floors. As I came up from the basement operating theatre to assess the wounded waiting in the Accident room, I had to wade my way among families lying and sitting all over the floor. In-patient numbers had increased from forty-five to over eighty by the small-hours. About eight were critically ill.

Throughout the night, the camps surrounding the Gaza Hospital were lit up by flares shot into the sky, and the shootings continued. I did not sleep that night, neither did the rest of the medical team. Among other operations, I amputated limbs, and opened chests and abdomens to remove damaged and bleeding organs. High velocity gunshot wounds were heavy going one at a time, but when they were piled up and pushed into the theatre along what felt like a never-ending conveyor belt, they were almost impossible to handle. One bullet through an abdomen could easily transect the intestines in several different places, explode the liver or kidney, and fracture both the spine and pelvis on its track in and out of the body.

To do a proper job on one high-velocity gunshot wound in the abdomen would take an experienced surgeon in a well-equipped outfit from four to six hours. But after the first few hours I realised I could devote no more than two hours to any one of the wounded, or I would not get through the work load. Dr Per Miehlumshagen, a volunteer orthopaedic surgeon from Norway, did the same. He did all the operating in the other theatre. The PRCS doctors and nurses were really good, and performed with such excellence throughout that I regretted I had no time to tell them properly how wonderful they had all been.

Per and I had been operating through the night into the morning of Friday 17 September. The rattle of machine-guns continued throughout. People wounded by gunshots continued to be brought in. At about seven o'clock that morning, Per came to tell me that we had almost caught up with the backlog of wounded, and that I ought to go and get some rest before it started all over again.

'What about you, Per?' I asked.

'I had some rest already,' said Per. I did not believe him, but was too tired to argue.

Although I put my head on my pillow, I was so jumpy that I could not possibly sleep. So I went off to look for Azziza, thinking that perhaps she would be able to tell me what on earth was going on.

'Something terrible is happening,' she said and that was all she could tell me. From her harassed and pale looks, I thought she probably had not yet had enough time to put two and two together. But Azziza told me that she must try to contact the International Red Cross. There was no food left, the place was filled with wounded, medical supplies had run out, and gunmen in the camps were terrorising and killing at will. She was going to appeal for more medical workers and medicines – and food for the many people sheltering in the hospital, and notify the International Red Cross of the presence of twenty-two medical workers from Europe and the USA. She also wanted to contact the Israeli Army which was surrounding the camps, appeal to it to lend protection to the foreign medical workers and ask it to control the terrorists now rampant in the refugee camps. She left at about ten in the morning.

After she left, I went up to the intensive care unit to look at the patients operated on over the last two days. The intensive care unit was packed with very ill patients, all on drip and some being ventilated. I grabbed Dr Paul Morris and asked him for a brief report. He told me that the mortuary was full of dead bodies. We went down to the mortuary. It was jammed with those who had died before we managed to operate on them. There were bodies of old men, children and women. They had to be piled on top of each other through lack of space. It just made no sense.

The ground floor of the hospital was packed full of people – some wounded and awaiting treatment, others trembling with fear. Most of them were so scared that they could not speak, all they could manage was to clutch at any doctor or nurse who passed by, as though we possessed some supernatural power to protect them. I still was not wholly aware of what had gone on, and why everyone was so frightened. The kids sensed I was unafraid and so they started to cling on to me, calling me a brave doctor. I was not brave at all, merely uninformed. Anyway I had been working so hard that I had no time to be afraid.

When Azziza returned at about midday, she told us she had done all that she had set out to do, but something very terrible was about to happen. She then told the camp folks hiding in the hospital that Gaza Hospital was no longer a safe sanctuary, and that at any moment, the Kata'ebs, or even worse, the Haddads, might move in. (Both the Kata'ebs and the Haddads were Lebanese Christian militias. The Kata'ebs – or Phalangists – were the Israelis' allies, but the Haddads were actually on their payroll.) On hearing this, the two thousand or so refugees evacuated rapidly. Many of the wounded were also carried out by their families, some with drips still running. She then proceeded to instruct the remaining handful of PRCS personnel – two resident doctors, and some nurses and technicians – to leave while there was still time. Some PRCS medics at first refused to go, and had to be firmly ordered to leave by Azziza.

At around 4.30 PM, she came to the foreign medical team, and told us that she too was going to have to leave. Although she carried Lebanese papers, she said she was in personal danger, as the hospital was already infiltrated. I did not even have the sense to ask her by whom.

The International Red Cross then arrived and brought some food and first aid equipment. Two doctors and two nurses from the Middle East Council of Churches had also come to help. This visiting delegation also included the Norwegian chargé d'affaires. He tried to persuade the Norwegian medical volunteers to leave, but they all chose to stay with the wounded and refused to go with him. The Red Cross team left with six very ill children and Azziza Khalidi, who promised to return the following day. She left us a large bunch of keys – to the kitchen, the pharmacy, the outpatients, the ambulance station, and the mortuary.

The hospital quietened down that night, although shelling and machine-gunning continued outside in the camps. The explosions came very close now, and the glass in the windows of the intensive care unit began to crack from the vibrations caused by the blast of the shells. More patients were now discharging themselves voluntarily and others were being discharged by their families. The last casualty of the evening was an eleven-year-old boy, shot three times by a machine gun, and left for dead under a heap of twenty-seven bodies. When the killers left, friends rescued him and brought him to the hospital. All he could tell us was there had been Israelis, Kata'ebs and Haddads. Then he went into shock. His arm, leg and index finger had been injured by bullets, but he survived his injuries.

In the theatre, I operated on a woman and a child. The woman had major surgery for a gunshot wound of the abdomen. It was a difficult operation, as I had to remove a third of her liver, and anastomose – or join together – transected large and small bowels. She was waking up from the anaesthetic, when the child was brought back from the theatre recovery room. I nipped back in to see both of them and remind the nurses in intensive care to give both of them blood transfusions. I was told that the packet of blood being transfused into the woman was the last one. There was no blood left for the child. We had run out. The child had been wounded by a hand grenade chucked into the midst of a group of little kids. He had lost a fair amount of blood through a severed splenic artery, but otherwise he was stable after his operation. Both needed blood and they were of the same blood group. The Palestinian woman overheard the nurses talking to me and asked us to give blood to the child instead of her. Then she asked for some painkillers and died shortly afterwards.

That evening, the foreigners held a meeting to discuss what to do if the Israelis, Haddads or Kata'ebs did come into the hospital. We decided that our priority would be to negotiate for the lives of our patients. I did not have any bright contributions to make during that discussion, as some of our little patients kept distracting me by asking me when Major Saad Haddad was coming into the hospital to kill them. At that time I did not have the faintest idea who Saad Haddad was, but I told the kids that if he was the troublemaker I would ban him from Gaza Hospital. The kids made me wonder if this Saad Haddad was responsible for all these casualties. But I did not dwell on that at all.

For seventy-two hours, from 15 to 18 September 1982, I was basically working flat out in the basement operating theatre of Gaza Hospital, inundated with casualties. I only managed to leave the operating theatre for a few minutes at a time to assess new arrivals so that we could decide who to operate on and who to let go.

That night, Paul Morris wrote a letter to his wife Mary, and then he asked me to deliver it if anything went wrong with him.

'Hey, Paul,' I said, 'you're talking as though you're going to die. You're joking, aren't you?'

But he was very serious, so I took his letter and promised to do as he asked.

On Saturday 18 September, an American nurse spotted some soldiers outside Gaza Hospital at 6.45 AM and one of the doctors was sent down to negotiate with them. After a little while I went down to join him and asked for the officer in charge. A young man with a moustache stepped forward and, in English, said, 'Do not be afraid, we are Lebanese.' His uniform was clean and well-starched, and it crossed my mind that he could not possibly be one of those who had been murdering people in the camps for the past three days.

I said, 'Of course I'm not afraid. What do you want?'

He asked us to assemble all foreign medical personnel to be taken for interrogation. After some discussion, he said he was prepared to allow a Swedish nurse and a German medical student to remain behind to look after the critically ill in intensive care.

We were escorted out of Gaza Hospital and down the main road of the camp, where we were passed on to a different lot of gunmen, who were rough, untidy and nasty. They kept poking us with their machine guns, and once or twice I nearly told them to get lost. We were made to walk along Rue Sabra. By the road were some bodies. At one point I was pushed so that I stumbled over the body of an old man. He was wearing a long blue gown and the white cap of a Haj. Thinking I knew him, I tried to look at his face. He had been shot in the head and his eyes had been dug out. On both sides of the camp road, groups of women and children had been rounded up by soldiers wearing green military uniforms, green baseball caps, but no insignia.

Our estimate was that eight hundred to a thousand women and children had been rounded up, some of whom had been hiding in Gaza Hospital the previous day.

Large bulldozers were at work tearing down shelled buildings and burying bodies inside them. I could hardly recognise the camps. The houses were now heaps of rubble. Within the rubble, I could see newly-hung curtains and pictures. The dynamited, partially bulldozed homes still had fresh paint on them.

Gunmen lined the sides of Rue Sabra while we were marched down it at gunpoint, and we could all see what was going on – the bodies, the smashed homes, the rubble, the terror in everyone's faces, the desperate mother who wanted to give me her infant – the baby boy which I held in my arms for a brief moment before it was cruelly snatched away by the gunmen. We knew what was about to happen. When, later, I was able to return, I roamed the length and breadth of the camps, looking for mother and child. I found neither. A Palestinian employee of the PRCS had come along with us from Gaza Hospital, but was discovered almost immediately, taken away and killed. It was as though they had been instructed to kill Palestinians but not foreigners, and kept to their orders.

I thought of all those who died, and the ones rounded up by the gunmen on the roadside. From the terror in their faces, they knew they were going to be killed once we left them. Suddenly I found myself wishing that the PLO fighters had not been evacuated. They could have defended their people! I felt myself getting angrier and angrier as we were marched further down the road. A doctor is a doctor, but a doctor is also a human being.

We were taken down through Shatila camp to the courtyard of the United Nations building on the edge of the camp, which was about ten minutes' walk away.

The United Nations building had been taken over by soldiers who claimed they were Christian Lebanese. In the courtyard of the building our papers were checked, and we were questioned about our political affiliations. Although they tried to impress on us they were Lebanese, I had my doubts. The place was full of newspapers and magazines in Hebrew, and tins of food and drink bearing Israeli labels. They took orders directly from Israeli army officials. They were no bandit army, for they never did anything without consulting an Israeli official, either directly or via the walkie-talkie.

We had no doubt of their hostility towards us: they shouted at us and insulted us for being friends and supporters of the Palestinians. One of the soldiers was a good-looking woman with long, black curly hair and icy blue eyes. Her behaviour was absolutely hideous: she was wild with rage when I told her I was a Christian. She shouted: 'You are a Christian and you dare to help Palestinians! You are filthy!'

They subjected us to a mock execution: I was so involved in a furious argument with them that I did not realise it was happening at the time. All I was thinking was that this awful bunch had dragged us out of the hospital so that they could kill our patients. My colleagues told me later: we were actually asked to surrender all our belongings, remove our white uniforms and stand against a wall. Two bulldozers were ready to knock the wall down over us. A group of soldiers with machine guns were standing as though they were ready to shoot us all down.

Thinking back, I realise that what they told me did

happen. I remember taking off my doctor's coat, and walking up towards a wall. I even remember looking to see if the bulldozers were trying to bury bodies behind the low wall. But I was blinded by anger, too angry even to be paranoid. Mock executions worked by creating fear. But on that morning I was too angry to be fearful. We were held in the courtyard for more than an hour. At about 9.15 or 9.30 AM, an Israeli officer came by and told them to take us to the Israeli headquarters, which was within walking distance, on a road parallel to the main road of the camp. This was a five or six storey building on high ground where I could see Israeli soldiers on the upper floors looking into the camps with binoculars.

In front of an Israeli film crew, we were assured that everything possible would be done to keep our patients safe. We were also assured that we would be helped to leave West Beirut, and we were given food and water. Two male doctors and one male nurse were allowed to go back to Gaza Hospital to help out, but the rest of us were taken by two Israeli Army trucks to the American Embassy outside the camps, and told to stay there. When more of us said we wanted to go back to Gaza Hospital, the Israeli officers warned us that it was highly unsafe, and only those three people were escorted back.

Back in the camps, the murderers were at work. The Swedish nurse who had been left in Gaza Hospital later testified that, half an hour after we had left, they heard continuous machine-gun fire lasting twenty to thirty minutes, accompanied by the screaming of women and children. That was followed by complete silence. That happened between 7.30 AM and 8.30 AM.

A BBC correspondent who arrived about 9.30 AM at Gaza Hospital said that heaps of dead bodies piled on top of each other – in groups of ten or more – lined the main road of the camp, the road down which we had been marched earlier on. Most of the dead were women and children. Half an hour later a Canadian film crew recorded

Rue Sabra with numerous dead bodies piled on top of each other on either side of the road.

Later journalists who arrived on the scene saw bull-dozers at work tearing down buildings and burying bodies in the rubble. The patients, the German medical student and the Swedish nurse left in Gaza Hospital were later evacuated by the International Red Cross.

The Israelis dropped us at the compound of the American embassy in West Beirut. I did not want to go into the embassy: I wanted to go back to the camps. But I knew that I could not. While the rest of the team went into the embassy, I decided I would walk to the Commodore Hotel to talk to the journalists there, to see if I could find out more about what had happened. Paul Morris came with me.

It was early in the afternoon when we got to the Commodore Hotel. We went to the press room, where TV crews had just returned from the camps, and were review-ing what they had just videoed in Sabra and Shatila.

First there were shots of the main road of the camp, the road we had been marched down early that morning. Heaps of corpses on both sides of the road. The people rounded up by the gunmen had been shot after we left. Then close-ups of the bodies filmed in the side alleys of the camp. Bodies piled on top of each other – mutilated bodies, with arms chopped off – bloated decaying bodies that had obviously died a day or two before. Bodies whose limbs were still tied to bits of wires, and bodies which bore marks of having been beaten up before their murder. Bodies of children – little girls and boys – and women and old men. Some bodies lay in blood that was still red, others in pools of brownish black fluid. Bodies of women with clothes removed, but too mutilated to tell whether they were sexually assaulted or just tortured to death.

I started to cry. For the first time I grasped the scale of what had happened. The truth hit me painfully. I had been so busy that I had no time to think. But now, I knew that while we had been trying to save a handful of people in the operating theatres of Gaza Hospital, the camp folks had been dying by the thousands outside. Besides being shot dead, people were tortured before being killed. They were beaten brutally, electric wires were tied round limbs, eyes were dug out, women were raped, often more than once, children were dynamited alive. Looking at all the broken bodies, I began to think that those who had died quickly were the lucky ones.

The machine-gun rattle that we had heard from the hospital was not fighting between PLO terrorists and Israelis as I had vaguely assumed, but had been the sound of whole families being shot dead in cold blood. The heavy explosive noises we had heard had been the shelling of the camp homes. The camps were completely sealed in by Israeli tanks, and not even a child could sneak out past them. When we asked the two thousand people hiding in Gaza Hospital to run away, they had nowhere to go. So they were all captured when they left the hospital, and indeed, many of them were murdered later that morning. People full of hope and life were now just mutilated corpses. These were the folks who after months of bombardment had come back from the bomb shelters to live in the camps. They had been so optimistic just a few days ago. They had believed the promises of the USA and other powerful nations that they would be left in peace, if the PLO left. They all thought they were being promised a chance of life.

I had watched them rebuilding their shattered lives and homes just a few days before. I had spoken to women who had watched their sons, brothers and husbands being evacuated with the PLO under the peace agreement and then had taken the guns they left behind to surrender them to the Lebanese Army or throw them away on the rubbish dump. I had eaten in their homes and had drunk Arabic coffee with them. My surgical skills had enabled me to treat a few people, to save them so that they could be sent out into the streets, unarmed, to be shot down again, this time successfully. I hated my own ignorance which had deceived me into believing that we all had a real hope of peace in Sabra and Shatila, a real chance of a new life. Like everyone else from the West, I thought things would be all right once the PLO left. I thought they were the ones whose presence caused all the attacks on the camps.

I had thought the old people could retire when the PLO went, and the children could grow up – instead of having bullets put through their heads, and having their throats slit. I was a fool, a real fool. It had never occurred to me that this would happen. It was a grim moment. I felt forsaken by God, by men, by a world without conscience. How could little children suffer the agony and the terror of watching scenes of torture, of their loved ones being killed, of their homes being blown up and bulldozed over. For these children, the mental scars, the psychological wounds would probably never heal. It was one thing to die suddenly. It was entirely different to watch loved ones being tortured and killed, while awaiting one's own turn.

I left the press room in the Commodore Hotel physically and mentally exhausted. I had no desire to see or talk to anyone, so Paul took me to a friend's place, an empty flat. I could be alone there. Why had this happened? My feelings were gone – it was as though my heart had died. It had been trampled on and murdered in the alleys of Sabra and Shatila, and buried there. To me, there was nothing worthy left in life any more. Everything was over now.

Per came to the flat to see me in the evening, and asked whether I was in good enough shape to visit the camps the next day. I cannot remember whether I said yes or no. But on the morning of the next day, 19 September, we were able to return to Sabra and Shatila. We saw dead bodies everywhere: whole families must have been shot together, and in one particular case we saw the body of a man (presumably the father) who had obviously tried to use his own body to shield his wife and children from the killers. They were all butchered mercilessly.

The total number of bodies counted by then was one thousand five hundred. We tried to go to the camp again that afternoon, but found it sealed by Lebanese tanks and troops: We also saw ten to fifteen Israeli tanks withdrawing from the scene.

Who was responsible for all this? It mattered little to me who pulled the trigger. It was who had organised the whole operation – and directed it. The Israelis were obviously responsible. They had invaded Lebanon. They had invaded West Beirut. It was meaningless to say that they had nothing to do with the massacres, because the killings happened precisely as the Israelis invaded West Beirut with the declared intention of flushing out Palestinian 'terrorists'. The Palestinian refugee camps had undoubtedly been their main objective. But it was not obvious that the individuals who had walked into the camps to slaughter their defenceless people were Israelis. So what? They took orders from the Israelis. They were fed on Israeli food, and they read Israeli newspapers. They were mercenaries of the Israelis. The camps were illuminated at night by Israeli flares shot into the sky above them, so that the murderers could get on with their crimes.

We were being asked to believe that the powerful Israelis had come into West Beirut precisely in order to get the Palestinians and had somehow forgotten their objective for long enough to let independent military forces sneak in under their noses and slaughter women, children and old men. It did not wash.

Some of us wanted to work out exactly what we had witnessed. In our anger, it was easy to blame the Israelis for the deaths, but the truth was that the murderers had not been wearing Israeli uniforms. On Monday 20 September, a few of us from the foreign medical team discussed the massacre, and we isolated various facts.

First, that on the Friday evening after the departure of the Palestinian hospital staff and Azziza Khalidi, a group of young men who were not known to the hospital workers entered Gaza Hospital. They were well-clothed, and unlike the camp folks they were not distressed. At first they tried to talk to the foreigners in Arabic, but then they switched to German when they failed to get across in Arabic. They asked for the whereabouts of the children 'whose throats were to be slit by the Kata'ebs in the morning'. They spoke pure German – 'klar deutsch', according to the German medical workers. Who were they?

Second, that a little child well-known to some of the foreign medical team was last seen alive between 10 AM and 11 AM in Gaza Hospital on the Friday, and was found dead in the stadium on the Saturday with other children. During our detention in the Israeli headquarters on 18 September, it was made clear to us by an Israeli General that the stadium was under Israeli protection and they had set up some clinic there. This little boy was killed after 11 AM on 17 September, in a place supposedly under Israeli protection.

Third, most of the area of the massacre in the Sabra and Shatila camps could be seen by the Israelis from their headquarters. So the Israelis had no excuse for ignorance.

Fourth, all the roads to the camps were controlled by the Israelis. It was they who blocked the camp people from fleeing. It was they who turned them back to the camps to be slaughtered by the murderers there. It was they who were in a position to allow the journalists in after the bloodbath was over.

Fifth, there were many attempts to give us the impression that the Israelis had actually tried to save us from the 'Haddads'. There were at least three instances where they (the Israelis) were obviously talking to the 'Haddads' in English to let us hear that they were negotiating our safety. This was a silly little game. Were they trying to impress on us that they had saved us from the Haddads? Then why had they been unable to save the defenceless Palestinians?

Sixth, we were given the strong impression that the

soldiers present on and around Rue Sabra, the main camp road, just before the massacre, were Haddad men with a few Kata'ebs. It was strange that both organisations went out of their way to make themselves noted by us and by journalists and people around the area, but that subsequently they *denied* their involvement in the killings. This made us doubt that the murderers were exactly who they appeared to be. Different official Israeli government statements have suggested that either the Kata'ebs or Haddad men were responsible. Surely the Israelis must know who did it – one may reasonably expect an army headquarters in the middle of a conflict to be aware of the identity of armed individuals visible less than a kilometre away. The camps were less than a kilometre from the Israelis' headquarters.

On Wednesday 22 September, two of us returned to Sabra and Shatila camp and spoke to the few survivors of the massacre. We learnt that many of the soldiers who did the killings did not speak Arabic and that among them were some black Africans. Who were these African-looking gunmen? Were they mercenaries imported by the Israelis to do this job? From where?

There were other indications that some of the murderers were not Arabs, and were thus not Lebanese. We found out that when the two doctors and the nurse left the Israeli headquarters on 18 September to return to Gaza Hospital, an Israeli Colonel issued a handwritten pass in Hebrew, and told the three medical personnel that this pass would enable them to enter the camps. They were taken in an Israeli jeep part of the way back to Gaza Hospital, and dropped nearby to continue the journey on foot. One of the doctors pressed for the Hebrew pass to be translated into Arabic as he assumed that the Haddads, being Lebanese, could not read Hebrew. The colonel said that the Hebrew pass was a guarantee of safe passage when shown to the 'Haddads', and it was only at the doctor's insistence that it was subsequently translated into Arabic.

Presumably whoever controlled the camps read Hebrew and not Arabic.

Also during our detention in the courtyard for interrogation, one of the woman medical workers had produced a written document to prove that she was not a PLO sympathiser. The document, written in English and Arabic, said that she was there to help the suffering people of Lebanon. The soldier to whom she showed the document struggled to read the English portion of the document but did not read the Arabic translation.

Today I still wonder who exactly were those gunmen who overran the camp alleys and killed the camp people. Quite a few of us came to the conclusion that the massacre was directed by the Israelis and whether they used mercenaries or their own army was a secondary issue. The reasons for trying to implicate the Phalangist militias were probably twofold – firstly to perpetuate Muslim-Christian animosity, and secondly to destabilise Lebanon. Those who planned the massacres knew they would have to leave one day. But the Haddads and Kata'ebs were Lebanese, and would always be there. Those who survived the massacres would live in constant fear even after the Israelis withdrew from West Beirut: they would have no peace of mind.

I hoped that the opposite would happen. I thought the Christian Lebanese would probably resent being made scapegoats by the Israelis in this matter. I hoped that the sacrifice of two thousand four hundred Palestinians and Lebanese from Sabra and Shatila camp (this was the official Red Cross figure announced on 22 September, which was derived from an actual body count) would not go to waste, but contribute to the unity of Palestinians and Lebanese in times to come.

CHAPTER 7

From their temporary refuge in the American Embassy, many of my colleagues left. I did not want to leave – I could not abandon some of my dearest friends not knowing if they survived or were killed, and if they were dead whether their bodies had been found and buried. And what about the Gaza Hospital staff? They had all disappeared. Were they alive, dead or imprisoned? I could not leave till I found out more about them.

I knew for sure that if I were Palestinian, I would have been slaughtered like everyone else. But they did not even bother to check my papers. No one could mistake a Chinese for an Arab. They just shoved me along with their machine guns and called me names. To be alive, to have survived, meant that I had a duty to speak up on behalf of those who were dead, whose bodies were buried under the rubble, and who could speak no more; to speak on behalf of those alive and suffering every mortal day, in silence, without voice. Not to lend my voice to those I had grown to love over the past few weeks would be a crime. I was not only a survivor, I was also a witness.

Those of us who decided not to leave got together and compiled a document detailing the events surrounding the massacres. Most of it came from my diary, with contributions from the rest of the team. To give it authenticity, I put

73

my name to it. It was not pleasant to put my name to a statement against the murderers. It would put me in some danger, but I had to be responsible for what I said, and so I signed it. Dr Paul Morris and Dr Per Miehlumshagen agreed to sign portions of it, which was a great help. They also decided it was time I got some sleep, and put me to bed. I wanted the statement sent out quickly, so that if I ended up dead, the world would at least have my record of what happened, including who I thought was responsible for the massacres. It was our testimony, it was a record of the truth. When a phone call came from London, asking for the statement, I got up and went to one of the charity offices to telex it to my husband Francis in London.

A dear Christian Lebanese woman typed out the telex for me. It took her forty minutes to send it. She was very upset over what happened to the camp folks. As we watched the returns of the telex emerge from the machine, I felt a great sense of relief, for our witness had gone forth. In it, I instructed Francis to circulate the statement as widely as possible, and warned him that if I did walk across a landmine, it would probably be no accident. I looked out of the window, and saw the whole street full of Israeli troops and their armoured cars and tanks. All their might, I said to myself, could not stop our statement from reaching the rest of the world now. When I left the offices of the charity, I was not anxious and bothered any more. From that moment, it would not matter one bit if I suddenly dropped dead. I had done what I needed to do.

The next day, I returned to Sabra and Shatila. More dead bodies were recovered from the rubble, and the stench of decaying human flesh filled the air, making me feel very sick. Yet people had come back to live in the camps. As Palestinians, where else could they go? After being uprooted from Palestine, they had been pushed from one Arab state to another, and from south Lebanon to Beirut. Most of them were tired of wandering around. They were all very upset by the massacres, but they knew their forefathers had lost their homes when they ran away from the massacres which took place in Palestine. They wanted to dig in this time in Sabra and Shatila.

Our return to the camps was a time of much sadness, as we learnt of the terrible things that had happened to our friends and acquaintances. But it was also a time of much rejoicing when we discovered that people we thought were dead had survived.

The cleaner of Gaza Hospital spotted me, ran up to me and threw her arms around me, relieved I was alive. Suddenly she spotted the crucifix round my neck, froze, and shrank away from me. Two of her kids had their throats slit by so-called Christians, and the symbol of Christianity had become a symbol of death to her. But she pulled herself together, and eventually accepted that the massacre had nothing to do with Christianity. God had not betrayed man: He never had, now or in the past. It was the other way round, man had once more betrayed God. I held her close to my chest, and she cried for a long, long time.

Gaza Hospital was devastated, and all its medical equipment had been pillaged by the gunmen who had invaded the camps. The fate of the hospital was now uncertain: the Israelis wanted to close down all Palestinian institutions. The Palestine Research Centre in Beirut was closed down. All its archives were taken away by the Israelis. They wanted to declare the Red Crescent Society illegal as well.

All over Beirut, the Israeli Army set up road blocks and stopped all vehicles, so that passengers could be screened and Palestinians taken away. Sections of roads were sealed off by the Army and house-to-house searches for Palestinians were carried out. Proprietors were ordered to turn in Palestinian tenants. Lebanese who tried to hide Palestinians were beaten up. All property owned by Palestinians was treated as war booty.

To hold a Palestinian identity card in those days meant that a person could be picked up without any reason. Many had disappeared. So you can imagine how relieved I was when I found a good number of employees of the PRCS alive on the sixth floor of the International Red Cross offices. I was especially glad to see three faces – Um Walid, the woman who was the director of the PRCS in Lebanon; Hadla Ayoubi, the PRCS's director of public relations, and my dear Azziza Khalidi, the administrator of Gaza Hospital. The International Red Cross had given all of them sanctuary in the Red Cross building to protect them from being picked up or murdered.

Their lives were hanging on a thread. Yet all of them remained so dignified and courageous. I cried when I saw them, but Hadla comforted me and asked me to be strong. After two days, they all voluntarily left the protection of the Red Cross to go back to work. It was not easy: they had to negotiate the legal status of the PRCS, the re-opening of Gaza Hospital, and the safety of the staff and patients.

Hadla Ayoubi was throughout the Israeli invasion the person responsible for co-ordinating the hundred or so foreign medical volunteers. This was a very difficult job as it needed a lot of patience, tact and understanding. The PRCS had suffered blow upon blow during the invasion, and many foreigners simply did not understand this. If Akka Hospital was bombed, and could not function until it was refurbished, there were two ways foreigners would react. Some were prepared to understand and might even help the PRCS staff clean out the rubble. But others would run to the Western press and tell them that coming to Beirut was a waste of time. According to them, the PRCS should not ask for foreign medical volunteers, since there was 'no work to do'. They did not explain that there were many medical needs to be met, but that the hospitals were demolished. I often felt like inviting them to clear the rubble and clean the floors, since that would help restore the clinics and operating theatres more quickly, and medical work could resume.

Such people were troublesome, always demanding

attention over trivial things, and were a drain on Hadla. Yet she was always kind and understanding. Sometimes she would laugh at me when I got upset with my volunteer colleagues, and remind me that anyone who bothered to come all this way to help the Palestinians must be treated with respect.

It was also Hadla who went round all the PRCS clinics and hospitals reminding the PRCS staff to observe strictly the ban on weapons in their institutions. No armed persons, be they Lebanese or Palestinians, would be allowed into a clinic or hospital if they insisted on coming in with their guns. They had to leave their weapons outside the hospital even at the height of the Israeli invasion. She explained to me that this was important as the medical institutions of the PRCS were entirely humanitarian, and not hang-outs for fighters. This policy of not allowing arms did not stop the PRCS hospitals and clinics being deliberately bombed.

Hadla conducts herself with great dignity. An exile from Jericho, she admits that she is a member of the Palestinian bourgeoisie. She is a lady who has given her life to her people through her work for the PRCS. Entirely disciplined, proper and gentle, she is a good person to deal with all the diplomatic aspects of the PRCS, and won the love and admiration of many of us. I often spoke of Hadla to my husband. When he finally met Hadla, Francis said: 'Hadla is a real lady.'

Gaza Hospital stayed shut, and all the patients were scattered once again in field hospitals. I was at work in one of these temporary hospitals, in the southern suburbs of Beirut. This was a converted shop, and was crowded and stuffy. Patients from Akka and Gaza hospitals who survived the massacres were all laid out in collapsible beds. The future of the patients was uncertain, and soldiers often burst in, and threatened them. Frequently, it was only through the intervention of the officials of the International Red Cross that patients were not arrested. A few days after I started work here, Um Walid and Hadla came round to visit the wounded. It must have been so difficult for them to talk to the patients, yet the two women put up a brave front. They distributed small amounts of cash to each patient, and they tucked the money under the pillows of those who were asleep during their visit. It all went quietly, and it was only when they turned to leave the field hospital that I saw Um Walid crying on the way out, and Hadla putting her arms around her to comfort her.

The Palestinians who had lost their homes were living in the streets, many of them simply squatting at street corners, outside cafés, department stores, sometimes laying mattresses and blankets out on the pavements. Each day more of them disappeared – they had been picked up overnight by the Israeli soldiers. Those were terrible days. I felt a compulsion to walk – walk from one end of Sabra to the other, from one end of Shatila to the other but at the same time I found it very hard to do. The woman with her baby who nearly became mine, the people hiding in Gaza Hospital – I just could not find any of them.

Instead, I found more destruction and more decomposed corpses laid out for grieving relatives to identify. I could feel the blood being drained away from the camps: they were now large patches of uneven ground, destroyed homes, where the living roamed listlessly, seeking out the dead. We all assumed that each mound of earth was a mass grave, and if we just followed the stench of decaying corpses, we would usually discover dead bodies. Relatives were not allowed to uncover the mass graves to identify bodies: instead, white lime was sprinkled all over the mass graves by the army to dissolve the last traces of human flesh. Sometimes a bracelet, a necklace, a dress was the only clue to the identity of a body.

Even after the announcement of the official body count of two thousand four hundred on 22 September, more bodies were found, mixed up with the rubble, in empty garages, in abandoned warehouses. Outside the camps, in

Akka Hospital, nurses had been raped and killed, doctors and patients shot dead. As I walked through the camp alleys looking at the shattered homes I wanted to cry aloud, but was too exhausted emotionally even to do that. How could little children come back to live in the room where their relatives were tortured and then killed? If the PRCS could not function legally, who was going to look after the widows and orphans?

Suddenly, someone small threw his arms around me. It was Mahmoud, a little child who had broken his wrist while trying to help his father rebuild their broken home. He had survived and his wrist had mended, but now his father was dead. Mahmoud cried, but he was glad I was alive because, from his hiding place during the massacre, he had seen the soldiers taking us away. He thought they had killed me.

Soon I was surrounded by a whole lot of children. Kids without homes, without parents, without futures. But they were the children of Sabra and the children of Shatila. One of them spotted my pocket camera, and wanted a picture taken. Then they all stood together, wanting their pictures taken. They wanted me to show their picture to the people of the world. Even if they were killed and the camps were demolished, the world would know that they were the children of Sabra and Shatila, and were not afraid. As I focused my camera, they all held up their hands and made victory signs, right in front of their destroyed homes, where many had been killed. Dear little friends, you taught me what courage and struggle are about.

As I walked home that evening to the Mayfair Residence in Hamra, where I had been given an apartment away from the camps, I walked past large Israeli tanks packed with soldiers. In my mind's eye, I could only see the Palestinian children of the camps with their arms raised defiantly in the victory sign. As long as there were Palestinian children, the Palestinians would keep on going. That evening, I sat down in an exhausted state and wrote a letter to my husband in London:

Dearest,

Physical exhaustion comes on and off, but I have no fear, no paranoia: our history has taught us otherwise. Would the slaves of yesterday have ever dreamt that one day they would be free and be called human beings? But this is our testimony – that historical trends are such that we will win. Maybe not today, maybe not tomorrow: maybe not this generation, maybe not even the next generation – but because we are human we will win, one day. Yes, it will take tenacity, discipline, sacrifice, a great price – but that which rightly belongs to us we will recover some day.

Darling, we are just two tiny individuals in this tide of historical liberation. Somewhere we may be washed away, forming the error margin – washed aside – but we know where the tide will flow, and nothing can stop it. It may sound rhetorical – but in the whole history of the oppressed people struggling for justice, nothing will ever sound rhetorical enough.

I cry like a young soldier would, one ready and prepared for a battle, but fallen even before the battle has begun. However, I laugh, laugh victoriously, for I know that there are millions that would carry on the struggle after me.

I looked into the face of death and have seen its power and ugliness, but I have also looked into its eyes, and seen its fear. For our children are coming, and they are not afraid.

CHAPTER 8

The inevitable happened: Gaza Hospital reopened on 1
October 1982. The Palestinian staff came back, at great
personal risk. Circumstances were very difficult. People
were picked up by the Army, and many of them never
came back. The PRCS was still not allowed to function as a
legal body. The Palestinians worked under the auspices of
the International Red Cross, which behaved honourably
by leaving the running of the hospital to the Palestinians.
What made things difficult, however, was the presence of
foreigners brought in to support the work of the hospital.
Many of them were new, and some of them were unable
to appreciate what the Palestinians had been through. This
created a fair amount of friction. It was difficult enough for
the PRCS to have to work covertly as an organisation. It
was even worse for the Palestinian doctors and nurses who
had been through so much to be ordered around by
foreigners, many of whom were not properly qualified, in
their own Gaza Hospital.

For many days after the news of the massacre broke,
Gaza Hospital was visited by taxis from Damascus. These
were sent by fighters who had been evacuated to Syria. The
driver would call into the hospital with a list of names, and
one of the PRCS staff would go with him to look for the
people on the list. They were usually the relatives of

evacuated fighters, who now wanted to take their families away from the camps in case another massacre took place. More often than not the taxis left the camp empty, heading back to the anxious fighters with the sad news that their loved ones could not be found.

I could only guess how the Palestinian fighters who had been evacuated must have felt. When they left their families behind, they entrusted them to the powerful Western nations who guaranteed their safety. They left Lebanon after ten weeks of bombardment so that Israel's attacks on Lebanon would end and Lebanese and Palestinian civilians would be spared. They had done so at the request of various Lebanese and Arab leaders. Tucked away now in Syria, Tunisia, Algeria, Greece and other countries, no doubt they felt betrayed and wished that they had stayed after all – whatever everyone else wanted. If they had stayed, Israel would have flattened Lebanon; when they left, their families were massacred.

The morale of the camp people had reached an all-time low. As Dr Morris said to some reporters, 'The massacre was the last straw.' In the afternoons and evenings, after work, I would visit the camps, just to talk to people and to listen to them.

I only knew Leila Shahid after the massacres. She is a Lebanese Palestinian, who at that time was working for the PRCS, and we met when she offered to help the foreign volunteers who had survived the massacres leave Beirut. I did not leave, and we got to know each other better after my colleagues left. She was extremely well-educated, multilingual, passionate and vivacious. I just took to Leila and adored her. She was very important in keeping me going after the massacres: I drew a lot of my strength from her. She would remind me to eat, insist I went to sleep, and try to comfort me when I got too depressed.

She took me to visit various Palestinians who had survived the massacres, and we recorded their statements.

I knew that such documentation was a vital although grim part of Palestinian history. Leila loves her people, and this affected me deeply. It was the way she would spend hours listening to survivors, even little children, that was so touching. She often cried when she heard the terrible things that happened to them. 'You know, the massacre is not only the mere killing of my people,' she told me. 'It is the destruction of our entire society. Our family unit was destroyed through the evacuation. The infrastructures which enabled our people to survive were also destroyed by the war – factories, workshops, training institutes, commercial companies. It took so much to build all these structures so that we Palestinians could live like everyone else. Now with them destroyed, many of us will be forced to return to living like refugees, depending on foreign aid. What are the survivors going to do to live?' My understanding of the Palestinians was scanty, and Leila patiently explained to me how the Palestinians were suffering not only in Lebanon, but also in the Israeli-occupied territories.

Leila, Hadla, Azziza, Um Walid and many other officials of the PRCS struck me as being very special women. They were not only capable and dedicated, but outstandingly human – always patient and approachable to people who needed their time. It was very interesting to see them work. They would be in their offices, with the door open, and people would just come in and take a seat around them. Each person would bring up their problems in turn to be 'solved', and took as long as he or she wanted. It was this ability to switch from person to person without being ruffled that amazed me, since some of the problems were indeed shocking.

On the evening of the day the hospital reopened, my friend Leila and I found ourselves in a little shop in Shatila camp, with Mouna's grandmother. Mouna was an eleven-year-old boy, the last massacre victim treated in Gaza Hospital before we were taken away by the murderers. He was the one who lay buried at the bottom of a pile of dead bodies pretending to be dead. Twenty-seven members of his family were killed. His wounds responded slowly to treatment, but his grandmother's wounds did not.

The seventy-year-old matriarch had walked twenty kilometres from south Lebanon to Shatila camp to visit her children and grandchildren. When she arrived, she found all of them dead, except her old husband and little Mouna.

Her oldest son, Abu Zuhair, was a Tel al-Zaatar fighter. A Palestinian refugee camp, Tel al-Zaatar was attacked and blockaded for six months in 1976 before a ceasefire was agreed on, to allow the camp civilians to be evacuated. But during the evacuation, three thousand Palestinians were murdered. There was very little international publicity about the Tel al-Zaatar massacre. Bulldozers came and flattened the camp and the bodies. White lime was sprinkled over the dead bodies, the flesh dissolved – and Tel al-Zaatar camp disappeared from the face of the earth.

Abu Zuhair escaped that massacre, and made his way over the mountains to Shatila camp. Mouna's grandmother, a Hadji, whose head was veiled with a large white Palestinian scarf, spoke with tears in her eyes, and Leila and I listened: 'Why did you die, Abu Zuhair? How could you come to me from across the mountains, all the way from Tel al-Zaatar with a Kalashnikov in your hand, only to be slaughtered like a sheep in Shatila camp? What is there left to say?

'Our doves are still here. Our carnations give fragrance. The sparrows sing their usual songs. Yet Abu Zuhair is nowhere to be found.

'Beirut, you took all I have. You took my last spark in life. My heart lies dead on your street.

'Abu Zuhair, the tall, young tree, was cruelly snapped off from his roots on your soil. May the blood of whoever murdered you mingle with yours. May his mother suffer the same agony.

'Who dug your grave, Abu Zuhair? Who brought this disaster unto us? What can I say in your memory?

'My heart is full of reproach towards this unfeeling world. Not even a hundred ships, nor two hundred stallions, would be enough to carry the load of pain in my heart.

'What can I say? "Mother," you tell me, "go visit our graves and pray for those they engulf."

'I go to the grave and tenderly embrace its stones. I implore it to make space so you can breathe. I tell it, "Please let your stones warmly embrace the bodies of my loved ones within, take care of them, I have entrusted them to you."

'I mourn your youth and mourn for all the young girls who never knew a moment of happiness or contentment: they went to meet life so hopeful and eager, and ended up being trampled and torn by its ferocity.

'Oh God, I can't go on. He was the handsomest of men and the strongest of youths. He used to pave the way for others, to facilitate their path.

'Your young body mingled with the earth too soon, your eyes filled with the sand.

'What else can I give to my country? My heart is full of agony and reproach to life.

'How I envy those of you who were there when my loved ones died. Did they die thirsty? Or were you merciful enough to give them a drink?

'I implore every passing bird to carry my anxiety and love to you, then to come back with news of my loved ones.

'My child, your body is strewn with bullets. Who sent you to me, crow of ill-omen? Why do you inflict disasters on me all at once? Spare them a bit, oh God. God – wait at least a year, then Thy will be done.

'I implore you, bearers of the coffins, move slowly. Do not hurry. Let me see my loved ones once more.

'I go to the graves and roam listlessly around. I call Abu Zuhair, then I call Um Walid (his sister). My calls remain unanswered. They are not there. They followed Um Zuhair (Abu Zuhair's wife) and the young ones. They all left one night by moonlight – all my loved ones.

'My child, you are near me no more. Mountains of distance are between us.

'Nabil (Abu Zuhair's nephew) calls his mother. "Mother," he says, "to whom have you left me?"

'Zahra answers, "I have left you in the care of your uncles. They should tell you of me and take you to my grave so my eyes can look at you and my heart reach out to you." But Abu Zuhair has gone and he can't carry out Zahra's will.

'Zuhair (Abu Zuhair's son) asks his father, "To whom have you entrusted me?"

'"Your grandfather will come for you. You are the continuation of his life."

'But life, what life is left to us? Our hearts have died. Our tears have dried, for all the young men and women who died.

'Where can I turn to? Where are my children?

'My child, may God show you the holy path, and may my love and care be a lantern to accompany you along the way.

'Almighty God, give me patience. Young men, please stay away: you renew my wounds and I am so weary. What can I say?'

The words of Hadji, the wife of Youssef Hassan Mohammed, reduced my Palestinian friend Leila to tears. She told me roughly what had been said. (I had my tape recording translated into English back in London.) Many Westerners thought life in the Middle East was less precious, and that one should not apply Western standards of life and death to the Palestinians. I hate people who say that, for they are both ignorant and racist. For anyone to say that Palestinians are immune to pain is evil. Each time I read the translation of Hadji's lament for her children and grandchildren, I cry, but I can never pretend that I can even feel a fraction of her pain.

That night, I left Shatila camp and got very depressed. Leila was leaving for London the following day, and out of desperation I wrote an open letter, a letter of appeal to the conscience of the world. The British press might refuse to print it, but at least I would have written it. What else could I do for the camp people?

OPEN LETTER 1 October 1982.

My name is Dr Swee Chai Ang (Mrs Khoo). I am a woman Orthopaedic Surgeon, a member of the British Medical Association, and a Fellow of the Royal College of Surgeons of London, and permanently residing in Great Britain. I left London on 15 August, 1982, in response to a Beirut appeal for an orthopaedic surgeon.

I am writing to you from West Beirut, from Gaza Hospital, the hospital for Sabra and Shatila camp. I am one of the members of the foreign medical team which worked right through the massacre of thousands of Lebanese and Palestinian people in the camps which took place between the 15–18 September, 1982.

I treated some of the victims, witnessed the shelling and bulldozing of the camp houses. These houses were the homes of thousands of Palestinian and Lebanese people.

Those who have died have already died, and none of us can bring them back to life again. I am now appealing to you on behalf of those who have survived the massacre – mostly women and young children.

Most of their homes have been bombed, shelled, bull-dozed and looted. There is no electricity for them, and a scarcity of safe water supply. Yet thousands have returned to live in these heaps of rubble because they otherwise will have nowhere to go to.

The Lebanese winter is coming, and thousands will have no roofs over their heads.

Then there is the problem of livelihood. With most of the male population aged between 15 to 60 years old either shot, arrested or asked to leave, the breadwinners for many families are gone.

I have seen many women from these camps soliciting in the streets to get some income to feed their little children. This, in the local culture, is the worst form of humiliation for these women – especially when their husbands' bodies are still rotting in the rubble.

While peace returns to Beirut, nightclubs, cinemas, brothels and entertainment parks re-open. High finance and banking return. Yet 250,000 people are living in utter misery and insecurity.

They have no rights, no work permits and live in ruin and rubble. Then these ruins and rubble are officially declared illegal and many are asked to quit their partially destroyed homes at short notice – not knowing where to go from here.

As one who originates from the Third World, I have seen much poverty and suffering. But this is the worst I have ever seen so far.

They need every help and support you can give. Many of them are emotionally prepared to starve or die of cold – but they have asked me to beg you to recognise them as human beings – like yourselves – and they wish to be accorded a human status.

If you have any room in your hearts for these people, please contact them – through me – at the Gaza Hospital. Thank you.

Dr Swee Chai Ang, MBBS, MSc, FRCS
Orthopaedic Surgeon
Gaza Hospital, Sabra and Shatila camp, West Beirut

There was no response at all to my letter, though Francis did manage to get the *New Statesman* in London to print it. The British press was not interested in printing the letter as it had 'no news value'. Neither my foreign-sounding name, nor the sufferings of the survivors in the camps, a mere two weeks after the Sabra and Shatila massacre, were of any news value. Back in Beirut, we plodded on.

The massacre and its aftermath had left me feeling very ill. I was running a temperature, and slept badly. It was only little by little that I managed to make my way about the camps – and the strain of discovering new horrors made every walk an ordeal.

Floor by floor, Gaza Hospital began to function. But Gaza Hospital was not only a hospital. The upper floors were occupied by the homeless camp families who had nowhere to go. Nor were all in-patients necessarily those who needed in-patient medical treatment. Many of them were kept in a hospital bed because they had no home or relatives. In the old days a hospital used to be a hospice as well, and Gaza was certainly performing both roles when it reopened, but the British administrators of Gaza Hospital did not like it at all.

One day, a colleague came up to me, and said in a sarcastic tone, 'Can you go and discharge some of the squatters? This is a hospital, and we are not here to provide charity for squatters.'

This made me furious. He had dared to call the Palestinians squatters, in their own Gaza Hospital.

'Why don't *you* go and discharge them yourself?' I said. 'You've been put in here and have the honour of being in charge – you do the work! Personally, I think all of them have good reasons to be here. Take old Professor Arnaouti. He is seventy-two. I know in the UK you can treat someone with bronchitis as an out-patient. But patients in the UK have homes to be treated in. Arnaouti's home and family are in Jerusalem. Of course, if you can arrange for him to go back to Jerusalem for treatment, you go ahead. But till you can do that, don't you dare ask me to discharge him, you ignorant, patronising bastard!'

My colleague was stunned at the viciousness of my tongue, and word went round among the expatriate crowd that I was a bloody-minded so-and-so. Indeed I was. The Palestinians could take abuse quietly when they had to, but there was no reason why I should. The expatriate administrators learnt I could be just as abusive as any British male when provoked. From then on they left me alone.

There was no peace within the camp. The trauma of the massacre remained fresh in the minds of everyone and they were now constantly harassed by the Army. Homes were searched, furniture smashed up and people were taken away to military detention centres. People were desperate.

Nightly, large tanks drove through the narrow camp streets at high speed.

One evening I saw one of these tanks suddenly stop in front of a partially damaged camp home, and without warning, fire a rocket at it, reducing it instantly to a heap of rubble. I walked on. The Shatila end of the main road of the camp was flooded. Over-zealous bulldozers had been tearing away at the homes all day, and had ripped apart the main water and sewage pipes of the camp. The drinking water was polluted by sewage effluent, and the place was just a big mess.

Turning into a camp alley, I walked towards the sports stadium. I had not found the strength to visit this area before. At sunset, it looked hideous. People had been killed here, people were buried here: I seemed to hear their voices echoing mournfully in the wasteland. This place had been pounded incessantly by Israeli aeroplanes during the siege. During the massacre, it was occupied by the Israelis, and the camp people told me that trucks of men, women and children were taken to the stadium by the Israelis, and many had 'disappeared'.

The body of a little child I had once treated had been found in the stadium on 18 September, the day of the massacre. With other little children, he had been blown up by a hand grenade thrown into their midst. All around the stadium I could see clothes, mostly women's clothes. Angry survivors told me large numbers of women had been forced en masse to undress, and were raped by the soldiers before they were killed. They said soldiers of the Israeli Army watched all this taking place, but did nothing to stop it. Indeed, it was the Israelis who had brought this group of soldiers to the stadium.

A Lebanese Christian who survived the massacre led me to his partially destroyed home, and gave me his testimony on tape. He lived near the stadium, and from his hiding place, saw what went on. He was furious that human beings were capable of doing this to others. He ended by shouting into the tape-recorder, 'No more! Even a seventy-year-old woman was brutally raped and killed.' He was shaking with anger, and his wife came out to calm him down.

Leaving the two of them in the ruins of their home, I hurried towards the hospital, in case I was needed.

Back in the emergency room at Gaza Hospital there was a young man anxiously waiting to see me. He had brought his wife. He thought she was severely disturbed. Indeed she was, and she had hardly slept for a month after seeing the massacre. She ate little, cried most of the time and broke into screams at night. I knew she needed a psychiatrist, but there was none around. I drew out a large syringe full of valium, and injected it into one of the veins of her arm. Turning to her husband, I said, 'That will make sure she sleeps for two hours. She might be less disturbed when she wakes up. Here are some tranquillisers. You should encourage her to take them until she manages to come to grips with herself. She is not mad. Anyone who saw what happened would behave in the same way.' He lifted her up in his arms and made his way back to the camps. There were just too many cases like that.

That night I heard the Arabic radio announce that Lebanon would be prepared to keep fifty thousand Palestinians: they would be deported to the Beka'a valley. But there were nearly half a million Palestinians in Lebanon. Where were the rest supposed to go? My thoughts were interrupted by the first thunderstorm I had seen in Lebanon – the rains were on their way. The bitter Lebanese winter was due in a few weeks. Where would the Palestinians spend this winter?

While the thunder rumbled in the distance, we heard the sound of a motor vehicle pulling up just next to the hospital. It was an armoured car, followed by a military jeep. A man in military uniform, presumably the officer, came out. In loud Arabic he asked for a doctor. Six of his men had fallen off the rooftop of one of the camp houses while arresting Palestinians. I asked him if he was Lebanese. He said he was, and that he was from Ba'albek.

I shuddered at the very mention of Ba'albek. During the massacre, the wounded had told me that the soldiers who broke into their homes were not Israelis but gunmen with a Ba'albek accent. Were these the same lot, then? These soldiers could have taken part in the camp massacre, and then have stayed behind to do house-to-house arrests. On top of that they now had the audacity to come into a Palestinian hospital and ask for treatment. I got angry.

It was time to get even, I said to myself. Then in a loud voice I told them there was no doctor around. It was easy to get them to believe me, as they assumed I was a little Asian nurse.

Then I felt someone gently tugging at my white coat: it was Azziza, the hospital administrator. She wanted to talk to me in private. 'Please, Swee,' she said, 'you have to treat these people. I know what you are thinking. But believe me, my family have suffered so much – and I ask you to do this, for our sake. We were forced to leave Jerusalem, then the siege, then the massacre – all these wounds are still sore, but we cannot deny anyone medical care. We are the Palestine Red Crescent Society, and our principles compel us to give medical care to all alike, even our enemies.'

I looked into the face of this beautiful Lebanese Palestinian girl, sad and heavy with all the sufferings she had been through, yet so gentle. My mind went back nine years to the oath I took upon graduation in Singapore: to treat patients irrespective of race, colour or creed. Yes, it was part of the Hippocratic oath all doctors pledge to honour. We were all idealistic medical students then. Azziza had reminded me of the very fundamentals of medical ethics. So I ambled back to Casualty, apologised to the officer from Ba'albek, said that the misunderstanding arose through my very poor Arabic and started treating his soldiers. Their injuries were fortunately minor, but all the same, they were grateful for the medical attention.

It was about 3 AM when we finished cleaning, stitching and dressing the wounds. They were given tetanus toxoid and prophylactic antibiotics. Towards the end, we became quite chatty, and I even started advising the officer that his boys were really working far too long hours. He told me they were very poorly paid, and worked long hours away from their families in Ba'albek. Perhaps the accident would be a good excuse, he said, for him to send some of them home for a short spell.

By the time the armoured cars pulled away from Gaza Hospital, the soldiers were showing me photographs of their families, and inviting me to visit their villages in Ba'albek, which they claimed was the most beautiful place in Lebanon. Surely incidents like this must contribute towards helping people understand each other.

All the patients were still awake. They had seen the two armoured cars, and when I went up to the surgical floors they asked what they wanted with the hospital. They offered me cups and cups of Arabic tea. I was truly fond of my patients, and it made me happy to be with them. But that night I was also very sad, because I had just heard that my contract with the volunteer agency was not being renewed. I was being advised by my Lebanese sponsors to leave the country.

They said there was 'no demand for an orthopaedic surgeon', but I did not think the laws of supply and demand came into it for a minute. I was running the Orthopaedic Department of Gaza Hospital and was the only doctor in the camps with an English Surgical Fellowship. There was a nightmarishly long list of war cripples waiting for surgery to straighten them out. I looked at my patients: those with infected, unknitted fractures awaiting operations, those with large raw wounds awaiting debridement and skin grafting or flap coverage; those with shrapnel and bullets needing removal; the women with fractured hips needing prosthetic hip replacements.

I knew that poor Abu Ali, the Palestinian theatre superintendent, had been risking his life crossing the military checkpoints over the past few days to get hold of

better orthopaedic surgical instruments to equip the
theatre for major reconstructive surgery. Any adult male
Palestinian between the ages of fourteen and sixty could be
arrested at any of the checkpoints as a suspected 'terrorist',
and join the ranks of the 'disappeared'. Abu Ali had told
me that the theatre would be ready for major orthopaedic
surgery by the end of the next week, and then we could
really get working on the old war injuries, some of which
were five months old. Now I was told that my employer
wanted me out by then. I did not even want to tell the
hospital staff and my patients this piece of bad news. They
had suffered enough, and I would only upset everyone
further if I brought out this nonsense of 'no demand for an
orthopaedic surgeon'.

I could guess the real reason for my dismissal easily
enough. It certainly had nothing to do with the PRCS. My
expatriate colleagues had no doubt complained that I had
been rude and vicious to them, and that I had put them at
risk by being openly anti-Israeli. They had probably
refused to work with me.

Meanwhile everyone was happy, and I tried to be happy
too. The women made tea, the children sat around, the
radio played Arabic music and we all talked and laughed.
For the time being, we managed not to think of the ugliness
of the real world. At 4 AM in Gaza Hospital, we were
happy.

The next morning Dr Amir, the Lebanese doctor, did all
the operating. I looked through the glass window of the
operating theatre and watched the enthusiastic young
doctor at work, and felt really proud of him. Downstairs in
the Casualty Department, a Palestinian doctor treated all
the fractures and sutured the wounds; and did the morning
ward round and instructed the nurses. Perhaps my sponsors had a point. Perhaps it was time to go. I asked my
Lebanese and Palestinian colleagues for the day off to visit
south Lebanon, and they were delighted to let me go.

CHAPTER 9

This was my first trip to south Lebanon. I left the camps together with Ellen Siegel, who was someone I had become very close to during and after the massacres. She was American and Jewish and came to work as a friend of the Palestinian and Lebanese people. She said, 'Gifts of shrapnel are not all that we in the United States can send to the people in Lebanon.' And she volunteered her skills as a nurse to the people in Lebanon. As a Jew, she was particularly concerned about the Palestinians, a people she said had been badly hurt by her own people.

Ellen was extremely lively and vivacious. She wore large, tinted glasses, through which one could just about see her green eyes and long eyelashes. Her hair was dark with large soft curls. She spoke slowly, with a deep American accent, and with her tall slender build, Ellen looked like a white middle-class American woman out of the movies. Everything about Ellen was beautiful; her movements were graceful, her conversation was soft and feminine. And she was one of the most courageous women I have ever met. She had to fight all her life against anti-Arab racism amongst Americans, and she had to put up with attacks by other American Jews against her because of her stand against Israel and her support for the Palestinians.

Fascinated by Ellen, I asked her how old she was. She told me she was forty. 'I can't believe that, Ellen,' I said. 'You look in your late twenties.'

'Oh,' she answered, 'it must be because I've spent all my life working for the Palestinians: I forgot to grow old. You are only starting, Swee. It is a long, long struggle. One day, you will also become forty, and you will not feel forty at all, because there is so much to do, and you feel as though you have just started.'

(Ellen was absolutely right. When I was forty I had spent six years of my life supporting the Palestinians. I did feel and do feel that I have only begun.)

After leaving the camp we went to Kola, the flyover near the Arabic University. Next to this flyover was an unofficial station where one could take a 'service' taxicab to the south. These were Mercedes cars which took up to five passengers to common destinations. The fare was then split five ways, making it cheap enough for people to travel. There were no buses or trains in Beirut. The very rich had their own private cars and either used them or went around in taxis – the rest of us walked or took the 'service'.

Saida and Sour were cities in south Lebanon: the ancient cities of Sidon and Tyre.

'Saida! Saida!' shouted one lot of service drivers, while the others, determined not to be outdone, shouted, 'Sour! Sour!' even louder. The place sounded like a fish market placed right in the middle of a busy junction.

Our service driver, after twenty minutes of touting, got his five passengers. In the back seat were Ellen, myself and another woman – we did not ask if she was Lebanese or Palestinian, as most Palestinians did not want to admit they were Palestinians at that time. She was middle-aged, wore a scarf round her hair, and was well covered with clothes and subcutaneous adipose tissue. She was jovial, friendly and cuddly. Travelling with her was a wire cage containing two noisily clucking white hens. In the front seat were two men, who started chatting to the driver as soon as they got in, as though they were old friends. They talked about everything under the sun, from their families to international and local politics, about Ayatollah Khomeini, the future of Lebanon, Mrs Thatcher of Britain, the Palestinians, and so on and so forth. What a case of verbal diarrhoea, I thought to myself.

The traffic on the Saida road was terrible. We crawled along in a long queue of cars in a dense traffic jam. The reason for the traffic jam? Bloody checkpoints. First, we were stopped like everyone else at the checkpoint of the 'official' Lebanese Army, where we all produced our papers and the boot of the car was opened and searched. Then we were stopped at the checkpoint of the Kata'ebs – the Lebanese Christian militia who were blamed by the Israelis for the Sabra and Shatila massacre. Then we were stopped at the checkpoint of the Haddads – Lebanese Christians who worked for the Israelis. They were mainly from south Lebanon, and were better known as the South Lebanese Army. Then we were stopped at the checkpoint of the Israeli Army; and yet another checkpoint of the Israeli Army; and so on, and so on.

Our driver cursed and swore at each checkpoint. No, that is not strictly true. As he approached a checkpoint, he would draw up by the soldiers with their M16 rifles and their tanks, and greet them in Arabic: 'God be with you.'

After we were through the checkpoint, he would start cursing and swearing: 'Bastards, sons of whores!' and let out a whole string of Arabic swear words beyond the decency of translation.

The traffic jam gave us the chance to absorb the view on both sides of the road. On one side we passed a devastated landscape: army barracks, large tanks and armoured trucks, whole villages bombed out of existence, large bulldozers with Hebrew letters on them, the same type we saw on 18 September tearing down camp houses and burying bodies under rubble in Shatila camp.

On the other side of the road was a long stretch of sandy

beach flanking the sea. There were people fishing and even sunbathing in certain areas! Lebanon was certainly a place of surprises.

The 'service' taxicab brought us to the city of Saida, and for another three Lebanese lira the driver took us to the Palestinian refugee camp of Ain al-Helweh, just on the outskirts of the city. Ain al-Helweh – 'beautiful eyes' or 'view', in Arabic – was the home of seventy thousand Palestinians before the Israeli invasion. As Ellen and I walked into the camp, what greeted our eyes was a big area of scorched earth, with small bits of brickwork standing no higher than three or four feet: no trees, no houses, no shops, not even partly bombed-out buildings. At one end of the camp was a row of recently-erected, corrugated-zinc huts. Within them were a few Palestinian families who were returning to the camp.

We said 'Hello' to the children. They had the same smiles as the children of Sabra and Shatila. I knew these kids would write the next chapter of Palestinian history for, just like the kids further north, they were not afraid.

The other camps near Saida were just as destitute, with very active bulldozers clearing away rubble, and Palestinian families watching the last bits of their homes being carted away.

It was getting late, and we would soon have to head north for Beirut. In Saida, we managed to visit two places of interest. The first was the citadel, a fort built into the Mediterranean Sea during the time of the Crusaders. It was next to the harbour, which was still busy with people hurrying to and fro. Apart from Israeli gunboats, there were no boats in the harbour. The citadel was now occupied by Israeli and Haddad soldiers. Groups of women and children were gathered round them. Women were asking for missing relatives, and the children looked like orphans seeking 'father figures', wanting to touch their guns and helmets. It was perfectly possible that some of the children had been made orphans by these very soldiers.

With freshly-painted road signs in Hebrew, and Israeli and Haddad checkpoints and soldiers in command at various junctions, it was clear that the south was under occupation, and would remain so for quite a long time.

The other place Ellen and I visited was Saida Mosque. This was the first time in six years I had been in a mosque, the last time being in the National Mosque in Malaysia. Saida Mosque was much smaller than Malaysia's National Mosque, but equally beautiful. Its tranquil atmosphere, symmetrical mosaics and perfect geometry reflected a different world – the heavenly world of God. Islamic culture might be beautiful and perfect and heavenly, but all around me was the real world Muslims lived in, a world of impoverishment, of suffering, of war – a world of hell.

After visiting Saida Mosque, it really was time for us to go north again. Ellen and I were both exhausted by the time we reached Beirut, and we decided to go back to the Mayfair Residence in Hamra instead of Sabra camp, as neither of us had slept or washed for a few days.

CHAPTER 10

It was a real pleasure to step into the apartment. Mayfair Residence was a fancy apartment block, with individual self-contained studio flats. Each apartment was complete with a large bed-cum-living room, bathroom, kitchenette, and a small balcony overlooking fashionable Hamra. From this balcony, I once managed to photograph two large tanks sealing off the entire street, and a truckload of soldiers entering houses to arrest people. Most of those arrested were Palestinian males between fourteen and sixty years old, but a fair number of Lebanese were also taken away.

One day there was a commotion in the reception of one of the blocks of flats. Ben Alofs, a volunteer from the Netherlands whom we called 'Big Ben', had grabbed the proprietor of the flats by the throat, shouting, 'You bastard, you collaborator!' and was shaking him up as if he was a kid. Ben was always soft-spoken and gentle, and once trained as a priest. It was something to see him so angry. The reason was plain – the proprietor had voluntarily betrayed a Palestinian family living in the flats to the Army. Despite the proprietor's collaboration, the flats were searched just the same.

Palestinians and their Lebanese friends were hunted down like foxes. Those fortunate enough to survive detention who were subsequently released bore horrible torture marks; some of them were crippled by the beatings. But they were luckier than those who simply disappeared without trace.

My flatmate in the Mayfair Residence was a young and pretty American nurse from New Jersey. We nicknamed her 'Mary Elizabeth Taylor' because of her good looks and the number of admirers she had. Mary was not only good-looking, but also kind and ridiculously generous. She arrived with the rest of the American women around the time I came to Beirut, with huge bags full of food, medicines, washing powder, batteries and other essentials which she then proceeded to share with anyone who needed them. Like the rest of the American medical volunteers, Mary came to help the people in Lebanon, and to take a personal stand against America's war aid policy in Lebanon. She told me, 'If our government hadn't sent those bombs, Lebanon would not be in this state.'

Although Mary wanted to work with us in the Palestinian refugee camps, she was directed by the British nursing administrators to work full-time in the American University Hospital. There was strong anti-American sentiment among the British section of the volunteers, some of whom blindly put all the blame for Lebanon's disaster on all Americans. The American nurses and doctors who volunteered their services to the war victims of Lebanon became the targets for attacks by some British volunteers, who made no distinction between aggressive American foreign policy, and the American citizens who came all the way here to take a stand on the side of those hurt by their government.

'Since you Americans caused all this trouble,' they told Mary, 'you might as well stay clear of everyone else and just stick to the American University Hospital.'

She beat the system by putting in a full forty-hour week in the American University Hospital, and then working an extra thirty hours in the operating theatres of Gaza

Hospital, helping Abu Ali set up the theatres and sorting out the surgical instruments.

My husband Francis and I have the following simple theory: generous people have Group O blood. Mary fitted our theory: she had Group O blood. She was also 'Rhesus Negative'. Her blood group meant that she could give blood to anybody. Unfortunately, no one was recommended to donate blood more than once in three months. Mary lied, and I found out to my horror that she sometimes gave blood twice a day. When I objected, she would just reply, 'Don't worry, Swee. My great-grandparents came from Ireland. We are all strong work-horses. Look, I am really strong – a work-horse.'

That was typical of Mary: I just cannot put into words how much happiness Mary brought to all of us by her generosity and her sunny disposition.

When Ellen Siegel and I got back from Saida that night, Mary was already back, and she had washed and bleached my overalls. She had also cooked us some dinner. 'Look, it is really no good being so late,' Mary said. 'The chips have all gone oily and soggy!'

As we sat down to eat Mary's oily, soggy chips, there was a phone call for Miss Ellen Siegel. It was about testifying before the Kahan Commission of the Israelis.

Ellen was the only one who was hot and bothered about testifying to the Kahan Commission. I dismissed it as one of those 'Israeli things' and had not given it a second thought. I knew that there had been a large demonstration in Tel Aviv, where four hundred thousand Israeli citizens protested against the invasion of Lebanon and the massacre in the refugee camps. A significant number of Israeli soldiers had been put in prison for refusing to serve in Lebanon. I also knew about the formation of the Commission of Inquiry by the Israelis, but commissions of inquiry were being set up all over the world, five of them to my knowledge.

I had seen more than enough of the death and

destruction Israel had brought to people in Lebanon.
'They have no right to set up anything,' I told Ellen when
she had finished speaking on the phone.

But Ellen was very serious about the whole thing. 'We
must all go to Jerusalem,' she told me, 'and testify before
Israel. We must let Israel know of her responsibility in this
whole business.' She showed me her own testimony, which
she had just written, and planned to give it to a journalist
friend who was going to Jerusalem to cover the hearings as
evidence to be considered by the Kahan Commission.

'Would you come with me, Swee?' she asked. 'It would
be wonderful if you came too, because you are like a
newborn babe in this whole business. You are not biased
through prior knowledge of all the rights and wrongs in the
Middle East. Your evidence would be important for the
Commission. Just as we should try to track down Nazi war
criminals, we must also help throw light on what happened
in Sabra and Shatila. If you are prepared to come along,
then perhaps the others like Paul, Louise and Ben might
come too.' Ellen was ever so persuasive, but I asked for
some time to think it over.

That night, I lay awake in bed and did some soul-
searching. I had to be careful not to confuse the war-
mongering and aggressive state of Israel – whose invasion
of Lebanon had made a hundred thousand people homeless and destitute – and the four hundred thousand Israelis
who demonstrated in Tel Aviv demanding an end to the
war. The Kahan Commission did not just happen, it was
formed under pressure. There had been so many massacres
of Palestinians since the formation of Israel – Deir Yassin
to Tel al-Zaatar, Jordan to Lebanon, southern Lebanon to
Beirut. This was the first time such an investigation had
been set up by Israel.

I thought about the plight of the people in the camps who
survived the invasion and the massacre and were now living
in utter misery; and about those whose bodies were buried
under rubble and in mass graves. I thought about how

desperately I tried to get the truth about the massacres out, and how so many Western news reporters did not want to hear. Because I was from the Third World, a coloured woman – they would not even give me an interview. I thought about how the Briton in charge of our volunteer team had tried to block my telex statement about the massacre. He – and others – made it clear they thought that health workers should do their work and keep quiet: to speak out the way I did was to go outside my 'proper' role. Furthermore, it was wrong for me to say anything anti-Israeli.

I thought about how they had wanted to shut me up. I had told them it would have been better if the massacre had not happened, because then I would not have to say anything against the murderers! For the first time, I realised a little of how the Palestinian victims must have felt. They have been wounded again and again, and denied the voice to state their case.

I made my mind up. Israeli politics might well be terribly complicated and sophisticated; the Kahan Commission might well have its own motives. In the final analysis, these things did not matter at all, just so long as testifying gave me a chance to put the case of the camp folks in front of anyone who cared to listen.

Early next morning, I told Ellen of my decision to come along with her. She was delighted. We then went to see three other members of the foreign team – Dr Paul Morris, Louise Norman, and 'Big Ben', the Dutch nurse. Ellen spoke to all of them in much the same way she spoke to me, and they agreed to come as well. Louise Norman was the Swedish nurse who was left behind in the intensive care unit of Gaza Hospital after twenty of us were ordered out on the morning of 18 September. We wrote down all our particulars and gave them to Ellen to be sent to the Commission via her journalist friend.

After two days, the Kahan Commission got in touch with Ellen. They sent her a telex via the International Red Cross saying they had received her testimony, and the names of the doctors and nurses in Gaza Hospital who wished to testify, and had instructed the Israeli Defence Minister, Ariel Sharon, and the Israeli Defence Force to locate us, and bring us safely before the Commission.

I was quietly amused: I could not wait until the people who had wanted to stop me telexing my statement heard about this!

At Gaza Hospital the next day, I came clean with the Palestine Red Crescent Society. I told Azziza my contract was not going to be renewed. More importantly, I told her of our decision to testify in Israel. My days with Gaza Hospital were now numbered, but I asked Azziza not to tell the patients about this because I could not cope with saying goodbye to them. I went on my usual ward round, stopping from time to time to take photographs of my patients.

The little boy with typhoid dysentery was much better now. A few days before, he had been suffering from melaena – bleeding from the intestines. He needed multiple blood transfusions, but there was a severe short-age of blood. The Palestinian male nurse looking after him came up to me one evening and told me that the hospital blood bank had run out. When that happened what we did was go to the Multinational Peacekeeping Forces and ask for donors.

So off we went to the French barracks to ask the officer in charge if there were any volunteers from among his men who had O positive blood. Unfortunately, all his men had given blood to another hospital the day before, and so they could not help. Then he suddenly thought of the Italians – they were just along the road and might be able to do something. He instructed one of his soldiers to drive us to the Italian barracks, and taught me the Italian for: 'We need O positive blood.'

Down at the Italian barracks, I had some difficulty

getting across to the officer. I soon found out that he was apprehensive about sending his men into a Palestinian refugee camp, even if it was just to donate blood. At the back of his mind he was probably scared that his soldiers' blood might help wounded terrorists. After a lot of persuasion, he finally agreed. Three Italian soldiers with O positive blood, escorted by three armoured cars, finally arrived at Gaza Hospital at five in the morning. I was once again reminded of how the world saw Palestinians as terrorists. Perhaps this was the first time the Italian boys had ever visited a Palestinian refugee camp.

At Gaza Hospital, I decided to take the Italian soldiers upstairs to see our little patient, who by now was really ill. The soldiers were embarrassed, having expected to see a wounded terrorist. They gave blood and left. For many days after that, they returned to the hospital to visit their patient, and brought him flowers and all sorts of little gifts. One of them became a close family friend. He even posed for a photo with the boy and his father, and I was the proud photographer.

I then went up to old Professor Arnaouti's bed. He was the 'squatter' from Jerusalem my British colleague had wanted me to evict. Arnaouti had been made homeless twice: once when he was made to leave Jerusalem; the second time when his Beirut home was destroyed by Israeli bombers. We called him Socrates, as he was one of the wisest persons we had met. He was multilingual, and politically well-informed. He was now an old man, and had no wish to go anywhere – except back to his birthplace, but he feared that he would die in exile in one of the PRCS hospitals in Beirut. He spoke perfect English with an Oxford accent. I wanted to say goodbye to the old Professor, but decided against it. I just wished him luck silently, and hoped that he would be able to see his beloved Jerusalem before he died.

Then there were the boys Milad, Mouna, Essau. There were the girls in the next cubicle, Leila, Fat'mah and their sisters; and the men and women who were wounded and expecting their operations next week. It was absolutely awful even to think of leaving them.

I had in my hand an appeal letter I had drafted to send to the President of Lebanon. It was signed by more than twenty foreign medical workers, all very concerned about the plight of people made destitute by the war and those arrested without reason. But the letter was never sent, as we realised that it would jeopardise the PRCS, since most of the signatories worked with them. This was no time to be provocative.

CHAPTER 11

Muslims hold a day of mourning forty days after someone has died, and 26 October was the fortieth day after the Beirut massacre. Ellen had suggested that we, the foreign medical workers, should assemble outside Gaza Hospital, and go down together to lay a wreath at the mass graves. We invited the press to cover this event, hoping it would draw attention to the camps. The wreath was bought and the press did turn up, but the procession was called off. The Lebanese Government was under heavy pressure from the Israelis to close down the PRCS. A procession which drew attention to the camps and the massacre would only provoke a reaction and provide a pretext to close down the PRCS. The procession was off, and we had to apologise to the press. A few of us slowly walked down to the mass graves to pay our respects.

The camp folks had already preceded us to the graves, and on the large pile of earth there were little clusters of flowers and a few black banners. Much of Shatila had already been bulldozed flat, like a football field – without the grass, of course. I spoke to a group of young widows. One of them told me they had seen a white dove rising at dawn from the mass graves, and that, she told me, was a sign that the souls of their beloved children and husbands had found peace. Incidentally, it was my birthday – a very sad birthday morning. Though the sky was clear blue, and the sun was warm and splendid, this did nothing to lessen the pain in our hearts. And not being able to publicly commemorate and mourn the dead made our sorrow heavier.

Ellen and I got back to the hospital just in time to halt arrangements for a farewell party. The hospital wanted to buy sweets and cakes.

'No need for all that – there is no farewell. We are just taking a trip to Jerusalem, and you'll be waiting here for us, and we'll come back to you,' we told our friends in the PRCS.

By this time, a small crowd had gathered outside Gaza Hospital. The camp people had heard that doctors and nurses from Gaza Hospital were going to Jerusalem to testify on their behalf. They were thrilled, and many of them started to talk about Jerusalem and about Palestine. 'Doctora, say hello to Akka, to Haifa,' they said, 'and kiss Jerusalem for us. May God protect you!'

In the course of history many groups have laid claim to Jerusalem. King David seized her from the original inhabitants, and then the Romans captured and sacked her, then came the Muslims and the Ottomans, the British and the Zionists. Many could lay claim to Jerusalem on religious grounds, or as part of an Empire.

But to these camp Palestinians, Jerusalem was very simply their home. They longed to be in Jerusalem to welcome us when we arrived: in exile they could not extend their Arab hospitality to us. Perhaps one day, they would be back in their parents' house, waiting to welcome their friends from abroad.

Ellen had packed her bags. We were ready to leave. We said goodbye to the hospital staff: to Hadla, Um Walid and Azziza, the three women who held Gaza Hospital together under the most difficult times, and to all the others who had struggled and had stayed strong despite every pressure, physical and psychological. When Azziza said goodbye, and had gone from view, my eyes dimmed with tears and I felt faint. 'Swee, you mustn't fall to bits,' whispered a voice in my ear. 'You won't be able to do anything for these people if you fall to bits like this.' It was dear Ellen. I pulled myself together, and we left for the Hamra apartment.

When we returned to Hamra, the first thing I heard was a British doctor gleefully announcing that I was booked on a flight to London on 30 October. My expatriate colleagues must have been really glad to get rid of me!

For the next two days, away from Sabra and Shatila camps, I had a taste of Beirut at peace. One afternoon I was walking towards the flat of Ama's mother in Hamra when a man rushed towards me. With my inadequate Arabic I grasped that he wanted me to go with him. Whenever someone asked me to follow him or her, it was always to visit some very ill patient, and so I immediately assumed he had a sick relative. But when he started pulling on my arm, and offering me one, two, three, four and finally five hundred lira, and started to talk about one hour, half an hour and so forth I realised he had mistaken me for a prostitute. This transaction came to an abrupt halt when I showed him my doctor's identity card. He vanished into the side streets, highly embarrassed.

Ama ran up to me. He had been watching all this from a distance, and was getting worried. Anyway, I assured him that I was a 'big' girl, and everything had worked out okay in the end. He took me up to his mother's flat and broke the story to her. This was my first introduction into the social and seedy side of Beirut.

Ama was Misha's friend, and Misha was a friend of Paul's, and that was how we came to know each other. But Ama's mother had become both my friend and mentor. Like most Palestinian mothers in Beirut, she was extremely worried about her two teenage sons. They were both over fourteen, and in Beirut, Palestinian males between fourteen and sixty were vulnerable to arrest and interrogation. And so there was no peace for Ama's mother. Her husband had fortunately fled in good time. During the Israeli occupation of West Beirut, her block of flats was searched a few times, but her boys managed to hide during these raids. Owning a posh flat in the expensive end of Hamra district did not spare them from harassment.

Ama's mother was a goldmine of Palestinian history for me. I eagerly devoured everything she told me about Palestine. We would spend hours going through the newspaper coverage of the recent events, and my questions to her were endless. Ama's father was a first-class Palestinian intellectual and political thinker, and it was my misfortune to have missed him. Ama's mother was mind-blowing enough. An aristocratic Syrian of Palestinian origin, fair and well-spoken, she never stopped embroidering, even when she was analysing the various international peace plans for me, and making projections of the Palestinians' future. Like the Palestinian women in the camps, she was embroidering on to a large piece of cloth a picture of the Palestine she recalled from her childhood.

'First the Palestinians in Jordan were put in tents, many years ago,' she said. 'Then a wall appeared around each tent. Quietly a roof was put up. A green plant appeared. Then more green plants. Then the sound of chickens, sheep . . . and in no time the camp became a village, with schools, shops and so on.' She paused for a while, and then went on: 'We make mistakes from time to time, and each time a mistake is made, our people pay dearly. Perhaps it will take a generation or two for the Palestinians to transform camps to villages, but once more that will happen.'

'Who is a Palestinian?' she asked. 'We are all over the place. Israel cannot wipe us out; no one can. Each generation is stronger than the previous one. We learn – really learn. Learn from mistakes, learn from strength. The aim is to win, not too soon, not too late, but just in time.'

Ama's mother had packed boxes and boxes of books ready to be shipped to Syria, where they would be safe from the Israelis. For her, these books were more important than gold and jewellery. 'They are the written records of the Palestinian struggle,' she said. I really treasure those moments with Ama's mother, and her flat became a second home to me.

My third home was the office of the World Students' Christian Federation (WSCF). Francis, my husband, was a staunch supporter of Singapore's Student Christian Movement (SCM), a branch of the WSCF. The Singapore SCM was under constant threat of closure by the Singapore Government. It had always supported the fight for the rights of the oppressed. Compared to many wealthy European organisations, the WSCF office in Beirut was much humbler, poorer, had less facilities, but its doors were open to an outcast like me. Yusef Hajjar, who ran the office, would make Arabic coffee, and he and his colleague Jacqueline would listen to all my noisy complaints patiently, even though they might not believe everything I said. I helped myself to their typewriters and their photocopier, churning out open letters and statements about the Palestinians.

It was in their office that I met Janet Stevens, an American journalist who some years later was killed in a bomb attack on the American Embassy in Beirut. Janet was always described posthumously as 'a beautiful American' by the Middle Eastern press. I remembered reading her reports on the invasion: as a journalist, her writing was uncompromising, and I respected her. She was a real and fearless friend of the Lebanese and Palestinian people. Times were very difficult then, and Yusef's office was probably watched as well.

It reminded me very much of Singapore's SCM office, where Francis and I spent many hours typing and photocopying statements and literature of oppressed groups. Yusef always used to say, 'When the chips are down, and the going gets tough, the Christians will be the only ones left to continue the struggle.'

And I used to reply sarcastically, 'A few Christians, you mean.'

On 28 October 1982, two days after we left Gaza Hospital, Ellen Siegel was asked to get in touch with the Israeli Department of Foreign Affairs spokesman, Isaac Leor. He asked us to make our own way to Ba'abda in East Beirut, where he was stationed. We were scheduled to appear before the Kahan Commission on 1 November. It was time for me to inform my sponsors of my intentions.

CHAPTER 12

The head of the organisation which sponsored me on my visit to Lebanon was a wealthy Lebanese Christian, who was married to an American woman. I usually felt too unimportant to take up his time, but he had asked to see me after hearing that I wanted to testify before the Israelis. I sat outside his office waiting while he was having a meeting with some diplomats. After a while, a couple of important-looking men walked out of his office, and when they were well and truly gone, his secretary told me I might go in to speak to him.

Seated in his air-conditioned office with its posh furnishings, he was looking away from me when I entered the room. He swung round on his swivel chair, motioned me to be seated, and looked at me out of the corner of his eye. 'Why do you constantly give me trouble?' he asked me glumly.

'What trouble?' I asked.

'Well,' he said, 'first there was your telex. That was bad enough. Then you managed to get yourself quoted in all the Middle East's magazines and newspapers. For the sake of your own safety, I suggested that you should leave, and you took it to mean we wanted to get rid of you, which was not our intention. Now I hear you want to go to Israel. I hope you realise that Israel and Lebanon are still at war, and your going to Israel to participate in such a commission of inquiry is not without its political implications.'

Looking back now, I realise he was absolutely correct in what he said. But I was stubborn, and refused to listen to his reasons. Instead, I argued doggedly that I should go. We reached deadlock, and his tone became more threatening. He reminded me of my contract with the British charity which had sent me. I was not an independent agent who was free to generate publicity against advice. My British organisation might want to take legal action against me for breach of contract. It was only then I understood that he must be under a lot of pressure from outside, and I must have been a real headache for him.

To absolve him from responsibility, I offered to resign. Then I could go down to Jerusalem as a free individual who was not attached to his organisation. This he accepted, but he warned me that it would be impossible for me to work in Lebanon again if I did that, since I needed to belong to a Lebanese organisation to continue my work with the Palestinians. He tried to persuade me that it would make more sense if I shut my mouth and was a 'proper surgeon' for the Palestinians. Furthermore, he reminded me that I was only a refugee and stateless; if I incurred too much unfavourable publicity, the British might even not let me go back to Britain, and then I would be in real trouble. But it was no use, I had made up my mind to go, and that was it.

As for the argument that charity workers had to remain neutral – I was not even interested. I remembered the poem by Pastor Niemöller which Francis once read to me. It was about not speaking up. The Nazis came for the Communists, the Jews, the trade unionists and the disabled – and no one spoke out. When the Nazis came for the others, there was no one left to speak out for them, since everyone else was killed.

I had to say something while I was alive and still had a voice. Ben and Louise, who were both sponsored by the same organisation, were made to withdraw their requests to testify. In the end there were only Ellen, Paul Morris and myself. Paul and Ellen did not work for the same organisation as I did, and were therefore not subjected to the same pressure.

Back in Mayfair Residence, I wrote to my sponsor, firstly to give him my official resignation, and secondly to tell him I had to lend my voice to the people of Sabra and Shatila and if that meant I had to pay the price of leaving Lebanon and jeopardising my own future plans, then it was just too bad. I also thanked the organisation for being a good host, for the truth was that they had been very good to the volunteers. I was sorry I had to upset them by acting against their advice.

That evening some British and European medical volunteers came to see me at the Mayfair. I do not know if they were acting under instructions, or came out of paranoia, but anyway they accused me of risking their safety by testifying in Jerusalem. 'Do you realise that by speaking up like this, all of us will get tarred by the same brush because of you?' one of them asked.

'You're endangering everyone's life,' said another, 'and the good work we're all doing here. If you go on being openly anti-Israeli and this whole place gets blown up by a five-hundred kilo bomb, you're the one who's responsible for it.'

The blackmail and the pressure from my own teammates was especially difficult to cope with. In the end, Mary intervened. She moved me down a floor to the apartment of her friend Jill Drew. Then she stuck a large notice on the door of our apartment, which said: 'Dr Swee has checked out of the Mayfair. She is no longer here.'

While I remained in Beirut, I was half hiding from my own colleagues, and Jill looked after me.

Was I really jeopardising the safety of the entire team, as some alleged? I had to do some more deep soul-searching. I had already resigned. I had officially left the Mayfair. I was doing this out of my own conviction and my desire to speak up for the camp folks, to lend them my voice.

Those of my European colleagues who protested the loudest had not visited the camps one single time. I recalled what my friend Leila said – the one who took me to see Hadji, the wife of Youssef Hassan Mohammed, in Shatila camp. 'Swee,' she had said, 'I am really sorry to say this to you, but some of your expatriate colleagues think this is a big picnic, and meanwhile our people are suffering and dying.'

It was well known in Beirut that some British volunteers had been insensitive enough to hold a disco party just as the news of the massacre broke. I was deeply offended by their behaviour. Jill, Mary, Charlotte and the other American nurses had played a crucial role in reassuring me that I was correct. I could not understand why the British volunteers hated me for going, while the American volunteers supported me.

In the end I decided that if one Palestinian from Sabra and Shatila objected to me going, I would call the whole thing off.

To cheer me up, Jill Drew did something very cheeky. While the rest of us got ready to listen in on the other phone, she rang Isaac Leor's number. At the other end, an Israeli soldier picked up the phone. Jill put on an Arabic accent and asked for Isaac.

When the soldier said Isaac was not in, she said, 'Please ask him to call Jamila. He knows my number. We have a date, and I'm waiting for him.'

Jamila was a popular Arabic name for girls, meaning 'beautiful'. We all burst out laughing at the vision of a red-faced and highly-embarrassed Isaac Leor receiving the message. It was terribly wicked, but it did a lot to calm me down.

That night we had dinner at Jill Drew's place, and sang Christian songs. We sang, 'When I needed a neighbour, were you there? . . . When I was hungry and thirsty, were you there?' We read the story of the good Samaritan again, and reminded ourselves of the need to renew our Christian commitment. I also quietly asked for God's forgiveness if I was making the wrong choice in deciding to testify, if I was being headstrong and refused to listen to advice. It was difficult to know what to do sometimes.

PART III

From Jerusalem to Britain

1982 – 1984

CHAPTER 13

Early the next morning, Ellen and I left. The American nurses came to say goodbye, as did Big Ben and Louise, but that was about it. We did not get the lavish farewell party usually thrown by the expatriates for a departing team. Dr Paul Morris was waiting for us outside the Mayfair. He refused to come into the Residence, because he did not want to have anything to do with the expatriate volunteers living there. Then Jill decided she would come with us as far as she could.

The four of us got hold of a taxi and asked the driver to take us to Ba'abda, East Beirut. We found the office of the Israeli Ministry of Foreign Affairs next to a large super-market. With all our personal belongings, we walked up to this office, which was full of uniformed Israeli soldiers. We were the object of much curiosity, having come from a Palestinian refugee camp.

Jill had to leave us. It was sad to part with her. She decided to walk back to the camps from East Beirut, to let the camp people know that we had made it safely. Her main worry had been that something awful might happen to us between West Beirut and the Israeli office, as that stretch of road was a bit of no man's land. Someone could throw a bomb at us, and kill us all, wiping out witnesses from the camps. Then they could even blame the

Palestinians for it. Fortunately this did not happen. Perhaps we were not important enough. From now on anything that happened to us would clearly be the responsibility of the Israelis.

This Israeli ministry was a large, bright building which reminded me of a large Singapore school hall. It was sparsely furnished downstairs, but with more sophisticated facilities upstairs. The colour-scheme was uninteresting and unattractive. Desks were metal, and painted blue grey. All over the ground floor hall were large stacks of cyclostyled leaflets.

There was a blackboard with chalk markings still on it. Obviously there had been a recent lecture. A quick glance at the writing on the blackboard and the printed notes suggested the lecture was on the 'cost-effectiveness' of the Israeli invasion. There were figures on US war aid, which ran into billions of US dollars between 1948 and 1982, and the efficiency with which the money was spent. How disgusting to think of the suffering inflicted on the Palestinian and Lebanese people in terms of 'cost-effectiveness'!

Isaac Leor introduced us to Avi and Egal, the two officers of the Israeli Defence Force who were to escort us safely to Israel. He warned us to speak the truth, but I said that was why I was going to Jerusalem. We were then shown to a blue Volkswagen van, specially rented for the occasion so that we would not be travelling in the usual military jeep. There were already three Israeli soldiers in it. Our security was provided by two Israeli armoured cars, with soldiers, who drove in front of and behind us.

We headed south, on the road we had used a few days earlier on our trip to Saida. This time, however, we were not stopped at the numerous checkpoints. The Kata'ebs waved us on, the Haddads waved us on, and the Israelis, apart from pauses at one or two checkpoints for some social chitchat with their fellow soldiers, also waved us on.

The road felt rougher and more bumpy than it had before. There were large potholes caused by shells and bombs, and the road surface was totally worn down by heavy military vehicles. The dust was thick and irritated my eyes, and the sun beat down relentlessly. I found a coat and covered up my face so that the sun and the dust could not get me. It also stopped any Palestinian seeing me travelling with the Israelis!

Egal and Avi were both around forty, and spoke good English. Avi was wearing civilian clothes, but had a fancy kind of gun hanging from his belt. Paul, who knew a lot more about guns, told me that what Avi was carrying was not a pistol but a miniaturised machine gun. How neat! I thought I would like to have something like that one day. Egal was in military uniform, and had stars pinned to his shoulders, so he must have been an officer. He was a jolly sort, and one could see how he could be very pleasant and friendly.

Avi, on the other hand, was incredibly quiet. He was also abnormally tall – at least six foot four, I reckoned. Paul told me that Avi was a member of the Mossad, the Israeli Secret Service. Even when I told him that he reminded me of Christopher Reeves in *Superman*, Avi did not respond to the remark. That lent weight to Paul's surmise, in my view.

The other three Israeli soldiers, by contrast, were all very young, probably in their late teens or early twenties. One of them kept looking at my news magazine *Monday Morning* but never said anything. In the end, I asked him if he wanted to have a look at it – he was delighted with the offer, and spent the rest of the journey studying the magazine. The other two were dragged into an argument by Paul, who launched into an attack on Israel's foreign policy in Lebanon. The argument went on and on, and became very irritating, because neither side was conceding anything. I tried to tell Paul to shut up and not to waste his time, but he persisted.

Nobody in the world could shut Paul up. A few days before he had been crossing an Israeli and Haddad checkpoint in south Lebanon. An Israeli soldier stopped him and wanted to see his papers. Paul said to the soldier, 'Who are you to ask to see my papers? You are a foreigner in this country, just as I am. You have no right to ask for my papers.'

Everyone went very quiet. Paul was giving a piece of his mind to a soldier armed with a machine gun, with more soldiers looking on from on top of two large tanks. He should have chosen somewhere safer to sound off. But the incredible thing was that he got away with it – he passed the checkpoint without showing his papers. Crazy people had crazy luck.

From my seat in the van, I could see the Mediterranean coastline. I had grown to love the Mediterranean sea dearly over these months. Her waters were calm, still, and blue, washing the coastlines of Lebanon and neighbouring Palestine. Throughout history, how much sorrow and bloodshed had she witnessed? Was she silent because she was unfeeling, or because in the depth of her wisdom she regarded human conflict as puny? The anguish of mortal humanity appeared lost in the deep blue calm.

I must have dozed off, for I woke up with a start. The van had pulled up at the side of the road. Above us was a large sign saying, 'Welcome to Israel'.

Egal got down and, in a loud, jovial voice, told the three of us, 'From now on, the roads will be nice and smooth and you can all relax.' Obviously he had not been enjoying the bumpy ride on the Lebanese trunk road either.

Indeed the road was nice and smooth, with no potholes and the surface well-tarred. Groups of pretty little school kids with bunches of flowers were all over the place, obviously on a picnic by the border. It had been such a long time since I had seen kids so happy. The sight reminded me of English kids on a day out. My mind immediately returned to the camps.

The Palestinian kids were around the same age: they

were all stuck in the camps, squatting among the ruins and rubble, many of them orphans. This would be a terrible winter for the homeless ones. At least the dead need suffer no more. What about the little ones in my orthopaedic ward, wounded by shrapnel and bombs? Many of them would never walk again. Yet the Israeli children were so innocent and happy – and I wished to God they would never, never find out that there were other children across the border who were miserable and suffering. Children all over the world had a right to be happy and secure, no matter what wicked things their elders had done. I could not help quietly praying for these Israeli kids, that they would not be punished for the misery and sufferings wrought by their parents and elders to other children. I prayed that they would not have to pay for the sins of others.

Our party stopped at a kibbutz hotel in northern Israel. We got down and, for the first time in months, I saw green grass. Ellen had become extremely upset. I followed her to the cloakroom, where she broke into tears.

'You know, Swee,' she said, 'this is terrible. Every house is built on top of someone else's house. The whole society here is built upon injustice.' This was too much for me to take in, considering that I had met my first Palestinian less than three months before.

Someone had presented Ellen with a bouquet of red roses in the morning before we set out. Now I followed her out to the fields and helped her plant them on top of the soil of what was once Palestine. It was dark by the time we completed this little mission, and we went back into the hotel.

Back in the lounge of the kibbutz hotel, we were introduced to Egal's superior officer, an important-looking official of the Israeli Defence Force (IDF). By this time, I was determined to work a few things out for myself. Right now I wanted to know what part if any the IDF had played in the invasion of Lebanon. I decided to ask Egal's chief.

'Sir,' I asked, 'what is the name of the Israeli army now occupying Lebanon?' In my ignorance, I figured that if the Israeli Defence Force were set up to defend Israel, there must be another section of the army which had invaded Lebanon.

Egal's chief was not amused at all: he stiffened up and answered, 'The Israeli Defence Force, of course. We in Israel have only one common army, not like the lot in the place you come from. Unlike Lebanon, with her seventeen armies, we are united and one.'

For the first time, I realised that 'defence' was a euphemism, and that the Israeli Defence Force was also the Israeli Attack Force.

After some refreshments in the kibbutz, we resumed our journey towards Tel Aviv. It was dark, but along the road I saw large luminous signposts pointing to Acco (Akka), Haifa and Jaffa. I thought of my Palestinian friends who had asked me to say hello to these places – presumably their places of origin.

We got into Tel Aviv really late. The Commission had booked us into the Moriah Hotel, a large five-star affair. I had never stayed in such a luxurious hotel before. The rooms were large, with two beds in each single room. 'It is ridiculous,' I said to myself. 'How could one person sleep in two beds? Perhaps they expect me to set the alarm at 3 AM, and switch beds.'

The bathroom was spacious, with hot and cold showers, a long bath, huge towels and lovely patterned green tiles all over the walls and floor. There were large glass windows with thick curtains. Ellen, Paul, Avi, Egal and I had a room each. Mine felt large, empty and pretentious, without the warmth and hospitality of the camp homes. Neither did it have the homeliness of the Mayfair Residence, where Mary's 'oily, soggy chips' greeted me each time I returned from the camps.

The dining room was equally sumptuous, with an amazing choice of dishes on the menu. But I had lost all desire for food – and had to hand over my mushroom omelette to Paul and persuade him to eat it for me. I had not learnt to waste food yet, not even Israeli food.

After dinner, Egal and Avi took us to the hotel bar and bought us beers. The two of them tried very hard to be good to us, and to be friendly. A folk band was playing, and Egal tried to entertain us with his own singing as well. Unfortunately, I was highly unsettled, and not very good company. I felt very, very depressed, and had to swallow a five-milligram valium tablet to get to sleep. None of us knew what to expect from the hearings the next day.

It was 1 November – Avi and Egal drove us to the university where the Commission of Inquiry was being held. It was an open hearing, and the press were out in full force. We were the only non-Israeli witnesses to offer evidence so far. Besides journalists, there were also large numbers of security and military personnel. As usual, I got the wrong end of the stick. 'So the Israelis think that we lot from Gaza Hospital have come here to blow up the lecture room and the tribunal?' I asked Ellen angrily, feeling quite insulted by the tight security. She explained that this was not the case, but there were lots of extremists in Israel who did not even want to see a Commission of Inquiry into a massacre in Lebanon. That was why the army and security were out to maintain order.

Bewildered by the large crowds and the incessant camera flashes, I could not help wondering if the publicity was being overdone. By now I had learnt that the Sabra and Shatila massacre was just one of many massacres against Palestinians since the 1948 Deir Yassin tragedy. How come this sudden publicity?

There was no time to wonder, for we were very quickly ushered into the lecture room where the judicial proceedings were being held. Ellen was the first witness, and she took with her a large plastic bag full of Hebrew newspapers and magazines which we collected from the United Nations building where we were detained on the morning of 18 September. The newspapers were dated 15, 16, 17 and 18 September, the days over which the massacre took place. As she rose to go into the 'court' room, she said to me, 'Israel brought all these things, now they can have them back.'

Paul and I sat outside waiting to be called. Then my turn came. As a doctor, I had been to court many times to give medical evidence for or against various parties. But I did not realise that the judges did the questioning in a Commission of Inquiry, and that there were no cross-examining lawyers. After taking the usual oath, the judges asked me to relate the events of the three days of the massacre, from the 15th until the morning of 18 September. By this time, I had lost interest in the audience within the room, the press, even the judges. I felt weary, because I knew only a handful among them at most cared anything for the camp people.

The press wanted its story, the Israeli lobby wanted to prove to the world their democracy was so excellent that they even gave the Palestinians a chance to have their say. The whole exercise should have been called the 'Inquiry into the Palestinian Refugee Camps Massacre', but the Commission instead called it the 'Lebanese Enquiry', refusing to mention the Palestinians.

So, even when murdered, the existence of the Palestinians was denied. I could hear my own hollow voice echoing, 'Palestinian, Palestinian', throughout, but even as I spoke, I knew this platform was a far cry from the justice I was seeking for the people I loved so much. Soon I went from being weary to angry, and told the Commission exactly what happened. The Israelis had said that they did not know, but we radioed them, pleading with them to stop the massacres. They stopped the foreigners from being killed, but did they order the killing of the Palestinians? We knew that those soldiers who pulled the trigger were totally answerable to the Israeli officials.

Afterwards I was told that my evidence contradicted that

of the IDF officials who had given evidence earlier on. 'In that case, they must have lied,' I told reporters waiting outside. 'I do not know what they have told the Commission, but what I said under oath was an exact transcript from my diary.'

The press persisted, taking on the role of the legal cross-examiner. I knew I did not have to answer any of their questions, but my love for the camp people compelled me to speak to anyone who would listen, including journalists who wanted nothing but their 'scoop', judges who probably saw me as nothing more than a 'PLO sympathiser' and members of a public who saw Palestinians as an inferior subhuman breed. I was already homesick for the Beirut camps, for the people I loved, for the sixth floor of Gaza Hospital.

I became increasingly enraged as I repeated myself to the journalists: 'Here were the twenty-two of us, who worked nonstop for seventy-two hours without food, water or sleep, to save a handful of lives while out there in the camps people were dying by the thousands. If only I knew, I would have run into the streets and done something to try to stop it.'

That quote went into all the papers the next day, but no one printed the more important message I tried to get across – that while there was nothing we could do to bring back to life those who were dead and gone, there was plenty we could do for those still alive today, facing terrible hardships. They were still living in ruins and rubble, they had no means of livelihood and were living in utter misery as winter approached. No one wanted to hear this in the Jerusalem of 1982. Perhaps the Kahan Commission was a triumph of Israeli democracy, but it did nothing to lessen the pain suffered by the Palestinian people.

On our way out, we were met by the British High Commissioner. He was very concerned about us, and took the trouble to come all the way to the university to make sure we were all right. But he was a bit confused as to whether I was Singaporean, Malaysian or British. I was not sure either, but after some thought I told him: 'I suppose the best way to put it is that if I died here, my body would have to go back to London, and that would probably be the concern of your department.'

Paul thought that was a very cheeky thing to say to the High Commissioner, but it was just a practical way of describing myself, and the only thing I could come up with at the time. The fact is that I had spent some time worrying about where I might be buried.

After giving evidence to the Commission, we were taken by Egal and Avi to visit some places of interest in Israel. For someone from South East Asia, the significance of a place like the Wailing Wall was not too obvious. The birthplace of Christ in Bethlehem had been transformed into a bustling tourist church. It was most unlike my idea of the manger where Jesus was born.

The Hadassah Hospital, a large Israeli hospital, was well organised and had modern equipment, like any large teaching hospital in Britain. No bomb holes, no crumbled walls, no shattered glass windows, no rubble like Gaza Hospital. With the exception of a handful of wounded Israeli soldiers, there was nothing to remind one of an ongoing war. The rest of the patients were exactly what one would expect in any hospital – cancer, diabetes, heart attacks, surgery cases and so on. No children with the 'Reagan-Begin' syndrome, no cluster bomb injuries, no burns from phosphorus. And there was water, electricity, potted plants, curtains, polished floors. I remembered Dr Habib's room in Gaza Hospital, which was supposed to be mine after he left. A large shell came through the wall one day, reducing the room and its contents to rubble, fortunately injuring no one.

We were then taken to visit Yad Vashem. Under normal circumstances I would not have wanted to visit this place, having spent many hours in the past weeping and having nightmares over the European persecution of the Jews, first by the Russian Czars, and then by the Nazis. But I did not want to offend my Israeli hosts, and so I went along.

It was just as well I did. A woman Israeli professor of history, herself a survivor of the awful Auschwitz camp during the second world war, had taken the day off to show us around. She was a kindly woman and got very upset when reminded of the Sabra and Shatila massacres. She turned round and took hold of my arm and said, 'Doctor, now you have seen the sufferings the Jews have been through. Please believe me, we were very distressed by what happened in Lebanon, to the people in the refugee camps. The news of this broke just before Rosh ha-Shanah and our whole village cancelled all celebrations. We were too upset to celebrate, many of us went into mourning instead.'

Her obvious sincerity, and the pain on her face as she said these words showed me that not all Israelis wanted to see the Palestinians persecuted and slaughtered. It must be cruel for Jews who had suffered so much under the Nazis to see their own people inflict suffering on others.

Here were two sets of people – the Jews and the Palestinians – with a great deal in common. At Yad Vashem I watched a film about how the Nazis indoctrinated their members with anti-Jewish sentiments, the first being to regard Jews as an inferior and subhuman breed. Some Israeli soldiers now regarded Arabs as inferior and subhuman. Why had they not learnt? Was it necessary for the creation of a home for the victims of Nazi persecution and European racism to be transformed into suffering for another people, the Palestinians?

Perhaps there is an evil being trying to play musical chairs or pass the parcel, making the Jews and the Palestinians suffer in turns. What if the Jews and the Palestinians both decided they were not playing this game, and threw the parcel back? There was absolutely no need for one set of people to have a home to the exclusion of the other. It must be possible for both to live together. Many said that Israel was too small to be home to both Jews and Palestinians. I think the idea of room or space is a relative one. Having been brought up in Singapore, one of the most crowded countries in the world, Israel or Palestine felt spacious to me, and it must be possible for a few million Jews and Arabs to live there as fellow citizens.

The population of Singapore was nearly that of Israel, and we managed to make homes for all our people in an area of only 226 square miles. Israel is many, many times the area of Singapore, so no one could use the 'over-crowding' argument to a Singaporean. Then there was Shatila camp, two hundred yards square, home for tens of thousands of Palestinians. There is an old saying: if you want the room, you'll make it. So it is not a question of room, but one of an ideology of intolerance.

As I bade the Israeli professor farewell, I looked at the boulevard of trees planted for the friends of the Jewish people, for those who helped to protect Jews from the Nazis, those who risked their own lives to save others, and I wept. Perhaps, if I had been born a generation earlier, in Europe instead of South East Asia, perhaps I, too, would be one of the many so overwhelmed by the injustice done to the victims of the Nazi holocaust, that I would become blind to the sufferings and dispossession of the Palestinians.

No 'ifs' and 'buts'! I had come from the living hell of the Palestinian Refugee Camps. While people here talked of 'morality' and 'conscience', 'righteousness' and 'godli-ness', there were broken bodies under the rubble and buried in the mass graves who had paid with their lives for this 'morality'. The living, homeless and destitute, had lost their birthright to pay for the foundation of the 'godly' state. The Palestinians held and tortured in prisons and detention camps paid with their freedom for the 'dem-ocracy' of the Israeli state. The stolen childhood and womanhood of the Palestinians paid for the 'progressive feminism' of the Israeli state which so appealed to the Western world.

Back at the Moriah Hotel, we got ready to leave. Ellen and I were leaving the Middle East, but Paul Morris was going back to Lebanon. Paul was totally unconcerned about the possible repercussions of our trip to Jerusalem. He wandered off to the Arab part of Jerusalem, and bought many toys for the children of the camp, including a drum for Essau, the boy injured by a cluster bomb. He had planned to tell Essau that the drum was a special present from Swee, for Essau loved me very much. This made the prospect of not seeing little Essau again a little less upsetting.

At this point we had a message that an Israeli lawyer called Felicia Langer was coming to see us. Avi, the IDF chap who we thought was probably Mossad as well, clearly did not like her. He told me how awful this Felicia was, how old and ugly and unkind she was. So I sat in the hotel lounge, and went up to every old and ugly woman to find out if she was Felicia Langer. Many of the women I asked were not at all amused. When one of the women asked me why I thought she was Felicia Langer, I almost let slip that it was because she was old and ugly.

Finally a woman arrived who was the exact opposite of Avi's description. Felicia was young, attractive and feminine. I turned round and gave Avi a hard, long stare. He was very embarrassed – blushing to his ears – and he quickly excused himself. I liked Felicia very much, and eagerly listened as she and Ellen talked. It was only very much later that I learnt that Felicia Langer was a true heroine, very committed to fighting for justice for the Palestinian people. I was ever so grateful for the chance to meet her and listen to her, and I gave her a copy of my statement on the massacre.

Although her visit was very brief, it had an impact on me, and brought me a strange inexplicable sense of joy.

Avi drove Ellen and me to the airport. By then, the poor chap had developed a nasty headache, probably through having to look after us three. He left the two of us at the airport, and drove on towards Lebanon with Paul Morris.

I knew what I had been told in Beirut was right: my days in Lebanon were over. But I was glad I had made the trip to Jerusalem. It was strange. Jerusalem was the Holy City, the meeting point of the three monotheistic religions. As a Christian I had long wanted to make my pilgrimage to Jerusalem, and now the Palestinians had brought me to her. Apart from having spoken up on behalf of the people of Sabra and Shatila camps, I also had the opportunity to meet Jewish citizens of Israel, those who were committed to struggling for peace and justice, who had taken a stand. Many of them paid dearly for that too. Members of the Israeli Defence Force who refused to serve in Lebanon were put in prison. Felicia herself would never know whether she would be assassinated the next day. Yet many like her continued with their work against the injustice within Israel. I saw the courage of both Jews and Palestinians.

We boarded the airliner, and as the plane door closed on us I had a vivid sense of déja vu. Tel Aviv airport reminded me of the airport in Singapore. As the plane took off, I felt exiled again – not from Singapore, but from the Middle East. Through the window I could see the sunset. Beautiful and golden, the setting sun cast its warmth and radiance over Lebanon, over occupied Palestine, over Beirut and Jerusalem, over victors and vanquished, faithfully and without bias, as it had done since the beginning of time. Now that I would be exiled from Jerusalem, I understood how the Palestinians must have felt.

Ellen seemed to have read my thoughts, for she started to talk to me about exiles and the right of return. Ten years before, she and a Palestinian woman, Dr Ghada Karmi, stood outside the Israeli Embassy, each carrying a placard. On the placard of the Palestinian woman the following words were written: 'I am a Palestinian Arab. I was born in Jerusalem. Jerusalem is my home. But I cannot return there.' The words on Ellen's placard read: 'I am an American and a Jew. I was born in the USA. Israel is not my home. But I can return there.'

'Think of the injustice of that, Swee,' said Ellen. 'Why should I have two homes, one in the USA, one in Israel, when the Palestinians have none? How can I exercise my right of return to Israel till the Palestinians are given the same right too?'

I looked out of the window: the sun had set. Beirut and Jerusalem were miles away. There was darkness outside, and I felt lonely and lost.

CHAPTER 14

I arrived at London's Heathrow Airport, and was greeted by my dear husband who had lost fifteen kilograms in weight while I was away. Only at that moment did I find out he actually thought I was killed during the massacre. The mistake arose because after the massacre a list of survivors was given to the major newspapers in Britain, and my name was omitted. I think I can easily explain that: I was a coloured woman and a refugee. The British correspondents probably did not include me in the list of British survivors and the charity which sent me probably did not see it as their responsibility to check whether I was alive. Francis telephoned the US State Department in Washington, who proceeded to contact the American Embassy in Beirut, who then tried to locate me, and even made inquiries at the office of my Beirut sponsors, although the message was obviously not passed on. I could blame no one, since refugees like myself were not seen as being the responsibility of anyone in particular. Mistakeş like that get made. But that was not good enough for Francis. After 15 September he had heard nothing whatsoever about me, except that I was in Sabra and Shatila, where thousands were slaughtered. The first he heard of me being alive and well was when he got my telex statement asking him to circulate it as widely as possible, on 22 September 1982.

My old friends were all delighted to see me back in London, although I was down to five stone in weight and fairly weak.

There was no time to lose. Many people had, like myself, learnt about the Palestinian people only because of Israel's invasion of Lebanon. The plight of the surviving Palestinians in Lebanon was very precarious indeed, and there might be very little time left. Another massacre or an attack on the camps could happen at any time, once the multinational peacekeeping force left. Every effort had to be made to publicise the plight of the destitute orphans and widows still living in the ruins. Their voice must be heard.

The massacres had brought home one painful lesson to me – the uselessness of my surgical skills. I might feel pleased about saving a handful of lives, but thousands of lives could have been saved if the rest of the world had known what was happening – if I had realised what was happening, stopped operating and publicised the fact that a massacre was taking place there and then. Now I knew, and there was no turning back. I owed it to those people whose lives I failed to save. In moments of despair, I was tempted to believe that people would have turned away even if they knew about and could help stop the massacres. If they did not know, it was my fault for not speaking up. But if I spoke up, and they knew, and still allowed it to continue, then it was they who would have to live with their own consciences.

I was not going to fall prey to cynicism. If there was to be another massacre, I was going to make sure no one would be able to say they did not know – they would have to admit they did not care. I was very tired and physically exhausted, but I was determined to talk to anyone who was prepared to listen, as long and as often as necessary. I had to make up for the limitations of being a doctor, a surgeon, by being a human being first.

That was the only time in my life I wished I had blue eyes and fair hair, and perhaps a name like Mary instead of

Swee Chai. Unfortunately my South East Asian features, foreign name and foreign accent, which had hindered me in getting a British surgical job in my early refugee days, now hindered me in doing publicity work for the Palestinians. With the exception of a few newspapers, no one wanted to interview me. In fact lots of reporters asked me if there were any British team members who would talk about the camps, as they would print interviews with British members of the team any time. I understood the position of the press. Who in Britain would want to hear about some refugees three thousand miles away from a strange, ethnic Chinese, woman doctor? There was only one British doctor who was willing to talk to the press: and that was Paul Morris, and he was unfortunately back in Lebanon, and therefore uncontactable.

At times I felt very resentful towards the other British doctors and nurses who had volunteered and worked in Lebanon, as they could so easily have helped the Palestinians by speaking up for them, but refused to do so.

So I had to go on a person-to-person campaign, and trudged all over Britain addressing small groups – in schools, universities, churches and mosques – and un-official gatherings like women's tea-parties, or groups of my own friends. It was not only tiring, but expensive. Francis had to pay most of my fares, since I was out of a job.

Within a couple of months I had done more than two hundred such meetings. Sometimes I would find myself talking to school children in London in the morning, university students at lunch time in the Midlands, and an evening meeting in some church in Scotland on the same day. I showed people slides of the camps which I had taken with my pocket camera, and told them the camp people's story. This inefficient way of campaigning helped me to meet a lot of very committed people, who really wanted to help the Palestinians, and it was worth all the trouble in the end. Francis had bought me a mini-slide projector, and I would arrange my slides to be shown on it, and the two of us laughed at this set-up, which he called my 'road show'.

An important thing emerged. People in Britain did care. Even though the country was in economic recession, people did respond to the plight of the Palestinians. Everywhere I went to give my road show, members of the audience would ask me how they could help. Many of them had never met a Palestinian in their life, but they would respond to the injustice done to the Palestinians and wanted to help.

People who offered to help came from all walks of life and had differing political backgrounds. Most of them were ordinary working people like myself, and wanted to help in what they saw as a human tragedy. The British people had a long tradition of generosity towards those in need, and their response to the Palestinians was not a one-off thing. They had given to Kampuchea, to Bangladesh, to places in Africa, and now in the same way they wanted to give to the Palestinians. Many did not know the politics behind the situation, and did not care who was right and who was wrong: they simply responded as good Samaritans. The unemployed, old-age pensioners, students, poorly-paid working people and ethnic minorities – all wanted to do something to help.

Eventually a group of us – Francis and myself, returned volunteers from Lebanon and Palestinians in Britain – got together to discuss how we could be of use to the camp folks. None of us were politicians, but many of us were medical and relief workers. We agreed to set up a medical charity to help people in Lebanon. We decided that this charity had to be non-sectarian, and help everyone in need; and be non-political and entirely humanitarian; and that it would be a channel through which the generosity of people in Britain could reach those who were suffering. The name 'Medical Aid for Palestinians' was chosen, so that we could avoid the political issue of Palestine, and could function wherever the Palestinians were, whether they were living under occupation or in exile.

CHAPTER 15

Ellen Siegel returned to Washington DC. A year passed, but she was unable to forget the people in Lebanon's refugee camps either. With the support of organisations in the United States, she organised a commemoration service on the first anniversary of the Sabra and Shatila massacres, and invited Ben Alofs, Louise Norman and myself to travel over to Washington in September 1983. This gave us the chance to remember the victims of Sabra and Shatila. It was my first trip to the United States, that powerful country across the Atlantic if one looks at the map from Britain, or the Pacific if one looks from Singapore.

The three of us were invited to Ellen's synagogue to attend the Yom Kippur service. It was a long service, and conducted in Hebrew. The whole service was entirely unintelligible to me. My American Jewish hosts told me it was about atonement for sins. For the Jews, sins of òmission were as grievous as sins of commission. It was good in a way not to understand the contents of the service, as I detected a very sad and heavy mood throughout, and it would probably have been upsetting, if I had understood what the rabbi was saying.

When I attended a service a few days later in Shiloh, a black Baptist church, it was too overwhelming. After I had thanked the pastor and his congregation for remembering

141

the camp victims, I broke down and wept in the middle of the song 'Amazing Grace'. This was the first time since Lebanon that I had broken down in public. The kind black lady next to me kept passing me pieces of tissue paper throughout the service. I had done all sorts of things in the hope of helping the people in the camps, but this was the first time I had remembered them before God, and prayed for them.

We gave the usual radio and television interviews. One memorable event was a press conference called on our behalf by the United Nations representative of the Palestine Liberation Organisation in New York. Jill Drew and I spoke at the press conference. The press room was packed with reporters, who had all come because they had misunderstood the press release sent out by the PLO representative. They thought they had come to hear the PLO comment on the events in Lebanon. The battle of Tripoli, in Northern Lebanon, was in the American headlines at that time. According to the press, the PLO in Lebanon had split into factions for and against the PLO chairman, Yasser Arafat, and the factions were fighting each other. This event had thrown everyone into confusion, and the press wanted to know what it was all about.

Instead, the PLO representative produced Jill Drew and myself – a nurse and a doctor, who spoke about the Sabra-Shatila massacres of a year before, and spoke about the hardships faced by the Palestinians. A few unsympathetic journalists were very annoyed, and attacked Jill and me for wasting their time with stories of no 'news value'! But, overall, it was a good press conference, and most of the African and Asian papers carried stories on the anniversary of the massacres, reminding readers of the difficulties the Palestinians were facing.

We had lunch with the UN Deputy Representative of the PLO in the UN dining room. It overlooked the sea, and was extremely pleasant. I remember nothing of the food we ate, but will always remember the bill our host received.

He signed his name, followed by 'PLO' in large letters. At least in this lunch room, I thought, in the middle of New York City, the PLO man was accepted and treated like all other diplomats, and not abused and called names as in many other places I had been. It was good to see the PLO treated with some respect.

All over the United States, people talked about Martin Luther King and his dream. The Palestinians, like the American Blacks, have their dream. It is a dream of peace with justice, freedom with security. It is a dream of things which all human beings cherish. 'Together, we will work and struggle to make that dream come true,' I told my American friends.

CHAPTER 16

Our charity, Medical Aid for Palestinians (MAP), came into being in 1984 – it took almost two years for us to get our act together. But once launched, MAP made steady progress, thanks to all sections of the British public who gave much of their time, money and substance. We kept in close touch with the Palestinians in the refugee camps. Because MAP was small, and had none of the funds larger organisations had, we always thought of ourselves as friends of the Palestinian people, rather than as some 'charity'. For those of us close to the camp folks, we knew they would find the idea of hand-outs offensive, but we were merely a channel whereby the goodwill in Britain could be directed to them. Our supporters did not give out of pity: like all supporters of a just cause, they gave out of solidarity, on a basis of mutual respect. We did not want to see a kind of paternalistic attitude emerge in us.

One thing made me especially grateful: the Palestinian experience had given me a chance to know the British people. It made me see beyond having a chip on my shoulder just because I was a small, coloured woman. Giving talks and raising funds for the Palestinians had brought me into contact with the real British people, and I would always want to remember their generosity, warmth and kindness to other suffering people, a side of Britain I was grateful to discover. Charity is not pity. The English word 'charity' originally meant 'love', and I discovered that many people in Britain were capable of loving, even a people they had never met.

MAP continued to raise small sums of money, and our limited resources were used to support health projects of the Palestinians. We would send small shipments of medicines and equipment from time to time or use the donations to help towards the education of health workers living in the Israeli-occupied territories. There were even a few occasions when we brought wounded people to Britain for treatment.

Milad Faroukh was the Lebanese boy wounded by Israeli bombs in 1982. He was the boy Paul Morris practically hand-fed back to life, as the little one refused to eat or drink after seeing his younger brother blown up in front of him. After Ellen Siegel and I left in 1982, Paul continued to work in Lebanon. He ran a clinic among the poor Muslims in Beirut, trying to continue his medical work. Unfortunately he was threatened, and had his clinic shot up, by a group of hostile militiamen. Paul left, but then revisited Beirut in 1984. He found Milad in the refugee camp. Milad was then eleven years old, and weighed only twenty-five kilograms – ten to twenty kilograms below the average for boys of that age. His heel wound was severely septic, and he still could not walk.

Paul had asked MAP to sponsor Milad's treatment in Britain, and we agreed. We had no money to pay for his treatment and had to raise the funds. Professor Jack Stevens, the head of the Orthopaedic Department in Newcastle-upon-Tyne, where I was working at the time, agreed to treat Milad free, so that we only needed to raise his air fare and accommodation expenses. Meanwhile Milad waited in Cyprus for his British visa, and the okay from London. While waiting, the stability of Cyprus helped him put on fifteen kilograms in a matter of three months. He not only grew quickly, but his foot also improved!

By the time he arrived in Britain, major treatment was unnecessary. Being away from wartorn Lebanon and having enough food to eat during the months of waiting had made Milad much better. Examination with .the radioisotope scanner revealed that the bones and blood vessels of Milad's foot were recovering rapidly. For once he looked fit and healthy.

It was a happy time for those of us who knew what Milad had been like back in 1982, and it was one of those rare stories with a happy ending. If only Lebanon had food instead of bullets, we would not have to bring kids like Milad thousands of miles to Britain.

PART IV

Return to Beirut

Summer 1985

CHAPTER 17

Spring came late to Britain in 1985. I was working as Senior Orthopaedic Registrar in a hospital called Dryburn, in beautiful, ancient Durham City, in North East England. I was beginning to leave the nightmares of Sabra and Shatila behind me, mentally putting away all the atrocities in the museum of my mind, reliving them only on special occasions, like the anniversaries of the camp massacres, when we mourn and commemorate. And, like everyone else who had survived 1982, I had to pick up the threads of my own life, and get on.

Milad had gone to school in Cyprus, having quite recently left Britain. He had lots of catching up to do on school lessons he had missed in Lebanon; and he had to grab whatever childhood he had left, before the years passed him by. Mouna, Nabil, Huda and Ali had all been able to travel from the camps of Beirut to visit him in Cyprus. I could feel the war wounds – like Milad's foot – slowly healing. For the first time since 1982, I had room in my mind to start a research project into the treatment of fractures, something which I could not have done if I were not mentally rehabilitated.

I had not been back to visit the people in Sabra and Shatila, but I knew that children had grown up in those three years; young people had married and babies were born. Shattered homes had been rebuilt and new ones had risen on top of those bulldozed flat. Separated from sons, fathers and husbands by the evacuation and arrests, women had picked up the pieces of their lives. The Palestine Red Crescent Society had fully restored Gaza and Akka hospitals. MAP had just offered some money to help reconstruct the sewage system in Sabra camp. There was always the threat of a new massacre, but the camp folks continued to rebuild their shattered homes, brick by brick, corner by corner, street by street, once again, with the same resilience they had always displayed.

In May that year, the trees started to blossom in full splendour. Because the winter was especially long and harsh, the glory of spring was out of this world. I was walking to Dryburn Hospital in Durham, along my favourite path. Beautiful clouds of pink and white lined the walk, while the tender green grass was as soft as velvet. In this happy state, I heard my long range bleep go off – long pips one after another. That meant an emergency. I ran towards the hospital, and picked up the nearest telephone.

'Miss Ang,' said the switchboard, 'long-distance call from Beirut.' What a relief, I thought, glad that it was not a surgical emergency.

A voice came on the line, 'Swee, they have attacked our camps again. They have taken over Gaza Hospital, shot our nurses and patients and burnt our medical supplies stores. We are very desperate.'

I was stunned. I had feared this would happen. In four months' time it would be three years since the 1982 Sabra and Shatila massacres, but now we had a new massacre. I did not yet know who the attackers were, but the right of the Palestinians to be in exile and their right to life were once again challenged. For nearly four decades, these camp people, deprived of their right to a homeland, had lived in exile. They had been threatened repeatedly with massacres, with bombs, with shells, with deportation. Many of them had been kidnapped and had vanished from the face of the earth. Yet they continued to labour against all odds to preserve their identity, and struggle to regain their lost birthright, their right to a home.

Each time it looked as though the old wounds were about to heal, new wounds were inflicted. How much persecution and pain could a people endure? How long would they be able to be strong?

The next day, my friend phoned again from Beirut. 'Swee,' she said, 'our women have gone back into the hospital and fought the attackers and we have now regained Gaza.'

But this triumph was short-lived. My friend never phoned back, but I learnt from the newspapers that Sabra camp's Gaza Hospital was lost once more. Most of the women who fought to retake Gaza Hospital were killed. Sabra and Shatila camps, and Milad's home, Bourj el-Brajneh camp, were surrounded by enemy tanks and shelled incessantly throughout May, the Muslim month of Ramadan. Just like the massacres of 1982, the siege on the camps was complete, and no one, not even the International Red Cross, was allowed to enter the camps to evacuate the wounded.

So after nearly three years of silence, the camps once again hit the international headlines! Lots of media commentators and experts on the Middle East deliberated on the situation. Was it a repeat of Tripoli, where the Palestinians were split and fighting each other? Or were there other explanations? The newspaper editorials went on and on.

But two facts emerged from the verbiage. The camps were resisting, and the resistance was united. Unlike the massacres of 1982, there was return fire. Unlike the 'Battle of Tripoli' in 1983, the Palestinians were not fighting each other. Along with terrible news of the dead, the wounded, the children dying of infectious diseases and lack of food, we heard that Palestinians risking death were saying, 'When I die, I do not want to be remembered as a member of this or that Palestinian faction, but just as a Palestinian of Sabra and Shatila.'

There were reports of teenage girls loading themselves with explosives and running into the enemy tanks. The newspapers called them 'suicide bombers': the camp people called them martyrs. The camps had dug in, to defend themselves to the last man, woman and child. Palestinian fighters were outnumbered twenty to one, and ill-equipped. They only had light arms and grenades with which to defend their camps against the tanks, shells and mortars of the attackers. A new chapter of Palestinian history was being written by the camps – the chapter of the resurrection of Palestinian resistance. To set the record straight, I too wrote an 'editorial', giving my version of the situation:

SABRA-SHATILA: SYMBOL FOR THE PALESTIN-IAN STRUGGLE

The Palestinian movement, born out of years of suffering, has two important pillars:
1) The will to resist.
2) The ability to unite.

In Beirut 1982, the Palestinians were united, but had much of their infrastructure destroyed. First, the families were split up by the evacuation of the men, then the women and children were massacred, the camp homes destroyed and bulldozed over. This was designed to eliminate all traces of Palestinian existence in Sabra-Shatila, Beirut.

Morale for the will to resist was therefore severely battered. This weakened one of the two pillars and hence distorted the strength of the Palestinian struggle. The will to unite was therefore also weakened, as demonstrated in Tripoli, Lebanon, 1983.

From 1982 onwards, the Palestinian struggle saw what would happen if they had neither 1) the will to resist nor 2) the ability to unite.

Sabra-Shatila 1985 has demonstrated to the whole world the resilience of the Palestinian people. They have regained the will to resist.

Therefore, when the enemies of the Palestinian people

sought to repeat a Sabra-Shatila 1982 massacre, they encountered fierce resistance. In addition, the courageous resistance of the camp folks inspired all Palestinians and revived the unity of the Palestinian movement.

In 1982, Sabra-Shatila was massacred without resistance. In 1985, Sabra-Shatila presents a united Palestinian people – united and steadfast in their resistance.

Sabra-Shatila may be physically destroyed in this battle. But the people will rebuild it once more. They have set the heroic standards to the rest of the world of unity, resistance, tenacity and courage. And that spirit of Sabra-Shatila will live on in every Palestinian and in people all over the world fighting for justice and liberation!

2 June 1985, UK

But after writing these optimistic words, I became very, very desperate. I feared that despite their heroism, Sabra and Shatila might be overrun, and the camp people massacred and deported. Palestinian history was full of heroic chapters – the 1968 battle of Karameh in Jordan, the 1976 siege of Tel al-Zaatar, heroic resistance struggles which were now the heritage not only of the Palestinian people, but of oppressed people all over the world. What should a doctor like myself do under the circumstances? I realised how precious Sabra and Shatila were to me. The Palestinians had been in exile and struggle from the year of my birth, 1948. Yet they remained completely human, under the most inhuman circumstances.

Tomorrow Sabra and Shatila might no longer exist, but for us – non-Palestinians honoured to be their friends – our duty was to respond in solidarity, before it was too late.

At the height of the 1982 siege of Beirut, there were nearly a hundred medical volunteers from all over the world working with the Palestine Red Crescent Society, looking after the injured in Lebanon. During the massacres of Sabra and Shatila, there were twenty-two foreign volunteer doctors and nurses in Gaza Hospital. We treated the wounded, and some of us spoke up to urge the world not to forget the camps.

Now the Palestinians were under attack once again.

From three thousand miles away, we could feel their pain and suffering. We wanted to go back to the camps.

But circumstances were different. The eyes of the world had shifted to the famine in Ethiopia. There was no longer a Gaza Hospital to return to: the hospital of Sabra camp had been burnt, looted and occupied by the new attackers. Akka Hospital was also surrounded by the militia, and although not burnt, could not function as a hospital. With these two hospitals out of action, the treatment of wounded people would be most difficult, if not impossible.

West Beirut – and Lebanon generally – had now become risky for foreigners. Westerners were particularly vulnerable to kidnapping. Beirut International Airport was embroiled in a hijacking incident involving a TWA airliner, and was generally no go for outsiders. Most flights out of Beirut were packed with foreigners fleeing Lebanon.

The camps were surrounded by tanks and gunmen, making it impossible even for the International Red Cross to evacuate wounded children. What chance was there for a doctor or nurse to get into the camps?

Our charity met to discuss how best to help. Someone suggested advertising for volunteer doctors and nurses to go back to the camps. Other members of MAP were astounded at this suggestion, because all of us were fully aware of the dangers, and someone else asked the woman who suggested advertising if she would like to go personally. That naturally created a bit of embarrassment, but we did conclude that we probably should look for volunteers from among ourselves to go first. I volunteered to go back to the camps, since I had been there before, and had a duty to respond now. I was also fully aware what kind of shambles the camps must have been reduced to, and would probably be able to cope. As a surgeon, I had performed operations in partially-destroyed buildings without water and electricity, and would probably be able to do the same again. Even if Sabra and Shatila were destroyed by the time I got there, I still had to visit the camp people to reassure them that we remembered them and had come back to see them. This was the least I could do as a friend.

We knew sending a team to the camps was a high-risk exercise which few British charities would be prepared to take on. Our charity was less than a year old, and most of us were very worried that we would be seen as being reckless and irresponsible. We spent hours arguing, and in the end decided to vote on it. Nine members were against my going back, and two were in favour. The two in favour were me and Francis, whom I bullied into toeing the line against his better judgement. My colleagues were very concerned for my safety, and that was why they voted against my going.

But in the end they changed their minds, and did all they could to support me in going back to the camps. We made a public appeal for volunteers, and were moved when dozens of doctors, nurses and technicians rallied round to offer help. They were prepared to come to Lebanon despite being warned of the dangers.

Within four weeks, MAP had mobilised a team of six medical volunteers and half a ton of medical equipment, and we were ready to leave for Beirut in early July. The medical equipment was for Haifa Hospital, in a camp just south of Shatila: Bourj el-Brajneh. Till this attack on the camps, Haifa Hospital had been a rehabilitation centre for paraplegics. During the siege, many people in Bourj el-Brajneh had died because there were no medical facilities in the camp itself and the sick and wounded could not leave the camp. So the PRCS planned to convert Haifa Hospital into a general hospital with operating theatres and an Accident and Emergency Department. Besides medical equipment, the British public also donated funds for us to buy an ambulance to serve as a mobile clinic. I told Dryburn Hospital that I was going on my summer vacation, and took my six weeks annual leave.

While we were making these preparations, we received word that a ceasefire had been called. After forty days of attacks and siege, the camps had refused to surrender. The ill-equipped and outnumbered camp people had fought back so bravely that one thousand of the militiamen who attacked the camps were wounded. Palestinian casualties were high, with six hundred and eighty dead, two thousand wounded, and one and a half thousand missing. The camps had been shelled and attacked with rockets for forty days and were reduced to rubble. Thirty thousand Palestinians had been made homeless. But the morale in the camps was high.

Our medical team included one British staff nurse, who was also a midwife – Alison Haworth; a trained nurse with a lot of rescue experience – John Thorndike; an anaesthetic technician – John Croft; a Lebanese friend from the days of 1982 – Immad; and good old 'Big Ben' – Ben Alofs, the Dutch nurse. Ben was fluent in spoken Arabic, and we all liked him very much. He flew in from Amsterdam to join us when he heard the terrible news about the camps.

CHAPTER 18

In 1982 the flight out had been packed with holiday-makers. This time the plane was largely empty, but then it was flying all the way to Beirut. We were able to land there after all. The airline had agreed to fly our medical and surgical equipment free.

As the plane landed, we could see the recently hijacked TWA jet parked beside the runway. The airport security was relatively slack: I did not even have my luggage checked. We were met by representatives of the Norwegian Aid Committee (NORWAC), an organisation we would be working with. NORWAC was well respected in Lebanon. They had been working here since the first civil war, and from the outset had been non-sectarian, rendering aid to all the parties in the conflict. This was difficult to do in Lebanon, as the country was very fragmented, but the Norwegians had managed to remain above the politics of the place.

The Norwegian co-ordinator, Synne, was the driver of the ambulance which was our transport. Fair, good-looking and in her early thirties, she was very dynamic and efficient. We were taken from the airport to the camps in the southern suburbs of Beirut. Bourj el-Brajneh was the first camp on that route. Although I had never worked there before, I remembered it as a camp with a large

Lebanese population as well as Palestinians. In fact, it was the largest camp in Beirut now, after the destruction of Sabra and Shatila.

But as we passed the entrance of Bourj el-Brajneh camp, a quick glimpse from the outside showed us an unreal scene: the apartments within looked like a series of open, irregular honeycombs. We could see that the camp was devastated: buildings were without walls, and collapsing. The camp entrance was guarded by a number of soldiers, armed with machine guns and rocket launchers. Synne told us that if we wanted to go into the camp now, it would take ages just to have all our luggage searched through, and as it was getting late, we should press on to see Um Walid, the PRCS Director in Lebanon.

Um Walid was known for her strength and for her ability to keep herself together under very difficult circumstances. In fact, I had never seen her become ruffled or lose control at any time, except the once – when she wept on her way out of the field hospital after the 1982 massacre. But this time the Um Walid who greeted us was very different from the Um Walid I remembered. The camp war must have taken its toll on the Palestinian woman. Although her first remark after we embraced was, 'Swee, are you still strong?' I could see that she had really been through a lot. She had been in Lebanon all these years. She had lost weight, and there were dark rings around her eyes, and her face had a sad look. Nevertheless, she had the air of one who refused to be defeated. She looked like a lighthouse that had taken a battering from the waves, but was still standing, and I was reassured to meet her.

'Yes, Um Walid, still strong,' I replied without thinking, though I could feel myself fighting back tears.

'We have lost Gaza Hospital,' said Um Walid. 'They burnt it, and none of us are allowed to go there any more. But you must not be too upset about that. All our efforts must be concentrated on building Haifa Hospital. Look, did we not raise Gaza Hospital from the ground? In the same way, we will open Haifa Hospital.'

With her words ringing in our ears, we wished her goodnight, and continued to the Mayflower Hotel, where we were staying the night. The Mayflower Hotel used to be quite a place in 1982. It was the overflow hotel for journalists, once the Commodore Hotel was full. Many volunteers and officials from non-governmental organisations and aid agencies also hung out there. I used to go to the Mayflower Hotel in 1982 to look for various people, including those from the various European commissions of enquiry into the Israeli invasion. The delegates from the International Committee of the Red Cross, and the co-ordinators of various health and relief agencies, used to spend time in the bar then. It was always so crowded that it was almost impossible to get a seat in the bar.

But now the Mayflower Hotel looked totally deserted. The six members of our British team, two Norwegians and four other foreigners made up the total complement of residents of the hotel. The hotel staff were the same, however – Abu George at the bar, all by himself this time; Moustapha at the reception. It was like old friends meeting again, but the circumstances were weird. The rest of the team had gone out for dinner, but I wanted to be alone, and stayed behind. The dining room was large and empty. I sat in the corner, alone. I asked for an omelette, and was told that the hotel had no eggs. This was not the Mayflower Hotel I remembered.

Abu George and Moustapha were not prepared to discuss the political situation with me, although I dearly wanted to know why the camps were being attacked, especially by the Amal, a Lebanese Muslim group which had once been an ally of the Palestinians. One of the hotel employees had recently been kidnapped, and so there was an atmosphere of unease. There was machine-gun fire outside, sounding like only a few streets away.

'No problem, Dr Swee,' they told me: 'The Druse and Amal are fighting each other. They'll stop soon.'

Right enough, after three-quarters of an hour or so the shooting ceased. Amal was a Lebanese party and so was the Progressive Socialist Party (Walid Jumblatt's Druse party). Political parties in Lebanon owned guns and tanks and rocket launchers, and instead of resorting to debate, they resorted to shoot-outs. In Beirut at that time, when a person signed up to join a political party, he was also given the option of belonging to the party's militia group. That meant he would be given a machine gun and a revolver, and probably some grenades too for good measure!

The word 'amal' meant 'hope' and Amal had originally been founded by the Emam Moussa Sadr, who had mysteriously disappeared. Moussa Sadr had founded the Amal movement as a movement to give the Lebanese Shi'ites, who were the majority of the Muslims in Lebanon, a chance to develop their higher human potentials, and the founder's aims were very noble indeed. During Amal's formative years, the Palestinians had helped and trained them. It was impossible for most of us to understand how part of Amal was now attacking the Palestinians.

The Shi'ites were themselves very deprived people, most of whom had known much suffering. Fortunately, not all of them were against the Palestinians. There were one million Shi'ites in Lebanon, and if they had all been against the camps, the situation would have been very much worse. The Palestinians were bitter about the Amal militia who attacked them, and who chose the holy Muslim month of Ramadan to do so, but they had no enmity against the majority of the Shi'ites, who had nothing to do with the attacks on the camps.

The next day was 5 July. We started early, because we were all desperate to see the camps. Sabra camp was mostly demolished, and had been turned into an Amal stronghold. Therefore the Sabra entrance was not a safe place to get into Shatila camp. The other entrance of Shatila, opposite Akka Hospital on the airport road, was a bit safer, since besides Amal militiamen, there were also official Lebanese Army positions. The Lebanese Army's presence was part of the ceasefire agreement. But there were still a few Amal checkpoints at which we had to stop. Because of the resistance from the Palestinians within, Amal had failed to overrun the camp, and were limited to controlling the entrance. The siege continued, even though there was a ceasefire.

The destruction in Shatila camp was appalling. Every single building had been damaged by the attacks. Some had one or more large shell holes. Some had several smaller ones. Some had bullet-riddled walls. Some had all of these. And there were heaps of rubble. Shatila mosque, untouched during the 1982 invasion, was destroyed beyond recognition – even its dome had been blown apart. There was a stench in the air – a mixture of dead bodies and garbage. The wounded and the dead were not allowed to leave the camp, and some of the bodies had to be buried in Shatila mosque. Flies hovered round garbage heaps. There were wounded people everywhere.

The NORWAC ambulance stopped beside a broken-down building which was to be the site of the Norwegian Clinic. While Synne and another Norwegian nurse were sorting out some structural plans for the clinic, including where to put the door, there being a choice of three large shell holes, my eyes wandered to the other side of the narrow camp road. A little figure emerged from the pile of rubble and garbage. Thin and small, probably no more than ten years old, wearing a white tee-shirt, and black pants. He waved at us, and smiled broadly. I did not remember him from 1982 – but he would only have been about seven then. Today this young 'man' was carrying a gun. He sure looked proud of himself and was going about with a strong sense of purpose. A bigger boy then appeared from behind him, also armed, and both of them disappeared in the direction of Shatila mosque. So these were the fighters who defeated Amal. These kids were the new Palestinian resistance fighters which Amal and their mighty tanks were trying to destroy.

Later that day, we arrived at Bourj el-Brajneh, the largest of all the Beirut camps. The road leading into the camp was partially paved with tar. The entrance was controlled by the Lebanese Sixth Brigade, a Shi'ite Brigade which again was part of the ceasefire agreement. A short way in, there was an Amal militia checkpoint. The road then forked, one path leading into the Lebanese part of the camp, and the other into the Palestinian part of Bourj el-Brajneh.

Further inside the Palestinian part of the camp, a checkpoint was manned by Palestinians. By this time, I was getting used to the idea of Palestinians carrying arms. After all, why not? Everyone else in Lebanon had arms, so why not the Palestinians? The ugly truth was that, without guns in the camp, a massacre at least as horrific as in 1982 would take place. Further on inside the camp, it was muddy and filled with puddles of sewage water.

Bourj el-Brajneh was very densely populated. The Palestinian part of the camp, about four square kilometres, contained a population of twenty-five thousand people. Buildings were close to each other, and many of them were two or three floors high. The blocks of houses were separated by narrow alleys, which in most places permitted the comfortable passage of one person, and would let two people by so long as they walked sideways. Open drains, rubble and a maze of water pipes followed the narrow alleys. The peripheral buildings of this camp were just as badly shelled as in Shatila, but as one got deeper into the camp, many of the structures were relatively intact.

Some way into the camp, next to a shell-damaged building opposite Haifa Hospital, we saw a group of people hovering round a large table. At the sight of new faces, they said to us in English, 'Welcome, what is your name? Come, look – a small present from our Amal brothers.' On the table was a display of bits of mortar, shell casings and bomb fragments, all in a large heap. These were samples of things lobbed into the camp by the Amal over the previous forty days. People had withstood the forty days of shelling and blockade, and morale was now very high. Feeling proud and victorious, the camp folks were lively and garrulous.

Haifa Hospital was partly destroyed, but by now my immediate reaction was to calculate what repairs were necessary to turn the rehabilitation centre into a functioning hospital. I could see that, although a fair amount of work was needed, Haifa Hospital was not beyond repair. There were three floors above ground and two floors underground. The top two floors were full of shell holes, and would need a lot of repair work. The first underground floor was to be converted to an operating theatre, with the casualty ward just across the corridor. The floor beneath that was to stay as a bomb shelter. The hospital staff was cleaning the building, and construction and reconstruction had begun. Our surgical equipment and anaesthetic machine had arrived, and for the rest of the day Alison, the two Johns and myself were busy with stocktaking. There was still nowhere in the hospital for us to sleep, and so we returned to the Mayflower Hotel, tired but satisfied, having spent a good and useful day.

CHAPTER 19

The next day, we visited Haifa Hospital again. The place was already looking different. The hospital was full of visitors from the camp. Beds had been put into the first-floor rooms, and they were starting to look like wards. One room had even been cleared and beds put in so that the British medical team could stay there. Palestinian women had brought us clean white sheets and had swept the room clean, and they had brought in tea and drinking water for us. It was ridiculously luxurious compared to the shambles of the camp outside. On the first basement floor, the Accident and Emergency room was packed full of patients, and two Palestinian doctors were already very busy working.

In the midst of all this bustle, Um Walid arrived. She had come to oversee the construction of the new operating theatre, and to pay the staff and construction workers. She went round the building floor by floor, giving plenty of instructions in Arabic, which, unfortunately, I still could not follow. Then she left for Akka Hospital.

Building work on the operating theatre began at once. On the basement floor, the builders – all from within the camp – started to knock down a wall to make space for an operating theatre. The din was incredible, and it was all made worse by an unannounced visit by journalists from the Associated Press, eager to cover the story of Haifa Hospital's opening. The reporter from the Associated Press was a bit surprised at first to find a Chinese woman leading the British medical team, but we got on quite well, and soon she went off to talk to all the team members, and some of the Palestinians as well.

The staff at Haifa Hospital were just as impressive as the staff at Gaza had been back in 1982, although there were less of them. Nidal, the hospital administrator of Haifa, reminded me in many ways of Azziza, except that she was about ten years older – in her late thirties or early forties. She worked incessantly and selflessly, and earned the respect of everyone. (She was to be killed by a large shell which fell on her home in Bourj el-Brajneh in May 1986. Her funeral was attended by over five thousand people in Beirut, but for many of us Nidal will never die. In our memories, her selfless devotion and courage will live forever.) She was well-loved by all. Hers was no easy job, having to cope not only with the day-to-day running of the hospital, but also with the added problem of opening an Accident and Emergency service.

She had to cope with the staff as well, and keep them working in harmony. The 1982 invasion and massacre had been followed by fighting in Tripoli in 1983. Medical staff had developed loyalties to different factions of the PLO. It was an eye-opener to see doctors from different factions working together harmoniously in a PRCS hospital. There was much talk of unity among the hospital staff, and three Palestinian doctors from three different factions invited me to take a picture of them standing together, shoulder to shoulder. They understood little English, and I understand even less Arabic, but they wanted the photo taken to tell me that they were united as Palestinians.

Dr Reda was the medical director of the hospital – young, enthusiastic, competent, hardworking and entirely devoted to his people. He was always in five places at once, as active and dynamic as Dr Rio Spirugi, but with none of

Rio's quick temper. Along with Reda, Haifa had five other young Palestinian doctors, and between them, they ran the casualty department, the out-patient clinics and the wards. I could see that they would become inundated with work once Haifa Hospital became fully functional. The camp population was swelling to nearly thirty thousand now with the influx of returning refugees.

By midday, when most of the patients had been treated and had gone home, the hospital staff sat down to lunch together. It was nearly three years since I had first eaten camp food, and I really loved it. When I was back in London, I had unsuccessfully spent many hours experimenting on foods, trying to cook them the way the Gaza Hospital cook did them. Camp food was something very special to me. The camp people had the ability to make any food delicious, even ordinary legumes and beans.

More precious to me than the camp food itself was the way everyone in the PRCS hospitals gathered together to share food, director and cleaner alike. It was so different from some NHS hospitals in Britain, where people were allocated eating places according to their social status and occupation. In one of the London hospitals I had worked in, there were at least six different dining rooms – one for hospital consultants and senior administrators, one for junior doctors, one for technicians, one for nurses, one for manual workers and one for members of the public!

During lunch in Haifa Hospital, we exchanged information and greetings from friends. I found out that the professor of surgery from Gaza Hospital, many of my favourite nurses and many other colleagues from Gaza Hospital were still alive, some not very well, but alive. In the Middle East, people greeted each other with the greeting: 'Al-Hamdullelah!', which meant 'Praise be to God!' Sometimes, a person could literally be on his death bed, and it was still 'Al-Hamdullelah!' Life itself was a gift, and a blessing from God. We could be sitting on a pile of garbage, but the fact that we were alive and with each other was a reason to praise God. Abu Ali, the theatre super-intendent of Gaza Hospital, was still working, and he was going to come to Haifa Hospital the following day to help set up the operating theatre. I rejoiced to hear that he was alive, and eagerly looked forward to seeing him the next day.

The afternoon was devoted to more stocktaking and organising. There was a fair bit of chaos, since pieces of equipment salvaged from Gaza Hospital before it was burnt out had all been thrown together. Orthopaedic sets had stainless steel and vitallium screws all mixed up. The anaesthetic machine from Gaza Hospital had bits missing, and it was difficult to find spare parts in the post-siege confusion.

The next morning I went to the Mayflower Hotel to give an interview to Visnews, a television network. This was a hilarious experience, as the interviewer did not understand English, I could not understand French – and there was no translator. The interviewer spoke a sentence or so, which I presumed to be a question, and I answered for as long as I liked on what I guessed he might have asked me. It turned out well, as I said what I wanted to say, which really amounted to two points.

Firstly, the British public had contributed their savings and efforts to help Haifa Hospital get established, because they wanted to support a health institution which treated all people in need. Through my years of association with the PRCS, I knew that it always operated under that philosophy, treating friends and enemies alike, without asking for payment, and hence I had no hesitation supporting them. Secondly, I was in Beirut during the difficult times of 1982, but I had seen then the best in humanity displayed by the Lebanese and Palestinians, working together to resist the Israeli onslaught and providing assistance to war victims. There was a fantastic unity between the Lebanese and Palestinians, in Beirut and South Lebanon. Why had all that fallen apart in 1985?

Last night, there were at least four battles going on simultaneously in Beirut – the Amal fought the Palestinians in Bourj el-Brajneh over some checkpoint problems; the Druse and the Amal were fighting in the streets of Hamra; while the Christians and Muslims were shooting at each other across the Green Line; and trails of missiles projected their tracks from various mountain positions. While the Lebanese fought among themselves and against the Palestinians, all was quiet in the southern border area, where the Israelis still occupied Lebanese soil.

Perhaps since people were not in a position to take on the Israelis, I said, they had resorted to getting at each other – what the locals called 'brotherly fighting'. I was sure the French reporter did not understand what I said, but he seemed delighted with the interview, and offered to drive me back to Bourj el-Brajneh camp. He drove like most Lebanese, and must have stayed in Lebanon for a long time to acquire the art of driving that way. He was fast, reckless and impatient, but his manner was entirely civil and charming.

When I arrived back at Haifa Hospital, I found that Dr Reda had already organised a whole convoy of orthopaedic patients to see me. Most of the wounded were now young, unlike in 1982, and had sustained their injuries defending the camp. They were mostly young men and boys, and some young women. The most common orthopaedic injuries were caused by high-velocity gunshot wounds, in other words, injuries from M16 rifle bullets. Compound fractures with damage to nerves and blood vessels were the rule when a limb was hit by an M16 bullet. Most of those with isolated limb injuries would have had their limb amputated by the time they got to see me. As the artificial limb centre in Akka Hospital had been put out of action by the attacks, the hundred and sixty-seven amputees from all three Beirut camps had to wait indefinitely till something was sorted out. The real difficulty was to get these wounded out of the camps. Most of them had fought to defend the camps, and were therefore wanted by the Amal militia, who still controlled the checkpoints and most of West Beirut.

At the beginning of the camp war, the International Red Cross had negotiated for a group of people to leave the camp for further medical treatment. They were captured as soon as they left the camp. Some of them were shot while they were being treated in Lebanese hospitals elsewhere in Beirut. For most of the wounded, the real hope was to have hospitals built inside the camps, so they could be treated without having to risk being abducted outside the camp. For the wounded in Bourj el-Brajneh, the setting up of Haifa Hospital was their hope of getting surgical attention.

The construction of the hospital was proceeding with gusto. I laughed and said to Dr Reda, 'At this rate the operating theatre will probably be complete within a week or less. In London, we'd probably only manage to draw up the plans in the same amount of time.'

'Ah, but this is PRCS construction, you see,' said Dr Reda seriously. 'We've had lots of experience building and rebuilding structures over the years.'

I had not forgotten how Gaza Hospital and Akka Hospital had been destroyed and restored so often in the space of a few months in 1982. The Palestinians had learnt to put together houses and buildings as fast as bombs and shells could demolish them. This was an experience acquired over the years.

Around lunchtime, Abu Ali turned up. I cannot describe how I felt on meeting this old friend: he had not changed one bit over the three years. He had just come from Akka Hospital, and had brought us some 'goodies'. From his two polythene carrier bags, he poured out a set of surgical instruments for major abdominal surgery, and then of all things a set of microsurgical instruments.

'Where on earth did you get that from?' I asked, completely amazed.

'From Gaza,' he said. 'They stole it at first, but now it is unstolen.' God alone knew how he had managed to 'unsteal' those instruments! He laid them out on a table, and started going through them: counting them out and looking at each pair of forceps, each needle holder and each retractor – most of the paired retractors had one of the partners missing by now – as though they were long-lost friends.

When he had finished packing all the instruments, I said, 'Come and see something – something very special.' I took him to the surgical storeroom which was now quite full of instruments and equipment from London. The theatre superintendent's delighted reaction to those instruments made all our efforts getting them out entirely worthwhile.

That afternoon, Abu Ali was busy fixing plugs to the plaster saw, labelling instruments and organising surgical packs. Later on he brought in Nuha, a very competent and soft-spoken Palestinian theatre nurse who had graduated from the PRCS Nursing School in Lebanon. Nuha immediately set about organising the hospital staff to make dressings, surgical bandages and laparotomy packs. Since I was relatively free, Nuha gave me a needle and some white thread, and showed me how to sew an abdominal pack. I had been a surgeon for ten years, and this was the first time I had seen abdominal packs sewn by hand. The hospital sewing machines had been looted by the people who attacked the camps. (When I went back to Britain, I told the nurses of Dryburn Hospital about these 'hand-sewn abdominal packs', and they chipped in to buy a sewing machine for the Haifa Hospital.)

CHAPTER 20

The next morning, a car from the British Consul in West Beirut arrived to take us to the Consulate to await the arrival of Sir David Miers, the British Ambassador, who was crossing from East to West Beirut to see us. The Consulate was situated near the coast, away from the camps.

It was a typical hot, sunny, Mediterranean morning. We drove through heavy traffic along crowded streets lined by shops and roadside stalls. In 1982, this half of the city had been full of bombed-out buildings, and the beaches, along with the coast-road, had been fully mined. I was glad to see that it had returned to some kind of 'normality'. However, the normality was only superficial. There were no longer air raids or shelling, but the security situation was far from satisfactory. There was no shortage of sectarian fighting, kidnappings and the violent settling of old scores.

The Consulate was a neat building which was heavily guarded by soldiers of the Lebanese Army. We were greeted cordially, after our papers had been checked. Then Sir David telephoned: he had tried to cross the Green Line that morning, but the crossing was closed. According to staff at the Consulate, that was Sir David's sixth attempt to cross from East to West Beirut in the past few days. Disappointed, we left the British Consulate to return to Bourj el-Brajneh.

We arrived at Haifa Hospital around 11 AM. Alison went to work in the dressing clinic at once. John, the anaesthetic technician, carried on the nightmare task of sorting out the anaesthetic machine rescued from Gaza Hospital, while the other John and I called at the emergency room, only to find ourselves mobbed by a large gathering of kids who had come forward to ask for pieces of shrapnel to be removed from all over their bodies. The average person in the camp might easily have twenty to thirty pieces of bomb or shell shrapnel lodged in his or her body. If they were small, these were usually best left alone, unless they happened to irritate a nerve or became septic. The larger flying shrapnel caused by an exploding bomb or shell would often amputate a limb or cause a severe internal injury. With the return of relative calm, kids loved to get their shrapnel taken out so that they could compare the metal 'souvenirs' from their bodies. I could see that John Thorndike enjoyed this sort of surgery.

'There really is a case for starting a proper shrapnel clinic,' he kept urging me. I knew we could not do this, however, because the operating theatre was nearly ready, and as soon as it was properly established, we would be doing other work.

Ben Alofs had meanwhile gone off to look at a proposed clinic right at the other end of the camp. It was formerly a school for Palestinian kids, but the Ramadan attacks had reduced the building to a pathetic structure with large holes in the walls and roof, and a crumbling floor. The PRCS hoped to convert it into a clinic to serve the needs of the people living at the far end of the camp, so that the out-patient load of Haifa Hospital could be eased. Besides his normal clinical duties in Haifa Hospital, Ben had also been assigned the job of painter-decorator, to work hand-in-hand with the camp construction team.

That evening, Alison and myself were going to take our turn sleeping in the hospital, and let the two Johns return to

Mayflower for a wash and change of clothing. In the late afternoon, we took a walk around the camp. It was only then that I realised how badly destroyed Bourj el-Brajneh camp was. Although the topmost floors of Haifa Hospital had been blown apart, that was nothing compared to what had happened to people's homes. Bits of roofs, walls and windows had been blown off by explosives and were lying on the floors of ruined houses. Wooden fencing and furniture were burnt black. There was a mass grave where eighty unidentified mutilated bodies were buried. Buildings were crumbling under the strain of the shell craters. From the scale of the destruction, the attacks must have been vicious.

Suddenly we found ourselves surrounded by a group of young men and boys. 'Hello, what is your name?' they asked. 'What are you doing here?'

We explained that we were medical volunteers from Britain working in Haifa Hospital. They were absolutely delighted to discover that people from the rest of the world knew about what was happening to the Palestinians, and volunteered to show us around the rest of the camp. One of the older boys, who wore a wrist splint for his injured hand, explained that he was a medical student from the American University of Beirut, but had not been back to college since the Israeli invasion. He would dearly have loved to continue his medical education but, being young and able-bodied, he believed it more important to stay in the camp to defend his people against attacks and massacres. It was a sacrifice he had chosen to make. He would not leave Bourj el-Brajneh camp, even if he was offered a place in college again, until he was assured his folks would be left in peace.

He showed us all the destruction and then turned round and asked, 'Why do people hate us Palestinians? Why do they want to destroy us like this?' I had no answer.

I tried to comfort him by comparing the resistance in the camps with the legendary battle of Karameh. The word 'karameh' meant 'dignity' in Arabic. Karameh was a

Palestinian refugee camp near Jericho, where in 1968 four hundred and fifty Palestinians fought the ten-thousand strong invading Israeli troops, and drove their invading tanks away. The Israeli military responded later by sending in their air force and bombing Karameh out of existence. But the Palestinian resistance was spawned and grew from there. The crowd was overjoyed to hear a foreigner talk about Karameh, to be reminded that there were those of us from the rest of the world who had studied and been inspired by the struggle of the Palestinian people.

We parted company on a triumphant note: these youngsters told me they would make Bourj el-Brajneh camp a fortress and would defend it to the last against any attacker.

That evening, back in the volunteers' room, for the first time in months – perhaps years – I felt confident and joyful. I got myself organised, and started to write a long letter to my husband in London. No sooner had I started, than I heard someone push open the door very quietly and come into our room. It was a young man in military uniform. He was very embarrassed at first to find Alison and myself, instead of John and Ben. Apparently, he was a member of the 'Ben Alofs fan club', which was growing daily. The camp people just adored Ben, but local culture was such that only the boys could visit him, and they frequently sought him out. I thought this young man wanted to listen to Ben's radio. After a little fidgeting, our friend settled down and accepted a seat. He was very young and small, probably five foot two inches or less. His face was boyish, with light brown, frizzy and curly hair.

Then Ben came into the room, and looked surprised and delighted. 'Hey,' he exclaimed, 'you didn't say you were a Fedayeen! Wow!' Ben beamed all over his face with a big broad smile. Ben's young friend was in full military uniform – green with brown patches, boots that were covered with camp mud. Slung over his shoulder was an old, rusty Kalashnikov. On seeing Ben, he looked relieved and spat out a mouthful of sunflower seeds so that he could speak.

He pointed to himself and said, 'I Makmoud.' Then he said, 'Amal very, very bad. Palestinians very, very good.' At this point, his reserves of English must have come to an end, for he turned to Ben and started talking in Arabic. We learnt that Makmoud was sixteen, that he was Lebanese and Shi'ite, but had been a Palestinian fighter since a young age. His family came from south Lebanon, and his home was destroyed by the Israelis. They fled to Bourj el-Brajneh camp. He considered himself a Palestinian, and would always want to be with the Palestinians. His mother felt the same too, and when his two older brothers joined Amal, little Makmoud and his mother chose to remain with the Palestinians in Bourj el-Brajneh.

He told Ben his mother was sniped at and wounded five days before, while trying to go out to get food for the camp. He saw the International Red Cross take his mother away in an ambulance, but was unable to follow her as he would certainly have been killed by the Amal once he was spotted by them. There had been no news about her, and he was very worried. Could Alison and I help him to locate his mother, who was probably taken to the Lebanese Makassad Hospital?

There was one little catch. For security reasons, he would not give us his family name. All we had to go on was that his eldest brother was Ahmed, and so his mother would be Um Ahmed (Um meant 'mother of'). He would bring us a picture of her in the morning, and would be grateful if we found out she was still alive. We agreed to do this for him. He immediately relaxed, and started talking and joking with Ben. Suddenly, he decided to impress us with his military prowess. He took off his shirt and showed us all the scars on his chest and arms, pointing to each one, saying, 'Look, here M16 bullet. Here, here and here as well. All M16 by Amal. But no problem, I am not afraid.'

I looked into the face of this Lebanese teenager, and

suddenly it was transformed into that of a heroic freedom fighter.

The following day saw Alison and myself doing a floor-by-floor enquiry in the Makassad Hospital, waving the small photograph of Um Ahmed and asking if anyone had seen this lady. Ahmed was a very common name in Lebanon, as common as John in Britain. No one in London would dream of going from ward to ward, department to department in St Thomas's Hospital, or any large hospital for that matter, asking if anyone had seen John's mother. The fact that she had been shot five days ago was no help, as loads of people got shot each day in Beirut. Mentioning that she was from Bourj el-Brajneh camp immediately caused people to lose interest. Who in Makassad Hospital bothered to remember a wounded Palestinian woman? In the end, they were so dismissive I decided to bluff them.

'Look here,' I said, 'this woman might come from a Palestinian refugee camp, but she is Lebanese and has two sons who are Amal fighters, and her family is looking for her.' At the mention of Amal, the charge nurse of the casualty department perked up, took a long look at her photograph and looked back at his patients' record book. The Makassad had received and treated this woman six days before, he now told me, but her injuries had not required hospitalisation, and the International Red Cross had transferred her to a Druse hospital to recuperate. The Druse Progressive Socialist Party was sympathetic to the Palestinians, allowed them to use their hospitals and also allowed camp refugees to shelter in their areas.

Beirut and indeed all of Lebanon were carved up into areas under the control of different political parties and militias. So when the Druse accepted Palestinian refugees into their areas, it gave the refugees some security against hostile militia groups. But it still meant that if the refugees accidentally wandered out of Druse-controlled areas, they ran the risk of being captured by other groups. Um Ahmed was safe for now, at any rate. We went back to report the good news to Makmoud, and return his mother's photograph to him.

On our way there, I thought once more of the Palestinians describing the Amal as their brothers, and thought how the camp war was especially painful for the Palestinians because when the Amal attacked them, it was like being attacked by one's own family. And when I looked at Makmoud's family, I saw the truth in this. The sons of this Shi'ite family were split into friends and enemies of the Palestinians, and the matriarch was wounded trying to help her Palestinian friends. The Palestinians could ask for no better friends.

The next few days were hectic days of rushing around between Shatila camp, Akka Hospital and Haifa Hospital. The PRCS was also trying to upgrade the medical services within Shatila camp so that if there was a new siege, the camp would be medically self-sufficient. In the past, the PRCS hospitals had usually been located at the edge of the camps, so that the PRCS could open its medical services to both the Lebanese public and the Palestinians. However, the recent Ramadan war had forced the PRCS to review its policies, as hospitals outside the camp could not look after the wounded trapped by a siege. Moreover hospitals outside the camps were vulnerable to attacks by various militia groups, and Palestinian employees were easily captured. The recent attacks on the camps proved to the Palestinian population that they were able to defend themselves. If there were adequate medical facilities during the siege, there need not be so many deaths.

Soon the NORWAC clinic in Shatila camp started to function. My Norwegian colleagues had asked me to do two orthopaedic clinics a week in Shatila camp. The NORWAC clinic supplemented the PRCS clinic in Shatila camp. The PRCS doctors and nurses in this clinic fought very hard to save lives during the siege, although there were then no facilities for treating battle casualties. It was hoped that the PRCS clinic could now turn over part of its

workload to the NORWAC clinic, while it underwent
structural changes to convert it into a hospital.

Much of my time was now dominated by administrative
work, which included running around with my NORWAC
colleague Synne trying to organise theatre equipment and
instruments, and fixing up meetings. The British medical
team was hard-working and dedicated, and overcame the
initial problem of adjusting to the situation. For Alison and
the two Johns, it was their first trip to Lebanon, and I had
nothing but admiration for the way they coped. Administrative responsibilities on top of the usual clinical work
made it harder for me to take time off for my cherished
walks in the camps, as I did in 1982. But the people of
Shatila camp I could see and feel, even through the walls of
my clinic room, through the muddle of various bits of
invoices. I did not need to speak to them to hear their
message; did not need to look at them to understand their
unconquerable spirit. I plodded on with my routine,
assessing the war-wounded and writing up detailed plans
for their proposed management. There were no facilities to
treat any complicated injury yet, so one would write
reports and recommendations as a substitute, and this
helped most patients psychologically; they despaired less,
but got impatient with waiting instead. This was probably
just as difficult for the medical staff to cope with.

One hot midday, I arrived at Shatila to see orthopaedic
patients in the NORWAC clinic after having done my round in
Haifa Hospital. It was weird – the clinic was locked and
there was no one in the main camp alley; all the homes
were empty too. Then a little girl came along and told me
that everyone had gone to Shatila mosque. It was the
forty-day ceremony for the fifty Palestinian martyrs who
died during the camp war. Tripping over bits of rubble and
concrete, I arrived at the ruins of Shatila mosque.

I stood there stunned: before me was a large crowd of
Palestinians – men, women, children; young and old.
Countless Palestinian flags were waving. Large pictures of

RIGHT: The ruins of
a West Beirut block
of flats, destroyed by
Israeli bombs in 1982.

BELOW: A cedar in
Lebanon

لجنة الصليب الأحمر الدولية

LEFT: Sabra and Shatila camps after Israeli air raids seen from Gaza Hospital. The view is of Rue Sabra, during the ceasefire in September 1982.

LEFT: Dr. Ang Swee Chai between two PRCS medics in front of Gaza Hospital in 1982.

RIGHT: The plume of smoke caused by shelling on the the morning of 15 September 1982, seen from the top of Gaza Hospital.

LEFT: Bodies in a Shatila alleyway after the massacre, 18 September 1982. *Ryuichi Hirokawa, Tokyo, Japan*

BELOW: The body of a child victim of the Sabra and Shatila massacre Gaza Hospital, 17 September 1982.

FOOT: Children of Sabra and Shatila after the 1982 massacre. 'We are not afraid. Let Israelis come.'

TOP: Youssef Hassan Mohammed.
ABOVE: Hadji, the wife of Youssef Hassan
Mohammed. 'They all left one night by
moonlight–all my loved ones.'

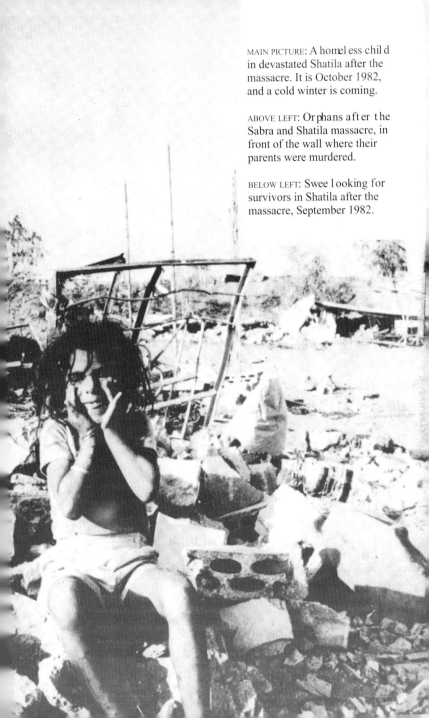

MAIN PICTURE: A homeless child in devastated Shatila after the massacre. It is October 1982, and a cold winter is coming.

ABOVE LEFT: Orphans after the Sabra and Shatila massacre, in front of the wall where their parents were murdered.

BELOW LEFT: Swee looking for survivors in Shatila after the massacre, September 1982.

BELOW: Gaza Hospital, which was burnt out on the first day of the Ramadan war, 1985.

RIGHT: The first MAP team leaving for Beirut, June 1985. From left to right: Immad, Swee, Ben Alofs, Alison Haworth, John Thorndike, John Croft.

FOOT: This 11 year old should be at school, not learning to defend his home and people – Shatila, 1985.

BELOW: Bits of the four hundred shells which hit Shatila in the course of one night in the 1985 Ramadan war.
FOOT: The forty-day commemoration of fifty martyrs who died defending Shatila in 1985.

LEFT: Nuha sewing laparotomy packs by hand – Haifa Hospital, Bourj el-Brajneh, 1985.

BELOW: Swee operating, without mask, gloves, anaesthetic or electricity – Shatila, 1985.

RIGHT: Swee fil ing X-rays in her special ist orthopaedic clinic in Shatila, 1985.

CENTRE LEFT: The Pal est ine Red Cr escent Society is a humanitarian organisation with staff from various political factions. The picture shows three Haifa Hospital doctors from three different factions, 1985.

CENTRE RIGHT: Um Wal id. PRCS Dir ect or in Lebanon and Vice-President of the executive committee of the PRCS.

FOOT: Part of t he mechanised effort t o flatten Sabra and Shatila, 1985

ABOVE: Major Nahla, who gave up nursing to defend Shatila. She died in 1987, with fifty-seven bullets in her body.

LEFT: Swee spent a lot of time taking wounded children out of the camps for treatment abroad. From left to right: Bilal Chebib, saying goodbye to Pauline Cutting, together with Samir Ibrahim el-Madany – the two boys are on their way back to Beirut with Dr. Ang Swee Chai.

ABOVE: Swee with children of Bourj el-Brajneh, saluting the uprising in the occupied territories, 1988.

RIGHT: Although this picture was taken in 1988, these primitive shelters in Beirut have been there since before 1982.

ABOVE: Dr. Chris Giannou
in the operating theatre of
Shatila Hospital.

LEFT: Swee in Shatila
Hospital. On the shelf behind
her are the remains of some
of the 248 shells which hit
the hospital over a six-month
period.

BELOW: 'Mama Rita' and
Swee distributing milk
to children in the refugee
shelters of West Beirut, 1988.

ABOVE: Dolly Fong with her patients in the Samir el-Khatib Clinic, often called 'Dolly's clinic' – Bourj el-Brajneh.

RIGHT: Dr. Kiran Gargesh teaching anaesthetic technicians in Rashidiyeh.

BELOW: Susan Wight on in the Samir el-Khatib Clinic, also called 'Suzy's clinic'.

ABOVE: Paying homage at the graves of those killed trying to get food to the starving people of Bourj el-Brajneh during the 1986-87 siege.

LEFT: Shatila in 1987, the International Year of Shelter for the Homeless.

martyrs were carried on poles and waved about. Drums were beating. Palestinian music sounded out. People were dancing and chanting militant slogans. I felt tears streaming down my face. I was crying because there was nothing but ruin and rubble all round, and so many had died, but yet today's memorial was not a memorial of sorrow, but one of hope and triumph. How could these Palestinians celebrate so triumphantly, I asked myself. Then I realised that only a vision of victory could remove the pain of death, destruction and separation. Today, there was this spirit of victory – in the midst of the broken walls and the rubble of Shatila camp, in the battered old mosque. This glorious sight – of victory, of jubilation, of confidence despite insurmountable difficulties – was something I will always cherish, and want to share with suffering people all over the world.

Shatila camp had been severely battered. For forty days and forty nights, shells and missiles poured down on this crowded camp of thirty-six thousand square metres. But Shatila had stood firm, and produced her martyrs. Today, the camp people were proud and victorious. They recalled how on one day alone, six hundred bombs, shells and rocket missiles had rained down on their homes, but they did not surrender. They recalled how, on another day, they ran out of ammunition; they put up a brave front and fired blanks, simulated explosive noises to create the illusion of return fire.

Rather than surrender, four Palestinian girls crossed the checkpoints in disguise and brought back thirty-five thousand rounds of ammunition – and the camp folks fought on. Today, Shatila did not weep over the mass graves of the 1982 massacres, but honoured the memories of those who had given their lives defending their homes.

After the memorial, I went back to the clinic, where I met Hannah, a nurse from Gaza Hospital I had worked with in 1982. She had got thinner, and her eyes were more melancholy. It was nearly three years, but I still could remember her in the accident room of Gaza Hospital; the expression of panic on her face when she discovered that the nitrous oxide cylinders were wrongly labelled as oxygen. She had stayed in Beirut even after the 1982 massacre for as long as she could, till she was arrested. Upon her release, she had gone abroad.

She had now left her studies in Belgium because of the attacks on the camps, and despite the risks she had returned. As I embraced the sobbing girl, I could feel how thin she was. 'Hannah, please, please be strong,' I said to her. That would usually pull people together.

But she dried her tears, looked up at me, and said, 'I try, but for how long?' I knew the answer, but decided it would be patronising for me to say too much. Fortunately a large crowd of patients had gathered around the clinic, and she immediately shook off her sorrow, and started to carry out her nursing duties.

Much later that day, when all the patients were gone, I asked Hannah about her close friend, Nahla. I found out that Nahla was wounded, and in hiding.

'She was forty days and forty nights fighting, fighting,' said Hannah. 'Then the camp had no bullets, and the four women went out to buy bullets. She was one of them. They tied the bullets round their bodies to pass the Amal to get back into the camp. Later the Amal found out, and were very, very angry. They want to kill her. You cannot pass by Nahla's place, because the Amal will follow you, and kill her.'

That was insane: Nahla was training to be a nurse in Gaza Hospital. Now she had earned herself a death warrant just by defending her people. Tall, fair and graceful, Nahla was easily one of the most beautiful women I had ever seen in my life. The thought of her fighting so bravely filled me with pride. But the realisation that she was wounded and had been hounded all over Beirut by Amal killers angered me. I would not dream of wanting to meet her; just the thought that I was her friend was a great honour.

The next day, Nahla's mother called in and asked to see me. Her daughter sent her love and a gift: a cloth tablemat on which was hand-printed the Palestine flag, and the rising sun. Nahla had asked her mother to give that to me. It was from her reading table, and her mother said that Nahla hoped that each time I looked at the colours of the Palestine flag, I would remember her. Then it suddenly occurred to Nahla's mother that she had not brought me a gift herself. She quickly rummaged through her cane basket, and found a fork and spoon to give me. I gave her a big hug, returned the fork and spoon, and kissed her many times. I now know where Nahla got her generosity and sense of self-sacrifice.

CHAPTER 21

The following day, I went to Hamra – the shopping area in West Beirut – and bought a bunch of flowers, intending to place them at the martyrs' graves in Shatila mosque. But I managed to lose the flowers between Hamra and the mosque. All the same, I went into the mosque to pay my respects. That was the first time I had been inside the ruins of Shatila mosque. As I entered through the door, I noticed how clean and beautiful the inside was. The fifty martyrs were buried in the main hall of the mosque. There were flowers everywhere. Instead of tombstones, photographs and Palestine flags marked the resting spot of each martyr. A quick look at the pictures revealed that all of them were very young. Not only were they young, but many of them were women – women who in the rest of the world would be planning a career, a husband and a family. Beautiful, smiling young people, who had given up their precious youth, their precious life for their people, their country, without reservation.

The patients of Shatila were a spirited lot. I often marvelled at their insight into their own condition, the way they knew exactly where each bullet or piece of shrapnel had gone through their body, and which vital structures had been destroyed. More than that, I admired their patience with me. Nearly all of them knew that there was no way I could carry out any major operations on them, given the lack of surgical facilities; yet they would keep their appointments to see me, and discuss their conditions with me.

The Belgian volunteer doctor who worked for NORWAC used to laugh at the way I allowed my Specialist Orthopaedic Clinic to deteriorate into one big social club. I found that letting a dozen patients sit together, listening to each other talk about their injuries, and learning to bandage each other's wounds and exercise each other's paralysed limbs, was a great morale booster, and helped to offset any despondency created by the lack of treatment facilities. Soon it reached the stage where patients were removing each other's plaster-cast before seeing me, bringing along voltage transformers so that the British plaster saw could use the electricity from the camp generator. I had no doubt that, given time, this lot would make excellent orthopaedic technicians, though I had reservations about what the British Orthopaedic Association would think of my unconventional and substandard clinic. But substandard or not, we did manage to function.

One day I had to remove a bullet from a young Palestinian's hand, which the bullet prevented from closing. It was lodged in the third metacarpal bone. There was no anaesthetic, and I had to operate without gloves, surgical mask or hat, and with a nurse holding a torch.

Before I started, I warned him, 'This is going to hurt – we have run out of anaesthetics.'

He answered in a matter-of-fact way, 'Doctora, you have forgotten I am a Palestinian.' What could I say to a patient like that? The operation was done without even a local anaesthetic.

After that operation, I began to do more and more operations with or without local anaesthetics in people's homes, on couches in sitting-rooms, or in the kitchen. One of the Palestinian nurses would come with me, and we carried with us a bottle of antiseptic, dressings, a scalpel with blades, sutures, a needle holder, dissecting forceps, and other items to perform minor surgery while visiting people in their partially destroyed homes. It was amazing how soon I learnt to manage with the barest of surgical facilities. But anything serious would have to wait till Shatila had a proper hospital.

Meanwhile the bomb shelter of Shatila camp was undergoing major renovations. It was being transformed into an operating suite, with theatres, resuscitation cubicles and recovery facilities. It would be annexed to the PRCS clinic, and together they would form the future Shatila Hospital. The camp people wanted to be ready and prepared the next time Amal attacked. John Thorndike, with his extensive experience in Accident and Emergency work, was diverted from Haifa Hospital to Shatila camp to help set up the place.

One afternoon I decided it was about time I visited Sabra camp, or what was left of it, and Gaza Hospital. I chose to walk back up the same road we had been forced to go down on the morning of 18 September 1982. I wished the rest of that team were with me to retrace our steps, so that the camp people could see that we had returned.

The pick-up or 'service' taxi dropped me at Akka Hospital, and after crossing the road, I was at the southern end of Shatila camp, at the beginning of Rue Sabra. The road was punctuated with checkpoints all within a stone's throw of each other. As I started to walk down the road, a voice cried out, 'The doctor who went to the Israeli Commission!'

People started yelling across the street to catch my attention, much to the bewilderment of the soldiers at the checkpoints. It was one big reunion. Oblivious of the bulldozers and the hostile gunmen, we embraced each other and exchanged greetings. The widows came out of their destroyed shelters, the orphans came out, the old men came out, and we were all overjoyed. Then the children lined themselves up once again in front of their bombed-out homes, raised their hands to make a victory sign, and demanded that their pictures be taken, just like the children in 1982. This time the victory sign was made with more resolve and defiance. The smiles were even broader – and the quality of the picture was better as my photographic skills had somewhat improved. I was invited into the camp people's homes, given coffee and cold drinks, while the rest of the camp folks came up to say hello.

Outside on Rue Sabra the bulldozers were working with a vengeance, destroying homes, churning up dust, rubble, bits of sewage and water pipes and electrical cables. The camp people told me that the bulldozers had come from Syria. The Syrians were apparently obsessed with the idea that Sabra, Shatila and Bourj el-Brajneh camps were connected by a system of underground tunnels. Since the Palestinians had always denied this allegation, the Syrians had threatened to bulldoze the camps flat to find them.

Forty Syrian bulldozers and five hundred Syrian construction technicians and engineers were in Beirut: their declared intention was to help rebuild the camps, but the camp people were dubious about this. And the tunnels? It was obvious that so far they had not uncovered them. They had only found sewage systems, water pipes, broken-down homes, heaps of rubble, and of course, a very defiant Palestinian population. Camp women and children would organise themselves to obstruct the bulldozers and try to stop them taking away the last brick and stone of what were once their homes. But as I watched the mess created by clean water and sewage welling up out of burst pipes and flooding the camp roads, I could not help but resent this insane treatment meted out to a people who had committed no wrong. They had just asked for what was every human being's birthright, a homeland.

An intended ten minutes' walk from Akka Hospital to Gaza Hospital took me two hours, stopping at various homes to greet people. Finally, I set eyes on Gaza

Hospital. For the first time, Gaza Hospital did not look like a hospital at all. It looked like a battered fortress. The walls still had soot on them, and the window glasses had been smashed on every single floor. The main door was locked, and the building was guarded by soldiers. The soldiers told me to go away. As I turned to leave, an old friend appeared, and I recognised him instantly as one of the administrative staff of Gaza Hospital. He must have made a convincing case to the soldiers, for they let me into the hospital.

This floor by floor tour of Gaza Hospital was one of the most upsetting experiences I had ever had, and I was grateful that Azziza and Hadla were not around to see the mess. Floor by floor, glass windows and doors were smashed to tiny bits, mattresses and pillows were ripped apart, wires and electric cables were pulled out and left loose on the floors. All the portable hospital equipment was gone. Things that were heavy and non-portable or of low resale value were smashed up. The walls were covered with thick soot and the floors were heaped with ashes. The soot and ashes got worse higher up.

On the sixth, seventh and eighth floors, I felt as though I was inside a large kiln that had not been emptied for years. The ninth and tenth floors had large holes punched through their walls – I was told these holes were made and used by the invading gunmen to shoot into the camps. I looked out through one of these holes, and saw that Sabra camp had been entirely flattened. On the floor, I picked up bits of bullets from MI6 rifles. Also left behind were empty ammunition boxes, labelled 'Made in USA'. The attackers of the camps in the 1985 Ramadan war carried American arms.

My initial anger passed, and I felt freezing – cold with tension.

'Doctora, never mind,' said my Palestinian friend. 'We will prepare this hospital again. We will wash the walls, bring in medicines and open this hospital again.' I knew from the tone of his voice that he meant every word he said. I had also heard these words and seen them put into action at least twice before, in August 1982, after the siege of Beirut, and in September 1982, after the massacres. I often wondered where these people got their strength from.

It was getting late, and I had to leave before it became unsafe to get across the checkpoints. 'Swee, please, please. My mother wants you to come up for coffee.' I turned round and looked. It was a young woman. I thought I recognised the face. Of course, it was Mona, Huda's big sister. She had grown so much. She was much taller and prettier now, but still recognisably Mona. It had been three years since I last saw her and Huda, and I loved being with their family.

I looked up at the tall block of flats opposite Gaza Hospital, and there on the seventh floor was a Palestinian lady standing on the balcony waving at me. She was wearing a white scarf round her hair. It had been nearly three years since I last visited them. I was so glad to see that their home was still standing. Mona and I ran up the flights of stairs, as the lifts were not working due to power cuts. Most of the flats in this block were deserted, as Palestinian families had fled from the attacks. But there were a good many Lebanese Shi'ite families living in the same block – it was their presence which prevented the entire block from being demolished. We reached the seventh floor, almost collapsing from lack of breath. The door was opened wide – and there to welcome me with warm kisses and an embrace was Mona's mother.

The flat was still like it was in 1982 – clean, tidy and well kept. But most of the nicer furnishings were gone, including the beautiful Palestinian embroidery done by Mona's mother. I could not bring myself to ask about the details of what happened. Mona's mother brought us Arabic coffee, and then sat down on a chair, looked at me, smiled again and again, and started to say verses of thanksgiving to Allah. I was made to sit on a large armchair. I supposed this was too big to be carted away by looters.

I remembered Mona's place as crowded. In 1982, father, mother, two daughters, four sons and two daughters-in-law all stayed in this three-room flat. Even then, it was spacious by refugee camp standards. Today, it looked ridiculously empty – empty of furnishings, and of people. There were only Mona and her parents. The rest were all missing.

This family had suffered much and given its fair share of martyrs. The two older boys were taken away to the notorious Ansar prison camp by the Israelis in 1982, and had not been heard of since. Initially, the family waited anxiously for their return; but as the days passed into months, and the months became years, they had come to terms with the realisation that the boys would probably never be seen again. It was difficult to have family members disappear. Families who knew that their loved ones were dead grieved, and thus learnt to accept the fact that they were dead. They buried them, and visited the graves, and prayed for their souls. But families would always wonder where the 'disappeared' were, and if they were alive. Supposing they were alive, the families would wonder if they were being tortured and suffering; and if they were dead, they would wonder where their bodies were. There would always be a question mark.

The third son was captured by the Amal on the first day of the camp war in 1985. He was lined up against a wall along with many others to be executed. Probably God was feeling kind, and heard the prayers of his mother. Some non-Amal Shi'ites intervened on his behalf, and pleaded for his release. He was taken to the Beka'a valley instead, and the family received news that he was alive. Mona took out her family album, and showed me their treasured family photographs. Happy pictures of her elder brothers' weddings, and of her brother who was now in Beka'a. There were also pictures of Huda and Hisham who were now, together with Milad, living in Cyprus with Paul Morris and attending school there. In the very end pages of the album were precious pictures which had turned yellow with time, pictures of her parents when they were young and happy in Palestine. Then her mother, who hitherto had only been sitting quietly, and giving me kind and fond smiles, suddenly spoke.

Mona said, 'My mother wants to know why you came back to Beirut – what you like about Beirut?'

There was only one truthful answer. I had not dared give it since arriving back in Beirut. But this time I needed to tell the truth. I said, 'I came back to see the Palestinians. . .' and then could not say any more.

'My mother says we love you more than all our Arab brothers.'

I always knew that: I only wished I were stronger, and able to be of more support to those who were suffering and struggling.

As I got up to go, Mona's mother stood up too, and took down a little basket. This she had woven by hand from telephone wires, and it was in the colours of the Palestine flag. There was nothing else of value in their home that she could give me. Everything else of any beauty or worth had been carried away by the soldiers when they came for her son. Though I really should not have accepted a gift from her, there was so much in this little item that I just had to hold it close to my heart. The national colours of Palestine woven with steel wires – that was the message this surviving family of Sabra camp wanted me to take home. It was painful to say goodbye to them. I had a premonition that we would not see each other again, at least not for a long, long time.

CHAPTER 22

In contrast to Gaza Hospital, Akka had miraculously survived physical destruction. The land on which Akka Hospital was built belonged to a Lebanese Shi'ite, Sheikh Cabalan. His influence had prevented Akka Hospital from being attacked and destroyed by the Amal militiamen who wreaked havoc on Gaza. Therefore the British medical team had the good fortune to see an intact building. Akka Hospital, which I had first seen after it had been reduced to rubble by Israeli bombs in 1982, had now been fully rebuilt. A beautiful building with white floors, three storeys above ground and two underground – it was complete with wards, biochemical and haematological laboratories, an X-ray department with imaging facilities, research rooms and libraries, wards, surgical operating theatres and a training school for the nurses run by the PRCS. However, Akka was unable to function as a hospital after the camp wars, because much of its space had been converted into a temporary refugee centre.

Moreover, hostile militiamen had cut off the hospital's water supply. It was in Akka Hospital, in the midst of the dislocation and the chaos, that I found a few old friends from 1982 – the staff of Gaza Hospital who had survived the attack, nurses as well as doctors, and old Professor Arnaouti, who was remembered by most of us as 'Socrates'.

The professor's grey hair had turned pure white now, but mentally he was still very alert. I sat down beside him and we talked about Palestine, about Jerusalem. He asked me if I sincerely believed that the Palestinians would really be able to return to Palestine, one day.

I said, 'Definitely, but I'm not sure whether you and I will be alive to see that day.'

My answer made him very happy: he was gladdened by my confidence. While I was talking to the old professor, someone came up and told me that Um Walid wanted to see me. I found Um Walid in her office talking to about twenty-four people on different things at the same time. After she had dealt with everyone else and they had left, she turned to Synne and myself. Um Walid wanted to see us to discuss the possibility of setting up some sort of operating theatre in Ain al-Helweh camp in Saida, south Lebanon.

Things in Ain al-Helweh camp were very tense, with the camp people living in daily fear of an attack and siege. The camp's seventy thousand Palestinians had no Accident and Emergency, or theatre facilities. If the camp was besieged and pounded with missiles, wounded people would have nowhere to go to, and many would die. The PRCS and the camp committee had already made plans to convert a cave into a hospital. All Um Walid wanted us to do was to transport things to Ain al-Helweh, since our chances of being kidnapped and killed at the various checkpoints would be infinitely less than those of any Palestinian.

So, once the ambulance was loaded up with chest drains, catheters, surgical instruments, a portable anaesthetic machine, operating lights, a plaster saw, blood transfusion bags and a dismantled treatment table, Synne and I headed south for Saida. The last time I had seen Saida was in 1982 when Ellen and I took a service taxi to the south. My last impression of Ain al-Helweh camp was a large, flat, bombed-out wasteland, much as Sabra camp looked in 1985. There was not a single building in Ain al-Helweh more than four feet high then – it was a tragic sight. Today, three years later, the Ain al-Helweh that greeted my eyes was totally different.

It had been rebuilt. It had neat brick houses, shops, electric cables and offices. The main road of the camp was properly tarred, with motor vehicles and bicycles busy making their way to various destinations. There was minimal dust, and certainly no dirt or garbage. The camp felt clean. The camp people looked well washed and had clean if modest clothes on. I would not have despaired so much in London if only I had known that Ain al-Helweh had been restored in this manner. It was a very happy day for me when I saw this resurrection of Ain al-Helweh town.

The proposed camp hospital would be in a cave sheltered from attack by hostile forces. Construction work had already begun, with great enthusiasm. There was a sense of urgency among the camp people to complete this hospital, to beat the 'deadline', to be ready to cope with massive casualties when the Amal chose to attack them. The hospital needed an X-ray machine, and we were glad that the British public had donated cash to buy a portable X-ray machine.

Shortly afterwards, I read in the papers that four of Ain al-Helweh's camp leaders had been murdered, and that there was speculation that this was due to problems between pro and anti-Arafat factions within the camp. This speculation proved ill-founded.

We were taking more medical supplies to Ain al-Helweh camp, and had a chance to speak to the one of the camp leaders who had not been killed. The press got it all wrong, he said. The camp folk had soon managed to arrest the murderers, who admitted to being on the payroll of the Israelis. The camp folks were outraged at the murders, and declared that they would make an even greater effort to achieve unity.

An Englishwoman who lived near the camp told us what the funeral procession of the murdered leaders was like. It consisted first of the coffin bearers – and the coffins were strewn with flowers and decorated with Palestine flags. These were followed by people with guns, shooting into the air. Then followed the camp people, marching shoulder to shoulder. Leaders from all factions of the PLO formed part of the procession. Everyone was shouting in unison. Though she could not understand what the people were shouting, she said they did so in one voice, and the message of unity was clear. If Ain al-Helweh were ever attacked, the Palestinians of Ain al-Helweh would defend it, with unity and steadfastness.

When we got back from the south, we found that Um Walid had actually fallen ill. This was hard to believe at first, because sometimes we forgot that Um Walid, for all her strength, was human. For the first time, Um Walid complained of difficulties. She had always been a tower of strength, and never let obstacles get in the way of her goals. Perhaps it was her high temperature that made her complain now, but it was more likely to be the outcome of a whole cumulative series of events.

There were just too many destitute Palestinians, especially widows and orphans. That was one thing, and then she could not seem to get a definite go-ahead for the rebuilding of Sabra and Shatila, despite hours of nego- tiations. Permission had only been given for two hundred homes in the camp to be rebuilt. How could thirty thousand homeless people fit into two hundred homes? Then with Gaza Hospital being destroyed, she had to find money to pay for private treatment for patients who would otherwise be treated free in Gaza Hospital. The out- patients clinic of Akka Hospital was now functional, but the conditions of work for the staff were anything but pleasant.

She was at Akka Hospital in the morning when trouble broke out at the dental clinic. There was a long queue of patients. Suddenly a man who claimed to be a member of Amal appeared and demanded immediate attention. The

Palestinian dentist refused to let him jump the queue, and a row ensued; the dentist threatened to commit suicide if he was pressurised any further. Um Walid had to sort out the situation and persuade the dentist to give this person preferential treatment, thus contravening the policies of the PRCS to treat all patients equally.

Next, the body of a PRCS nurse, missing for a week, was found in a rubbish dump. She was murdered after being brutally raped by many different men. Then the entire laboratory of Gaza Hospital which the Amal had stolen during the camp war was put on sale, and the PRCS had to buy it back.

She got home to learn that the family who lived up the road had all been shot dead for no apparent reason. They had never been involved in anything. It was one event after another – nearly all of them unpleasant and nasty, and they had all taken their toll on this brave and strong lady.

The following day I met Um Walid again and although she was still weak she was in control and back to her usual self again.

It was nearly time for me to leave Beirut, but before I went I called in at Shatila camp in the hope of seeing Hannah once more to find out if Nahla was all right, and also to say good-bye. By the time I got to the camp, it was getting late, and I had just missed her. But a kind person offered to take me to where he thought Hannah might be. We went past Shatila mosque, through a maze of narrow camp alleys, with rubble and partially destroyed homes on both sides. We finally arrived at one of the camp homes.

At first I thought this must be Hannah's home, but later learnt that this was the office of the General Union of Palestinian Women (GUPW) in Shatila camp. My guide thought Hannah would have been here because one of the members of the GUPW was to have been married that day. However, the wedding celebration had been cancelled by the couple. They had planned this great day many months

ago, but now there was no way they would have a
ceremonial wedding when so many people from the camp
had died, and the wounds were still fresh. I met the young
couple and wished them the very best.

As I was getting ready to go, someone came and said that
five Palestinians had been kidnapped by Amal at the
checkpoints and that the camp was surrounded and
besieged. It would be very dangerous to cross the checkpoints now. It was just as well I could not leave, for that
gave me a chance to get to know the women, who invited
me to share their dinner. The General Union of Palestinian
Women was very active in many ways. During the
Ramadan invasion, they had organised themselves to look
after the camp, tend to the sick and wounded, feed the
camp and support the camp resistance. During peacetime,
they ran kindergartens and vocational schools, and helped
organise the women to do Palestinian embroidery, which
was not only a source of income for the camp, but also
preserved the art and culture of their homeland in items
like cushions, tablecloths, scarves, dresses, handker-
chieves, bookmarks and flags. Wherever there was a piece
of cloth, a needle and a piece of thread, the memory of
Palestine became transformed into a reality.

They had diligently compiled lists of people kidnapped
and missing since the camp war started. These totalled one
and a half thousand from all three West Beirut camps.
There was strong evidence that they were taken away to
torture centres, and systematically tortured and murdered.
Some bodies of those taken away were found, but there
were still fifteen hundred who were unaccounted for. They
had simply disappeared. At this point, a young woman
called in, the wife of a martyr. Then an older woman called
in – she was the mother of two martyrs. The meal was
unpretentious, consisting of potatoes, unleavened bread,
and hummus – a dip made of chickpeas and garlic – but the
honour of eating with these women was overwhelming. It

was no exaggeration to say that each one of them was a heroine in her own right.

I suddenly remembered I was on a small mission. Before I left London, the representative of a Miners' Support Group in Yorkshire had called on me and had given me twenty-four greeting cards, from twenty-four mining families in her village, to take to the people of the camps. The coal-miners of Britain had been out on strike for a year, stretching from 1984 into 1985. Conditions were very difficult throughout the strike, and many mining families had to sell their furniture and possessions to survive. During the strike, the British miners had their equivalent of the General Union of Palestinian Women. The miners' wives, mothers, sisters and grandmothers organised themselves into Miners' Support Groups, and these women ran soup kitchens to feed the community, travelled all over Britain on fundraising tours, and kept everyone's morale up during the darkest moments. Like the Palestinian women, they formed the backbone of the community. The British press scorned the ending of the strike as a 'defeat', but my Palestinian friends in Shatila camp called it a victory. Their reasoning was simple: any group who could hold out for a whole year under those conditions won a great victory.

So while the British commentators talked of the defeat of the miners, the Palestinians of Shatila camp saluted the miners for their heroic and victorious year-long strike. Perhaps the Palestinians knew too well what struggle was about, better than the British press. One of the women told me the Western press had dealt with the Palestinians the same way they had dealt with our miners.

'They consistently distorted or refused to publish our case,' she said. 'However, even if the newspapers won't print our story, it will still be written: it will be written with the blood of our martyrs.'

The notice board of the Women's Union had been bombed, but they decided to display the greeting cards from Yorkshire on the wall alongside the photographs of their martyrs.

Haifa Hospital in Bourj al-Brajneh camp had expanded at an incredible speed. The operating theatre was fully functional now; the wards were filled with in-patients, the Palestinian medical staff were well-organised – it was another successful chapter of Palestinian construction and reconstruction. I had only one more job left – to find an ambulance for Haifa Hospital. Once the ambulance was put on the road, I would have effectively used up all the money raised in Britain, and would have no more administrative responsibilities. The British people had been extremely generous – and most of the cash raised during the camp war appeal had not come from the wealthy, but from ordinary people. Most of the money sent over from Britain had gone into the purchase of the X-ray machine, and theatre and resuscitative equipment.

On this, my second visit to Lebanon, I learnt that much had changed. Even as a foreigner, it was easy to see how fragmented a society this had become. It was really very sad. A twenty-one-year-old Lebanese patient died one day, and I could only thank God for ending his suffering. He was from a poor Shi'ite family, and was paraplegic – paralysed from the waist down – because of a wound sustained in the 1982 Israeli invasion. For the last three years Haifa Hospital, which till recently had been a rehabilitation centre, had been his home.

Unfortunately, during the Ramadan attacks on Bourj el-Brajneh camp, he – like many others – contracted severe gastro-enteritis. The camp, under siege for forty days, had been denied water, food or medicines. The constant bombardment meant the camp people had to be crammed into severely overcrowded bomb shelters for days on end. Under these conditions, infectious diseases like gastro-enteritis (diarrhoea and vomiting), skin and respiratory tract infections simply ran wild. A normal healthy adult would usually count himself or herself lucky to survive such conditions. For a paraplegic, to contract infectious diarrhoea simply meant death.

The lower half of his body could not feel what was happening, and he must have sat for hours, perhaps days, in a pool of his own diarrhoea fluid. When the siege was over, he was totally emaciated, and large ulcers had developed on his bottom. He had constant diarrhoea, which meant that the pressure sores could not be kept clean. Gaza Hospital was destroyed, Haifa Hospital was undergoing major renovations, so he was transferred to Akka Hospital. But it was impossible to treat someone like that in Akka Hospital. It was just beginning to sort out the aftermath of the Ramadan war, and worse than that it had no water supply! The logical solution would have been to transfer him to one of the private Lebanese hospitals, which had piped water, facilities for intravenous feeding and enough nurses to look after him.

Since he was Lebanese, we thought we might approach various Lebanese charitable foundations to sponsor his treatment in one of these hospitals. I found out how difficult it was for the Lebanese poor to get medical care. Charitable foundations for Sunnis, Christians, Druse or Shi'ites would only help their own community – and they usually already had dozens of cases to sponsor. The Shi'ite foundation we approached wanted to know which village he and his family originally came from, as there were Shi'ite villages in south Lebanon, in Beka'a and other parts of the country. When furnished with that information, the foundation advised me to see some Sheikh who came from that area, to see if he would help. The Sheikh politely declined to see me. So the young man continued to suffer, and the nurses of Akka Hospital continued to wash him with bottles of water strictly reserved for drinking.

We had applied to the Ministry of Health a long time ago – but God alone knew when or if help would be forthcoming. He finally sank into a deep coma, and died – a skeleton covered with broken skin. His death was a deep and sobering lesson for me. The Israelis did inflict the first wound, but he died in such an inhuman way because of all the obstacles in West Beirut. Two days before he died, he pleaded with me to take him back to Haifa Hospital, once the wards were opened. It was impossible to honour his request now.

My experience in West Beirut during the Israeli invasion of 1982 was that the Lebanese were warm, generous and friendly. They had never discriminated against the Palestinians, nor among themselves on the grounds of religion or sect. But in 1985 they seemed to be obsessed with differences among themselves. Now a Shi'ite taxi would not go into a Sunni area, and vice versa. And to mention the phrase 'Palestinian refugee camp' to a service taxi driver meant that one would be put out of the vehicle straight away. As I passed the Lahut – the Near East School of Theology – I recalled how it was converted into a field hospital in 1982 through the joint efforts of the Lebanese and the Palestinian people. Hundreds of lives must have been saved as a result.

Nobody then was asked if he was Palestinian or Lebanese. Lebanese were not asked whether they were Christian or Muslim. Muslims were not asked whether they were Sunni or Shi'ite. Today, that warmth, generosity and unity seemed to have been replaced by sectarian hostility, cynicism and a sense of helplessness. Money could buy many things now: arms, the loyalty of the various militiamen, favours, medical care, and perhaps even principles.

Lebanon had made me very sad. This place had seen too many tanks, too many guns, too many wars. Young people, instead of going to school or work, had to carry arms and fight for a living. Instead of money being spent on health and welfare, cash was being diverted into the pockets of arms dealers. In the words of a Lebanese friend: 'Lebanon has become a battlefield for various outside political forces, and the sons of Lebanon their cannon fodder. Life has become worthless. If a person is shot dead, few will even ask why, or who did it.'

More disturbing was the way young men and teenagers could only relate to power, often in the form of a gun, and membership of a militia. These thoughts were jostling in my mind as I passed Mayfair Residence, where we stayed in 1982. Suddenly someone called from across the road, 'Doctora, doctora!'

I did not recognise the man, but he said he knew I was one of the doctors who worked in the Lahut in 1982. He invited me to have coffee with him, and introduced himself as a doctor. He was a member of the Progressive Socialist Party of Syria, a name I did not know at all. He patiently explained his party-political line to me. Most of what he explained was of little concern to me, except that his party was non-sectarian. It was incredible to find a non-sectarian political party in the Beirut of 1985!

Under the glass top of the doctor's table lay a picture of a beautiful young woman. I had seen her face on posters stuck up on walls all over Beirut and even in south Lebanon, and I had often wondered who she was. Now the doctor told me that she was the eighteen-year-old woman who drove a suicide mission into the Israeli barracks in the south, the first Lebanese woman to have carried out a suicide attack on the Israelis.

The doctor spoke very fondly of the second woman to go on a suicide mission. He told me how she came to see him one morning and brought him a beautiful bunch of flowers. She told him that she was going somewhere, but could not tell him where. She was going to 'make something good, something beautiful for Lebanon.' It was only after the suicide mission that he learnt where she had gone.

Many westerners dismiss the people who carry out suicide missions as crazy or 'terrorists'. The more charitable among them just sigh and say, 'What a pity! What a waste of a life!'

But to many people in Lebanon, they were heroic

martyrs. Like their Palestinian counterparts in Shatila mosque, these two young women were so beautiful. They could have chosen a happy marriage with an adoring husband and pretty children. But they had chosen to give up their lives for the liberation of their people and country. My eyes were brimming with tears, and I had to leave before it became too embarrassing. I felt sorry for my nasty feelings against Lebanon of a few minutes before. These two young women had erased all the ugly sectarianism I had experienced during my stay here. They had not chosen to 'attack the Palestinians to appease the Israelis'; they had also not put up all sorts of excuses for Lebanon's troubles. They had chosen to confront their enemy, and they did so with courage and self-sacrifice.

It was really time for the British medical team to leave. Much publicity and fund-raising work awaited us in Britain. We also saw the need to start a long-term medical programme in Lebanon, and this was something which should be discussed with MAP back in London. For instance, once Haifa and Shatila hospitals were completed, surgeons would be needed to carry out operations on all the wounded who were already waiting. If further attacks on the camps took place, we would have to mobilise further medical support to deal with the victims.

On the eve of departure, in August 1985, I found out that Immad and Alison had got engaged. I must have been a careless and insensitive team leader not to have known they were in love. But Alison had worked so hard throughout her time in Beirut. If only I had known, I would have tried to persuade them to take some time off together. But the incredible thing was that Alison was now refusing to leave Haifa Hospital, and wanted to stay on to help the camp people. I had always respected her dedication, but what about Immad, who was coming back with the rest of the team to London? She talked Immad into letting her stay on; the hospital needed her help, and he had to respect her wishes.

She was sniped at and trapped in another camp siege. In the end, she had to be evacuated from the camp and flown back to London, ill from pneumonia and having suffered a severe loss of weight through overwork. That Alison survived was entirely due to the mercy of God. If anything had happened to her, I would probably have had to hold myself responsible for agreeing to let her stay behind.

CHAPTER 23

When you read this chapter, you will wonder who Nabila Brier is, and why I suddenly choose to write about her. Like many people who work with Palestinians, I have learnt not to ask too many questions about their personal backgrounds, or take their photographs. Often, I take my Palestinian friends for granted, until suddenly I hear they have been killed. Only then do I begin to appreciate them – too late. Perhaps I must learn to tell those I love and respect of my feelings promptly, while they are still alive and able to hear me. Like Nabila – we always called on her whenever we wanted her help, and yet I hardly thought of her when I started to write this book.

It was only when she was gone that the part of our lives we shared became a gaping hole, and I began to think about her, quickly trying to make sure her face would not blur over the passage of time. When we are alive and together, we always have too much work to do, and are often too busy to spend time on one another. We always promise that one day we will sit down together and talk about things not related to work, that we will find out about each other. Then suddenly, one of us learns that this is not going to be possible any more. . .

Nabila Brier was shot dead on 18 December 1986, in West Beirut. Most of us who knew her were too stunned to think of what actually happened. I remember my first meeting with Nabila ever so clearly. It was some time in July 1985, near the end of the month. The British public had donated some cash towards the purchase of an ambulance for Haifa Hospital in Bourj el-Brajneh camp. For a whole month, I had been trying to get hold of a second-hand ambulance, a nearly impossible task. It was just after the Ramadan war, and there were simply no decent second-hand ambulances to be had in Beirut. We had a few offers of rotten vehicles which broke down just two kilometres down the road. In the end, my Norwegian colleague told me to see Nabila Brier, the UNICEF field officer in Beirut.

Nabila had just returned from the 1985 Nairobi Women's Conference, where she spoke as UNICEF representative from Beirut. I was told to turn up in her office between 7.45 AM and 8 AM to discuss the ambulance. When I turned up just before eight, Nabila was already waiting for me in her office. She was an attractive Palestinian, in her thirties, with extremely intelligent eyes. Nabila had an ambulance in her custody which had been donated by the people of Denmark to the General Union of Palestinian Women. It was not the rescue type of ambulance, but was suitable for transporting non-ambulant day-patients from one hospital to another. In other words, it was more a minibus than an ambulance. It was for the women to transport children and women patients to and from home, to kindergartens, hospitals and treatment centres.

It was brand new, from Europe. Because the Lebanese government had put up the vehicle tax to 50,000 Lebanese lira (£2,500 Sterling), the women's union could not afford to put the ambulance on the road. Moreover, the security situation in West Beirut was so bad, with Palestinian institutions subjected to such open persecution, that the General Union of Palestinian Women had found it almost impossible to function openly, and had gone partially underground. They decided to donate their ambulance to us, so that we could use the money raised in Britain to pay the vehicle tax. After all, the money we had was not going to be enough to buy an ambulance, but would be enough for the tax.

Nabila was brave and courageous, and it was only much later that I realised what tremendous pressure she was under. She had lost many members of her family. She told me, 'My family have paid our share of their blood debt in Lebanon.' Strange words to many people, but those familiar with Palestinian history knew that numerous Palestinian families in Lebanon had lost many members.

The press often .asked: 'Are the Palestinians bitter towards the Amal?' This question was a loaded one. People wanted to know whether the pain inflicted on the Palestinians by the Amal was the worst. Those who persecute the Palestinians always love to point out that the suffering they mete out is by no means the worst. Thus the Israelis would be quick to point out that the Arabs were equally cruel to the Palestinians.

The average family in a Palestinian refugee camp in Lebanon would have lost members through attacks by the Israelis and the Arabs. And Nabila's family was no exception. But she was wrong when she thought that enough of her family's blood had been spilt – little did she realise that one and a half years later she would be the next to be sacrificed.

Four gunmen murdered Nabila. What a disgraceful, sick action! Did it take four cowards with machine guns to face this brave Lebanese-Palestinian, who was armed with nothing but courage and truth? With Nabila dead, perhaps her family had poured out enough blood to satisfy these devils. I can only take comfort from the fact that she died instantly, that she was not tortured or raped, that her body was not mutilated, as was the usual practice of such murderers.

What had Nabila done to deserve to die? She was a Palestinian, and she worked for peace. As a doctor, my dealings with her were limited to organising medical supplies to Lebanon, not only for the Palestinian camps, but also for Lebanese humanitarian groups. Large crates of medicines and relief supplies such as blankets and clothing would arrive from all over the world labelled 'Mrs Nabila Brier, c/o UNICEF, Beirut'. These would be channelled to people in need – the Palestinians in the refugee camps, the Lebanese Shi'ites from the deprived areas, and people in need of help. There was no commission charged, no tax, no cuts, no bribes – so common among corrupt customs officers in Beirut.

The death of Nabila was a threat to many relief workers. So, after all, humanitarian and relief work could result in the loss of one's life. That was probably the aim of these mischief-makers, to scare people off from helping the deprived communities in Lebanon. During the attacks on the camps in 1985, nobody was allowed to speak up. Journalists were threatened if they reported on the situation in the camps. I was threatened for speaking up against the attacks on the camp. Those who murdered Palestinians did not want any witness to speak up against their crimes.

To make sure that I had all the relevant information regarding the camp war, Nabila came to see me in the Mayflower Hotel on the morning of my departure in 1985. She handed me the UNICEF report on the recent attacks on the camps. Details of the number of Palestinians made homeless, the destruction of the camps, including schools, kindergartens and clinics, were carefully documented in the report. Nabila's visit to me would have been watched by those who attacked and destroyed the camps. The more she tried to get the truth out, the more she would endanger her own life. But without people like her, the situation would be much worse. Crimes and atrocities would not reach the outside world. If there was anyone who would put her life on the line to get the truth out, it was Nabila.

They had been after Nabila for some time. In December 1985, her husband was threatened with kidnapping, if the two of them remained any longer in Beirut. They left Beirut, and came to see us in London. Phil, the Irish anaesthetist who worked in Gaza Hospital in 1982, invited all of us to dinner. It was such a lovely little dinner, and it was so good to see Nabila in London. Much of the conversation was about the needs of the camp people – like how to send clothing to those who were homeless, how to make the Lebanese winter slightly more bearable. That dinner was the last time we met. Nabila was soon back in Beirut, continuing her work with UNICEF, despite the threats directed against her.

The death of Nabila shocked us all. My friend Phil was too numb to react. But after a little while, she burst out: 'How I wish I never knew anything about Palestinians or Lebanese or Israelis! Not a moment of peace at all!' Phil broke into large sobs on the other end of the telephone – she was in the middle of her ward round as an anaesthetist in charge of the intensive care unit in a large London hospital. Her colleagues must have thought Phil had gone crazy – she went off to answer the telephone, and came back sobbing. Indeed, the whole situation in Beirut was insane. God Almighty, please give us patience, and give us strength.

Now, more than ever, I understand what struggle is about. Today we are together, sharing with each other, laughing and crying together; tomorrow, one of us is just taken away from the rest of us forever. Yet we go on, we continue, that is the only way we can honour those who have so generously laid down their lives.

Next to my bed was a box, containing many photographic slides. These were slides of ornate musical instruments, embroidery, fishermen at sea, jewellery, portraits of dancers, peasants, orchards . . . They were beautiful slides, colourful and exquisite, of another people and another culture. They were slides of Palestine and her culture. Nabila gave them to me, and wanted me to show them to people all over the world. Her instructions to me are now very painful to repeat. But I remember clearly her concluding remarks: 'Our friends only know us through our sufferings. But it is also important that they know Palestinian history is not only full of massacres. We have culture too, we appreciate beauty and art like everybody else.' Perhaps we must remember Nabila in that way: the beautiful, enthusiastic Palestinian woman, articulate, cultured and brave – there is nothing the enemies of the Palestinian people can do to take that away from her and from the rest of us.

PART V

From Beirut to Jerusalem
1985 – 1988

CHAPTER 24

Our medical team returned to London in August 1985. While
.we had been away, there had been an overwhelming
response from members of the public in Britain wanting to
support the work of our charity. Dr Rafiq Husseini, the
director of MAP, had worked himself flat out during our
absence. He is a Palestinian born in Jerusalem, married to an
Englishwoman. Prior to becoming the founding director of
MAP, he qualified at Loughborough and was a researcher in
microbiology in the University of Birmingham. He gave that
post up to be the person responsible for providing the
direction and executing the policies of our charity. He is also
a cousin of Dr Azziza Khalidi, the Palestinian woman who
ran Gaza Hospital in 1982. Like Azziza, he is gentle, patient
and chronically optimistic in the face of the worst disasters.

Before our departure, the charity had placed a small
advertisement calling for medical volunteers, and this had
attracted over sixty applicants. Money had poured in.
Although our funding from large institutions was minimal,
we received a huge amount from individuals. The office
was flooded with donations: a one-pound note from an old
age pensioner, a five-pound note from a widow, another
from an unemployed person, and so on.

The donations were usually accompanied by letters. A
typical example would be:

'Dear Medical Aid for Palestinians,

'I read of your efforts in Lebanon. Please accept my small gift of £2 to support your good work. I am sorry I can't give any more, as I am unemployed. God bless you all. From. . .'

The letters that came with the donations convinced me that generosity was inversely proportional to wealth. The poorer a person is, the more he or she is ready to give. The first time we received a cheque for fifty pounds it came from an unemployed person, and I wept. The 'dole money' was about twenty-one pounds a week, so his cheque represented two weeks' livelihood. The second time, we received a donation from an old age pensioner with a note: 'Dear MAP, Please accept this to support your work. I am sorry it isn't more. . .' The third fifty-pound donation came from a woman who wrote: 'Dear MAP, I am a widow. But I want to give this for the children in the refugee camps in Lebanon, because their need is greater than mine . . .'

The office also grew. Many people came in to help: they licked stamps, did the mailings, looked after the collection boxes and organised fund-raising events for the Palestinians. It was our supporters who kept the whole Lebanon project going, who raised the money and did the work. Often when people in Lebanon thanked me for all the work I had put in, they did not really appreciate that the work of the medical team was only made possible by all those people in Britain. They were the true friends of the Palestinians and Lebanese, although they never had the chance to meet them.

In 1986 MAP moved to new premises. To save on rent, Rafiq Husseini arranged for us to rent the basement of an office building in London. It looked like a dump before we moved in, but some hard work gave it a very respectable appearance, with cream paint on the walls, proper carpeting on the floor, effective ventilation and decent lighting. Here we set up offices with word processors, a design room and an exhibition and sales hall, putting in eight phones, a telex and a fax.

As MAP relies heavily on volunteers, there were lots of tables and chairs in the main hall where volunteers could sit and work. They made out receipts, wrote thank-you letters and packed sales items such as printed tee-shirts, mugs, greeting cards and pieces of Palestinian embroidery. The walls were usually hung with paintings donated to MAP to be sold to raise money.

Between 1985 and 1987 our charity sent more than sixty medical volunteers, of nine different nationalities, to Beirut. Lebanon could be a very dangerous place at times: bombs, shells and snipings were the facts of life. But for European men, there was the special danger of being kidnapped. On more than one occasion, we had to evacuate our people from Lebanon as their lives were directly threatened. Nevertheless, doctors, nurses and health workers continued to come forward, volunteering their skills and willing to risk their lives in order to look after sick and wounded people in Lebanon.

The living expenses we provided for the volunteers were extremely low, just enough for subsistence in the refugee camps. We were able to select the best people, those who came forward from a sense of commitment, rather than those who thought working in Lebanon would just be one more paid job. Our doctors and nurses sometimes even offered to pay their own way in the Lebanon.

All our people had to undertake to treat anyone in Lebanon, regardless of race, colour or religion. There was already enough sectarianism in the country, without foreign health workers making the divisions worse.

The 'bureaucratic' aspect of the Lebanon programme was vitally necessary. We had to be sure we explained the situation in Lebanon to those who volunteered their services. We had to be systematic about it. The risks had to be spelt out, and volunteers had to sign a release form stating that they understood the dangers and were taking the risk of their own volition.

Although we did not pay the volunteers much, we had to pay a lot to insure them against war, civil war and invasion. Those clauses added a great deal to the usual insurance premium. Even worse, we were unable to find any insurance company willing to provide a policy which covered the risk of being kidnapped in Lebanon.

A constant dilemma faced us: should we go on sending volunteers to such a risky and volatile area? But we saw it as our duty to act as a channel between those in Lebanon who needed help and those in Britain who wanted to help. It would have been irresponsible to sever the link between them. So we continued with our volunteer programme, and tried to cope with the nightmares it caused. Rafiq bore the brunt of the responsibility that went with the volunteer programme: but some of us, like myself, still went to sleep every night half-expecting to be awakened by a long-distance S.O.S. call from our volunteers. By this time I was back in my Senior Orthopaedic Registrar post in the Royal Victoria Infirmary, Newcastle-upon-Tyne. The clinical responsibilities attached to this post were demanding enough, but the added responsibilities of the Lebanon programme continued to take up whatever energies I had left.

Rafiq was away from the MAP on a visit to his family in Jordan when disaster struck. In January 1987, our office received a shocking telex from our volunteers who were working in Bourj el-Brajneh camp. It read:

We, as foreign health workers living and working in Bourj el-Brajneh camp, declare that the situation in the camp is critical and conditions inhumane. The camp has now been under siege for more than 12 weeks and we and the 20,000 residents are being subjected to conditions of deprivation and misery. Drinking-water is the most basic human need. Most houses do not have running drinking-water and it has to be collected daily from taps in the streets and at great risk of personal safety. Several women have been shot and killed collecting water for their families. Food stocks have been completely depleted. There is now no baby-food or milk and babies are drinking tea and water. There is no flour and therefore no bread, no fresh food so pregnant women and children are suffering undernourishment. People are eating stale food and suffering vomiting and diarrhoea. Many families now have no food. It is winter and the electricity was cut off from the camp two and a half months ago. People are cold and have chest infections. There are huge piles of garbage which cannot be cleared and rats are thriving. One old lady who was bedridden was unable to get help when her foot was eaten by rats for three consecutive nights, before she was rescued. The constant bombardment of the camp forces the people to crowd into poorly ventilated shelters with no sanitation, or to risk being blown up at home. Hundreds of children have scabies and many have severe skin infections. Approximately 35 per cent of homes in Bourj el-Brajneh have now been destroyed. In the hospital, many medicines have run out and we have no more gauze. The hospital building is rendered unstable by repeated shelling and patients and nurses have been injured by shrapnel. Water is dripping down the walls and mould is growing in every room.

We declare these conditions to be inhumane and on humanitarian grounds we call for the lifting of the siege and the admission of food and medicines by the international relief agencies.

DR PAULINE CUTTING, BRITISH SURGEON
BEN ALOFS, DUTCH NURSE
SUSAN WIGHTON, SCOTTISH NURSE. 23 January 1987.

Mike Holmes contacted me and asked me to come to the MAP office to discuss the situation. I came in, and we read the statement. 'Swee,' said Mike when we had finished reading the message, 'what are we going to do about this?'

Mike was our newly appointed publicity officer. An ardent supporter of the Palestinians, he had just come down from Scotland to join us at MAP. Like many others who have spent hours working in the office, raising funds and generating publicity for the camps, Mike had not been to the Middle East before.

'I don't know, Mike,' I replied. 'But it looks as though the whole lot are slowly dying because of a really long blockade. Today is Friday. We'd better spend the weekend launching an urgent appeal, and get everybody in. Could you let Pauline and Suzy's folks know what is happening?'

'Sure,' said Mike.

'Oh, and we'd better make sure we keep all the people who talk all the time and never do any work from coming into the office and getting in the way.'

Mike immediately set off to get things going. What was so infuriating for us was that the siege seemed to have been going on for at least three months, but there had been no coverage of it in the British media. We assumed our volunteers in Bourj el-Brajneh must have been trying to reach us and had been prevented from getting through because of the siege. We knew that Rashidiyeh, a Palestinian refugee camp near Sour, was under siege, and we had been working out ways to help the people there, but never realised that the Beirut camps of Bourj el-Brajneh and Shatila were also being attacked and besieged. The western press concentrated on the PLO's storming of Magdoushe, a Christian village near Saida, but nothing was said about the camps.

We were very upset to read the declaration of our three volunteers, and were angry with ourselves for not realising how bad things had become. It was particularly difficult to tell the families of our volunteers the truth, but we knew we had to. One of our volunteers in Bourj el-Brajneh camp was an Austrian physiotherapist called Hanne . Although he had been working in Bourj el-Brajneh camp he had not signed the statement. We knew he was still alive as the NORWAC co-ordinator in Beirut had managed to speak to him on the radio after the statement was sent out. One day the police came to our office in London: they had been asked to find out about us by the Austrian police. Apparently Hannes' mother was convinced that her son was dead and we were hiding the truth from her! So we had to make sure that all the families, including his, knew what was going on.

Soon we received another desperate message from our volunteers in Beirut:

> We declare that the situation in the Bourj el-Brajneh camp has become intolerable. The camp has been under siege for more than 14 weeks. Two weeks ago we sent out a declaration that there soon would be no more food in the camp and that the situation was critical. We are still under siege and now the people are beginning to starve. We have seen children hunting in garbage heaps for scraps of food. Today one woman was shot while trying to collect grass on the outskirts of the camp to be able to feed her seven children who no longer have any food at all. Some women and children are taking the risk of leaving the camp and many small children have been taken prisoner. Some of those who have no food now eat dogs and wild cats to survive. We appeal to all parties in this war to stop fighting, and we appeal to the United Nations to take steps to achieve a ceasefire immediately, so the international relief organisations can get in with food and medicines to stop this massacre.

The people in our London office got very desperate on receiving this message. I had a very unpleasant feeling that something awful would happen soon. It brought back all the horrors of 1982, when the camps had been sealed off. We had called for help then, but no one had answered. When the siege was lifted in 1982 and the outside world was allowed in, the roads were strewn with dead bodies. This time, the camps were defended, so a massacre could not happen so easily.

But it had become a long, drawn-out war of attrition. Maybe the camp would be starved into surrendering, and then as they came out of the bomb shelters, they would get gunned down. This had happened before: the siege of Tel al-Zaatar in 1976 had ended after six months in a massacre of three thousand people, just when the camp had agreed to a ceasefire and was about to be evacuated by the

International Red Cross. A journalist friend told me what it was like immediately after the siege of Tel al-Zaatar. He had visited the camp, which was being bulldózed. Dead bodies were everywhere. The bulldozers drove over the bodies and incorporated them into the earth.

Hunger is an effective weapon, as those of us who had starved before knew. Hunger could drive even the Palestinians to surrender. Then there is thirst. I remember the story told by an orphan from Tel al-Zaatar: 'At night the mothers went out to get water. The wells were in open squares which were under fire the whole time. The mothers kissed their children goodbye before going out of the house, because they didn't know whether they would ever see them again.' Of the ten women who went to get water in Tel al-Zaatar one night, only four returned: the rest were killed.

Late in January 1987, news arrived at the MAP office that the Palestinians in the camps had asked for a *fatwah*, a dispensation from their religious leaders, allowing them to eat dead bodies. It smacked of imminent death for all in the camps. Even at the height of the 1982 Israeli siege, no one had had to eat cats and dogs; in 1987 people were even thinking of eating human bodies.

I went to the filing cabinet in the office and pulled out the file marked 'Medical Volunteers'. Inside it there were four completed sets of forms, with photographs of Ben Alofs, Pauline Cutting, Susan Wighton and Hannes. I felt sick to think I might never see them again. Ben I had known since 1982, Pauline I had only met once, Susan and Hannes I only knew through what Alison, who had been with us on our first medical team to Lebanon in 1985, had told me about them.

Yet as I studied the forms and their pictures again and again, I felt as though I had known them all my life. Four wonderful young people who had only gone out to help others – what had they done to deserve such a fate in the camp?

It was in August 1985, in a tiny room packed with reporters, that I first met Pauline Cutting. I had just come back from Beirut, and was addressing a press conference on the situation in the Palestinian refugee camps. Being so tiny, I could not be seen by anybody, and so the president of our charity, Major Derek Cooper, brought me a chair to stand on while I was speaking. While I was taking off my shoes to get up on to the chair, Major Cooper whispered to me, 'There is a wonderful young lady surgeon who wants to volunteer for Lebanon. Will you talk to her after this?'

That was how Pauline and I met. Now it was nearly a year and a half later, but I remembered her so well. She had a sensitive face, and looked as though she felt the sufferings of others instinctively. God forbid that anything should happen to her now!

It was no use being fearful for the safety of our volunteers in the besieged camp, or feeling guilty that things had got to such a state. We had to do something, had to push as hard as possible to publicise the situation, had to campaign for the lifting of the siege, and we had to bring our people home. I decided to forget my job as an orthopaedic surgeon on the National Health in Britain until all this got sorted out.

At the beginning of February 1987, events in Lebanon once more attracted the attention of the British media: some hostages were threatened with execution by kidnappers unless their demands were met by a certain deadline. Terry Waite had just been kidnapped. Mike Holmes managed to wangle an invitation for me to appear on a BBC television programme to discuss hostage-taking in Lebanon. Of course I regarded our volunteers trapped in the camps as hostages too. In fact all the Palestinians trapped by the siege of Shatila, Bourj el-Brajneh and Rashidiyeh camps were hostages.

After the programme, I introduced myself to the editor of the BBC foreign news, and showed him a copy of our volunteers' statement. An ex-hostage himself, he understood the plight of those caught in the siege. I said to him, 'The lives of twenty-five thousand Palestinians and our volunteers depend on your publicising the situation.' He agreed to give the camps coverage, and as a result our little office was thrown into chaos by journalists over the next few days.

In spite of the massive international publicity, the siege was not lifted. Every time Nabih Berri, the leader of the Amal militia besieging the camps, announced that the siege would be lifted and food allowed into the camps, his promises were followed by the news that relief convoys had been turned back and even shot at.

Friday 13 February was one more of those days when the morning news announced that Nabih Berri was going to lift the siege to allow food into the camps. The Cuttings came to the MAP office hoping that we would be able to contact their daughter, Pauline, via a radio link. They were extremely courageous and understanding people. We all knew how anxious they must have felt – but they never once blamed us for letting Pauline get into such a dangerous situation, and they were always very supportive of everything our charity did. Whenever asked about their daughter, they would always point out that she was just one of the thousands under siege.

We did finally get through to Pauline at nine o'clock that night. The siege had not been lifted, and the hospital was inundated with casualties. Fourteen legs had been amputated that day. There had been six deaths and eighteen wounded. The food convoy had been fired on, and the driver had been shot in the head.

Our volunteers told us, 'We will stay with the people of the camp until the danger is over. We will remain with them – to live or die with them.'

I was very proud of them, but when I looked across the room at Pauline's parents, and thought of Suzy's parents and Hannes' mother as well, I knew it was about time I returned to Beirut myself.

CHAPTER 25

We had to get a team together to replace Pauline and company in Bourj el-Brajneh camp, and we had to raise funds to pay for medicine and equipment to replenish those used up in the camps. The next few days were really hectic.

Replacing the medical team was not just a simple matter of swapping two groups of people. A lot had to happen before it became possible. It needed a ceasefire, the partial lifting of the siege and a safe escort out for the besieged team while their replacements went into the camp. There was no indication any of these things would actually happen. The situation in the camp deteriorated as the siege tightened still further and there was even more sniping and shooting. To make things worse, an awful civil war had erupted outside the camps among the Lebanese of Beirut: the flare-up was the worst such war for years.

So we asked for four thousand 'blood bags', half of which were to be given to the Lebanese Red Cross, and the other half to the Palestine Red Crescent. We also got hold of anaesthetic drugs, surgical instruments, antibiotics, plaster of Paris, and all sorts of things we knew the hospitals needed – about four tons in weight. We put together a team of eight medical volunteers. To make kidnapping less likely, we picked medics who carried non-British passports.

We left for Beirut on 2 March 1987, via Cyprus this time, as Beirut airport was closed again. Unfortunately, I went no further than Cyprus, as I was refused a Lebanese entry visa. It did not surprise me to be singled out by the official Lebanese authorities in this way. It was only too obvious that those attacking the camps would not want the Palestinians to be joined by friends and supporters and they would know my name. They must have put pressure on the Lebanese Embassy not to give me a visa.

We got news that Pauline Cutting had received death threats. Everything had become very grim, and I felt helpless. *The Guardian* newspaper in Britain did a profile of me entitled 'Angel with Clipped Wings'. I thought it a very apt headline, at least as far as the clipped wings were concerned.

The rest of the team continued by boat to Lebanon, with thirty-nine crates of medicine and equipment. They were led by Major Derek Cooper, President of MAP. When they arrived in East Beirut, Major Cooper and Lady Pamela, his wife, were advised by the British Ambassador not to cross the Green Line. All British passport holders were kidnap targets in Lebanon. The Ambassador had enough on his plate with Terry Waite and John McCarthy having been kidnapped, and Pauline and Suzy being stuck in the siege of the camps: he could do without Major Cooper and Lady Pamela being taken hostage as well.

So the five volunteers who did not carry British passports, none of whom had been to Beirut before, went on to West Beirut without the Coopers. Their job was to get the thirty-nine boxes of medical supplies across the Green Line, make their way to Bourj el-Brajneh camp, negotiate a ceasefire and get in to replace the team who had been trapped by the siege. They bravely volunteered to go on their own. As team leader, I must have been crazy to let them do so!

Meanwhile, I took a plane to Egypt. I figured few people in Cairo would know about my support for the Palestinians. Maybe Lebanese representatives there would give me a visa. The British consul in Cairo wrote a supportive letter to the First Secretary in the Lebanese Foreign Interest Section of the French Embassy, asking them to speed up matters so I could get to Beirut on a humanitarian mission. I did get my visa, on 30 March 1987, twenty-eight days after setting off from London.

When I spoke to people in London, I found out that the MAP team of five had not yet managed to enter the camps. The siege had not been lifted, and sixty-three women had been sniped at and wounded while trying to bring food into the starving camps. Twenty-one of the women had died. Shatila camp had run out of fuel, and they were burning furniture to keep warm. The young men of Shatila camp had volunteered to starve so that the women and children might be fed. Pauline had received a death threat in writing.

The Syrian peacekeeping force had moved into Beirut and had put an end to the civil war outside the camp. Syrian troops had not, however, been deployed around the Palestinian camps, and the Syrians seemed content to allow Amal to continue the siege and to go on sniping at women and children. Pauline's parents had sent a telegram to Hafez al-Assad, the President of Syria, begging for the siege to be lifted so that they could have their daughter home. Nothing had happened. The Syrian peacekeeping force kept its distance, and the siege went on.

I thought Damascus probably held the key to the situation. The Syrian peacekeeping force had just moved into Beirut and stopped the Lebanese from fighting each other. If the Syrians were powerful enough to put a stop to the civil war between the Druse, Amal and other Lebanese factions, surely they could stop Amal attacking the camps. President Assad had taken the position that Palestine was part of Greater Syria: in that sense he had adopted the Palestinian cause.

Although the relationship between Syria and the PLO

was very strained at that time for a number of reasons, Syria would understand there was also a humanitarian case for imposing a ceasefire and allowing provisions in for the starving. Many of us recognised that for Syria to stop the attacks on the camp would strain Syria's relationship with Amal, one of her major allies in the fight against the Israelis. But for the sake of human lives, President Assad might consider it a reasonable price to pay. But would he?

Sooner or later I was going to have to talk to the Syrians to arrange an escort out of the camp for our people. I decided I might as well start immediately, in order to lay the groundwork before arriving in Beirut, so I wrote a letter to President Assad:

His Excellency
President Hafez al-Assad.   30 March 87

Your Excellency,

I hope you have received the telegram from Dr Pauline Cutting's parents, begging for the siege to be lifted so that they may have their daughter home.

I am the Leader of the International Medical Team, which left London for Beirut on the 2nd March 87. The British people has sent us, hoping that we could relieve Dr Cutting's team, currently in Bourj el-Brajneh Camp in West Beirut. It might seem imprudent for me, a foreign doctor, to address Your Excellency so directly, and I do beg your forgiveness and your patience to hear me out.

I first set foot in Lebanon in 1982, having volunteered my services to the suffering people in Lebanon, then victimised by the Israeli invasion. I have seen much suffering and cruelty then, and was one of the doctors who was trapped in Sabra and Shatila camps during the massacres. Having been brought up a Christian, it was then that I found out, at first hand, the true story of the Palestinian people – and that story was written with blood. I then went to testify before the Israeli Kahan Commission on behalf of the people of the camps. I felt I had to lend voice to those innocent women and children killed so brutally while the Israelis occupied the camps.

This time the cries of the Palestinian women and children in Shatila and Bourj el-Brajneh camps have again reached me, and not only me, but the International Community including the people in Britain.

Five months of siege on these camps have resulted in starvation, death and misery. Those wounded continue to suffer and perish. The International Community and people in Britain have responded overwhelmingly to the plight of the Palestinians. We have now medicines for the sick, surgical equipment to treat the wounded, food for the starving. Doctors and nurses from all over the world have left their own countries and volunteered their services to the Palestinians, knowing full well of the risks to their own lives in so doing.

All over the world, people follow with interest the entry of the Syrian peacekeeping forces, and look forward to the lifting of the siege on the camps so that relief could be brought to the Palestinians who have suffered for so long. Instead, news on the camps takes the form of women being sniped at and killed while trying to go out and buy food for their children, relief convoys being shot up while trying to bring food into the camps. These acts must have been committed against the wishes of Your Excellency and your peacekeeping forces.

The International Community can continue to donate food and medicines. Doctors and nurses can continue to volunteer their services. Dr Pauline Cutting and her team can work themselves to exhaustion in the besieged Bourj el-Brajneh camp, till the entire camp perish through hunger, disease and injury. But only Your Excellency could bring an end to this insane suffering.

In 1982, at the height of the Sabra and Shatila massacres, we appealed to the Israeli Defence Forces to stop the massacres – but our plea went unheeded, and the massacres continued. I brought this fact to the attention of the Israeli Kahan Commission. Today in 1987, I appeal to Your Excellency to do all in your power to bring an end to the sufferings of the Palestinians in the besieged camps, and the lives of women and children to be spared. I also beg you to grant protection to Dr Pauline Cutting and her team, and allow the new medical team already in West Beirut for nearly a month to safely replace them. In this way, Your Excellency has not only honoured the wishes of anxious British parents, but also the British people who sponsored the whole relief effort. I eagerly await your instructions, and would personally call at your Embassy in Cyprus this week.

Dr Swee Ang.

In order to get the letter to Syria, I faxed it from Cairo to Mike Holmes in the London MAP office, and asked him to take the letter to the chargé d'affaires of the Syrian Interest Section of the Lebanese Embassy in London. The Syrian Embassy had recently been shut down, and the Lebanese Embassy was looking after the Syrian Government's interests. Mike also took along a few newspaper clippings about me, so that the whole lot could be sent in the diplomatic bag to the President.

I knew that whoever opened the President's mail in Damascus might think I was crazy and just file the letter in the wastepaper basket. To make sure this did not happen, I told Mike to tell them that I was prepared to have the letter broadcast on Arabic radio: then the whole of the Middle East would hear it, and the President would have to hear what I had written. On the same evening, I learnt that Mike had already gone to see the chargé d'affaires and had told him exactly that. Now all I had to do was make my way back to Cyprus and check in at the Syrian Embassy to find out what was going on.

On 2 April I called at the Syrian Embassy in Cyprus to see if there were any developments. No one there seemed to know about a British medical team trapped in the siege of Bourj el-Brajneh, but the First Secretary kindly offered to check with Damascus. Leaving my phone number with his secretary, I went off to await developments.

The next morning at nine o'clock, the Syrian Embassy telephoned and asked me to call at the Embassy immediately with the original of my letter to the President, together with my travel document. They wanted to send the letter to the President that morning. The letter Mike had produced in London had not been an original and was not signed by me, and now they evidently wanted it done correctly.

After hanging around for nearly a month just trying to get a visa from Lebanese representatives, I must admit that I was very impressed by the efficiency of their Syrian counterparts. The First Secretary of the Syrian Embassy advised me to wait a few days for things to happen.

Three days later, on 6 April, the morning bulletin on the World Service of the BBC announced that the Syrian peacekeeping force was going to move in and take over Amal positions at Shatila camp in order to enforce a ceasefire. This meant food would be allowed into Shatila camp. Two days later, the Syrian peacekeeping force imposed a ceasefire at Bourj el-Brajneh. The next day, the First Secretary at the Syrian Embassy in Cyprus urged me to leave for Beirut and to go to Bourj el-Brajneh to see our people. He must have grown tired of me hanging around the Syrian Embassy every day, asking him if I could see President Assad, and asking if there was a reply to my letter.

He assured me that there would be no problems once I reached Syrian-controlled areas in Beirut. Off I went and bought myself a ticket for the overnight ferry from Larnaca to Jounieh.

It was precisely seven in the morning of 10 April when the ferry from Cyprus docked in Jounieh harbour. The sun had already risen, and I looked out to sea. Lebanese soldiers came into the ferry, and lined the side of the road leading out of the harbour. The security was tight, but they were not rude. Women passengers hurriedly put on lipstick and sprayed themselves with perfume as they looked out at the eagerly waiting crowd. People jumped with joy and blew kisses at their loved ones from both sides of the gangway. A young soldier shouted loudly across in English: 'I love you!' An embarrassed young lady blushed and tried to conceal a smile. The weeks of worry and uncertainty, capped by the rough and sleepless night on the crowded deck of the ferryboat, probably contributed to the sense of unreality I experienced on finding myself back in Beirut.

Had I really made it? Was this the East Beirut harbour where I had arrived in 1982? I cleared customs and the security checks, and as I walked out I spotted the fair hair and faded blue jacket of Øyvind, the NORWAC co-ordinator. He waved vigorously and I waved back. 'Welcome, Swee!' Øyvind shouted from across the crowd. Tall and in his mid-thirties, he was very patient and soft-spoken – this was a legacy of his training as a clergyman. He laughed a lot, and his smiling eyes showed that he was a man who was in love with life and people.

Øyvind took me to a taxi waiting by the roadside, and we put my large suitcase – the same one I had used in 1982 – into the boot. The taxi set off. East Beirut appeared much more prosperous and tidy than in 1982: the roads were smooth and there were traffic lights which people were obeying. There were shops and offices, and large pictures of the Lebanese President, Amin Gemayel, were everywhere. We drove towards the Green Line: Øyvind decided to use the civilian crossing, which was open and free from snipers. The traffic jam at the crossing was awful. We decided to get down, walk across the Green Line with my luggage, and pick up a different taxi on the West Beirut side. East Beirut was just another city in the Middle East to me, but once I crossed the Green Line into West Beirut and saw the bullet-riddled walls, the bomb-damaged buildings, the streets full of dirt and dust, and the anarchic traffic, I knew this was no dream: I was back on home ground. 'Hello, Beirut,' I thought. 'Here I come!'

The taxi whizzed through narrow streets. I was going to be able to stay with our Norwegian friends in the NORWAC flat in Hamra. He asked, 'How does it feel to be back?' Øyvind knew I had been refused visas in the Lebanese embassies in London, Rome, Athens and Cyprus. He understood that I had nearly not made it.

'Fantastic!' I said. That was the best and only word I could summon up to describe my feelings. Even after all these years of war, Beirut was still a very beautiful city. The driver asked me, 'Do you love Beirut?' I said I did, and he continued, 'The first time I drove my little son up to the mountains and showed him Beirut from the mountaintops, he cried. He asked me why people are trying to destroy such a beautiful country.'

CHAPTER 26

The Lebanese people were still warm, friendly and hospitable. When they were bitter, the bitterness was no longer directed at each other. It was terribly sad that Lebanon had been a battlefield for so long. Much of the economic infrastructure had been destroyed by successive wars. The Lebanese lira had collapsed almost completely. Over the years, great efforts had been put in to destabilise and cantonise Lebanon, and to turn her children into cannon fodder. Wages were low, and jobs hard to come by. Most young men were forced to fight for a living. They joined various militias, and when they were on duty they shot at each other. But once they were off duty, they did not have to kill. It was then that one really appreciated their good qualities – remnants of Arab courtesy and warmth which stood out against being brutalised. In dreams, I could hear myself shouting out loud: 'Leave Lebanon alone, give the children a chance to grow up. No more guns, no more tanks. Leave them alone!'

After thirteen years of war, I sensed people wanted peace. The level of tolerance was amazing. There were no traffic rules – people just drove through the streets with a lot of give and take. If there was an accident in which no one was injured, it was 'ma'lish' – never mind. If someone was injured, it was 'al-humdullelah' (Praise be to God) that no one died. Here no one had to preach forgiveness – it was built into the place.

There were many people I wanted to see, people I had not heard of for two years, both Palestinians and Lebanese. Øyvind assured me that the MAP team in Bourj el-Brajneh was alive and in reasonably good spirits. We called in at the PRCS clinic in Mar Elias camp. This is a small Palestinian refugee camp, which started off as a camp for the Christian Palestinians, a group of significant size. In recent years, most of the Christian families had left, and Mar Elias had become the administrative headquarters of nearly all the Palestinian political parties, like the Fatah Intifada – the party of Abu Musa who split from the mainstream Fatah; Sa'iqa; the Democratic Front for the Liberation of Palestine; the two parties of the Popular Front for the Liberation of Palestine; the party of Nidal – the Fatah Revolutionary Council (Abu Nidal); and so on – all except groups loyal to Arafat. Those loyal to Arafat had to function underground since the Syrians were actively arresting them.

Along with these political offices there were those of the various European relief agencies and the United Nations Relief and Work Agency (UNRWA). And of course, the PRCS. Although Um Walid was still in charge of PRCS work in Lebanon, there were now regional directors – like Dr Mohammed Osman in Beirut, Dr Ali Abdullah in Saida, and so on. It was good to see Um Walid again, and to be introduced to Dr Osman. The PRCS clinic in Mar Elias treated a hundred and fifty to two hundred out-patients daily; now a new hospital was being constructed. Wherever you went – in Lebanon, in Egypt, in Sudan – the PRCS would be putting up a building, a clinic or a hospital, whether there was peace or war.

The Syrians had imposed a ceasefire and the camps were not being attacked, but they were still under siege. The entrances to the camps were closed, and were guarded by President Assad's Special Forces and the Syrian Intelligence. Palestinian women were now being allowed to go out to buy food for their families and to carry their rations back. Before the Syrians moved in, women were shot at when they tried to enter or leave the camps to buy food and fetch water and many had been wounded and killed. No one dared shoot at the Palestinian women in front of the Syrian peacekeeping forces. It was amazing how everyone feared the Syrians – both Lebanese and Palestinians!

It was noon before I left Mar Elias, but I wanted to visit Shatila and Bourj el-Brajneh. According to the ceasefire agreement, women did not need special permission from the Syrian Intelligence to enter or leave the camp – so I decided I was going to chance it. I bought a scarf, tied it round my head and arrived at the Sabra end of Shatila camp.

Sabra market was bustling with life and there were people buying and selling. As well as clothes, shoes and toilet items, there were stalls stocked with fish, meat, fruit and vegetables. It all looked fine, and the visitor who went no further into Shatila camp would probably not realise the true situation. Some western papers had printed cruel lies that the markets and shops of the camps were packed with food. But the market was not inside the Palestinian part of Sabra – it was in the Lebanese part of the camp. In 1982, Sabra and Shatila camps were the homes of both Palestinian and Lebanese people, who had lived together for many years. When the Israelis invaded and sent in their mercenaries to massacre the camps, both suffered. But after 1985, when the first camp war started, it was a deliberate policy of the attackers to isolate the Palestinians.

Sabra camp fell in 1985, and most of the Palestinian families either fled or were killed, leaving only the Lebanese families as sad witnesses of what was happening to their Palestinian neighbours in Shatila. The part of Sabra where most of the Palestinians had lived was near Gaza Hospital. Palestinian homes there were destroyed, so that even if there was a ceasefire those who escaped had nowhere to come back to. The homes had not been rebuilt. Across the road, Shatila camp put up a fierce resistance and did not fall. Instead it was besieged from 1985 onwards.

The siege had been total for nearly two years now – from May 1985 to April 1987 with only partial lifting at one point for a couple of months. All the entrances and exits to the camps were surrounded by tanks and militiamen so that no one could enter or leave the camps. There were full-scale attacks on the camps, raining shells and rockets on to the homes of people. At other times there were ceasefires, and the situation was more like a tight curfew. Throughout the last six months of the siege on Shatila camp, the market continued to see all kinds of delicious fruits, meat and vegetables, while the Palestinians in Shatila camp starved. When they asked for food, they only received bullets and mortar bombs.

When Muslim religious leaders granted the starving Palestinians in Shatila a dispensation to eat human corpses during the siege, the camp people replied to the world:

> Throughout history, countries and communities have been wiped out through wars, natural disasters and epidemics, but not through deliberate starvation in the way we are being subjected to. Are you using hunger as a weapon, to starve us into submission? Where is the conscience of the twentieth century? If we perish in this way, let it go down in human history that the world which allowed the Sabra and Shatila massacres less than five years ago also let us die in this manner.
>
> You said we could eat the flesh from human corpses. But how could we eat the bodies of our loved ones, of our brothers, sisters, fathers, mothers and children.

The young men of Shatila volunteered to starve to conserve food for their old, their wounded, their women and children. Shatila was slowly dying. But they were proud and dignified as they awaited death. It was clear that nothing – not the massacres, not the two-year siege and not the food blockade – could break the spirit of Shatila camp. The siege tightened and the shells continued to rain down day and night on to the ruins and the debris. Early 1987 meant starvation, disease and the bitter cold and floods of the Lebanese winter. I wondered if Shatila would make it.

This little camp, two hundred yards square, had become a symbol of steadfast Palestinian resistance – it had become the Alamo, the Stalingrad, of the Palestinian people.

In the West, there had been relatively little news about Shatila. I did not know exactly what to expect, and my heartbeat quickened as I turned off from Sabra market to head towards Shatila camp. Uneven and muddy, the road was partially flooded, with bits of rubbish floating about. I could see the back of Gaza Hospital, and it looked deserted and desolate. As I walked on, the front of Gaza Hospital, covered with soot, came into view. The neighbouring buildings all looked empty – the families must all have fled, I thought to myself.

Suddenly there was a shout: 'Stop!' An armed man in plain clothes materialised from nowhere. He was an Amal intelligence officer in his twenties, slimly-built. I suppose I might have thought him good-looking, but I noticed his bloodshot eyes and trembling hands and automatically started diagnosing what was wrong with him. Coarse tremors – bloodshot eyes – he smoked hashish, more than likely, and maybe took some stimulant as well. His manners were nasty. I was in an unpleasant situation: the Amal gunman and I were the only living beings in sight. Taking a quick look at his pistol, I noticed it had no silencer. Well, at least if he shot me, someone would hear it.

It was a case of hoping for the best, as I really had no idea what he was up to. Thank God I was carrying some letters addressed to residents of Shatila camp. They were family letters from Palestinians in Europe to their relatives in the camps – all of the mundane 'How are you? I am praying for your safety' type. The man spoke reasonable English.

After giving me a bad time, going through my handbag, my papers, my shoes, he suddenly seemed to decide I was not smuggling guns into the camp, and was telling the truth when I claimed to be on a social visit. He let me pass. The incident was so nasty I never wanted to venture near that part of Sabra camp again without a very good reason.

As I continued towards Shatila camp, I kept being stopped by members of Amal, some in paramilitary uniform and others in plain clothes, but all armed. It was a stressful walk. I thought of the women of Shatila having to walk this way each day to get to the market to buy food for their families, and then having to return the same way laden with shopping. If the Amal people could harass and intimidate a newly-arrived doctor who was obviously a foreigner, I could only guess what it was like for the Palestinian women. The ceasefire was in force, but I was sure that if it was not for the Syrian troops, I would have joined the ranks of the 'disappeared', or would just have been shot.

After being stopped 'unofficially' by these people, I finally arrived at the official station of the Amal militia. This was a block of flats, about four storeys high, which had been damaged by shellfire. Through the shell holes, I could make out stacked up sand-bags, and soldiers with machine-guns. On the wall outside there was a large portrait of the Amal leader, Nabih Berri. A dozen or more Amal soldiers were manning the checkpoint. My travel document and belongings were taken for inspection. Inside the tall building, more soldiers were visible. They were a hideous bunch: I was completely terrified. I had never experienced such terror before – not even during the mock execution in September 1982. I was actually trembling, my knees felt as though they were giving way and then suddenly they seemed to have vanished. As a foreigner I could be kidnapped, and as a friend of the Palestinians, I could be shot dead. They seemed to have read my thoughts, and one of them loaded his machine-gun, and pointed it at me.

I had to do something before I trembled to the ground. I drew a deep breath, threw my shoulders back and told them as loudly as I could manage that I had an appointment to see the Syrian officer at Shatila checkpoint. At the word 'Syrian', they relented, gave me back my travel document and belongings and motioned me to go to the Syrian checkpoint.

This incident taught me the usefulness of a particular sentence, one I was to use on subsequent occasions whenever stopped by Amal: 'I have an appointment with the Syrian officer at the checkpoint.' It regularly got me out of trouble.

As a doctor, I found it interesting that my legs, which had almost failed to support my weight a second before, now decided of their own volition to take off at an embarrassingly high speed towards the Syrian checkpoint at the entrance to Shatila camp. I wanted to slow down, so no one could see I was afraid, but my legs would not allow me even that bit of self-control. The Syrian checkpoint was only a stone's throw down the road: I told the Syrians there that I wanted to hand some letters over to people in the camp. They opened all the letters and read their contents and finally decided to let me visit the camp for no more than one hour. They kept my travel document, telling me they would tear it up if I stayed longer than their authorised sixty minutes. That, to me, was a decent deal, after the treatment I had had from the Amal. I thanked the Syrians and went into Shatila camp.

The place was physically unrecognisable: it was a demolition site. Everywhere there were ruins, collapsing concrete, rubble, dereliction and destruction. Palestinians were standing on both sides of the camp road. This time no one waved or shouted at me to grab my attention. There was no laughter, there were no greetings. Nobody moved. I had never seen Shatila camp frozen like this. It was impossible to accept: it was diabolical. What had happened? Then I walked past the first Palestinian on the road. He still did not move, but he muttered a welcome under his breath: 'Ahlan, Doctora, ahlan.'

It was the same as I made my way on into the camp. Standing up or sitting down, Palestinians greeted me very, very quietly, without moving at all.

Remembering the way vaguely from my 1985 visit, I turned left into one of the narrow camp alleys towards Shatila mosque. Once I was in the alley, and shellfire-damaged buildings obstructed the view from Amal and Syrian military positions, some children and a woman came up to me, and guided me to Shatila hospital.

'What is your name?' asked the children.

I turned to them, and asked, 'What is your name?' The smallest of them, a cute little girl, gave me a big smile, put her hand into her mouth and blushed. The whole party escorted me to Shatila Hospital, telling me to see Chris Giannou, a Greek Canadian doctor.

Chris and I had met once before, in 1983 in Paris. He had a long history of commitment to the Palestinians, and was arrested by the Israelis at the beginning of the 1982 invasion. Chris went to Shatila camp in 1985 to set up the hospital, and had remained inside the besieged camp for nearly two years. If ever there was a foreign doctor who had given everything to the Palestinians, Chris Giannou was that person. His surgical skills, his administrative abilities, his patience and courage, even his personal life all belonged to the Palestinians.

'Hello, Chris!' I said.

When I tried to give him a big hug, I broke down and cried. It had been just over four years since we last met. Now Chris was no more than a human skeleton covered with skin.

'It's all right, dear,' he said. 'Don't worry about us. How is Francis? Come, I'll show you the hospital. We have everything. It is going to get better for everybody. Look, the women even managed to bring back a box of chocolates. Have one, will you?' He offered me a piece of chocolate.

'No, you have it, Chris,' I said. 'You need feeding up more than I do. Have you seen yourself in the mirror?' Almost at once I realised what a stupid thing it was to say, and both of us burst out laughing. There was no mirror for him to look into.

A quick tour of Shatila Hospital revealed how much it had developed from the little shelter of 1985. It was now housed in a number of separate blocks. The main hospital was built over the underground bomb shelter. The shelter was now converted into an efficient, well-kept operating theatre, above which were two wards for in-patients. The top floor was badly shelled and put out of action. The operating theatre was clean, and all the items neatly arranged. Here the surgical team had performed over three hundred life-saving operations over the last six months. The floor space was limited, thirty by twenty feet at most, but the theatre was divided so that two operations could be carried out at once.

The out-patients and emergency department was in the old PRCS clinic of 1985, separated from the operating theatre and ward block by a narrow alley. It also contained the X-ray department. The small portable X-ray machine had been put to full use, and had been skilfully adapted to produce intravenous urograms and other specialised contrast films. There was a laboratory, a blood bank, and a room for dentistry. The pharmacy stores and dispensary were in yet another building. Across from this was Chris Giannou's office – the kitchen pantry. There Giannou, the chief surgeon of Shatila camp and the Director of Shatila Hospital, would sit on a wooden stool behind a small square wooden table and carry out his administrative responsibilities. Visitors would have to find themselves seats on sacks of rice, on the floor or on large containers of cooking oil, paraffin or detergent.

'Mine is a low-cost outfit,' said Chris with a chuckle. The next room was the kitchen proper, about twenty feet square, and from here eighty hospital meals were churned out three times a day. The staff dining room, next to the kitchen, was half its size. It had a long wooden table and two rows of wooden benches, where hospital staff sat to eat, and also had meetings. This hospital was the most compact and efficient set-up I had ever come across. Many of the PRCS staff recognised me, and here in the hospital, out of the view of the Amal, we were free to embrace and kiss each other.

As I hurried to leave, I heard people saying from all around, 'Good, Doctora Swee, we are very good. Please don't worry. Come back and see us again.' With these words of reassurance in my ears, I hastily left for the Syrian checkpoint, to pick up my travel document and leave Shatila.

CHAPTER 27

That evening, back in the NORWAC flat in Hamra, I felt drained and exhausted, but I could not sleep. When I did manage to sleep, I was crying in my dreams. Shatila camp now had food, but would the Palestinians be strong enough to rebuild their broken community yet again? They had been imprisoned in their ruins for nearly two years. Shatila was now a terribly deprived and dangerous place – a concentration camp. Deprived, because it was little more than an open demolition site, without water, electricity or any semblance of social life. Dangerous, because Amal could fire bullets and shells into the camp at any time without warning.

I lay in bed thinking of my friend Nahla, whom I had hoped to see this time. In 1982 she had been with me in Gaza Hospital, training to be a nurse. In 1985, when Sabra and Shatila were attacked, Nahla gave up nursing and fought to defend the camp. When Shatila camp ran out of ammunition, Nahla braved the Amal tanks to buy bullets. Four women brought thirty-five thousand rounds into the camp. In 1985, Nahla had been wounded and in hiding. I could not visit her, because she was on Amal's 'wanted' list.

While I was on my way to Beirut in April 1987, I learnt that Nahla was dead. Now the reunion we planned would never take place in this world. I kept asking myself if Nahla's fate was a reflection of Shatila's. But Nahla had been strong, and though her military career was short and she died young, she had already become a major when she lost her life. I just could not sleep that night, and I wrote a poem to Nahla. In the poem, I mourned her death, and especially how I had missed being by her side when she died. At the time of her death Nahla had just become engaged, and I thought of the bridal gown she would never put on.

Time passed slowly until, just before dawn, I gave up the idea of sleeping. I got up, washed myself and waited for Øyvind to wake up. We were to go to meet the Syrians today, to negotiate a safe conduct for Pauline Cutting and her team out of Bourj el-Brajneh camp. Amal had formally threatened to kill Pauline and Susan once they ventured out of the camp. We knew that they meant what they said. Only the Syrians could stop them, and so Øyvind and I were going to negotiate directly with General Ghazi Kanaan, the head of the Syrian Intelligence in Lebanon.

We arrived at the Beau Rivage, once a famous Beirut hotel, now taken over by the Syrians as their military intelligence headquarters. General Kanaan had gone to Damascus, but his deputy agreed to see us. After my hassles with Amal at Shatila the day before, the Syrians seemed very civilised indeed. I gave the Syrian official standing in for General Kanaan a copy of my letter to President Assad, and asked if they would escort our medical team out of the camp. It was difficult to communicate, as the Syrian officials in this particular office only spoke Arabic and French, and Øyvind and I could only come up with English, Norwegian and Chinese. But they seemed to guess what we were after and sent for Major Waleed Hassanato, the Syrian intelligence officer in charge of the Beirut camps, so that he could take me to Bourj el-Brajneh to see the MAP team.

In his early thirties, Major Waleed had a round face with

a well-trimmed moustache. My first impression of him was that his manners were pleasant and cultured. It was difficult to imagine him dealing harshly with Palestinians on his wanted list, but many in the camps said he could be an absolute terror when exercising his power as the intelligence officer in charge.

Major Waleed decided to drive Øyvind and myself to Bourj el-Brajneh camp to ask Pauline Cutting and our trapped team if they wanted to leave. We were shown to his car, and set off. The whole situation was very bizarre. In a way it was lucky that I had forgotten nearly all my Arabic, because I was able to maintain very polite relations with Major Waleed, who spoke nothing else.

About all I could say in Arabic was, 'Thank you,' so I said this whenever it seemed appropriate. Major Waleed was very kind and proper, and each time replied, 'You are most welcome, doctor,' in Arabic.

He dropped us off at an office belonging to a pro-Syrian Palestinian faction in Bourj el-Brajneh and said he would be back at 1 PM to collect us. That would give us time to speak to our people. After Major Waleed left, I went to Haifa Hospital to look for Pauline and company. The hospital was still there, but it was in a terrible state. Pauline Cutting was very, very thin. So was Ben Alofs. And I met Susan Wighton and Hannes for the first time. They were all in good spirits.

It was difficult to tell them it was time to go back home to be with their families, because in fact none of them wanted to go. The people of Bourj el-Brajneh would be upset too. For a moment, I wondered if I had any right to raise the question of the team leaving. In the end I decided to be unpopular. Six months in this dreadful siege was enough, and they needed a break. If they wanted to come back after they had seen their families, MAP could always send them out again. After warm embraces and greetings, I pulled myself together and asked, 'When do you people want to leave? Your families are all very worried about you. I have to make arrangements with the Syrians.'

There was complete silence. I felt that I had uttered the unutterable. But then Pauline suggested that they could leave on Monday 13 April. They said they wanted to spend a few days in Mar Elias camp to be with friends, and were obviously convinced that Mar Elias camp was very safe. They seemed to have forgotten that some of the team had received clear death threats, not to mention that scores of journalists were waiting to get hold of them once they were outside the camp.

'I'll have to discuss that with Um Walid and the people in Mar Elias,' I said; 'but if we work on you leaving on Monday morning from here and perhaps going to Mar Elias camp – we can take it from there. I'll also have to contact the British Ambassador to take you across the Green Line to catch the boat – Beirut airport is still closed. I suppose all your visas have expired by now?'

We all agreed to this plan, and I went to have a look round the hospital. The top two floors had been blown off by shells, and the rest of Haifa Hospital had neither water nor electricity. The walls were dark, damp and mouldy. But I was glad to find many old friends – Nuha, Dr Reda, Ahmed Diep the anaesthetic technician and others. They were all PRCS medics, and had been through four camp wars over the past two years. I had first met Dr Reda, the director of Haifa Hospital, and Nuha the theatre sister in 1985. I had known Ahmed Diep since the days of Gaza Hospital in 1982: he was one of those who worked many long hours in the basement operating theatre during the Beirut massacres, till Azziza ordered him to leave on Friday, just before the hospital was overrun by the murderers. He was an excellent anaesthetist, and I could trust him to anaesthetise poor risk patients for very major surgery. My friends all looked exhausted, but were eager to tell me about the recent camp war.

As we were talking, someone suddenly came up with a message for me: 'Doctora, Major Waleed has arrived, and wants you to leave now.'

Ben Alofs stared at me with astonishment, and said, 'This is Waleed Hassanato, the Syrian?'

I knew why he was surprised, but it was impossible to explain everything in a short time. 'Yes,' I said, 'Major Waleed Hassanato. He has agreed to provide security for your leaving, you see.'

Ben looked even more astounded. Because Syria supplied the Amal besiegers with arms and advice, many people in the camps saw the Syrian Army as the allies of Amal. Syria justified its support for Amal by stressing their reputation as a significant part of the anti-Israeli 'South Lebanese Resistance'. This fitted in with Syria's anti-Zionist stand: the Israelis had occupied South Lebanon, Palestine, the Golan Heights and neighbouring Arab territories, lands which Syria claimed were historically part of 'greater Syria', and so Syria supported Amal in their fight against the Israelis.

Nobody ever gave me a convincing explanation of how tanks and guns supplied to Amal to fight the Israelis ended up being turned against the Palestinian refugee camps. My own suspicion, after asking many different groups, was that Amal was under pressure from the Israelis to attack the Palestinians. In the south, the Palestinians had accused Amal of making a deal with the Israelis to empty out the Palestinian population, thereby ensuring the security of Israel's northern border. Amal of course denied it. But the Palestinians said that they had arrested three Israeli advisers working side by side with Amal when Palestinian fighters captured the village of Magdoushe, near Saida, in 1986. If that were true, then Amal obviously collaborated with Israel, and that would explain why they were so vicious towards the Palestinians.

But Amal had their own explanation for the camp war. Many times, I had been pulled up short by Amal officials and told that the Palestinians brought just too many disasters to Lebanon. If it were not for the Palestinians, they told me, Lebanon would never have been bombed and destroyed so cruelly by the Israelis. Lebanon had suffered enough playing host to the Palestinians. Amal feared a repeat of the full-scale Israeli invasion of 1982. They were especially annoyed that the Palestinians in the refugee camps dared to arm themselves. One Amal person asked me: 'Tell me, doctor, which Arab capital would ever allow a group of refugees to carry arms?'

Of course, he did not realise he was talking to me, a survivor of the 1982 Sabra-Shatila massacres, which happened precisely because the Palestinians were dis-armed. I had seen the state of Shatila and Bourj el-Brajneh camps in 1987. How could anyone ask the Palestinians to surrender their right to self-defence, so that a repeat of the massacres of 1982 could take place? Teenage Palestinian fighters in Shatila camp could never be persuaded to surrender their Kalashnikovs, not after the bitterness of 1982 and the last two years of siege. They had lost their right to a homeland, to security in exile, and their very existence was now being challenged. Who would dare ask them to surrender the right to life? One woman fighter in Shatila camp told me: 'They have to recognise us, because we fight back. They want to make us anonymous, wipe us out and bury us in mass graves, but we will die fighting.'

The last few decades in the Middle East have seen at least four major conflicts. These are between Iran and Iraq, between the Israelis and the Arabs, between the Israelis and the Palestinians and between the Arabs and the Palestinians. With the exception of the Iran-Iraq war, the conflicts revolve round Israel and Palestine.

The conflict between the Israelis and the Arabs has resulted in a number of wars between Israel and Arab countries. Israel has invaded and occupied not only the Gaza Strip and the West Bank, but also the Golan Heights, which are part of Syria. The Israeli air force has attacked various Arab countries – Iraq, Tunisia, Syria, Lebanon and Egypt are a few examples. I have heard Israeli politicians boast that they have fought and won five major wars against their Arab neighbours: 1948, 1956, 1967, 1973 and 1982. The last of these was not really a 'genuine' war between Israel and one of its neighbours. Although Lebanon is still suffering from the phenomenal damage to the country's economy and society, the 1982 war was really between Israel and the PLO.

The Palestinian-Israeli conflict exists because Israel could only be created over the destruction of Palestine and the expulsion of its people. In 1988, the State of Israel celebrated forty years of existence; while the Palestinian exiles remembered the loss of their homeland. For Israel to flourish, all traces of Palestine had to be obliterated. The wounds inflicted by Israel go on festering; Israeli bombs cause death and destruction; torture and mutilation in Israeli detention camps, such as the Ansar camps, will take more than a lifetime to fade from the memory. And Israelis complain that the Palestinians refuse to 'recognise' the State of Israel. After being forced to give up their country, their homes – even their lives – the Palestinians are being asked to surrender their souls to the victors.

The Palestinian-Arab conflict is still more complicated. Some argue that it arises from the conflict between host countries and refugees. But the Palestinians are *exiles*, not refugees, and they want to go home. The host countries support them, in principle, at least. But when the Palestinians use the host countries as bases to launch attacks into Israel, the host countries suffer Israel's revenge: one rocket fired into Galilee would mean the flattening of dozens of Lebanese villages by Israeli air raids. This has led to Palestinian-Arab conflicts, but it is a tribute to the courage of the Arab people that in spite of the price they still supported the Palestinian struggle. A further complication in the case of Syria arises from an unresolved issue. Is Palestine part of Greater Syria? Does Arafat – the Chairman of the PLO – or Assad – Syria's leader – have the right to speak for the Palestinians?

I am not an Arab, nor am I a Muslim. I am not a

European, and I have neither the difficulty of living with the guilt of Nazism, nor responsibility for the British Mandate in Palestine. For me, supporting the Palestinians is not a political matter: it is my human responsibility. They seek to return home. Failing that, they demand the right to a decent life in exile: the right to exist. Their demands are just. I support them. Because I have no political angle, I was able to ask the Syrians to protect our medical volunteers so that our work in the camps could continue.

Some people discussed the fact that a few days earlier Syria had been supporting Amal's attacks on the camps. Now Syrian troops had taken control of the camp entrances to stop the Palestinian women being sniped at, and were escorting food convoys into the camps. I did not have the luxury of wondering about the whys and wherefores of it. If the Syrians were now the friends of the Palestinians, then they were my friends too, for the time being. I did not speculate about the next day, or the next week. It was all as fragile as desert moisture, but while there was time to breathe, to eat and to live, people had to seize the opportunity. Women made repeated trips back and forth bringing food and water for their families. While the ceasefire imposed by the Syrians lasted, they were making the most of it.

When we arrived back at the political office where the Syrian major had arranged to pick us up, I could see a large crowd which had congregated to greet a United Nations relief convoy loaded with sacks of flour. Children and women were clapping and cheering as Syrian troops escorted the convoy on its way into the camp. Meanwhile, behind the political office, the body of a woman had been dug out of a temporary grave to be taken to the cemetery. She was one of the women killed while trying to get food for the camp during the siege. As her exhumed body, wrapped in a large plastic bag, was carried past, its stench was evil. It reminded me of the mutilated, decaying corpses of the 1982 massacres. Was the camp celebrating the ceasefire, or mourning the loss of loved ones?

Øyvind and I told Major Waleed that our people would be ready to leave on Monday 13 April. He asked us to contact the British Ambassador and request him to provide security across the Green Line, as the Syrians did not control Christian East Beirut. So Pauline and the rest of the MAP team would be the responsibility of the Syrians from Bourj el-Brajneh as far as the British Consulate in West Beirut, and from there to the ferry at Jounieh they would have to be the responsibility of the British Ambassador, John Gray.

Having made these provisional arrangements, we bade Major Waleed farewell. The British Ambassador kindly met me, and agreed to provide security for Pauline, Susan, Hannes, Ben – and Chris Giannou, if he decided to leave as well. Chris's mother had contacted Um Walid, and expressed concern over her son, and Um Walid thought that it was about time Chris left Shatila camp for a break.

So Monday 13 April was to be the day of the great team swap. New foreign nurses and doctors were going into Bourj and Shatila, and those who had worked so tirelessly throughout the siege were going to be able to leave. I was told to call at Major Waleed's office at nine in the morning. His soldiers showed me to his office, and I found him just getting out of bed. He was acutely embarrassed at my bursting into his office while he was trying to put on his shoes and socks. I tried to assure him everything was all right. Not only was I a doctor, but I was so happily married. I pulled out of my wallet a picture of my husband Francis with his precious black-and-white tabby cat, Meowie.

The major's soldiers all studied the picture closely, and then declared their admiration for the beauty of the Meowie cat, and the kindness of my husband's face. Then they expressed their regret at the fact that I had not produced any children for my husband, so that the poor man only had a cat for company while I was away. They even suggested that Francis should find himself a good Syrian wife so that she would give him many, many children. I found their advice totally unacceptable. But I guess they were only winding me up.

The Syrian intelligence officers first went to Bourj el-Brajneh to get the foreigners out, and drove them to Mar Elias camp. We then went on to Shatila camp to ask Chris Giannou whether he wanted to leave or not. I had sent a message to Chris the night before asking him to be packed and ready if he wanted to leave for Canada. Major Waleed stopped his car at the camp checkpoint and told me through an interpreter to go and fetch Chris. I found him in the hospital kitchen, and told him Major Waleed was at the checkpoint, waiting to escort him to the British Embassy.

Chris refused point blank to come. 'Look,' he said, 'I just can't leave. There is too much to do. Apart from that, if I left now it would be very bad for the morale of the camp. I'll try to talk to my mother and reassure her that I'm okay.'

'Well, Chris,' I said, 'I must say I'm really proud of your commitment, but at least will you go out and thank Major Waleed for coming all this way to get you, otherwise I am going to look like a fool.'

So he came out with me and we went to the checkpoint, where he spoke to Major Waleed in Arabic, before walking back into the besieged camp. Major Waleed was not too pleased that Chris had turned down his offer of help, but the glimpse of Chris Giannou as we drove away, skin and bones covered with a tattered old blanket, proudly walking back into Shatila, on the morning of 13 April, will always stay in my mind.

On Easter Sunday, I persuaded Øyvind he ought to take a day off, and go up to the mountains. I wanted to be alone in the NORWAC flat to read the Bible, to pray and thank God for getting Pauline and her team safely home, having heard on the BBC World Service news that they had arrived safely in Britain. I turned to the letter of the Apostle Paul to the Roman believers. I read, 'Nay, in all these things we are more than conquerors through him that loved us. For I am persuaded, that neither death, nor life, nor angels, nor principalities, nor powers, nor things present, nor things to come, nor height, nor depth, nor any other creature, shall be able to separate us from the love of God, which is in Christ Jesus our Lord.' (Romans, VIII, 37–39). Over the years, I have seen much destruction and death, but I have seen so much love and faith that I am fully assured God is still there.

After my meditations the Lord brought me a wonderful visitor: old Dr Said Dajani. I had first met him in 1982, and had always respected him. He founded the PRCS nursing school in Lebanon, and was the medical director of the PRCS doctors in Lebanon for many years. He taught in numerous medical schools in Lebanon, and many of those he taught have now become well-known specialists. He was nearly eighty, and his hair was pure white, but his face still carried the wonder of a young child. We had a long, long chat and the poor old man cried. The past four and a half years of hell had just been too much. His PRCS nursing school had been closed, and opened, and closed again so many times. At the moment it was closed. His wife had breast cancer, and his knees were full of arthritis. But then he said something wonderful: 'It has got into my head that somehow I will die in Palestine – so I cannot possibly die here.'

Then he spoke enthusiastically of Palestine. What a wonderful thing it would be if old Dr Dajani was back in Palestine, and we could all go to visit him there! I looked at the face of this kind and gentle Palestinian doctor and thought of the pain and anguish he must have suffered over the years. Yet there was no bitterness or hatred – just faith and a radiant smile when he talked about Palestine. He told me of three battles he had won in his life.

The first, not a peculiarly Palestinian problem, was

giving up smoking. He used to smoke ninety cigarettes a day. He had a major battle with that, but won, and gave up smoking.

Then he had a more moving story to tell. In 1947, Dr Dajani was on his way to the United States to attend a medical conference as medical director of the Palestine Medical Services. Stopping over in Paris, he heard the news of the decision to partition Palestine and he knew there would be great trouble in his country. He knew he could go on to the United States and call it quits – or return. It was a great struggle – one voice said, 'Dajani, you are a coward, running away.' Another said, 'No, you are not a coward, you are going back.' He finally returned to Jaffa to direct the medical services during those very difficult days. War, chaos and many wounded people awaited his return.

Then there was the time after 1983 when the American Embassy in West Beirut was bombed. The Americans retaliated by shelling and bombarding West Beirut. It was a terrible time, and friends from Australia, Denmark and Spain offered to get him out, but eventually he decided to stay. 'Run away?' he asked me rhetorically. 'No, I am not a coward.' So he stayed. Then came the camp wars, and the Amal's reign of terror against Palestinians. He stayed on. Today, he was talking enthusiastically about reopening the School of Nursing which had been closed down during the camp wars. I felt proud to meet a senior colleague of such great moral strength and courage.

Dr Dajani told me about when he was setting up medical services in Sour city in south Lebanon, then an area of great poverty. One day, he passed a house and heard children crying. He pushed open the door. The parents were too embarrassed to tell him why the kids were crying, but it was obvious they were hungry. So Said Dajani went out, got bread, cheese and olives and fed the kids. The children then started to laugh and play, but the doctor and their parents wept.

Before the Sour hospital was built, he used to spend

nights sleeping on the sand. One morning, he woke up to find that someone had covered him with an old blanket. He was very grateful, but had never found out whom he had to thank. This story is typical of Lebanon – a place where kindness and generosity abound in the midst of poverty and war.

Then I told him about all the trouble I had trying to get a visa. He was very upset and said, 'They refused you a visa because they didn't want you to come to help the Palestinians. Is helping the Palestinians a crime? How cruel can people get?'

But I told him not to worry: they would have to try harder before they could stop me being a friend of the Palestinians. He laughed at my cheek, said goodbye and wished all of us well.

CHAPTER 28

The following days were chaotic and hectic. It was fortunate that the Italian Dr Alberto Gregori was able to work as MAP's volunteer surgeon in Haifa Hospital while I ran around doing other things. Alberto was great, and was loved by the camp people, who nicknamed him 'Abu Garfil' – after his toy cat, Garfield. Soon he began to look like a Palestinian – and was in fact stopped at the checkpoint for questioning because the Syrian intelligence thought he was a Palestinian disguised as an Italian doctor.

His MAP volunteer colleague, an Australian anaesthetist called Dr Murray Luddington, had meanwhile gone into Shatila camp. Murray caught the Palestinian 'bug'. Within a few days of entering the camp he wrote his letter of resignation to his British hospital – which till then had kept his job open for him. He asked them to look for another anaesthetist, because he had chosen to stay with the Palestinians in Shatila camp. He soon began to look more scruffy than the camp people, and they had to get him decent clothes to wear. His Arabic improved, and before long he could argue with the hospital cook, and answer the Amal at checkpoints with not so polite words. He was never mistaken for a Palestinian, but his large beard often got him nearly arrested. In those days, only members of the

Lebanese Shi'ite Hezbollah (Party of God) wore beards – and neither the Syrian Army nor Amal got on too well with Hezbollah.

Soon Alberto left, and I had to take up the post of surgeon in Haifa Hospital. It would have been great if only I could have stayed in Haifa Hospital to work properly as a surgeon. But at that time the Palestinians needed more than a surgeon. They needed someone to run around and organise the bringing of medical supplies, negotiate arrangements for fuel and food to come into the camps, and evacuate wounded people out of the camps to different European countries for specialised medical treatment. As team leader, I found myself doing all this during the day, and doubling up as resident surgeon at night as well. This was important, as people were still injured at night, and needed surgical attention. As the siege was still in force they could not be transported out of the camp for treatment.

Spending the night in the camp after a hectic day's running around was not always easy. Whether I slept in Haifa Hospital, or in the clinic at the opposite end of the camp, I would usually find myself either talking late into the middle of the night, or being kept up by people with all sorts of complaints, not necessarily medical. The atmosphere in the camp remained tense. I would jump when a door slammed shut, thinking an explosion had gone off. An innocent event such as the loudspeaker of the Bourj el-Brajneh mosque asking for blood donors would find me racing uphill from the clinic to Haifa Hospital thinking that fighting had broken out, and the wounded needed attention. It was usually just an open call for blood, not an emergency. I really had no reason to be so neurotic and on tenterhooks, as the PRCS doctors were extremely competent. They had worked through the long siege, and had saved so many lives, and there was nothing I could do which they could not do better.

One morning, Ahmed Diep, the anaesthetist, knocked

frantically on the clinic door at 4 AM: 'Doctora Swee,' he shouted, 'urgent laparotomy in Haifa Hospital.'

We ran uphill towards the hospital on the uneven, winding camp alleys, tripping over rubble, water pipes, and puddles of water. In the emergency room of Haifa Hospital was a young man who had shot himself in the abdomen. The PRCS doctors had already resuscitated him, set up a drip and organised blood for him. Nuha, the theatre sister, had already got ready for a major abdominal operation. Dr Nasser, the surgical resident on duty that night, was already changed and scrubbed in theatre. They only sent for me because some of these gunshot wounds could be very nasty, and it would be good to have an older surgeon around to give a hand.

Dr Nasser did most of the operation, with me assisting. The bullet, as one might have predicted, had gone through the front of the abdomen, hitting the small intestine in two different places, the edge of the liver, the large intestine in three different places, and coming out through the pelvic bone behind. Ahmed Diep gave an excellent anaesthetic; and Nuha and Dr Nasser both performed extremely well.

The only mistake was mine. I decided to take the chance of not doing a 'defunctioning colostomy' – a procedure regarded by many surgeons as mandatory in these circumstances. This meant pulling a loop of large bowel out of the body at a point before the injuries and making a hole in it, so that all intestinal contents drained out through this opening. In this way, no fecal material would pass through the injured portions of the bowel, thereby minimising contamination, as they slowly healed. I took a stupid risk, and even told Dr Nasser that at worst, the patient would develop a fecal fistula (or abnormal passage) through the exit wound of the bullet, and we would face the problem when it arose. The patient of course did exactly that, and had to undergo a second operation for a defunctioning colostomy and resection of fecal fistula.

Thank God the patient survived. Nuha gave me the

scalpel towards the end of the first operation thinking that I would do a colostomy, and nearly dropped to the floor when I said, 'It is probably going to be all right, Nuha. Let's take a chance.' Now I sheepishly remembered the words of the surgeon who first taught me surgery: 'The thing to do is to anticipate trouble and avoid it. Do not deliberately get into trouble and then try to get out of it.' Nuha still laughed kindly at me whenever we talked about this, months later.

As all the camps were still besieged, every piece of equipment had to be brought in by special negotiation and with written permission of the Syrian Intelligence, who in turn had to inform Amal they had authorised it. Life was very, very miserable. For instance, just to apply for permission for a Palestinian doctor to leave Shatila to visit his father in a West Beirut hospital outside the camp could take me up to five visits to the Syrian military intelligence. On each visit I might have to wait three or four hours, often in the hot sun, sometimes late into the night. This was bureaucracy carried to unprecedented lengths.

The Palestinians did not need my medical skills, because the PRCS had many well-trained doctors and nurses. At the height of the camp war, as many as sixty PRCS doctors and nurses were trapped in the camps. This was not surprising, if one bears in mind that before 1982 the PRCS provided medical care on demand to West Beirut and all of southern Lebanon. Now there was a ceasefire, what the camp hospitals needed was to replenish their stores of medicine, oxygen, nitrous oxide and surgical equipment, and to stock up in case of a new attack on the camps. Someone had to cross the checkpoints with stores for the hospitals. Only the Palestinians could have persuaded me, a British-trained surgeon, to take on the job of a truck driver, and to spend hours at the Syrian intelligence office waiting for permission to bring things into the camps.

The first permit to bring an ambulance-load of medicines into the camps took ages to obtain. The permit had to come from the Syrian Intelligence, and so the bureaucracy swung into action. Once the request was tabled, days passed with no response. I threatened to fly back to Britain with all the medicines and announce to the British public that the Syrians were preventing medical aid getting to the camps. They were furious with me, but in the end relented. The four tons of medicines, gifts donated by the British public, got into the camps bit by bit.

The Palestinians in Bourj el-Brajneh camp fixed up an old, battered ambulance for me to drive around fetching food, medicines, electric cables, blankets, paraffin, furniture – and even a coffin on one occasion – in and sometimes out of the camp. When I had time to think about it, I shuddered to think of what my medical colleagues back in Britain would make of me, a woman Fellow of the Royal College of Surgeons of England, reduced to an ambulance driver – no, even worse, a truck driver. I was very happy to be a truck driver, but in class-conscious Britain doctors are respected and truck drivers are not.

As it happened, I was not even a good truck driver, because I was born with a very poor sense of direction. Quite often, I drove east when I meant to go west, and in Lebanon that could be dangerous. One day, I drove the wrong way along the coast road and found myself on the non-civilian crossing on the Green Line. This was the 'Museum Crossing' and only vehicles with special permission from the military were allowed to pass. I was promptly detained at the checkpoint and questioned. After a while, the soldiers were convinced that I was genuinely lost, and one of them jumped into the ambulance and directed me back to where I wanted to go. From then on, I took care to carry a compass with me wherever I drove.

Driving a new car in West Beirut was not the easiest thing in the world. To drive a battered old ambulance without any signal lights or mirrors and a gearbox that was about to fall off was a real challenge. There was no glass in the windscreen, but the windscreen wiper miraculously survived and sprang into action at the slightest provocation. The first time I drove it out of Bourj el-Brajneh camp, the Syrian soldiers at the checkpoint were astonished to see this 'thing' come out of the camp and they ran towards it. Only then did they realise that it had a driver. I was so small that they could not see me, and thought the old heap of rust had taken off on its own!

Driving that ambulance was difficult for yet another reason. People from Britain were accustomed to driving on the left. You were supposed to drive on the right in Beirut – but in practice you drove wherever you could. When you approached a junction, the thing to do was not to stop, otherwise you would be waiting all day to cross. You simply had to keep going and expect the other vehicles to stop. It was a test of nerves. None of the principles of good driving learnt in the British School of Motoring applied. If the traffic lights went red, you put your foot down and got across quickly, or else the driver behind would get really irate. Pedestrians would cross the road anywhere, and often walked straight in front of cars.

I used to stop at the Syrian checkpoint, and show the intelligence officer my permit for driving the ambulance, signed by Major Waleed Hassanato, which might read: 'Doctora Swee is given permission to drive the ambulance out of the camp and return with it with five oxygen and five nitrous oxide cylinders and thirty boxes of medicines for Haifa Hospital. She and the ambulance have to be searched thoroughly as she leaves and enters the camp. Date. . .' The permit was good for one trip only, and I would have to apply for a fresh permit each time I made a trip to fetch supplies for the hospital.

Once the intelligence officer was satisfied that my permit was not a fake, he would let me go. The Syrian soldiers would then usually walk on to the airport road and stop the traffic so that I could turn right into the main road without crashing. I suppose they trusted neither my driving nor the dodgy vehicle.

Heading north along the airport road, after a couple of

turns, I would soon arrive at Kola, the flyover near the Arab University. This is if the ambulance did not fall into a shell crater and become stuck, in which case some kind person would have to help me lift it out. On the way I would pass Akka Hospital, the Sports Stadium, the Fakhani entrance of Shatila camp and several checkpoints. Apart from stopping at each checkpoint to show my identity card, I also ended up treating patients, examining them and giving out medications, or writing out referral slips for them to be seen at the PRCS clinic in Mar Elias.

The Amal soldiers, the Syrian soldiers and all sorts of other people on the roads in the southern suburbs of Beirut soon found out that the driver of the battered old ambulance was also a doctor. They knew I would stop at various checkpoints to treat people for their skin diseases, coughs and colds, diarrhoea and vomiting, aches and pains. The ambulance always had a generous supply of 'checkpoint medicines', and sometimes I would make an extra trip and return with more. (To get to Shatila camp, for instance, I had to drive past all the Amal checkpoints, which meant driving past the families of the Amal men. To start with the soldiers would make me halt and threaten me with their rocket launchers, but after a while they brought their children or wives to see me for medical advice. Then the Syrian soldiers did the same too.)

If the weather was not too hot, I wore a large Hezbollah scarf round my head. This signalled to everyone that I was a believer in God, and not a loose foreigner. It stopped curious male strangers wanting to know my name, and whether I was married or looking for a boyfriend. Nobody dared to look at me.

The stretch of road from Kola to Mar Elias camp was always bad for traffic jams. So it saved time to drive along the back streets on the wrong side of the road. If the army stopped me for driving on the wrong side, I would just say: 'Maa bariff, ana ajnabiya.' (I don't know, I am a foreigner.)

Mar Elias camp was a sort of headquarters for me, as the four tons of medicines and surgical equipment was stored in the PRCS warehouse there. My ambulance was small, and Major Waleed would never allow me to load it up fully. There was still a siege, and Amal would only allow small quantities of medicines to be brought into the camp each time. In fact, they were very cross that the Syrians had allowed me to drive things in and out of the camps at all, and had threatened to fire on the ambulance when I passed Amal areas. But I believed my life was in the hands of God, and tried not to be fearful. I also trusted that the Syrians would probably take action if I was killed on errands they had authorised. In fact, when the security situation around the camps was bad, and fighting had broken out, Major Waleed's men would often stop me from going near the camps. When things calmed down, they would then instruct me to go ahead.

Once the ambulance was loaded with medical supplies from Mar Elias, I would leave for the camps, either for Shatila or Bourj. Sometimes when the ambulance carried oxygen cylinders I was really worried, as one bullet fired into them would explode the whole outfit. Fortunately no one had tried that yet. At the camp checkpoint, I would stop, get down and show my permit to the Syrian officer. Then each box of medicine had to be carried down from the ambulance, opened and searched. The doors of the ambulance would be tapped, the wheels and seats inspected. The camp women would then come out, and carry the boxes of medicines, intravenous fluids and surgical supplies on their backs to the hospital. Palestinian women had to carry these by hand as under the ceasefire and provision of rations agreement, only what a woman could physically carry was allowed into the camps. This was a most inefficient way of doing things, and I sometimes spent up to two or three hours at the camp checkpoints. But it was a tremendous improvement over a total siege, and we were thankful for any way of getting things done.

Life in the besieged camps was still miserable. While the city of Beirut lit up at night with electric lights, the Palestinian refugee camps remained discreetly dark. Children often tripped over rubble and twisted cables in the darkness, and broke their little ankles. There was no electricity. Even dry cell batteries and accumulators were kept out of the camps. The electric generators in the camps were old and overworked and they slowly packed up, making life even more difficult. The Palestinians had managed to tap or 'siphon' electricity from the homes of Amal families living near the camps. They never told me how or when this was done, but a frequent request was for me to obtain permission for x metres of cable to enter the camp, so that they could wire up the clinics and hospitals to the electricity of Amal.

Once, I really put my foot in it. There had been a changeover of Syrian troops, and Alberto took the new lieutenant to have a look at Haifa Hospital. Being new, he was flabbergasted at the terrible conditions there, and asked if he could do anything to help. The hospital administrator asked him if the generator could be taken out to be repaired. With electricity, the hospital would at least be lit up, and people could clean and wash the walls. The Syrian lieutenant said he could not authorise that, but suddenly had the bright idea of letting Haifa Hospital 'siphon' off electricity from the Syrian station about half a kilometre down the road. I was asked to procure a kilometre of 25-cm diameter composite cable, comprising four individual cable bundles, for the hospital to use to tap electricity from the Syrian station.

Major Waleed got back from Damascus just in time to scupper the whole exercise. We were all hauled up for a real telling off from him. Haifa Hospital continued in darkness for some time. The major's anger worried me, for he could easily suspend my permit to drive the ambulance and transport medical supplies into the camps. So far, he had allowed me to do many things for the Palestinians which he considered 'humanitarian'.

Major Waleed asked me several times if I was trying to help 'pro-Arafat' Palestinians. The Syrian Government was opposed to the PLO head, Yasser Arafat. But I said I was here to help all Palestinians. Indeed, I told him, if I was prepared to treat Amal people – who had attacked the camps – it should be clear that I was not about to discriminate in favour of those Palestinians who supported Arafat. That was an internal problem of the Syrians and Palestinians, in which I had no power or even right to interfere. That reply was perfectly satisfactory to the Syrian Intelligence.

Eventually the Syrians granted us permission to take the Haifa Hospital generator out of the camp for repairs. The truth was that the generator was beyond repair. The Syrians knew that I was taking it out to dump it, and that a new one would be brought into the camp, but they were so sick of me pestering them day and night they agreed to let us take it out.

Kazeem Hassan Bedawi, a friend who was also the administrator of the Palestine Red Crescent outside the camp, was told by Dr Osman to help me with the generator. Kazeem is tall and light-complexioned, with brown eyes. A statistician by training, his services to the PRCS were greatly valued. Kazeem and I first met in 1985, in Haifa Hospital over lunch. While we were eating, he suddenly took off his shirt, and showed me the scar on his abdomen. Alison, who had just arrived in Haifa Hospital and was still settling in, was stunned to see me trying to examine him with my mouth stuffed full of food. In 1987, Kazeem had been transferred from Haifa Hospital to work in Mar Elias camp, which was not besieged.

We went out early to hire a forklift to take the old generator out of Haifa Hospital. We then returned with the new one. We had finished unloading it from the forklift and we were about to leave the Hospital, when someone came with a message saying that Major Waleed wanted to see us. We started towards his office, on the outskirts of the camp.

A couple of Syrian intelligence officers intercepted us round the corner from Haifa Hospital and abducted Kazeem. They took him away. The two of us had been so pleased at being able to replace the generator that we both forgot that Kazeem was a male Palestinian, and should not go anywhere near the Syrian intelligence. We had not realised this was a trap. I have not seen Kazeem since that day. I learnt from his friend that he was beaten up, accused of being an Arafat supporter and carted off to jail in the Syrian capital, Damascus. His Lebanese wife was six months pregnant at the time, and she has since given birth to their first child.

This incident shook me to the core, and I was unable to function at all for a few days. But then a Palestinian lawyer I knew had a few words with me. She told me I must stop thinking of Kazeem and get on with supplying the camps. Somewhat younger than Um Walid, and a very strong personality, my lawyer friend looked at me sitting there miserably and said, 'Swee, I know how you feel. But you must stop yourself from feeling bad. The Syrians did this, first because they wanted Kazeem anyway, and second because they want to intimidate you so that you will stop working for our people. To work with us Palestinians, you have to be able to contract to this small.' She held her thumb and index finger together. 'And at times you have to be this big,' and she stretched out her arms to their full span. She gave me a big hug, and continued, 'There is a lot of work only you can do, and you must carry on.'

Of course she was right, and I pulled myself together and continued loading up the battered ambulance with food and medicines for the camps, putting that dreadful incident behind me. But sometimes when I walked past Kazeem's office in Mar Elias camp, his words echoed in my mind: 'Can you wait for me till I come back from Waleed Hassanato's office?'

I went up to the office of the Syrian military intelligence several times to demand an explanation. There was none.

Another job I did not particularly enjoy was arranging for wounded Palestinians to go abroad for specialist treatment. First, few Palestinians in the camps had travel documents; they carried only refugee identity cards with their names, places and dates of birth. The identity card had to be submitted to the Lebanese authorities so that proper travel documents could be drawn up. The procedure was lengthy and complicated, unless it was speeded up by bribing officials.

Once the travel document had been obtained, the next problem was obtaining visas. Most Western countries have reservations about granting visas to Lebanese Palestinians, and only do so if they receive instructions from hospitals or specialist centres, together with financial guarantees. As the postal system had broken down in Lebanon, even a simple letter of recommendation had to be sent by courier.

Once the visas had been fixed up, then someone – me, for example – would have to call in at the Syrian Intelligence with copies of the clinical case reports and photocopies of the travel documents with the visas. The Syrians would then make sure that the patients applying to leave the camp for treatment overseas were not on their list of people wanted for pro-Arafat activities. This would usually take a few days, and if the patient was 'in the clear', permission would be granted.

If the patient was on the wrong side politically, I would be called to the Syrian Intelligence office and told not to help Arafat supporters escape. Most times, I would be let off lightly, as I was a foreigner, and ill-informed about Palestinian factional politics. Sometimes, the Syrian intelligence officer would be so astounded by my ignorance that he would tell me: 'Look, Doctora Swee, we all want to facilitate your efforts to help the wounded. But we notice that you're playing into the hands of Arafat supporters, and this is a very bad thing.' I would usually listen attentively to a long lecture, via my driver-interpreter, and then apologise profusely at the end for being naive.

Occasionally, after a long lecture, the Syrians would grant permission for even Arafat supporters to leave the camp. For instance, Major Waleed once allowed four bilateral amputees from Bourj el-Brajneh camp to leave for treatment in Europe. He explained that although they were all Arafat supporters, they were not a threat to the security situation since they had no legs. On humanitarian grounds, he allowed them to leave.

Once written permission was received from the intelligence, air tickets had to be arranged. The families were informed, and then the International Red Cross was notified, so that its delegation could come into the camps and transport the wounded to the airport. Only when the plane actually took off could I be sure my patients had left safely. Until then there was always the possibility that they would be kidnapped or arrested at one of the checkpoints on the airport road.

Only when the MEA plane had gone would I heave a sigh of relief and head back for the camps, accompanied by crying relatives of the departed patients. The rest of the family would usually have no travel documents or visas, let alone the financial means to join the wounded person abroad. It often occurred to me that they would not see each other for a long time.

Bilal Chebib and Samir Ibrahim el-Madany were two boys paralysed by snipers in December 1986. Bilal was from Bourj el-Brajneh and a patient of Dr Pauline Cutting's. Samir was a Lebanese boy. It was the policy of MAP to be non-sectarian and to try to help both Palestinians and Lebanese equally, if possible. The Spinal Centre in Stoke Mandeville Hospital in Britain offered to treat these two kids. Pauline contacted me from London late in April 1987 and asked me to send the boys, as the arrangements in Britain were ready.

But much as I hurried things up in Beirut, the boys and I were unable to leave before 4 June 1987. Although the boys were both under ten years of age, I still had to go through all the bureaucratic procedures. As they were both paralysed from the waist down, I had to fly back with them myself. We were booked to fly on 2 June. But Beirut International Airport shut down that day because of the assassination of the Lebanese Prime Minister, Rashid Karami.

Our London MAP office sent me a long telex complaining about the inconvenience I had caused everyone by delaying the trip. When I received the telex, I tore it up out of frustration. With the assassination of Rashid Karami, another civil war might break out. Everyone was on full alert, including the Syrians. I certainly could not help the airport being closed down. Fortunately everything calmed down after forty-eight hours, and I left with the boys on 4 June. The only hiccup on that day was that I forgot to inform the Red Cross of our travel arrangements. I had to drive our battered old ambulance with the boys and their wheelchairs to Beirut International Airport.

We arrived at Heathrow in the evening, and I was relieved to be able to hand the boys over to Pauline.

I returned to Beirut once more. Summer passed, and the camps continued in semi-siege. Palestinian men inside the camps were still not allowed to leave the camps without special permission. If they were outside, they could not return without special permission. Officials of the Red Crescent were threatened and harassed. One day, six plain-clothed, armed men charged into Um Walid's office in Akka Hospital. They locked the door and threatened her with their guns. One of them said, 'Um Walid, we know you, you are an Arafat supporter.' In her office hung a huge portrait of Yasser Arafat – probably the only such portrait hanging openly in Beirut.

She replied, 'I am a Palestinian. If I do not support Arafat, who is the head of the Palestine Liberation Organisation, who else can I support? You are Syrians – you support your President, Hafez al-Assad. If you are prepared to support Arafat, then perhaps I will consider supporting your Assad.'

The gunmen left her alone. A few weeks later, she was arrested and her office equipment confiscated. Because she was the head of the PRCS in Lebanon, they could not torture her physically. But they picked on Dr Amir Hamawi, the well-loved Lebanese doctor who was once in charge of Gaza Hospital. They brought him in and they beat him before her eyes. But she did not flinch and told them they ought to be ashamed of themselves for torturing a doctor. She was released and returned to her office in Akka Hospital the next day to continue her work for the PRCS in Lebanon. Her arrest did not shake her one bit.

As September approached, morale in the camps plunged even lower than before. The Palestinians of Shatila camp began to hold demonstrations against the siege. It had now lasted more than two years, and people could not take it any more. When the Syrians had imposed the ceasefire a few months before, hopes were boosted. The camp folks thought that they could pick up the threads of their lives once again. But no such luck. The schools remained closed. Amal forbade them to rebuild their homes, and prohibited the transport of building materials into the camps. Two years of attacks and siege had destroyed social institutions like schools for the children, work for the men, home life for the women, and had turned the camps into prisons whose life had congealed into a frozen immobility.

In the camps there was no future, no hope, no security, no laughter. Things must have been terribly hard for the Palestinians to admit to me, 'We feel as though we have nothing left to give.'

Every day saw more cases of depression and mental stress. One day, a Palestinian doctor came in and punched the hospital wall again and again with his clenched fist, then he shouted, 'Why do they let us go on like this? We want to know how long it will take for someone to die in this way.' Like others, he had not left the camp for two and a half years. He had worked through four camp wars, and was a survivor of the 1982 Israeli invasion and Sabra-Shatila massacres. He lost his family in the Tel al-Zaatar massacres.

Shahaada, a lively and attractive Palestinian nurse, was one of my new friends in 1987. She brought her little nephew to see me one day. The poor child had lost both parents in the 1982 massacres. He kept waking up with fear in the middle of the night dreaming of his mother, crying that he could not remember what his parents looked like, except that his mother was fair and beautiful. Shahaada tried hard to compensate for her nephew's loss by being a surrogate mother.

Some days later I heard that they had taken Shahaada too, so the little boy had lost his last relation. Yet when I drove the nurses of Shatila Hospital to buy food for the hospital, I never failed to marvel at their resilience and far-sightedness. For instance, tins of canned beans ordered for the hospital might be labelled: 'DATE OF EXPIRY – 1989'. Then the girls would object and refuse to accept the beans, saying they would only settle for food which would last five years. Two years was not enough: mentally they had already dug in for yet another siege. There was not the slightest sign of surrender, and they were bracing themselves for further endurance.

CHAPTER 29

September 1987 was the fifth anniversary of the Sabra and Shatila massacres. The camp situation remained grim, and as the Lebanese winter approached, we all experienced the same misery as before.

The MAP team had expanded to include volunteers from Malaysia. Dr Alijah Gordon, a Malaysian resident of American origin, had launched a nationwide campaign for volunteers in Malaysia. Through her tireless efforts, the Malaysian people were able to channel their support for the Palestinians in Lebanon by sending medical aid and volunteers. Within a couple of weeks of launching the appeal, Alijah had recruited and sent four medical volunteers to work with us in the camps. There was now no shortage of foreign medics volunteering to come to the Palestinian refugee camps in Lebanon. By this stage, over seventy people from ten different countries had been recruited by MAP. The Western media had given the sufferings of the Palestinians a lot of coverage too. Both Pauline Cutting and Susan Wighton had been honoured by Queen Elizabeth with British awards for their work with the Palestinians and for sticking it out during the siege.

But for the Palestinians in the Beirut camps, everything had ground to a halt. They still had no water, no electricity, no building materials to patch up the large shell holes.

People had no future, no security; children had no schools to go to, men no freedom to venture out. If the camp homes were not repaired and rebuilt, the winter would be a disaster for those in the camp. For those who fled the dreadful situation to find shelter in empty warehouses, garages, staircases or on the roadside in Lebanon, the winter spelt utter gloom. Women who tried to smuggle in bits of cement and building materials with their food parcels were arrested. It was a deadlock – the Syrians were unable to force the Amal to allow building materials into the camp. I thought of driving sacks of cement labelled as flour into Shatila camp, but when I saw two Palestinian girls with the same notion being made to eat bits of cement at the checkpoint, I gave that idea up.

Susan Wighton returned to Bourj el-Brajneh camp. Despite threats to her life, and advice to the contrary, she came back to continue her preventive medical programme work in the camp. Susan's return was very important to the depressed morale of the camp people. She took her medal from the Queen and placed it in the mosque in Bourj el-Brajneh camp. She said, 'That's where it should belong.'

In early September, I planned to leave for Europe, to raise some publicity for the camps around the fifth anniversary of the Sabra and Shatila massacre. Before leaving, I wrote an appeal:

> The survivors of Sabra and Shatila, 5 years after the Israeli Invasion appeal to you for your help. These two refugee camps once held 80,000 Palestinians. Since 1982, following the Israeli Invasion, the Massacre, and the last two years of attacks on the camps, Sabra camp had been demolished, and Shatila reduced to rubble. In addition to those killed, wounded or missing, thousands have fled.
>
> In 1987, 30,000 Palestinians now live in what is left of Shatila and its vicinity. They are now homeless, living either by the roadside or squatting in the ruin and rubble of what is left of Shatila camp. Shortages of water, electricity, medicines, even food and the fear of new attacks on the camp have made life totally unbearable.

Now these people have to face the cold, wet and bitter Lebanese winter with no homes, no warmth and no future. This is the International Year of Shelter for the homeless. . .

My writing was interrupted by a voice: 'Doctora Swee. . .'

That brought me back to the real world – I was in a hospital which had been hit by two hundred and forty-eight shells during the last attack. Its wards were ventilated and lit by gaping shell holes. The hospital had no water, no electricity and it flooded when it rained.

'What's the matter?' I asked.

I turned round, and saw an eight-year-old girl lying in bed, having her dressings changed by a Palestinian nurse. Her legs were severely burnt and practically all the skin on the shins had disappeared. She had been waiting weeks to be taken to Europe for specialist treatment. When she called me, I thought she wanted to know if the arrangements were going ahead.

How wrong I was! She only wanted to kiss me. As I bent over her bed and held her head in my arms, I saw how beautiful she was. Instead of looking at the terrible burns on her legs, I looked at her beautiful, dark eyes and her curly black hair. Despite all her suffering her face remained wonderfully loving and human. She was a child of Shatila camp.

'You come and see me tomorrow?'

'Maybe, God willing,' I said.

I knew that was a lie. Tomorrow I would be off to Europe to do some lobbying, perhaps in a posh conference room with large glass windows and polished tables, talking to comfortable politicians and budget-makers who would explain how and why they could not help. Yet I would have to try. After five years, I had become thick-skinned and persistent.

I never did say good-bye. In the Palestinian refugee camps, life, death and separation are all so mixed up that we never said good-bye. People live in hope of a better tomorrow. The expression which sums it up is: 'We are waiting. Next year in Jerusalem.'

While I was back in Europe, trying to organise publicity for the camps, I met Yasser Arafat, the head of the Palestine Liberation Organisation. He came to address a conference of 240 non-governmental organisations in Geneva. The participants in the conference were afterwards invited to a reception held by the PLO. Like everyone else I went to the reception. During the reception, which was packed with representatives of European NGOs, Yasser Arafat awarded some people the Order of the Star of Palestine, the highest award given by the PLO. I did not know exactly how to react when my name was suddenly called out – the Chairman of the PLO wanted to award it to me! How could I receive such an award when so many Palestinians I knew were more worthy of it than I was, when so many other friends of the Palestinians were giving more than I could ever dream of giving? I did not move. When my name was called out the third time, I had to go up to the Chairman to save embarrassment all round.

I felt highly honoured, yet humble, and said to him, 'Like the Palestinians, I also come from a movement with no individual heroes or heroines. This honour which you are giving me should go to the heroic Palestinian people who are now under siege in the refugee camps of Lebanon, the martyrs of Palestine, to Nahla, Nabila and Nidal, and the many others who laid down their lives for their struggle. And to those who are suffering in the prisons of the Israelis, and to the children who will write the new chapter of Palestine history, to the friends of the Palestinians all over the world who continue to stand in solidarity with the Palestinians under the most difficult circumstances. And to the people of Shatila, who have no roofs over their heads in the coming Lebanese winter, who have stayed strong despite attacks and massacres. Thank you for honouring me, but I know to whom the honour should really go, those whose actions continue to inspire us daily, and I can only receive it since they are not here to receive it in their personal capacities today. . .' I found it difficult to continue, but the Chairman put his arms around me, and kissed me.

That evening I thought about how the Palestinians always tried to thank their friends, even though there was really no need. Nor was there any need to bestow awards or honours. Their confidence and trust in me was more than I could ask for. And by giving me the Star of Palestine, the Chairman had actually given me honorary Palestinian status. I wondered if he knew he had given the award to an exile from another country, from Singapore.

While I was in Europe, trying to organise publicity for the camps, I kept in close touch with the situation there. The temperature plunged in October. Then came November: the rain started to pour and the camps were flooded. Partially bombed buildings collapsed on children and injured them. The skies were grey, and the mood in the camps even greyer. It was cold and wet all the time. Not a single building in Shatila camp was watertight. Torrents of rainwater poured in through shell holes and the rain dripped steadily from the smaller bullet holes. Everywhere I went in Europe I tried to impress upon people the right of the Palestinians to have a roof over their heads.

The hospital was by far the least destroyed of all the buildings in Shatila, yet Dr Kiran, one of the volunteer anaesthetists from MAP who worked in Shatila, slept on a wet floor with his mattress dripping with water. Media attention faded. It was not news any more. Away from the cameras and the tape-recorders, hidden from the news reporters, the Palestinians continued to suffer in silence, forgotten and forsaken by a world without conscience.

Once again I returned to Beirut, having failed to marshal enough international support to bring about the reconstruction of the camps. Like everyone else in the camps, I became very depressed.

Then something happened. On a gloomy, wet December day, when the floodwater in Shatila was up to mid-calf, we got news that the Palestinians in the Israeli-occupied territories of Gaza and the West Bank had risen up against the Israeli Army. It was 9 December 1987. The news bulletin said that Palestinians in the occupied territories were demonstrating against the Israeli occupation, and little children were throwing stones at well-armed Israeli soldiers. This news was a breath of fresh air in the depressing Beirut camps. Suddenly, everyone in Shatila was talking about the 'Uprising in the Occupied Territories'.

Not long before, I had watched children in the camp drawing dead bodies on the walls with some gentian violet – a skin antiseptic lotion – which they had taken from Susan Wighton's clinic. The pictures were their testimony of a stolen childhood. But now all the children gathered around listening eagerly to the adults talk about the uprising in the occupied territories. They made 'V' signs in the alleyways at anyone who passed by.

I had always suspected that Palestinians in exile and Palestinians under occupation were two parts of one divided body, longing to be reunited; that a victory for one would inspire the other. Now I had my proof. The exiles around me in the camps of Lebanon were uplifted and inspired by what was taking place in the occupied territories. They heard of the growth of the resistance of their brothers and sisters living under occupation. They rejoiced.

It was twenty years since Israel occupied the West Bank and the Gaza Strip. The Palestinians living under Israeli occupation had lived in utter misery and wretchedness for two decades. But now they were standing up and telling the occupiers that they were not taking it any more.

Like many Palestinians in the camps of Lebanon, I could not visit the Israeli-occupied territories. But I wanted to know about them, and I listened to people who had visited or came from those areas, and learnt what life under Israeli occupation meant. I asked a Palestinian friend from the Gaza Strip what it had been like there. For her, life was difficult. On top of harsh living conditions – bad, crowded housing, poor sanitation and poverty – there were also the oppressive conditions imposed by the occupying authorities. There were curfews, arrests, restrictions of movement, threats by the Israeli Army to close down camps, and the arbitrary demolition of people's homes. She was engaged to a Palestinian abroad, but was refused permission to leave Gaza to marry him. Now and then the Israelis would call her up for interrogation – sometimes just to mock her or threaten her, sometimes making her hope she would be allowed to leave, for the enjoyment of watching her disappointment when she was told that it was all a mistake.

One day she received a message from the Israelis to call in to get her exit permit. She thought it was the usual false alarm, and so she was totally unprepared when she arrived only to be told to leave occupied Gaza by land across the Sinai desert into Egypt. She was told she could not return to her family in Gaza ever again. My friend told me she had to leave on the spot, before her exit permit was withdrawn by the Israeli authorities. After four years of waiting, she had to go in such a hurry that there was not even time to say goodbye to all her friends and family. It was a one-way ticket from the occupied lands to exile with her husband.

The best land was taken over by the Israelis. From another friend I heard how Palestinians in the West Bank who tried to hold on to ancestral lands were squeezed out by all sorts of pressure. Some people's homes were demolished, while others were sealed by the Army, and evicted families were forced to live in tents. To dry out the farms and olive groves of the Palestinians, the Israelis sank very deep wells which drained away all the subsoil water, diverting it to irrigate the playgrounds and gardens of the newly-arrived settlers from the United States and Europe. It was illegal for any Palestinian to sink a well, and they were forced to pay the Israelis for the water stolen from them.

Each morning at about four o'clock, able-bodied Palestinian males would assemble at various centres to await selection. Israeli owners of factories, construction projects and farms would arrive to select their Palestinian labourers for the day, taking away the Arabs they had chosen like slave owners in medieval times walking away with their chosen slaves. Slave owners were stuck with their slaves, but the Israelis would return their workers at the end of the day after having extracted their labour from them. Over 100,000 workers would be selected each day. So the Palestinians, robbed of their homes and lands, were now reduced to daily wage slaves in what could have been their own land. What of decency, of morality, of godliness? What of God's commandment to the tribes of Israel in the Old Testament, concerning their relations with those outside the tribe: 'But the stranger that dwelleth with you shall be unto you as one born among you, and thou shalt love him as thyself: for ye were strangers in the land of Egypt: I am the Lord your God.' (Leviticus XIX, 34) This was not honoured in the Israel of the twentieth century.

The whole idea of Palestine was outlawed. People caught in possession of items in the colours of the Palestine flag would be jailed, never mind if they supported the PLO. Children as young as three or four years old had been arrested for being anti-Israeli. Most Palestinians who had been arrested and had spent time in Israeli prisons, would tell similar stories of the free use of torture by the Israelis in prison. Many of them, including children, were also sexually assaulted by their Israeli interrogators. My friends could have gone on describing the crimes committed by the Israelis against the Palestinian people.

When I tried to comprehend how the Palestinians coped with all this brutality, I was told of an Arabic word which was part of the daily vocabulary of the Palestinians living under occupation – 'sumud'. It meant steadfastness, endurance. For me it came across most clearly in the translation of this song, which expressed the feelings of the Palestinians when they were beaten, when their homes were blown up by the Israelis, when their lands were confiscated, when they were deported and threatened with death:

I AM ENDURING

I am enduring, steadfastly, I am enduring
In my homeland, I am enduring
If they snatch away my bread, I am enduring
If they murder my children, I am enduring
If they blow up my house, O my house
In the shadow of your walls, I am enduring.

With pride, I am enduring
With a stick, a knife, I am enduring
With a flag in my hand, I am enduring;
And if they cut off my hand and the flag
With the other hand, I am enduring.

With my field and my garden, I am enduring
With determination in my beliefs, I am enduring
With my nails and my teeth, I am enduring;
And if wounds in my body should multiply
With my wounds and my blood, I am enduring.

This was a song which was sung by Palestinians living under Israeli occupation, by people who had to face the most well-equipped army in the world with only their bodies and stones. But after December 1987, televisions in homes all over Western Europe and the USA showed scenes of little Palestinian children braving Israeli tanks and armoured cars with their stones. David and Goliath had come to mind during Israel's invasion of Lebanon in 1982, but this really was the story of David with his stones and the mighty Goliath all over again. The more the Israeli army tried to smash the uprising, the more concerted became the resistance. Nasty scenes of Israeli soldiers beating up

Palestinians and deliberately breaking their limbs, of pregnant Palestinian women being kicked by soldiers, of the liberal use of tear-gas against anti-occupation demonstrators and of live ammunition being used against unarmed Palestinians shocked the civilised West – twenty years after the process first started.

Liberal Israelis expressed concern at the level of violence in the occupied territories – they were afraid that their army recruits might become brutalised by beating up Palestinian women and children. Just like beating up animals, it brutalised those who did it repeatedly.

Until quite recently, I shared the widespread belief that the super-efficient Israeli Army did not inflict extreme brutality: I thought it was incapable of doing this. In early 1983, when I first returned to London after the Sabra and Shatila massacres, I was interviewed by the editor of a Saudi magazine. He was a very quiet man, and listened very carefully to everything I said. At the end of the interview, he asked me, 'Do you ever cry when you think of the Palestinians?'

'By God, you bet I do,' I said. 'If I do not even do that, I am an animal.'

'I know that, doctor,' he said. 'Thank you for being our friend.' And then he rolled up his shirt sleeve, and there on his arm was a large ugly scar from an old machine-gun wound. 'I was ten when this happened,' he said. 'The Israelis came to my home in the West Bank.'

There were no television cameras on the West Bank then, and so atrocities were perpetrated unnoticed. It had taken twenty years for the Western media to publicise the case of the Palestinians in the occupied West Bank and Gaza. It took the massive uprising which started in 1987 to expose the true face of the occupation.

CHAPTER 30

It was a long, unpleasant winter. One morning, I woke up in the clinic in Bourj el-Brajneh. When I opened my eyes, I looked into the smiling face of Dolly Fong. 'Good Morning, Swee. Did you sleep well?' She greeted me with a cup of coffee. It was a typical Sunday: there would be no routine work, but if the camp was attacked, then the clinic would become a resuscitation centre for the wounded. Except for the times when Susan Wighton came back, Dolly was the only foreigner in this clinic, and had held the place together since July 1987. The camp people always referred to this clinic as Suzy's clinic, or Dolly's clinic, after their two devoted foreign medical volunteers. But its proper name was the Samir al-Khatib Clinic. The PRCS built this clinic in 1985, and named it after a doctor of theirs killed by the Israelis.

Dolly Fong was one of the eleven medical volunteers sent by the Malaysian people to work in Lebanon. For me, the Malaysian volunteers were very special. They were hard-working and undemanding, and they instinctively felt with and for the Palestinians. Most of them had given up jobs or business opportunities to work in Lebanon.

There was Mathina Gulam Mydin, a Malaysian nurse working in the south with both the Palestinians and Lebanese Shi'ites. I can remember the night when she received news that her grandmother had died. Mathina was very close to her grandmother and had been scared that she would never see her again once she left for Lebanon. Her fears proved well-founded, but she was not bitter at having lost the opportunity to say goodbye to her grandmother, and she behaved positively. Very few of us knew that she sat up the whole night crying, because she continued work the next day as though nothing had happened.

Then there was Tengku Mustapha Tengku Mansoor, a Malaysian pharmacist who was also a prince. But some prince he was – he had never accepted any of the money which came with his birth. He had worked and earned his own keep, as well as providing for his wife and kids, and his fifteen cats. When he heard of the need for medical personnel in Lebanon, Tengku left his family and dispensary and came. The camp people loved him. I remember vividly those nights when he was on duty. Until one or two in the morning, his Palestinian friends would call through the broken windows of Haifa Hospital, 'Mustapha, Amir Mustapha, please come and have coffee with us.' Amir was the Arabic word for prince.

The others, nurse Pok Lui, Dr Naidu, Dr Hor, nurse Hamidah, nurse Hadji Rosnah, Dr Yussef and paramedics Buddit and Ahmed, were all people with hearts of gold. It was good for the Palestinians to see people from the Third World who had responded out of solidarity, free from the paternalism that European volunteers sometimes showed.

For me, it was not simply a matter of being extremely proud. I was born on the beautiful Malaysian island of Penang. A crystal-clear rapid, Ayer Itam, flowed down from near our home to join the large, lazy river which drained into the sea. Grandfather's garden was filled with large gardenia bushes, tall fruit trees and red and blue flowering plants whose name I never learnt. My younger brother and I loved the tamarind trees best. The mango, jackfruit, rambutan and starfruit trees were absolutely forbidden to us kids, but we were allowed every liberty with the tamarind. Its fruits were always too sour to eat, and handfuls of them were surrendered to the grownups to be used for cooking at the end of the day. That was my childhood home: a tropical paradise. For eleven years I had lived in exile away from South East Asia: I could not even visit my grandfather's house in Penang. Now the Palestinians had brought the Malaysian people back to me, in a wonderful way.

After I had my coffee, Dolly Fong looked at me. I knew she wanted to say something, but like most Malaysian girls of Chinese origin, she was naturally shy. I was kept guessing for a minute or two. Finally it came out: 'I wonder if you have time to prune the roses on the rooftop? You have lived in England for so many years, and if you could do it like how the English do their rose gardens, would you mind?' What an assignment in the middle of besieged Bourj el-Brajneh!

The clinic had become Dolly's home. She and Susan had planted all sorts of flowers on the rooftop. We called it the 'rooftop', but it was not exactly a rooftop. It was the upper floor of the clinic – blown apart by shells. The roof was demolished and two walls were missing. Thank God nobody had ever died when the clinic was hit by incoming shells. Now it was to have a roof garden. Like the Palestinians, Dolly and Suzy were determined to turn the bits of concrete into a home, and the shell-damaged top floor into a garden.

As I was clipping away at the rose plant, I thought of Rashidiyeh camp in south Lebanon and of how, during the siege and bombardment, the Palestinians had built a hospital. At first I did not believe it possible, but when I sneaked into Rashidiyeh camp, I saw the newly-built hospital. The bricks and cement had been brought into the camp just before the siege started. The siege of Rashidiyeh was as nasty as in the Beirut camps, but still the people of Rashidiyeh had managed to build themselves a hospital while the camp was being attacked and besieged. So a rose garden for the Samir al-Khatib Clinic was not mad at all – it was entirely reasonable.

In January 1988, more than two and a half years after Amal's first attacks on the refugee camps, Nabih Berri, their leader, announced the lifting of the siege from all the camps. He said this was to express 'solidarity' with the uprising in the occupied territories. More than two thousand Palestinians had been killed in the Amal attacks on the camps, but they had been unable to crush the Palestinians. International pressure had forced the Syrians to call a ceasefire. No Arab leader could marshal popular support from his people by taking an overt anti-Palestinian stance. The Arab masses saw the Palestinians as the heroes, and the cause of Palestine as sacred, and were taking to the streets to demonstrate their solidarity. The Lebanese people, as always, wanted to support the Palestinians. The people of Syria wanted to support the uprising. The popularity of the Palestine cause, and the courage of the Palestinians in the occupied territories had forced Berri, the leader of Amal, to remove the check-points from the camps!

That same month, I flew back to London. This time Beirut airport was open, though the flight was delayed for six hours. Back in London, I was just in time to see Mike Holmes and Susan Rae off at Heathrow Airport. Susan was the fundraiser for the MAP office in Scotland. Both of them were on their way to the occupied territories, and this was Mike's first trip to the Middle East. Nearly a hundred Palestinians had been killed since the beginning of the uprising, six weeks before, and hundreds more had been wounded. Mike was taking out a cash grant to help some of the injured people pay their hospital fees. Each time a Palestinian needed hospital admission, the Israelis charged a fee of more than a thousand US dollars as initial deposit. Palestinians unable to pay did not get treated.

When I looked at Mike's brand new passport, I laughed.

'How are you going to convince the Israelis you're a bona fide tourist, and not a supporter of the Palestinians going specially because of the uprising?' I asked, knowing that Mike was constitutionally incapable of lying.

It was also funny watching Susan and Mike check in at London's Heathrow Airport with a whole lot of Israelis and Christian pilgrims who were boarding the flight for Tel Aviv. As I was waving them off, I shouted, 'Kiss Jerusalem for me!' A few Israelis turned round and stared at me – they must have wondered what on earth this Chinese woman had to do with Jerusalem.

They were met by Susan Wighton at Tel Aviv airport. Suzy, who had worked in the occupied territories before, was very worried about her Palestinian friends when she heard of the brutality of the Israeli soldiers and the killings of Palestinians, and so she went ahead of the other two to visit people.

Unable to visit the occupied territories, I waited desperately for Mike to get back to hear about events there. The news bulletins in London showed Israeli atrocities against the Palestinian demonstrators, but I wanted to know the spirit of the people in the uprising. If I could not be with them, I wanted to feel with them.

At the back of my mind were many questions. How long would the Palestinians under occupation be able to sustain the uprising? How long could they stand being beaten up, being imprisoned and being hungry? If the general strike there continued, how were they going to live? Who was going to bring milk to the Palestinian children? Were these people as strong and steadfast as the people of Shatila camp? What could we do to support them?

As I was eager to hear Mike's report of his trip, I arranged to meet him in MAP's London office. Mike shared his office with the telex and because he was MAP's publicity officer his phone rang a lot. He also had an open-door policy and so volunteers wandered in and out of his office.

One tip I picked up from the journalists who had interviewed me was to use a tape recorder, so I brought one along with me. We settled down in his office and switched the recorder on. Mike told me his first day in the occupied territories was a 'baptism of fire'. He told me that he had learnt more about Israeli occupation and Palestinian courage from experiences in those twenty-four hours, than in his whole life. Susan Rae and he arrived at Tel Aviv Airport at 5 AM, 17 January 1988. By 9 AM, they were driving towards the ancient city of Nablus, which took its name from the time when Napoleon invaded. The people of that city resisted, and hence it became 'the city Napoleon could not take'.

On their way they almost drove into a demonstration by the Palestinians, with Israeli soldiers firing into the crowd. As he told me about this, Mike gave a shudder. He said that for a moment he thought they were going to get caught in the demonstration and risk being beaten up, shot at and arrested like everyone else. Fortunately the demonstration drifted away in the opposite direction, followed by the Israeli soldiers, and the party continued on their way to Nablus.

'How did you find Nablus?' I asked.

'I had my first whiff of tear gas there, and I must say it wasn't very pleasant. But the Palestinians really weren't afraid at all,' Mike said. 'When we got to Nablus, Israeli soldiers were firing tear gas into the homes of Palestinians. It wasn't just CS gas, it was new versions – CS 515, CS 560, worse than the original CS gas.' He showed me a photograph of a tear-gas canister. 'Look, this was made in Pennsylvania,' he said. 'Look at the date on it. It says 1988. Even if it came out of the factory on New Year's day, it took less than three weeks to get to Israel and be fired at Palestinian demonstrators.' Mike got visibly upset and stopped to light a cigarette before continuing.

'Soon after we got there, Palestinians came out to see us, and one thing they showed us was their personal collections of rubber bullets. People think rubber bullets are pretty harmless. But they're not that harmless at all. While we were there, a four-year-old boy was shot in the head with a rubber bullet. He became unconscious, and one pupil started to dilate. Palestinian doctors said that the rubber bullet had caused internal bleeding into the brain, and he had to be transferred to the Hadassah Hospital for brain surgery.' This was the hospital Paul Morris, Ellen Siegel and I visited in 1982, after testifying to the Israeli Kahan Commission. I knew it was an excellent hospital, and I asked Mike what the outcome was.

'I don't know if the boy survived. It takes at least an hour to get from Nablus to the Hadassah. If I'd a fragile head, which was bleeding internally, the last thing I'd want would be to be driven along a bad road for an hour. And a lot of time was wasted between the referring Palestinian doctor and the admitting Israeli doctor over the telephone. Instead of asking for the patient to be sent quickly, the doctor at the Hadassah kept insisting on the child's folks bringing 1,200 Israeli shekels as initial deposit, otherwise the kid would be sent back.'

This 'cash on delivery' style of dealing with the wounded made Mike furious, especially since the little boy had been wounded by Israeli soldiers.

Just then Clare Moran, one of our most efficient and reliable workers, came in, and started typing at sixty words per minute on the typewriter in Mike's office. We gave up, and went to sit on the table by the coffee machine at the bottom of the staircase, hoping to get some peace and quiet.

'We were still at Nablus,' continued Mike, 'and were invited to visit the office of the General Federation of Trade Unions. They'd a list of names of all the people wounded so far, and wanted to know if MAP could help with their treatment. There was one point when we were talking, that I could have sworn the wall of the building moved towards me. I was stunned, but the Palestinians laughed – it was only Israeli aeroplanes breaking the sound barrier. They do this all the time to intimidate the Palestinians.' Mike started to laugh. He was still a bit embarrassed at not having been able to tell the difference between a bomb exploding and planes breaking the sound barrier.

'Then we went to another home, but unfortunately Israeli soldiers spotted us. They knew we were foreigners and they wanted to get hold of us. Then a whole lot of Palestinian kids motioned us into a house, and the owner locked the soldiers out. But the soldiers stood outside, banging on the door, and talking on their walkie-talkies. After about ten minutes, the soldiers left and the kids knocked on the door and told us it was safe to leave. The kids had gone round the back of the house, and started to throw stones at the Israeli soldiers, who then went after the kids, and forgot about us! We were saved by Palestinian kids! They were really magic. They were everywhere, and not afraid of anything.'

'So you have fallen for the Palestinian kids, Mike?' I asked.

'How could I not? They saved our bacon,' he said with a smile. He then went on. 'We visited Palestinian families, many of them living in absolute squalor. One man said to us, "Look at these miserable conditions. I brought a family into this world for Palestine. Look at my sons and daughters – their bodies were bruised and broken by the beatings of the Israelis. But when the bandages came off, they went out again to demonstrate against the occupiers. I am so proud of them." And when we spoke to the children, they said the same thing about their parents.'

At that point we were joined by three students who had volunteered to help with our new ambulance appeal. One of them, a young woman I loved very much, who was delighted to see me back from Lebanon, rushed up to me, knocking over Mike's coffee and putting the tape recorder out of action. The poor girl was very embarrassed, but soon we were all roaring with laughter. Mike and I adjourned to the room where the photocopier was, and he continued his colourful description of the occupied territories, while I took notes in long hand.

'We visited Ballata camp,' he said. 'There we saw how the lives of the people were made absolutely miserable by the occupation. There were open sewers, and the smell was awful. One thing the television cannot get across to viewers is the stench. They're not allowed to have covered sewers under the law of the occupation. But there's no hatred against the ordinary Israeli. We met the father of a man who'd been deported a couple of weeks ago, and whose wife and daughter had been beaten up. He said they didn't hate the British or the Americans, they didn't even hate the Jews. He said, "They're not our enemies. Our enemies are the soldiers and the occupation. Remove them, and we'll live in peace as we did before." He was so broad-shouldered!'

This was what I knew to be the case. Over the years, the Palestinians had been portrayed as a bitter people prone to hatred. Like Mike, I found the reverse. Most of the Palestinians I knew were ready to forgive and forget. Sometimes when I went on and on about the Sabra and Shatila massacre, my Palestinian friends would ask me to put it behind me, and get on with life, but I found a great quote for them in Yad Vashem in Israel. It said: 'Forgetfulness leads to exile, while remembrance is the secret of redemption.' I urged them to learn from Jewish wisdom.

Sometimes, when Mike talked about the Palestinians who had moved him, he would say something like, 'You know, when I heard him say that, I felt a lump in my throat.' I would dutifully make a note in the margin – 'lump in the throat' – to remind me when I got down to transcribing the notes that Mike was on the verge of crying at that point.

'This anxious Palestinian mother had to go to the Israeli Security to ask for the release of her nine-year-old son, who'd been captured for throwing stones. Not so long ago, the boy's father was detained by the Israelis, and he was still on the wanted list. So the boy's father couldn't go to claim his son, and had to send his wife instead. She was a teacher. The Israelis told her, "You're a teacher. You mustn't teach your nine-year-old son to hate." She replied, "A nine-year-old should never hate anyone. The occupation taught him to hate the soldiers, I did not teach him that. Remove the occupation, and let my son learn to love your people."

'Palestinian kids appeared all over the place, making victory signs with their wee hands. The kids knew no fear. The Israelis arrested a three-year-old boy for throwing stones, and they threatened him: "You're only three and shouldn't know how to throw stones at us. Someone must have taught you. Tell us who taught you, or else. . ." The little boy replied, "My brother." That was it. Fully-armed Israeli soldiers picked up the toddler and stormed into his home looking for his brother. They found him in a corner playing – he was only one year older than his baby brother!'

As Mike got really carried away, his Scottish accent became stronger and stronger. Sometimes I had to stop him and ask him to repeat what he said. At this he would throw up his hands in despair, call me a 'bloody foreigner' and start all over again.

The party then went down to Gaza and visited the hospital and some clinics there. It was difficult for Mike properly to assess the medical needs there, as he was not a medical person, but he tried to make a mental note of the kind of injuries he came across. The casualties of the uprising seemed phenomenal. Most of them could not get proper treatment. The deliberate policy of breaking the limbs of the Palestinians meant that victims would be crippled for a long time. A fractured limb takes a good few months to mend, and then an equally long time to be rehabilitated to full functional status. As an orthopaedic or bone surgeon, I know that there is no way to hurry the process of bone healing. If all four limb bones are broken, then the injured person will be quite useless for up to a year. Meanwhile, if he was the sole breadwinner, his family would starve.

'The Shifa Hospital in Gaza City was packed with wounded Palestinians,' Mike told me. 'The whole place was a heap of bruised and bashed up people. People with broken arms, broken legs, crushed chests and tummies. A seventeen-year-old who was on his way to visit his aunt got shot in one leg, and was brought in pursued by Israeli soldiers hurling tear gas at him. As though that wasn't enough, they came into the hospital and smashed up his other leg. As he was put into bed, he shouted: "I don't like the Israeli soldiers. They should leave Palestine and give the Palestinians their rights!" He was laid down next to a forty-five-year-old Palestinian who had both his testicles crushed by the Israelis. Next to the forty-five-year-old was his thirteen-year-old-son, both of whose arms were broken by soldiers.

'One thing a lot of people told us was this: "If Shatila could resist three years of continuous attacks and siege, we too can resist the occupation." '

And he produced a clipping from a local English-language paper. There, in bold type, was just what he had just told me. To me, this was most telling – it linked the struggle of those in exile with those living under occupation. Were these people as strong and steadfast as the people of Shatila camp? I now had the answer. The momentum of the uprising was founded on the steadfastness of the Palestinians in Lebanon. Shatila had journeyed from exile to home, from Beirut to Jerusalem.

CHAPTER 31

If I were writing a romantic story about the Palestinians and wanted a good ending, this chapter would not be necessary. It would be so much more satisfying emotionally for both the reader and myself just to end with the uprising which has captured the imagination of the world. Unfortunately, this is not possible. The tragedy of the Palestinians in Lebanon continues, and as their friends, we continue to live in their broken lives and homes. There are half a million Palestinians in Lebanon, whose misery you will now understand. The uprising gave them dignity and a new meaning to life, but as 1988 unfolded, the same forlorn situation persisted. The siege was reimposed once the media attention faded. The MAP medical volunteers in Lebanon continued working quietly in the refugee camps and the shelters. They too began to ask me: 'How much longer?'

Spring returned to Lebanon. It was April 1988, and I returned to Beirut again, for the sixth time. This was to be a short trip, mainly to assess the situation, so that MAP could work out where our limited resources would best be deployed. I also wanted to see our volunteers and talk to them. Many of them had stayed for a long time in the wretched conditions of the camps, enduring through air raids, shelling and homelessness with the Palestinians through the long winter.

The wretched misery suffered during the winter of 1987–88 could only really be understood by those who lived in those camps. The walls were full of large shell holes, roughly covered with small pieces of polythene. Rain and cold winds came through. The last wooden doors and window shutters were burnt during the depth of the previous winter, when people ran out of fuel and firewood. A year had passed but repair and reconstruction of broken homes was totally forbidden. So the windows still had no shutters. Nevertheless, another year had passed.

On this trip I did a fair amount of travelling, covering the Beka'a valley, Beirut and south Lebanon. The largest camp in the Beka'a was Bar Elias, controlled by the Syrians. Most of the Palestinians came here from south Lebanon or from Beirut, mainly after the 1982 invasion and the camp wars of 1985 to 1988. Some of us visited the head of the PRCS there to discuss how MAP could best support them, and I was impressed by how well run the hospital was, despite the lack of facilities and equipment. There were about 100,000 homeless Palestinians living in shelters around the camp, in degrading conditions. Just up the road was Anjar, the detention centre run by the Syrian Intelligence where Palestinian detainees were interrogated and tortured before they were carted off to Syria.

Spring meant that the bitter rains had ceased, and the sun warmed the mountains and beaches once again. But back in Beirut, when Rita Montanas, a seventy-five-year-old German public health worker, who was the latest recruit to join MAP, started her daily routine of distributing milk to the refugees living in shelters all over the ravaged city, there was nothing to remind us of the beauty of spring – apart perhaps from Rita's radiant smile.

There was still no rebuilding allowed in the devastated camps: the blockade of construction materials continued, and the people remained homeless. The International Year of Shelter for the Homeless, 1987, had come and gone. Apart from various resolutions at international conferences, there was nothing to show for it. Resolutions stating that everyone had the right to a home meant nothing to people whose only choice was between the rubble of their camps and the wretched refugee shelters outside the camps in the streets of Beirut.

The people in the shelters called Rita 'Mama Halib'. Halib means milk in Arabic. They changed her name to 'Mama Rita' when they realised that she brought more than milk for their children. She brought them clothes, books, medicines – and most of all, she brought much-needed friendship into those grim and God-forsaken shelters. I knew that God had given Rita her warm heart and smile to bring a bit of happiness into the squalor of the shelters and she also had the gift of patience – to carry on working as long as she could be of service to others. Leila Shahid, my Palestinian friend, once said to me: 'Sometimes when I look at the friends we Palestinians have, I begin to believe that God understands that we suffer too much. At very dark moments, we were given very special friends.'

The shelters were very humiliating: the ultimate insult to the Palestinians. They had converted tents to houses, they had turned camps into exile townships. Now their towns were destroyed, their identity was crushed, and they were forced to squat in these shelters. Each shelter was partitioned by black drapes into small spaces for individual families. A floor area of fifty feet by fifty feet would easily hold a few hundred people in shelters. In these darkly lit squats, there was never enough light to see, but one could smell the overcrowding. An oppressive atmosphere was created by the overproduction of carbon dioxide, the damp, and the depression. I thought of a book by my friend Rosemary Sayigh. It was called *Palestinians, from Peasants to Revolutionaries*. These shelters made me think, sadly, of writing another book: *Palestinians, from Revolutionaries to Refugees*. In these squats, Palestine seemed so far away. Here struggle seemed to cease, and with it life as well.

But I was wrong. The helplessness was more apparent than real. Once the checkpoints were removed, people from the shelters returned to live in the destroyed camps! They made a choice between being refugees with no identity and being prisoners with dignity in the ruin and rubble of the Palestinian camps. The people in the shelters had not forgotten they were Palestinians. It was the start of transforming refugees to exiles all over again. So the population of Shatila, Bourj el-Brajneh and Rashidiyeh increased again. Shops started opening, children asked to go to school. Women began to produce Palestinian embroidery – all over again.

The PRCS picked up the pieces in the camps. They set about repairing their hospitals and clinics all over again. Shatila Hospital and Haifa Hospital were both being refurbished.

I wanted to visit Rashidiyeh hospital and the MAP team working there. Øyvind and I took an ambulance-load of supplies and drove south to Rashidiyeh camp. Our route was along the same bumpy road down which Ellen Siegel, Paul Morris and I had been driven by the Israeli Defence Force on our way to Jerusalem in 1982. On our right, the waves of the Mediterranean Sea lapped lazily along the coast. To our left, the fields and orchards had recovered from the assault of 1982. Now there were stretches of green, dotted by oranges and tangerines. The fragrance of lemon blossoms and jasmine flowers filled the air. The fields were covered with bright yellow daisies. Located near Sour, Rashidiyeh was about three hours' drive from Beirut, provided the many checkpoints were not unduly troublesome.

The checkpoints had changed hands since 1982, but they were still there. From Beirut to the River Awali, just north of Saida, the checkpoints were now Syrian. From the Awali to just south of Saida, the checkpoints were controlled by Sunni Lebanese belonging to the Nasserite party of Moustapha Saad. From there all the way to Sour, the checkpoints were controlled by Amal. Further south would be Unifil and then the Israeli-occupied areas.

There were other camps near Sour as well as Rashidiyeh. The smaller camps were Qasmieh, Al-Bas and Bourj el-Shemali. Although these camps were not under siege, the Palestinians living in them had no peace, as there were regular kidnappings and occasional murders.

Rashidiyeh camp is a mere seventeen kilometres from the border of Israel, or 'Occupied Palestine', as the people in the camp call it. Unlike Shatila camp, it is spacious. People are able to grow vegetables, fruits and flowers inside the camp. One boundary is the Mediterranean Sea, with stretches of sandy beach. The other boundary is provided by orchards planted with oranges and lemons. It was thanks to its orange trees and numerous plants that Rashidiyeh did not starve to death during the siege.

Like Ain al-Helweh camp in Saida, Rashidiyeh was demolished by the Israelis in 1982; like Ain al-Helweh, it was rebuilt. It was badly shelled by Amal during the recent camp war of October 1986 to April 1987, and its entrances were still guarded by Amal gunmen. The people of Rashidiyeh had already started picking up the pieces. The rubble from the blown-up homes was collected and used as building blocks to repair the damaged areas. Men, women and children were busy working in the fields. Vegetables were growing. Little shops opened. In this camp, you could use a bicycle instead of walking because the distances were fairly large. Most of the original Rashidiyeh was built on higher ground, but there was a newer part of the camp towards the beach, with rows of one-storey brick houses which had been heavily shelled and destroyed. Beyond that area was the soft sandy beach of the Mediterranean coast. In the past, it was possible to fish, swim and sunbathe here, but the war had destroyed that source of food and recreation. It was covered by snipers round the clock.

Dr Salah, the PRCS director in Rashidiyeh, was busy helping to paint the hospital, which was nearly ready. Like other male Palestinians, Dr Salah had been under siege for a very long time. Because the siege of Rashidiyeh was so sudden and unexpected, Dr Salah found himself the only doctor in a besieged camp of seventeen thousand people throughout the whole of the last war. He treated the wounded, tended the sick, took charge of building the hospital during the siege, and looked after the medical needs of the camp. He looked extremely tired, but was kind and patient. He had earned the respect of all in the camps, including the MAP volunteers.

The MAP volunteers were Dr Kiran Gargesh and Susan Bernard, a theatre sister. Kiran is an Indian anaesthetist who first joined MAP in 1986. The PRCS desperately needed someone to set up anaesthetic services in the newly-built hospital in Ain al-Helweh camp. I remember our first meeting very well. A gentle, vegetarian doctor arrived at the London MAP office to see me. He had a terrible cold, and so did I. But ill as I was, something told me that he possessed a quality of selflessness which so many of us lacked. He left for Lebanon in 1986, and had since then worked tirelessly and quietly, not only as an anaesthetist, but also as a teacher of anaesthetics. He had worked in Ain al-Helweh camp, Shatila and now Rashidiyeh.

Kiran and Susan had managed to get into Rashidiyeh during one of the few days when the siege was partially lifted. They wanted to help the PRCS set up an operating theatre in the camp. Susan had set off from the MAP office to come to Lebanon for a three-month stint, but finding it difficult to leave, had chosen to stay on in Rashidiyeh. She was now busy setting up the operating theatre. Kiran had once again started to train anaesthetic technicians for the PRCS in Rashidiyeh. I sat through one of his classes and enjoyed every minute of it.

It was good to talk to Kiran again. He is absolutely stable mentally, and it was very reassuring for me to know that even mentally stable individuals could fall helplessly in love with Palestinians. I often wondered if I was crazy – that was the only way I could explain my obssession with the Palestinians. In the summer of 1987, I was going back to Beirut with four new Malaysian medical volunteers. We went via Cyprus, and stayed in a hotel while waiting for a flight into Beirut. The hotel manager recognised me, and he started on at me: 'You're not going back to Lebanon again, are you? And with all these new medical volunteers. Why do you keep doing this? You know they're all crazy in Lebanon, and it's so dangerous.'

The Malaysians looked at me – they had already been briefed of the dangers they were likely to face in Lebanon. After a short silence, I replied, 'Yes, I know they're all crazy. But we're crazy too.'

The manager burst out laughing, and ordered drinks for all of us. As long as doctors and nurses from all over the world selflessly continue to offer their lives and skills to the people in Lebanon, I will continue to be inspired by this madness. But Kiran was always so balanced – always a doctor, full of faith in life, and love for the Palestinians. No matter how depressing conditions had become, like during the siege, or throughout the Israeli air raids, during which some of his dearest friends died, he remained quietly confident. Perhaps it is his Indian philosophy, I do not know, but I am grateful for his calm temperament.

We were entertained in style by the Palestinians in Rashidiyeh. The PRCS and the women's union got together and gave us dinner. Representatives of the popular committee of the camp also joined the dinner. We spoke of the uprising, the need for a Palestinian homeland, the future of Palestinians in Lebanon. The food was wonderful, and had been grown in the camp. Deep fried eggplants, delicious salads, freshly baked Arabic pitta bread, rice cooked with garlic, cardomoms, almonds and fresh lemon. To go with it was mint tea and Arabic coffee. There were also Arabic sweets and puddings to finish with, but I did not try them, as I do not like sweets. We went on till the small hours, and then parted. Rashidiyeh had no electricity, and I had to use a torch. However Kiran and Susan had learnt to move with great agility in the darkness.

We returned to the medical volunteers' flat in Rashidiyeh. This was the upstairs of a building which had been hit by shells, and there were bullet holes in the walls. But it was decent accommodation under the circumstances. Susan made us more coffee – this time 'Nescafé'. It had become quite chilly, and we washed with really cold water scooped out with plastic buckets from a well nearby. Lighting was from a little kerosene lamp. The stove was a gadget Susan got from Sweden. It was hard work to make a cup of coffee, as Susan had to spend a good half hour pumping away to build up enough pressure for the paraffin to ignite. But their outfit was homely, and we sat talking till we could no longer keep our eyes open. I have learnt that such rare moments are precious, and it seems like a crime to have to sleep.

The sniping and shelling in Rashidiyeh had taken its toll. There was a large new graveyard where all those who lost their lives during the last attacks were buried. Moreover, this was one of the camps harassed by the Israeli air force, sometimes merely breaking the sound barrier to intimidate its inhabitants, sometimes actually dropping bombs. It was badly damaged during recent attacks, but its people remained stoic. Rashidiyeh stood firm. The Israelis had bombed Rashidiyeh camp on many occasions – but each time the camp was rebuilt. The children of Rashidiyeh stood and posed for me victoriously – like their counterparts in Shatila.

Anniversaries of massacres and wars succeeded each other: the Palestinian calendar was full of such events. We remembered and mourned friends. At about 7 AM on 16 April 1988, I was at the NORWAC flat in Hamra, having returned from the refugee camps the night before, and was about to leave for Bourj el-Brajneh. A Palestinian friend arrived at the flat just before I set off. 'Did you hear the news?' he asked me.

'What news?' I asked. I had not listened to the BBC that morning.

He said, 'It is much better you hear from me now before you go about the day. Abu Jihad has been assassinated.'

I did not know whether to believe it or not. I had never met the Palestinian leader Abu Jihad, but I had met his wife Um Jihad at a meeting in an international conference in Geneva. We switched on the radio, and listened to the news. Gunmen had broken into Abu Jihad's home in Tunis, and had murdered him and three other people in front of his wife and his three-year-old son. The murderers even videoed the killing. The thought of his family having to live with that made me sick.

Everyone in Lebanon was stunned – the PRCS, the people both inside and outside the camps, Palestinians and Lebanese alike. People were emotionally paralysed for the first couple of days.

The Israelis alleged that Abu Jihad was the leader of the uprising in the occupied territories. The Palestinians accused Israel of killing him to put an end to the uprising. To the Palestinians in Lebanon, whose morale had been lifted by the events in the occupied territories since the end of 1987, the death of Abu Jihad was a crushing blow. I went to see Um Walid on the day the news of the assassination broke. It was the first time the two of us sat together for more than an hour without talking. She just cried, and I watched her quietly. Like the other Palestinians trapped in semi-siege in the camps of Lebanon, she could not even attend his funeral. Where would he be buried? No one knew at that stage. Abu Jihad remained an exile in life and death. The people in Bourj el-Brajneh camp borrowed the large table from the Samir al-Khatib Clinic and draped it with a Palestine flag, and held a memorial service. Speeches and prayers were broadcast through the mosque loudspeaker.

The more I spoke to Palestinians, the more clearly one message emerged. The Israelis thought there was only one Abu Jihad. But the Palestinians told me: 'In the refugee camps of Lebanon and among the massive uprising in the occupied territories we are all Abu Jihads.'

The people in the occupied territories responded to the murder by escalating the uprising. More were killed, wounded and arrested by the Israelis, but more stood up against them. Palestinians in Shatila told me that MAP must give priority to the uprising. They wanted all aid to go to the occupied territories even at the expense of Shatila. It was very painful for me to hear that from Shatila, as I knew how badly they were suffering and how much they needed all our support. I knew how much they needed the rebuilding of their destroyed homes. Their morale was low, as the siege had still not been lifted, three years after it started, and nearly six months after Berri announced that it was being lifted. But the last bit of strength they had they wanted to give to the uprising.

Then another dimension seemed to open up. Syria allowed Abu Jihad's body to be buried there. Dozens of bus-loads of people left Beirut for Syria to attend his funeral. Did this mean the beginning of a new dialogue between the Syrians and the Palestinians? In less than a month's time, my friend Kazeem Hassan Beddawi would have spent a whole year in prison in Syria. I had often thought of visiting his wife and their baby boy, but had not done so – for fear that she blamed me for his arrest. Kazeem was not the only Palestinian imprisoned: there were at least two thousand Palestinians held as political prisoners by the Syrian security. Would they be free at last? But hopes had been shattered before, and I have learnt of necessity to accept the disappointments.

Israeli bomber planes were breaking the sound barrier in south Lebanon. Villages in the south, as well as the Palestinian refugee camps, were attacked. In May 1988, two thousand Israeli troops crossed into southern Lebanon. People in Lebanon told me: 'The Israelis failed to stifle the uprising in the occupied territories, so they take it out on us by threatening to invade Lebanon again.'

It was a multi-pronged attack on the Palestinians in Lebanon. Saida and the south were bombed by Israeli aeroplanes, and shelled from the sea by Israeli gunboats. The Beirut camps were attacked from the mountains, not by the Israelis, but by anti-PLO forces. Shatila and Bourj el-Brajneh were shelled incessantly from the month of May 1988. Both camps were flattened; homes and hospitals demolished.

Shatila finally collapsed on 27 June 1988, followed by Bourj el-Brajneh a few days later. I got the news of the fall of Shatila in London, having just returned from a fund-raising trip in the Gulf countries. People all over the Gulf wanted to support the uprising and build hospitals and clinics to mend the wounds of the Palestinians. What can I say? Each time I think of Shatila, I still cry. It was nearly six years since I first met the people of Sabra and Shatila. My understanding of the Palestinians began with them. It was they who taught a naive woman surgeon the meaning of justice. It was they who inspired me to struggle incessantly for a better world. Each time I felt like giving up, they would strengthen me with their example.

The memories of the 1982 Israeli invasion, the days following the evacuation of the PLO, when I shared with them their hopes in rebuilding their lives, only to be shattered by the massacres; the following years of siege on the camps, each time a new wound, gaping, deep and bleeding which a surgeon could not mend – these were now part of my daily consciousness. Sometimes I wondered why living was so painful. Sometimes I wondered why I was not buried in the mass graves, the rubble, along with everyone else in 1982. At other times, I wondered if, had I been shot dead in 1987 trying to get things into the camps, I could have been put beside my friends in Shatila mosque.

But these were just empty musings. I was alive, and I

knew that as long as I kept living there was much to be done. Living or dying, I just wanted to be true to the Palestinians. Now, with Shatila gone, the light had gone out. It had defended itself to the last person. The Israelis had failed to destroy Shatila; for three years Amal under the leadership of Nabih Berri tried, and failed as well. But after six years, the recent onslaught by Syrian-backed factions finally flattened whatever was left of this little patch two hundred yards square. When the camp was overrun, there were eight people who refused to surrender. Among them was Amni, the head of the General Union of Palestinian Women in Shatila. She was one of those in Shatila who told me to hold fast on the uprising.

The fall of Shatila was a blow to us all. But that would not stifle the uprising and the demand for a Palestinian homeland. In 1982, I had witnessed the crucifixion of Palestinians in Beirut. From 1985 to 1988, I had witnessed their resurrection. I had seen their indestructible spirit in defending their dignity in their besieged camps in Lebanon. Today, they have carried their struggle for existence back to their ancestral homeland. I was no longer frightened or pessimistic. I remembered Amni telling the people of the Gaza Strip that Shatila was fighting for Gaza. The people of Gaza replied that they were fighting for the people of Shatila. After laying the foundation for the uprising, Shatila was demolished. But the physical survival of Shatila is not the point. Shatila lives in the hearts of every one of us. One day, we will rebuild it on the soil of the Palestinian homeland. Till that day, we shall honour the martyrs of Shatila with our continued support for the people in the uprising.

How long would the Palestinians under occupation be able to sustain the uprising? That question does not matter now. What matters is that it has started.

A new generation of Palestinians has grown up in the occupied territories and in the camps of Lebanon under the most dreadful conditions. They have forgotten the meaning of fear. They have chosen to die standing, rather than live on their knees. One song to emerge from the struggle in the occupied territories is by Mustafa al-Kurd and is called 'Stone and Onion'. With a stone to confront the Israeli military, and an onion to lessen the effect of tear gas, the Palestinian demonstrators have conquered fear. The song goes:

> The fear is dead which dwelled in our hearts
> Which killed the hopes and blocked the paths
> Which put the lights out
> The fear is dead and I buried it with my own hands
> Fear was the monster which oppressed us
> Which was cruel to us
> Which broke the jar and spilled the oil
> The fear is dead and I buried it with my own hands.

They have a dream. And I share their dream: the dream of a world just visible through the smouldering ruins of the refugee camps and the tear gas – a world where an eleven-year-old boy need not learn to use a Kalashnikov or rocket-launcher to defend his family – a world of peace, justice and security, where I will never have to tell a child, 'Go to school,' only to learn that the school has been bombed, or tell a girl, 'Go help your mother get the dinner ready,' only to have her return to tell me her mother and family have been murdered – a world where we do not have to fear being buried alive in collapsing rubble, where I will not have to patch up broken bodies only to see them being blown up again, or hold the broken body of a child in my arms and ask, 'Why?' or hear people ask, 'How much longer?' – a world where there are no prisons, no torture, no pain, no hunger and no refugee identity cards, where I can put my head down in my own home and listen to my mother's songs as I close my eyes at the end of the day. That place is our dream, our Jerusalem.

ADDENDUM

Francis sitting with the delegation to the 2010
Commemoration of the Sabra Shatila Massacre.
He was actually reading some of his poems to them.

LIFE WITH FRANCIS

My publisher for the Chinese edition of *From Beirut to Jerusalem* wanted me to include a chapter on my late husband, Francis Khoo Kah Siang, one of the founding members of Medical Aid for Palestinians (MAP). After his death, MAP started the Francis Khoo Award to be given bi-annually to someone for lifelong service to Palestine. My dear friend Dr Runa Mackay was the first recipient in 2012. Runa served the Palestinians as a medical doctor in Nazareth for 30 years. When she retired from her hospital in Nazareth, she joined MAP as a volunteer doctor in the Palestinian refugee camps of South Lebanon. Dr Mackay also founded Scottish MAP. In 2014 it was awarded to the Qattan family for their enormous humanitarian service to Palestine.

Unfortunately the adorable Grand Matriarch of the Qattan family, Leila Qattan passed away on 27 January 2015. The news of her death shocked us all and had not even reached the Palestinian community at large. Yet, a couple hundred close friends stood next to the grieving family on a freezing bitter February day to pay their respect as Leila was laid to rest at Mortlake Cemetery in London. The late afternoon sun appeared just in time to melt some of the overnight snow and frost. It turned the grass and pathways muddy and slushy. Our collective pain and loss was palpable. Leila in life was generous, kind and warm to all. None of us believed that she could die. Our love for her made us forget that she too was mortal. Yet, in death she remains our inspiration and our icon. As her family surrounded her grave to pray for her, I could hear friends standing next to me whispering quietly "What a disaster! How can she leave us? How are we going to carry on? How can we cope?" It seems yesterday when I embraced her and thanked her for her steadfast support of MAP. She was a true friend who supported us through very difficult times, mobilising her family to help us at every turn. No words will ever adequately express our gratitude for all she had done during her lifetime for the Palestinians and MAP. Her children and grandchildren have so much to be proud of and so much to live up to.

I wanted to tell Leila's husband, Abdel Mohsin that Leila will always live among us, but it was difficult in the midst of such a large gathering. It is going to be difficult for him to lose his precious lifelong companion. They have been married for more than 60 years. But I pray that he will learn what I learnt. That soon he will discover that it is not life without Leila, but life with Leila. She will always be with him, just as Francis is always with me.

Francis died on 20 November 2011 unexpectedly. I returned home from a speaking trip in Malaysia and found him dead. In a state of shock and disbelief I wrote his obituary.

Francis and Swee, with friends in Beirut.

"FRANCIS KHOO KAH SIANG,
23 October 1947 to 20 November 2011

It must be so bizarre that the one person who loves you beyond words and whom you also love the most in this world goes on to make you a widow – and without polite notice!

So it is the case with my beloved. As I stepped off the plane, I received a text message sent a few hours ago that he "cannot come". As I came into the house, I smelt delicious chicken macaroni soup freshly cooked in the kitchen. There was some left in a bowl which he must had eaten from to stem his hunger as the plane was delayed. But there was no answer to my call, except from our agitated cats. Yes, my beloved had died in the room upstairs.

Did he choose to die before I got to him to spare me the pain of resuscitating him? Was it Divine Mercy that he was taken home to God so painlessly, silently, and alone before medical science complicated his humanity? Was it to spare his wife anxious moments waiting at the hospital intensive care? Could I not just cradle him in my arms in these last precious moments on earth? Only at our re-union with our Maker and with each other can these questions be answered. For now, I am grateful to be able to look after him on this last lap of his earthly journey as he returns to the One who created him.

As news of his death broke out, thousands of emails, letters, text messages, phone calls, flowers poured from all parts of the world and all walks of life. From heads of states, diplomats, politicians, and friends employed and unemployed. I am not only overwhelmed by the volume but by the affection and admiration they held for him. Friends and family are flying in from all over the world. I have managed only to reply to just over a thousand messages over the last 48 hours. The rest might have to wait for their reply until the funeral is over.

So who was this Francis Khoo?

He was the fourth generation of an established Singapore Peranakan (Straits born native) family. It is a close knit family. As a boy he sang in the Singing Khoos with his brothers Lawrence and Victor, and the family is devoutly Catholic. As he grew up he began to acquire a strong sense of justice – beyond merely legal. Of course he was a lawyer, but even in University as Vice President of the Students' Law Society, he served a greater justice. He opposed the introduction of the Suitability Certificate, the abolition of the jury system, and later on the heavy bombing of Hanoi on Christmas day. His other interests include photography – he patented a pocket camera at the age of nineteen. He loved drawing, writing and ran the St Joseph Institution school paper and the university Undergrad.

Despite all the above "distractions", he qualified and was called to the bar. Within months of arriving as a junior lawyer in his firm, he took on the legalities of forming a Citizens' Co-op to save the Singapore Herald, the liberal English daily closed by the government.

In 1974, I met him at a Justice and Peace meeting. His deep commitment to social justice was to him a Christian obligation. The first commandment is to love God; the second is to love your neighbours as yourself. Two weeks later I read in the Straits Times that my new acquaintance was to defend a controversial trial in which factory workers and a student leader were charged with rioting. I called him to ask him to re-consider since he might invite personal repercussions. Despite being Malaysian born, I had lived long enough in Singapore to be a "*kiasu*" (law-abiding. timid, please do not rock the boat) coward. I sensed that the government wanted the workers and the student leader imprisoned, and to defend them would be seen as being anti-government and the consequences would be dire!

He patiently explained that everyone is entitled to legal defence – and no one should be deemed guilty until proven beyond reasonable doubt. These workers were poor and established lawyers would not take their case on and someone just got to do it, in the interest of justice. If he had to pay the price of doing so, he would accept it!

I am still not sure when my admiration for him turned to love. In 1976 when I sensed that he might be detained under the Internal Security Act I asked him to marry me, so that if he were to be arrested I can visit him in prison and at least be his link to the outside world. We married on 29 January, 1977.

The arrest came, and he managed to escape. I was detained shortly afterwards and questioned about him. Upon my release I joined him in exile in the United Kingdom.

Francis started his life in exile as a cleaner in a Central London Hotel. He then went on to work as an administrator in a British Charity, Medical and Scientific Aid for Vietnam. Two years later he was journalist for an international third world magazine, South. From there he went on to direct War on Want, a prominent international NGO founded by the late British Prime Minister, Harold Wilson and Lord Fenner Brockway. Apart from chairing numerous charities he was co-founder and Vice Chairman of the British Charity, Medical Aid for Palestinians from 1984 to 2007. He had to step down as new British Charity Commissioner Legislation advised against office bearers serving more than 9 years. He had served 23 years!.

From War on Want he returned to legal practice in London until his failing health forced him to stop work. Despite this, his work for many charities continued.

He wrote many poems, songs and articles. He sang for many including the wives of the striking miners. One of his songs Father Christmas in the Slag Heap brought the whole of Hemsworth, a town faced with pit closure, to tears during their poverty stricken Christmas in 1984. He also sang at canteens catering meals for the aged. His songs and writings are available to the Singapore public for those who are interested.

He suffered renal failure from 1998, went on dialysis, but had a successful renal transplant on the British NHS in July 2011 – the generous gift of an anonymous British woman donor. The day before his death he was at the Annual General Meeting of Living Stones, a charity to which he was trustee. His diary is full of future engagements including the Haldane Law Society, charities for the homeless, Medical Aid for Palestinians, the Scottish Parliament, and the House of Commons – plus supporting me in dozens of public lectures and talks. It is full of engagements until end of September 2012.

His untimely death left a huge void in all our lives. We are all in a state of shock. But by God's grace, time will make it possible for his memory to overwhelm the pain of our loss. My tribute to him will be to continue to serve the cause of peace and justice. I also hope to be the widow who will take his ashes back to his beloved Singapore after his 34 years of exile.

Dr Ang Swee Chai (Mrs Francis Khoo),
22 November 2011"

഻഻

Francis' funeral and cremation took place on 25 November 2011, five days after his death. The days following his funeral were hectic as I refused to postpone any public speaking and engagements. As Francis' widow I also took on some of his engagements as well. I know I must continue to serve the cause of freedom and justice as this would be what he wanted. I cannot honour him as a widow by withdrawing and suffocating under a cloak of tears and grieve. He had long taught me that we are not to allow personal circumstances to excuse ourselves from our responsibility of supporting others. I returned to my patients at the Royal London Hospital the week following Francis' funeral, and did not cancel a single public engagement. I wanted to honour and remember him through my continued support for the Palestinians.

The year following Francis' death was 2012 – the 30th anniversary of the Sabra-Shatila Massacre, which took place in September 1982. My personal loss was subsumed in the remembering of this horrendous reality. It also marked thirty years of my returning to London from the massacre and its aftermath. That first visit to Sabra-Shatila in 1982 was shocking and unforgettable. It resulted in the loss of 30% of my body weight while out there. Upon my return, Francis did not molly coddle me, but immediately with the help of Major Derek Cooper, his wife Lady Pamela Cooper, Dr Fathi Arafat (the late President of the Palestine Red Crescent Society), several British Palestinians and supporters, plunged me into the hard work, often into the early hours of the morning, of forming MAP. He arranged for me to speak to dozens of meetings, groups – churches, politicians, trade unions, universities, schools, and even pubs – about what happened to the Palestinians. In early December 1982, a scarce three months after the massacre, the British media had already lost interest in Sabra-Shatila and the Palestinians. Hence it really was a case of campaigning at the grassroots, talking face to face to people on a personal level. The majority of people in the UK only knew of PLO terrorists and never heard of Palestinian refugees. I doggedly repeated the story of Palestine and her people to everyone who was prepared to listen. Francis insisted I never turned down any opportunity to speak about the Palestinians and that included travelling hundreds of miles just to talk to half a dozen interested supporters. I was often exhausted and so was he. He came to listen to all my talks, and critique every sentence. The support for MAP steadily grew and the hostile attacks on us could not stop us from telling the British public the truth about the Palestinians.

Francis wrote the first constitution and the mission statement for MAP. He also filled in the forms for the British Charity Commissioner to get MAP registered. He gave the charity its name Medical Aid for Palestinians. When it was suggested that we should drop the word Palestinians he fiercely opposed it. He argued that Palestinians are not terrorists but the victims of terror. They are a people who were forcefully driven out of their homeland Palestine, denied their identity, their basic rights as human beings, and, for the people of Sabra-Shatila finally denied the right to life. They died as refugees on foreign soil. MAP would not change its name.

Journeying with the Palestinians without Francis' physical presence is difficult. I miss him every step of the way. He was lawyer, political advisor, critic to my articles, protector and on top of all an extremely joyful and hopeful companion even in times of devastation and despair. He loved singing, and wrote many poems and songs. He more than made up for my tendency to be melancholic and pessimistic. He wrote songs while "on the run" from the Singapore secret police. I remember him quoting Bertol Brecht "Will there be singing in the dark times? Yes there will be singing about the dark times". So there was a song for every occasion and if there wasn't, it would have to be written.

One of Francis' most beautiful and encouraging poems was called The Rebel and the Revolutionary. It is a poem which constantly helps me to see beyond hopeless situations and stay the course.

"THE REBEL AND THE REVOLUTIONARY

> a rebel hates
> a revolutionary loves
> a rebel hates injustice
> a revolutionary loves justice
>
> a rebel negates
> a revolutionary creates
> a rebel reacts
> a revolutionary acts
>
> a rebel divides
> a revolutionary unites
> a rebel says :
> 'my rights'
> a revolutionary :
> 'our duties'
>
>
> a rebel attacks
> the singer
> and is deaf to the song
> a revolutionary retrains
> the singer
> and rewrites the song
>
> a rebel sees red

all vision blinkered
by the burning grass
a revolutionary sees
the wondrous colours
that is the rainbow
which follows the deluge
which quells the flames

for a revolutionary knows
where promises lie
when hopes are false
how rage is disciplined
why the grass has roots

a rebel asks '*why*?'
a revolutionary, '*why not*?'

a revolutionary is an individual
but never individualistic
is sometimes alone
but never lonely
a rebel perceives
the winter
of today
a revolutionary conceives
the spring
for tomorrow

for tomorrow shall dawn
dreams will come true
the nightmare will end
when a rebel
matures
into a revolutionary

francis khoo 1987"

Francis with Yasser Arafat.

In 2010, Francis' kidneys failed completely and he was on the last stretch of peritoneal dialysis. Peritoneal dialysis allows the patient to dialyse with bags of fluid while travelling. I became concerned since I knew as a doctor that this was his last stretch of freedom to travel. The next step would be haemodialysis which meant Francis would not be able to travel at all, as he had to be connected to the hospital's kidney machine every other day to have his blood "cleansed" of toxic byproducts. Since the formation of MAP, Francis had never had the opportunity to visit Sabra-Shatila. With typical humility and obstinacy, he always insisted that he should not go on any delegation since he was not a doctor or politician and unable to help anyone. Finally he succumbed to my forceful insistence that he owed it to himself to meet the people he had supported for 28 years, and he was paying his own airfare anyway. He was not using MAP's money.

His visit in 2010 was on the twenty eighth anniversary of the Sabra-Shatila Massacre. That visit to the Palestinian refugee camps of Lebanon and to Sabra-Shatila was for Francis like a home coming. He was already familiar with the names of all the places he was due to visit. Just like a Palestinian child who learnt the names of places in Palestine while growing up in exile in a refugee camp in Jordan, Lebanon or Syria, Francis learnt the names of the places in Shatila, the hospitals in Lebanon, the names of all the Palestinian refugee camps in Lebanon and their history. He met people whose names he already knew and many more whose names he learnt. He sang for all of them and invited them to join him in the singing.

In 2011, Palestinians in Lebanon invited Francis to visit them again. However he just had a successful kidney transplant in July 2011 and his doctors told him that he must not travel abroad for a year while his condition stabilised. That year was also the beginning of the Arab Spring. He was full of hope for the Palestinians, the

Middle East and for his own Singapore. He told the Palestinians in Lebanon he would be with them in 2012. His untimely death in November that year was a shock to all. But I am grateful he did not live to see the "Arab winter" which followed.

The following year 2012 marked that thirtieth anniversary of the Sabra-Shatila Massacre. I got news that Pope Benedict XVI was to visit Beirut and he had chosen to be there on 14-16 September 2012 – the thirtieth anniversary itself! Israel and the Western Press had always blamed the massacre as the work of the Lebanese Christians. But for those like me, who had lived through the events first-hand, we know that although a couple hundred Lebanese Christian militiamen working with the Israeli Army were inside Sabra and Shatila, the massacre was under the control of the Israeli Army. The Israelis sealed the camp so none could escape, supplied bulldozers for burying the bodies, shot military flares to allow the murders and rapes carried out by the Lebanese militia to continue throughout the nights. They supplied the weapons which made it possible. The couple hundred Lebanese Christian militiamen were trained by, and in, Israel. Still, this does not mean that the Church should ignore Christian culpability. Well in advance of His Holiness' visit, I wrote to him via his ambassador in London the following letter. In the letter I reminded the Pope that my late husband Francis was a devout Catholic, and I was writing as his widow. I wanted the Pope to acknowledge the victims of Sabra-Shatila.

ॐ

"His Holiness
Pope Benedict XVI
26 August 2012

Dear Holy Father,

It fills me with joy and hope to learn that you are planning to visit Lebanon in September. This September is also the 30th anniversary of the massacre of 3,000 Palestinians in the refugee camp of Sabra and Shatila in 1982. That event had cut through my heart, but slowly by the grace of God, the pain is healing.

In June, 1982, while still a fundamentalist, born-again Bible Presbyterian, I was shocked when I saw devastating scenes of Lebanon being destroyed by Israeli war planes. My church was entirely pro-Israel, but God made me wept when I saw innocent people, many of them children killed and thousands of homes destroyed. A month later, I left my hospital and volunteered my skills as a surgeon to work for the war wounded.

When I arrived in Beirut, I was sent to work in Gaza Hospital in Shatila Palestinian refugee camp, and that was the first time I met Palestinians and learnt of the injustice committed against them since 1948. A few weeks after my arrival, Israeli tanks invaded Beirut, and a contingent surrounded and sealed Sabra and Shatila on 15 September 1982. With all escape routes from the camps blocked, the Israelis sent in a group of Christian militiamen into the camps. They slaughtered unarmed women, children and old people. They raped and mutilated their victims, carving crosses on their bodies.

To add to the hurt, they identified themselves as the Kata'ebs, known to be Roman Catholics.

Although there was historical enmity between the Christians and the Muslims, that massacre was unique in its brutality. Deep within me, I have difficulty believing that Christians are capable of doing this to other human beings also made in the image of God. For many days after the massacre I found it difficult to put on the crucifix which Pope John Paul the Second had blessed. It was given to me by my late mother-in-law, a devout Catholic. By God's grace, and through her prayers and the steadfast love of my late husband I did not lose faith and I now attend Mass at Corpus Christi Church in Covent Garden, London, and receive Holy Communion there.

God has opened my eyes and heart to see and understand that the crimes committed against the innocent in Sabra-Shatila are also my crimes, for up to that point I have also been prejudiced and full of hatred towards the Arabs. I lived in spiritual blindness, thinking wrongly that I was righteous. I belonged to those who made such crimes possible. I asked God for forgiveness and in my repentance asked Him to give me the rest of my life to help the Palestinians. God, in His grace, has granted that and I am still working this out.

The Palestinian refugees in Lebanon are the most deprived of the 4 million which grew from the 750,000 driven out of historic Palestine in1948. They have no civil rights, no state, no homes, no passports, no future, and even no right to life.

While I pray that your visit to Lebanon will bring great blessing to the Christians in Lebanon, it has come on the 30th anniversary of dreadful massacre. Lack of recognition for the 450,000 (250,000 official and 200,000 unregistered) Palestinian refugees would mean that Christ's own vicar failed to acknowledge them. They are certainly the least among us all in the eyes of the world.

I know Your Holiness leaves on 16 Sept, two days before hundreds of us, Palestinians and non-Palestinians will pay our respect at Martyr's Square, the mass grave where a thousand of those slaughtered were buried.

I also understand that for security reasons, you have been advised not to visit Shatila Camp where the refugees continue to live in squalor. But I wonder if it is possible for you to send a representative to join us on the day of the commemoration – the 18 September with either a prayer, or a blessing for the victims? If this happens, we will truly feel the love of the Lord Jesus on that day, and the deprived and the dead will be truly blessed.

Holy Father – your visit will be packed with events, and like everyone else we will be praying for you and your team, that the visit will glorify God. But please let me know if you will be sending a representative to the commemoration on 18 Sept 2012. I arrive in Beirut on 13 Sept 2012 to help with the commemoration, and can be contacted through Miss Ellen Siegel who will be staying at the Casa Dior Hotel, Hamra, Beirut.

Look forward to hearing from you.

Your loving sister in the Lord

Dr Swee Ang, Consultant Orthopaedic Surgeon
Founder and Patron, Medical Aid for Palestinians"

As-Safir, the largest Arabic newspaper in Lebanon translated this into Arabic and published it during the Pope's visit. As anticipated, the Pope did not join the commemoration though his Cardinal in Lebanon did email me a few days after the Pope's departure.

Francis was not around to critique and edit my writings anymore, but he had taught me basic writing skills. I had to grow up and continue writing on my own. As Lebanon's Palestinians plunged into deeper despair and oblivion, I wanted to write something to encourage them. The following piece is called "Lesson on Hope" and was published on the eve of the thirtieth anniversary of the Sabra-Shatila Massacre.

"A LESSON ON HOPE
On the 30th anniversary of the Sabra-Shatila massacre, 2012

This year, while the Palestinians in Lebanon are preparing to commemorate the 30th anniversary of the Sabra-Shatila massacre, Lebanon is receiving thousands of refugees fleeing the fighting in Syria. We pray that, with international resolve, the conflict will end soon and the Syrian refugees will be able to return.

Sixty four years ago, in 1948, Lebanon received another group of refugees – some of the 750,000 Palestinians fleeing the massacres and the destruction of the villages and towns in Palestine. They were put in tents and promised the right of return to their homes. But Palestine was renamed Israel. The refugees and their children remained in Lebanon, dispersed in 12 refugee camps, forming part of the 4 million Palestinian refugees worldwide today. For them, there was no enthusiasm from the Western powers to address the root cause of their dispossession and no support for their returning to their ancestral homes.

Each September, hundreds of Palestinians and friends from worldwide meet in Shatila, at Martyr's

Francis, Swee with MAP's CEO and Lebanon Programme Director
at Martyr Square.

Square, where a thousand of those killed in Sabra-Shatila were buried. We mourn and remember those whose lives were cruelly cut off. In so doing we ensure they will not be forgotten and we also pay homage to their families.

Thirty years ago, in August 1982, I arrived as a young volunteer surgeon to work in Gaza Hospital in Sabra-Shatila Palestinian refugee camp in West Beirut. As a born again fundamentalist Christian I grew up an ardent supporter of Israel. That summer I watched on television the relentless bombardment of Lebanon by Israeli war planes. Countless were killed, among them many children. Hospitals, factories, schools and homes had become heaps of rubble. My pro-Israel Christian friends were unable to convince me that people in Lebanon deserve to suffer and die since they harbour a terrorist group known as the PLO (Palestine Liberation Organisation). Somehow I wanted to help the people in Lebanon. So when Christian Aid sent an appeal asking for a surgeon to help look after the wounded, I resigned from my British hospital, and left for Beirut.

That was my first visit to the Middle East. I never knew Palestinians existed until then. The western popular press only told of the terrorist PLO, which hated Jews, planted bombs and hijacked planes. They said this group had built their base in Lebanon and that Israel was helping Lebanon flush them out, even if Lebanon had to be flattened to achieve this. One Israeli spokesperson announced "To make an omelette, one have to first crack eggs"!

I arrived in a Beirut that was devastated after 10 weeks of heavy air bombardment. There was scarcity of food, water and medicine due to the military blockade. Homeless families flooded abandoned car parks, schools and even slept on the road-side. I was taken past Akaa Hospital; a five storey hospital reduced to rubble and mangled wires. This hospital was at one end of Rue Sabra, the main street of Shatila. At the other end was Gaza Hospital, which was still standing, despite the tenth and eleventh floors being wrecked by shells. Both were state of the art Palestine Red Crescent Society hospitals, and both were targeted despite flying International Red Cross flags. I was placed in Gaza Hospital to head the orthopaedic department and facilitate its re-opening.

Soon after my arrival the PLO evacuated. It was the price demanded to stop further heavy aerial bombardment of Lebanon and lift the continuous military blockade. Fourteen thousand able bodied men and women from the PLO evacuated with the guarantee by the Western powers that their families left behind would be protected. Some of those leaving were fighters, but others were PLO civil servants such as doctors, lecturers, trade unionists, media personnel, engineers and technicians. The PLO was the government in exile of the Palestinians. Thus fourteen thousand families in Lebanon lost their breadwinner – often the father or the eldest brother, in addition to those killed by the bombs.

This ceasefire lasted only three weeks. The multinational peace-keeping force, entrusted by the ceasefire agreement to protect the Palestinian civilians of Beirut, abruptly withdrew. On 15 September several hundred Israeli tanks drove into West Beirut. Some of them ringed and sealed Shatila Camp to prevent the inhabitants from fleeing. The Israelis sent their allies, a group of Christian militiamen, into the camp. When the tanks withdrew from the perimeter of the camp on the 18 September, they left behind 3,000 dead civilians.

Our hospital team, who had worked non-stop for the previous 72 hours, was ordered to leave our patients at machine-gun point, and marched along Rue Sabra out of the camp. As I emerged from the basement operating theatre, I learnt the painful truth. While we were struggling to save a few dozen lives, people were dying by the thousands. Some of the bodies were already rotting in the hot Beirut sun.

The images of the massacre are deeply burnt into my memory. They include dead and mutilated bodies lining the camp alleys, bodies which only a few days before were living human beings full of hope and life, rebuilding their homes, trusting that they would be left in peace to raise their young ones after the evacuation of the PLO. These were people who welcomed me into their broken homes. They served me Arabic coffee and whatever food they found, simple fare but given with warmth and generosity. They shared with me their broken lives and how they came to be refugees in Lebanon. They showed me faded photographs of their homes and families in Palestine before 1948 and the large house keys they still kept with them. The women shared with me their beautiful embroidery, each with motifs of the villages they left behind. Many of these villages were destroyed after they left.

There were patients we failed to save and those brought in dead to the hospital. They left behind orphans and widows. A wounded mother begged us take down the hospital's last unit of blood from her to give to her child. She died shortly afterwards. Women raped before being killed left cruel psychological scars on their children who survived.

The frightened faces of families rounded up by gunmen; the desperate young mother who tried to give me her baby to take to safety; the stench of decaying bodies as mass graves continued to be uncovered day after day will never leave me. The piercing cries of women who discovered the remains of their loved ones from bits of clothes, refugee identity cards, as more bodies were found continue to haunt me.

The people of Sabra-Shatila returned after the massacre to rebuild their homes once more. Gaza Hospital re-opened. But their courage was rewarded with yet more violence. Shatila, Burj-el-Brajneh, and Rashiddyeh camps were held siege and attacked from 1985 to 1988, killing 2,500 and making 30,000 homeless. Nahr-el-Bared Camp in the north, home to 40,000 Palestinians was flattened in 2007 and yet to be rebuilt. The Palestinian refugee camps of Lebanon became the most squalid and deprived in the Middle East.

Add to this the Lebanese law prohibiting Palestinians from taking up 30 professions and 40 artisan trades outside the refugee camps, and it is not difficult to see how the younger generation despair, Some youngsters drop out from schools in search of manual labouring work. Palestinians are also prohibited from owning or inheriting properties. With these unjust laws in place, they are confined to the refugee camps with no escape. Denied the right of return to their homes in Palestine, they are not only born refugees, they will also die refugees and so will their children.

For me, one painful question needs to be answered. Not why they die, but why did they die refugees? After 64 years, how can we allow a situation where a person's only claim to humanity is a refugee identity card? This question has haunted me for 30 years. It has yet to receive an answer.

But in recent years, as we journey along Rue Sabra as part of our annual commemoration of the Sabra and Shatila massacre, our weary footsteps are suddenly lightened by the influx of hundreds of young Palestinians. They are the post-massacre generation, reminding us that there is life after that horror.

Full of eagerness and courage, in defiance of those who worked so hard to obliterate them, they have survived and will survive.

Is there hope for the Palestinians? They had lost their country 64 years ago and found themselves on alien land which would not even grant them basic civil rights. Those who live in Gaza and West Bank find themselves under siege and imprisoned behind the Wall. Palestinian land is gobbled up daily for Israeli settlements and military use. In Shatila, the younger generation enter this world in the shadow of the ugly massacre. The wounds have not healed.

But there is hope. As a people they have survived against all odds. If you talk to the youngsters in the refugee camps, you will know that they have never forgotten Palestine. They will tell you that even though they might not make it back to Palestine in their life-time, their children will.

Supporters and friends from round the world increase daily, inspired by their courage and resilience.

For those of us who are privileged to enter into their lives and receive their generous hospitality, our gratitude knows no bounds. We discover true friendship. We have learnt that poverty and deprivation are no obstacles to human dignity. We admire their courage in their daily struggles. When their children embrace us, new life and hope return.

One such occasion was last year when a group of young Palestinians put on an event for those of us who came to join the commemoration of the Sabra-Shatila massacre. They had no money and no sponsors, so they held the event in Martyr's Square in the evening. It was poetry reading with hip-hop; instant painting of the silhouettes of their friends onto the whitewashed walls; and traditional dapke dancing. Nearly all of them were born after the massacre, so they asked me to give them my firsthand account.

I recalled the events of 1982, ending with the following:

"A few days after the massacre, I walked down Rue Sabra towards Gaza Hospital. The stench of decaying human flesh was unbearable. Survivors were identifying the remains of their loved ones. A group of kids spotted me and called out 'Doctora Sine' (Chinese Doctor). Most of them were orphans, destitute and homeless. Suddenly they stood in front of me and asked for their pictures to be taken. As I released my camera shutter, they raised their hands in a victory sign and said 'We are not afraid'. That picture has as background broken buildings, mass graves, and hopelessness but the children in the foreground defied them with their hands raised in a victory sign. I have been back to Lebanon many times but have never found those children again. They might have perished. But they will always be my inspiration. During the darkest hour, I will see them with their hands raised up, defying intimidation and death, poised to regain the dignity they had been robbed of."

Since then, I have met many more children in Gaza and the West Bank. They are just as courageous and precious as their counterpart in Lebanon. They have suffered so much but remained fearless and steadfast.

This anniversary we must reflect on how the Palestinians build and rebuild their lives courageously over the last 64 years, and how we as friends can support them in their struggle for justice. We will look through our tears to see the wonderful young generation. Life has returned to Shatila. After thirty years with the Palestinians, I have learnt this lesson on hope.

Dr Swee Chai Ang, September 2012
Author "From Beirut to Jerusalem"
Patron and co-founder, Medical Aid for Palestinians."

In 1984, inspired by our 7 years as political refugees and being stateless, Francis wrote "Passport" for the Palestinians. As a fellow traveller and a kindred spirit, with no passport, he understood the meaning of statelessness too well. It was translated into Arabic and Italian on the thirtieth anniversary of Sabra-Shatila. The stateless, passport-less Palestinians in the refugee camps of Lebanon love his poem dedicated to them.

"PASSPORT

> what is a passport
> but a scrapbook galore
> boasting faraway places
> you have travelled before?
>
> what is a passport
> but a hassle to you
> what with visas and fees
> for you to renew?

what is a passport
but duty-free fags
and airports and customs
and samsonite bags?

but where is my passport
my right to have one
that mark of my birthright
my place in the sun?

where is the passport
for those kept behind
for family and patriots
within the 'green line'?

where is the passport
for sabra, shatila
for millions in *menfa*
ejected diaspora?

where is that passport
for al'quds, ramallah
nablus, jabali'yah
tulkarm and rafah?

when can a passport
cry out 'palestine'?
this land ain't your land
for this land is mine

but this is my passport
the one i hold dear
a flag, a rock
a chequered *keffiyeh*

for soon i'll go
where *za'ter* grow
dance the *debkeh*
come what may

so come that day
my karameh
so come that day
my karameh

francis khoo   27.7.84

Francis died an exile, a fate shared by many Palestinians. The younger generation of Palestinians only know too well this will happen to them unless a just solution can be found in this generation. As a special concession the Singapore government gave me a one trip travel document to take Francis' ashes home to be laid next to those of his parents and his older brothers. The exile had returned home.

After this single trip, I left Singapore to continue my life in exile in London, and with my orthopaedic surgical practice and Palestinian support activities. Emotionally I steeled myself to being alone. But as I entered into my fourth year as a widow, I suddenly realised that Francis is still very much with me. When I was asked to write this chapter I thought I would be writing a memorial, and originally the title was Life without Francis. But as I wrote and re-read what I wrote I realise that he is still here with all of us. That is why this chapter is called Life with Francis.

Feb 2015

THE WOUNDS OF GAZA

I returned to Gaza in January 2009 when it sustained the worst attack since the Six Day war in 1967. The Christmas week of 2008 was rudely interrupted by shocking scenes of Gaza being bombed by land, air and sea. In just three short weeks, 1,400 Palestinians were killed, nearly half of them children. In this tiny part of Occupied Palestine, there were 5,450 casualties, severe enough to require operations; many remain in a critical state today. Over 21,000 homes were destroyed, 4,000 of which were flattened to rubble by the deployment of implosion bombs. Other buildings were not spared – 40 mosques, hospitals, clinics, schools, even United Nations warehouses. The scale of attacks matched that meted out to the Lebanon in 1982, or indeed, during the 2006 invasion, with similar intensity, ferocity and breaches of international law.

I have known Gaza since the days of the first *intifada*, twenty years ago. Indeed, *From Beirut to Jerusalem* was written during the six months I had to spend waiting for the Israelis to grant my first visa into Gaza. A surgeon was urgently needed to treat the untold injuries sustained

333

by unarmed Palestinians during that uprising, and I volunteered.

The enforced wait proved productive; it enabled me time to pause my work in Beirut, produce these memoirs and then head for the Gaza strip when the visa finally came in 1988. I spent the next six months as the only foreign orthopaedic surgeon in the Anglican hospital of Al-Ahli in Gaza city.

I first met Palestinians in 1982 when I responded to an international appeal for help following Israel's invasion of the Lebanon. I was warned by my Church these people were 'terrorists' and the Philistines of the Bible. In the refugee camps of Beirut, however, I found camp people who were warm and generous and who kept telling me of a home their young had never seen. Of a place called Palestine they were forced to flee in 1948. And of their determination to return one day. From Beirut, they would return to their Jerusalem. That their wish to exercise their right of return remained undimmed through the passing years and that the Palestinian nation was indivisible. Those in the diaspora was one with those under occupation.

They told me the hospital they named 'Akka' in Shatila camp was to remember the coastal city many came from. And 'Gaza' the hospital in Sabra camp I worked in was named after the tiny strip of land just 147 square miles in Palestine.

In September of that year, thousands of unarmed men, women and children of the camps were massacred in Sabra and Shatila. That massacre forced me to acknowledge Palestinians existed and their story of exile was true. This book was written in dedication to those who died and to all survivors who remained steadfast in their determination to return to Palestine.

I returned to Beirut many times and was there in 1987 when news of the Intifada emerged. Palestinians rose up in an uprising of civil disobedience against the Israeli occupation of the West Bank and Gaza. The Israeli army responded brutally to put down the uprising. Many of my friends in the Lebanon were anxious for their families who remained behind and did not flee in 1948 and 1967. But they were also proud it had finally happened after decades of occupation. I told my friends I would go to Gaza and promised to report back on a Gaza most of them had not seen.

They were full of hope that morning in 1987. The Uprising was a declaration to the whole world of the refusal of Palestinians in the West Bank and Gaza to live under Israeli occupation. TV coverage worldwide showed Palestinian children confronting Israeli armoured cars and tanks with stones. Women and old folk were not afraid anymore. It was David and Goliath, my favourite Bible story.

Occupied Palestine was telling the world, "We will die standing; we will not live on our knees". Their courage captured the sympathy and imagination of the world.

To crush the Uprising, tear gas was fired into unarmed demonstrations, into homes, schools and hospitals. 'Plastic' bullets and 'rubber' bullets were fired at very close range into the eyes and heads of demonstrators, causing blindness and death. Israeli soldiers were filmed on TV beating a captured Palestinian to death. As Yitzchak Rabin, the then Prime Minister boasted openly that when Israel was through with the Palestinians, they will be a nation of cripples.

Because of the large numbers of casualties, the UN asked for an orthopaedic surgeon. I responded and left the Lebanon for Gaza a year later. Despite UN sponsorship, Israel took six months to allow me in.

I remember how I first heard of the news of that uprising. I was on a routine morning round with 'Mamma' Rita, an 80 year-old retired German ambulance driver and paramedic who volunteered with our charity Medical Aid for Palestinians. We were doing a daily morning milk round, providing milk, basic medical care and advice for the homeless in Beirut. Each family was partitioned from the other by a blanket and had to contend with a living space of 3 metres by 3 metres. Thus a small basement garage was shared by dozens of families. You could smell the overcrowding. I remember that December morning in 1987, wet, cold, dark and damp. The floors of the shelters were flooded; there was no electricity and running water. Here you saw despondency and their sense of helplessness was palpable.

The intervening years gave no respite to the suffering of the people of the camps who survived the massacre. Indeed, their conditions deteriorated and morale sank to a low. These were people who had little to look forward to, the children had lost their smiles and laughter, their homes were destroyed in the camp wars of the mid-80s and many families were sheltering in abandoned car parks and basements.

But that December morning, something was different. Glued to their radio, they heard the first news of the Intifada. Explaining in broken English to me, I saw a sparkle in their eyes as they spoke of the Intifada. Their smiles began to return. They were beginning to regain their dignity.

They told me their grandparents said Gaza was very beautiful. They could only imagine and dream of going to live there one day. They were told of the olive and orange groves and the blue Mediterranean sea. The wanted me to confirm Gaza's beauty. They were indeed correct; Gaza, despite the suffering and devastation, is a truly beautiful place.

❧   ❧   ❧

In the course of that first Intifada, hundreds died, thousands more were injured and tens of thousands imprisoned.

I worked in the Al-Ahli hospital in Gaza city. It was a small hospital founded in 1891 by Christian missionaries and was the only independent medical centre not under Israeli control at that time. In all the other Israeli controlled hospitals, wounded Palestinians brought in for treatment were open to scrutiny and subjected to arrest. Doctors had to report stone throwers shot by the Israeli soldiers. It was understandable why wounded demonstrators preferred the security of Al Ahli.

As we refused the Israeli Defence Force automatic access to our hospital, we were hostilely treated. If they wished to arrest one of our patients, they would surround the hospital with armoured vehicles. Soldiers would take up positions on our rooftops pointing at us with loaded automatic weapons, ready to snipe into the hospital. Indeed, my clinic was shot into. Ground commandoes would advance into the hospital. Sometimes soldiers would storm in while women were in labour.

On one such occasion, I was finishing an operation on a patient who was shot in the shoulder. Soldiers marched straight into my operating theatre – guns and all – and demanded I surrendered him for interrogation. I refused to let them do so. Taken aback, they promised to return later to take him once he recovered from his anaesthetic. They had probably never had to contend and row with aggressive Chinese women before!

They did return that night but could not find the patient. Except for the foreign doctors' rooms, the whole hospital was searched to no avail. My foreign anaesthetic colleague had hid him in his room. Our patient escaped but the hospital saw no end of harassment for the next few days.

But the staff continued to plough on, treating and operating on more and more wounded.

❦   ❦   ❦

The entire Gaza Strip was regularly put under curfew. These curfews were prolonged and often lasted for weeks on end. Children were locked up in their homes and not allowed to go to school. They were not even allowed to look out of the window. They risked being shot at if they did so.

May 1989 was an abnormal month for me. Israel was celebrating its Foundation Day and placed the whole of Gaza under military curfew. I was out in Jerusalem to buy medical supplies and, as a UN official, was exempted from the curfew. As I drove through, I saw how Israel was decked out with blue and white flags, and preparations for celebrations were well in advance. There was an atmosphere of gaiety in Israel but as I advanced back into Gaza, my heart was heavy. Gaza had remained silent, like a ghost town. There was a curfew, no music was allowed, no one was allowed out of their homes. My ambulance was the only moving object as I drove through Gaza city. It was eerie.

I remember only too vividly 6 May, 1989, a day of blood. It was Eid – the ending of the Muslim fasting month of Ramadan – and it was usually a time when everyone broke their fast, visiting each others' homes, showering gifts and offering well wishes. But as worshippers emerged from their mosques, Israeli helicopters appeared and started firing live rounds at them. Children and young men angrily responded by stoning the ground Israeli soldiers. They responded by shooting back. In that few minutes, 343 injured Palestinians were brought into our tiny hospital and 6 of them died while awaiting treatment. We operated on the wounded all day and throughout the night and into the next morning. As I emerged at dawn, I was told to go off for a shower and have something to eat.

It was then that I had a distinct sense of *deja vue*. At 7.00 am, 18 September, 1982, years before, I was ordered out of the basement operating theatre of Gaza hospital in Beirut's Shatila camp. I walked into the bright sunlight and learnt the truth and scale of what happened over the previous three days. I was a witness and survivor of the Sabra-Shatila massacre.

But on that 6 May 1989 morning, something was different. As I left the hospital operating theatre that morning, the tree in the hospital courtyard greeted my eyes. Overnight it had put out pink blossoms. Against the bright May sky, it looked bizarre and beautiful. When I reached my quarters on top of the hospital pharmacy, I knelt down and burst out into sobs. Memories of that earlier massacre in Beirut and what I experienced the night before in Gaza and my six months there overwhelmed me.

The tear gas and the shootings, the sheer humiliation forced upon families, the open cess-pools, the realities of life under occupation. "God, are you still there?" I asked. But then I looked out of my window. The tree in full blossom seemed to tell me that He had not forgotten. Spring was in Gaza, as beautiful as it always was.

❧ ❧ ❧

When Israel withdrew its settlements from Gaza in 2006, it created a large prison for all one and a half million people. It put Gaza under military siege. No one was allowed to enter or leave Gaza without Israel's permission and a blockade arose.

Visitors, especially those from the West, usually visit the West Bank and tend to bypass Gaza. It was for a start, logistically difficult, given the extra security ringed around Gaza by the Israeli army. Personally I had spent hours at the Israeli Erez checkpoint trying to gain entry into Gaza in the intervening years. Likewise there was no guarantee I could get out at a chosen time after each visit. This belied the myth that Israeli withdrawal at that time gave Gaza unprecedented freedom. Many westerners also believed Gaza was poor and uninteresting and teeming with Islamic zealots and suicide bombers. This belief is untrue.

வ   வ   வ

When the latest attack on Gaza started in December 2008, Dr Ghassan Abu-Sita, a young Palestinian surgical colleague of mine in London, became concerned about the level of destruction and the fate of his family. Ghassan comes from a distinguished Gazan family and was desperate to go there to assess the medical needs and plan for long-term medical help. While we were both surgeons, we realised our role was not to perform operations – Gaza had superb and skilled local Palestinian surgeons. What they needed was medical supplies and further training. We wanted to know what the best way of supporting them was.

Throughout the 22 days of bombardment, Gaza was hermetically sealed off by Israeli troops. We figured that we had a narrow window of opportunity to get into Gaza from the south, at the Egyptian-Rafah checkpoint. The normal entry through Israel was hopeless as too many visitors found to their cost. But the Egyptian side in the south also proved difficult as Egypt could not open the Rafah crossing without Israeli authorisation. Our hunch was correct.

As we had anticipated the Israelis declared a temporary unilateral ceasefire on the eve of President Barrack Obama's inauguration. The Israeli general election was also due to take place soon. We left London for Egypt.

The road from Cairo to the border at Rafah was punctuated by at least ten Egyptian military checkpoints. Despite many of them being unmanned, it still took more than five hours to reach Rafah. Along the route, various trucks heading for Gaza were turned back. One of these was a truck with cement; building material was not allowed for Gaza. The bombed out hospitals, schools and homes must remain ruin and rubble. The crossing had just been open for doctors to go to do humanitarian work. A long convoy of trucks with medical supplies and equipment were held up in line at a separate goods crossing near us. Each truck's contents were carefully searched, causing enormous delay.

The British Embassy in Cairo warned us it was reckless to go and that we were going against the advice of the government. Everyone was nervous about the prospect of being allowed in. The previous day saw dozens of medical doctors turned away. So it was rather surreal that three hours of frustrating wait finally ended and we were waved on to the bus taking us into Palestine.

Once we entered Gaza, it felt like a home-coming. The atmosphere was completely different. The Palestinians meeting us carried our luggage without wanting any tip and we had our passports stamped with Palestine entry visas. Thirteen Palestinian young men who wanted to leave Gaza were turned back by the Egyptians and were denied permission to leave Gaza. At least 25 Palestinians were denied exit permits to study abroad, despite all being awarded international scholarships to do so.

A Palestinian health ministry liaison person came to meet us. We said we came from Britain to assess the medical needs of Gaza for a medical charity. He was very pleased and arranged an ambulance to take us to the taxi-stand at Rafah. That evening, Gaza radio announced that the first British medical team had arrived. Ghassan thought it very funny, what with him being a Palestinian from Gaza and I a Chinese. Fortunately, we were joined by Dr Sonia Robbins, a British plastic and hand surgeon, the next day. So, with her, we now had an Anglo-British component, a truly rainbow coalition.

We stayed with Abdel Daim, Ghassan's father-in-law who came to pick us up at Rafah. I had been on the road leading from Rafah in the south to Gaza city in the north many times during the first Intifada. I remember the road being crowded with buildings and shops on either side. But this time, as Abdel Daim drove us I was surprised the road was flanked by open spaces – fields and clear areas. It was apparent that since the second Intifada in 2001, many buildings were destroyed by Israeli military action. As Gaza had been under siege most of the time, rebuilding was not possible, so these clear spaces became fields over time. Further north, there were recent bombed-out buildings – heaps of rubble, collapsed concrete, mangled cables – the devastation of the latest invasion. This was very much like Beirut in 1982. And what Al-Jazeera TV in London was showing during the preceding three weeks – factories, schools, playgrounds, petrol stations, mosques and homes were bombed out and gone.

I looked at Northern Gaza – how often have I driven down Sal-Uddin Road, the main road from Gaza City leading to the Israeli Erez checkpoint, in 1988 and 1989. I remember every turn and corner. I know the citrus orchards, the farms and the homes of people with beautiful gardens. Often I would stop my ambulance to give a ride to the farm workers and they in return would give me freshly picked lemons and oranges. I now see it completely laid waste by Israeli explosives. Northern Gaza 2009 resembled the nuclear devastation of Hiroshima after the Second World War. The entire area was obliterated.

"Look at our petrol stations!" Abdel Daim exclaimed. "Where?" I asked. There by the road-side was a man squatting. Surrounding him were several jerry cans – plastic containers for carrying water – filled with petrol instead. "From the tunnels", remarked Daim. The tunnels also brought in food, medicines, cigarettes, Coca-Cola and other items. Ghassan bought a can of Coke still covered with tunnel sand.

As he drove, Daim continued, "They pound us from the sea, shelled us from their tanks, bombed us with F16s and helicopters – they have killed and wounded so many. But they have not recaptured one inch of our territory. Welcome to Free Gaza!" Wow! I thought. What a defiant spirit. He went on, "I will not leave. If they want to, they can come and kill me on my land."

Yes. How can I forget? In the first Intifada, I spent six months with them and found the same steadfastness and courage. I had completed *From Beirut to Jerusalem* and wanted to share with them the story of their Palestinian relatives in the Lebanon. I had brought along only six copies with me but the nurses in the hospital carefully spliced the book into four or five sections and shared it out among the others so more could have access to the book. They were hungry for news on the Lebanon. While the Beirut hospitals were named after places in Palestine, those in Gaza, in turn, named their places after Telazater and Shatila, in honour of the refugee camps in the Lebanon. There is no better example than this to prove that the Palestinian people are one and indivisible, that there is no distinction between those under occupation and those in exile.

Daim turned off the main road and into a narrow road with several pot-holes. On the one side was a cemetery. "You remember Mohammed – the little boy killed by the Israelis at the beginning of the Intifada? The picture of him being cradled in his father's arms was seen on world TV. He is buried here as this is where he lived". Beyond the cemetery were olive groves and destroyed houses still occupied by people. It was off the beaten track with donkey-drawn carts as the main form of transport. Yet everyone seemed to know Daim and they waved at him as he drove past.

On the left side was a field with two peacefully grazing ponies. Yet another turn brought us closer to the olive trees. Daim pointed to a large field, "The Israelis came one night and destroyed all the olive and apricot trees on 60 *dunums* of land. Most of those trees were over 50 years old and planted by my mother. The area is named after my mother, Magbule, who dug the first well here. She came at the age of 17 years from Jordan to marry my father, the Municipal Judge in Khan Younis." Daim later took us to the graves of both his parents on his farm and the grave of his olive trees. The remains of the olive trees were neatly piled together, the huge trunks reminiscent of those in the Garden of Gethsemane in Jerusalem. On his farm, even murdered olive trees deserved a grave.

When we finally reached Daim's home, flanked by palm trees, bougainvillea flowers, hibiscus, jasmine and honeysuckle, I found it difficult to believe suc' a beautiful garden stood in the midst of such destruction. An arrogant cockerel made his presence felt. But he was outdone by a peacock that fanned out his tail in huge grace and glory. "Oh, we have 30 of them in the farm," explained Daim. The house is a bungalow with a flat roof top. I started to climb to the roof but was immediately stopped by Daim as there were Israeli drones (robot spy aircraft equipped with rockets and mechanical snipers) surveying the area. Anything that moves would be shot at. I did not need convincing as I beat a hasty retreat.

Daim is a tall dignified Palestinian of about 60 with silver grey hair, moustache and long eyebrows to match. Beneath the stern appearance, was a kind man with a great sense of humour. He had been arrested and imprisoned four times, and although tortured, never betrayed his friends. He came from a Bedouin family in Beersheba and they were renowned for their strength and loyalty. The family was driven out and became refugees in Gaza. Aida, his wife, is a young looking and attractive lady, who decorated their home with beautiful Palestinian embroidery pieces. I first came across such embroidery in Beirut in 1982, in Shatila camp. Each village has its distinct motif. Women sat on the floor embroidering colourful and ornate motifs, each village distinct from the other. Despite the demolition of their villages, memory and heritage lived on through these colourful silk threads sewn on black cloth. It is very labour intensive, but soon I was able to pick the various motifs like the Star of Bethlehem, the Rose of Jerusalem, the Cedar tree, the Olive branch, and the rich red and orange of the Bedouin communities. Now in Aida's home, I saw all these once again displayed on cushion covers, pictures framed on the wall, cloth covering tables, the sofas and wrapped around vases. The beauty of the embroidery and the garden brought to life the real beauty of Palestine. Diaspora Palestinians always told me their Palestine was beautiful. I always dismissed this as mere sentimentality. But on this farm house, I know it is.

Although their home was spared total destruction, every single window pane was shattered. Many neighbouring buildings were also destroyed. Aida had tried to seal off the home from the cold, wintry Gaza air by pieces of polythene.

When the cold wind blows, the polythene 'curtains' flap and send a chill across the house. The family's warmth and generosity also concealed the dark history of Khan Younis. One evening, Aida's mother told me of the massacre of Khan Younis in 1956 under the command of Ariel Sharon. Nearly all men were killed, resulting in the women and children having to dig their graves.

How can I repay such hospitality of this Palestinian family? Each morning, before we embarked upon our visit to the hospitals, there would be Arabic coffee, home baked pastries, cheese and bread waiting for us. When we returned, there would be a cooked dinner. Just days ago they were eating bread with salt while Gaza was pounded by bombs. One day, we found that they had killed one of their turkeys and two chickens for us. As if it were not enough, Daim would leave one morning to buy us fresh fish. He could not allow us to leave Gaza without tasting their famous fish. It was extremely delicious, but I remember Gaza's fishermen were often shot at or even killed by Israeli gunboats if they strayed outside the three-mile waters of their own coast. My eyes still brim with tears as I recall that fish dinner.

We managed to visit all hospitals and saw the extent of damages to schools, clinics and UN buildings. We introduced ourselves as the 'British' medical team. We spoke to the medical personnel and administrators whom we found to be extremely disciplined and dedicated. Like the parting of the Red Sea some thousands of years ago, we left in time before the barriers were lowered and Gaza was once again sealed off from the world.

In Gaza, we wrote a quick report of our findings. We wrote it on a morning when Israeli bombs fell hard and fast in southern Gaza. We put the facts down and sent it out immediately. It was our witness and was published in the medical journal, the *Lancet Global Health Network*. It attracted a great deal of attention. Excerpts read:

The wounds of Gaza

The wounds of Gaza are deep and multi-layered. Are we talking about the Khan Younis massacre of 5,000 in 1956, or the execution of the 35,000 prisoners of war by Israel in 1967? Yet more wounds of the first Intifada, when civil disobedience by an occupied people against the occupiers resulted in massive wounded and hundreds dead? We also cannot discount the 5,420 wounded in southern Gaza alone since 2000. Hence what we are referring to below are only that of the invasion as of 27 December 2008.

Over the period of 27 December 2008 to the ceasefire of 18 January 2009, it was estimated a million and a half tons of explosives were dropped on Gaza Strip. Gaza is 25 miles by 5 miles and home to 1.5 million people. Prior to this, Gaza has been completely blockaded and starved for 50 days. In fact, since the Palestinian election, Gaza has been under total or partial blockade for several years...

On the first day of the invasion, 250 people were killed. Every single police station in Gaza was bombed killing large numbers of police officers. Having wiped out the police force, attention was turned to non-government targets. Gaza was bombed from the air by F16 and Apache helicopters, shelled from the sea by Israeli gunboats, and from the land by tank artillery. Many schools were reduced to rubble, including the American School of Gaza, 40 mosques, hospitals, UN buildings, and of course, 21,000 homes, 4,000 of which were demolished completely. It is estimated that 100,000 people were made homeless.

A. Israeli weapons – In addition to conventional weapons and high explosives, four categories of unconventional weapons could be identified –

i.   Phosphorus shells and bombs – eyewitnesses speak of bombs exploding at high altitude scattering a large canopy of phosphorus bomb lets which cover a large area.

During the land invasion, eyewitnesses describe the tanks shelling into homes first with a conventional shell. Once the walls are destroyed, a second shell, a phosphorus shell, is then shot into the homes. Used in this manner the phosphorus explodes and burns the families and the homes. Many charred bodies were found among burning phosphorus particles.

One area of concern is the phosphorus seems to be in a special stabilising agent, resulting in the phosphorus not completely burning out. Residue still covers the fields, playgrounds and compounds. They ignite when picked up by curious kids, or produce fumes when farmers return to water their fields. One returning family returning to water their field met with clouds of fumes producing epitasis. This makes the phosphorus an anti-personnel weapon against children.

Surgeons from hospitals are also reporting cases where after primary laparotomy for relatively small wounds with minimal contamination, they find on second look laparotomy increasing areas of tissue necrosis at about 3 days. Patients then become gravely ill and by about 10 days those patients needing a third relook encounter massive liver necrosis. This may or may not be accompanied by generalised bleeding, kidney failure and heart failure and death. Although acidosis, liver necrosis and sudden cardiac arrest due to hypocalcaemia are known to be complications of white phosphorus it is not possible to attribute these complications as being due to phosphorus alone.

There is real urgency to analyse and identify the real nature of this modified phosphorus as to its long term effect on the people of Gaza. There is also urgency in collecting and disposing of the phosphorus residues littering the entire Gaza Strip. As they give off toxic fumes when coming into contact with water, once the rain falls the whole area would be polluted with acid phosphorus fumes. Children should be warned not to handle and play with these phosphorus residues.

ii. Heavy Bombs – the use of DIME (dense inert material explosives) was evident though it is unsure whether depleted uranium was used in the south. In the civilian areas, surviving patients were found to have limbs truncated by DIME, since the stumps apart from being characteristically cut off in guillotine fashion also fail to bleed. Bomb casing and shrapnel are extremely heavy.

iii. Fuel air explosives – Bunker busters and implosions bombs have been used. There are buildings especially the eight-storey Science and Technology Building of the Islamic University of Gaza which had been reduced to rubble no higher than 5-6 feet high.

iv. Silent Bombs – People in Gaza described a silent bomb which is extremely destructive. The bomb arrives as a silent projectile at most with a whistling sound and creates a large area where all objects and living things are vaporised with minimal trace. We are unable to fit this into conventional weapons but the possibility of new particle weapons being tested should be suspected.

B. Executions – Survivors describe Israeli tanks arriving in front of homes demanding residents to come out. Children, old people and women would come forward, and as they were lined up they were fired upon and killed. Families have lost tens of their members through such executions. The deliberate targeting of unarmed children and women is well documented by human rights groups in the Gaza Strip over the past month.

C. Targeting of ambulances – 13 ambulances have been fired upon killing drivers and first aid personnel in the process of rescue and evacuation of the wounded.

D. Cluster Bombs – Dropped on the Rafah border crossing with Egypt. The first patients wounded by cluster bombs were brought into the Abu Yusef Najjar Hospital after the ceasefire.

Since more than half the tunnels in the border with Egypt have been destroyed, Gaza has lost part of her life-line. These tunnels contrary to popular belief are not for weapons, though light weapons could have been smuggled through them. They are the mainstay of food and fuel for Gaza. Palestinians are beginning to tunnel again. However it became clear that cluster bombs were dropped on to the Rafah border and the first was accidentally set off by tunnelling. Five burn patients were brought in after setting off a booby trap kind of device.

E. Death toll – as of 25 January, 2009, it is estimated 1,350 were killed with the numbers increasing daily. This is due to the severely wounded continuing to die in hospitals. About 40 per cent killed were children.

F. Severe Injuries – The severely injured numbered 5,450 with 40 per cent children. These are mainly large burns and poly-trauma patients. Single limb fractures and walking wounded are not included in these figures.

Through our conversations with doctors and nurses the word holocaust and catastrophe were repeatedly used. The medical staff bear the psychological trauma of the past month living through the situation and dealing with mass casualties which swamped their department and operation rooms. Many patients died in the Accident and Emergency Department while awaiting treatment. In a district hospital, the orthopaedic surgeon carried out 13 external fixations in less than a day.

It is estimated that of the severely injured, 1,600 will suffer permanent disabilities. These include amputations, spinal cord injuries, head injuries, large burns with crippling contractures. There are 400 amputees of which 88 are bilateral.

Special factors to consider – the high death and injury toll is due to several factors.

No escape – Gaza is sealed off by Israeli troops. No one can escape the bombardment and the land invasion. There is simply no escape. Even within the strip itself, movement from north to south is impossible as tanks have cut off both halves. By contrast, it was possible for people in the Lebanon in 1982 and 2006 to escape from an area of heavy bombardment to an area of relative calm. Gaza does not have this option.

Gaza is densely populated – The bombs used by Israel have been precision bombs, they have a hundred percent hit rate on buildings which are crowded with people, such as the central market, police stations, schools, the UN compound used as a shelter from bombardment, mosques (40 of them destroyed) and the homes of families who thought they were safe as there were no combatants in them. In high rise flats, a single implosion bomb would destroy multiple families. The pattern of consistent targeting of civilians make one suspect that the military are but collateral damage, while civilians are the primary targets.

Quantity and quality of the ammunition – as described above.

Gaza's lack of defence – against the modern weapons of Israel. Gaza has no tanks, no planes, no anti-aircraft missiles against an invading army. We experienced that first hand in a minor clash of Israeli tank shells versus Palestinian's AK-47 return fire. The forces were simply unmatched.

Absence of well constructed bomb shelters for civilians – Unfortunately even if these were present they would be no match for bunker busters possessed by the Israeli army.

Conclusion

The next assault on Gaza would be just as disastrous. The people of Gaza are extremely vulnerable and defenceless in the event of another attack. If the international community is serious about preventing such a large scale of deaths and injuries in the future, it will have to develop some sort of defence force for Gaza. Otherwise many more vulnerable civilians will continue to die.

❧ ❧ ❧

The report stayed on the *Lancet Global Health Network* for 28 days – from 2 February to 2 March 2009. It was taken off the website due to massive pro-Israeli protest accusing it of factual inaccuracies. However, in those 28 days, it had found its way into many other publications and as of March 2009, has been translated into ten languages.

Dr Ang Swee Chai
March 2009

GAZA 2014

It was the last week of August 2014. I looked out through the large glass corridors on the twelfth floor of the London hospital where I worked. The late summer sun had cast its golden gentle rays over the whole of East London. Within this long glass sealed hospital corridor where only staff with special authorisation can pass, all is still. But the few trees outside this sealed building were gently swaying with a light breeze. Their movements broke the calm. For a split second I forgot my own deportation and that of my young surgical colleague by Israel a week ago, and the 50 days of nightmare, pain and destruction suffered by the people of Gaza from Israel's Operation Protective Edge. Gaza was bombed from the air, shelled by land and sea for 50 days and nights.

I also heard news that there was a ceasefire in Gaza pending further negotiations. The people of Gaza were celebrating the ceasefire through the night. It brought them hope that the enormous suffering of the last eight years imposed by the blockade, with the four major military assaults on this tiny strip of land would soon end. I respect their hopefulness, but a large part of me would always be sceptical since they had been betrayed again and again. I cried with pain over the loss of lives, destruction of homes and institutions – the price Gaza had paid to even reach this ceasefire. While the bombs were falling there was huge international protest and outcry, but it had not change the minds of those in control of political, military and economic power. So once the media attention faded I feared it will be a return to the status quo of the last 8 years of draconian hermetical blockade of food, medicines, fuel, essential raw materials – with regular bombardment by F16s, assault helicopters and tank shelling. Any eight year old child in Gaza would have lived through four major Israeli military assaults, plus countless air-raids in between these frightening and brutal assaults. He or she would have known of nothing else except the military blockade and the various military attacks.

I also heard that for the first time in 7 years a United Nations Food Convoy had passed through the Rafah Crossing from Egypt – so is the blockade actually over?

This was not to be. Rafah Crossing was rapidly closed again and remained close even at the time this article goes to press. The tunnels through which some essential goods like bicycles, food, medicines and even refrigerators were smuggled into Gaza were completely closed by the new Egyptian Government. That lifeline vanished.

The fifty days of military assault on Gaza, the Israeli Operation Protective Edge, had resulted in more than 2,100 deaths though many more bodies were still buried under the rubble. The dead included the annihilation of 91 Gazan families with parents, children, young infants and grand-parents killed together. There were more than 11,000 wounded, many crippled for life. Fifteen hospitals, forty five clinics. 8 fire stations and the main ambulance station were all targeted. Many were destroyed beyond repair. These were just part of the 76 health institutions targeted and destroyed. Eighty thousand homes were destroyed, making 500,000 people homeless.

Health institutions are supposed to be protected by international law. They are sanctuaries where the sick and wounded can be treated in a secure protected environment. Health is a human right. But this has never been the case for the Palestinians. In 1982, every single one of the Palestine Red Crescent hospitals and clinics in Lebanon were targeted. Most were reduced to rubble burying alive the patients under treatment within them. During the First Palestinian Uprising, I worked in Gaza treating civilians wounded by the Israeli Army. The Christian Hospital where I worked in and my operating theatre were regularly invaded by Israeli soldiers with the declared intention of abducting patients under treatment. They got away with that and continued to destroy hospitals and clinics in Operation Cast Lead in 2008-2009 and this time on an even bigger scale in Operation Protective Edge. No country dared to sanction Israel for their actions. There was total lack of political will.

I have to register my admiration and respect for the Palestinians doctors, nurses and health workers of Gaza who continued to work under fire, often to exhaustion, often silently bearing the grief of losing their own family and friends through this senseless massacre. Many foreign doctors volunteered to go to Gaza to help. But only a handful was allowed entry. Denial of entry and deportation were the rule.

When Dr Asif Chaudry, British consultant upper gastrointestinal cancer surgeon and I tried to go to Gaza to help them we were denied entry, detained and deported.

The pettiness of the Israeli security towards us was beyond belief. What could a couple of doctors do to alleviate the situation in Gaza except to provide a token gesture of friendship and solidarity? The interrogation was threatening, insulting, demeaning and degrading. They knew how to practice psychological victimisation to a fine art. It brought back to me the memories of my detention without trial by the Internal Security Department of Singapore in 1977. Among the usual accusations and scare tactics was the insinuation that I was having a relationship with my colleague who is young enough to be my son. This was not only an affront to the two of us but also to the honour of my late husband. But what was this compared to the historical and contemporary injustice and brutality committed against the Palestinians?

After the interrogation we were taken to Ramle Prison and detained overnight pending deportation. Ramle was a Palestinian village flattened during the Nakbah and the Prison was built on razed and confiscated Palestinian land. Apart from a few tall trees left in the neighbour-hood of the prison, there were no witnesses to what was before. Palestinian Ramle was wiped off the map.

Our detention and deportation was just Israel's attempt to teach us a lesson. They had to drive home the message that they as Occupier with superior military power can do anything they like. Asif and I wrote an account of our deportation and detention for the benefit of those who intend to go to Palestine. I have included our statement, Deportation Timeline, in Appendix 1.

But there is one thing they cannot do. They can humiliate us, imprison us, deport us but they can never stop us from supporting the Palestinians. We will support them where ever we are, and will speak up for them.

For me, my life is divided into two chapters – before I met the Palestinians and after I met them. I grew up in Singapore supporting Israel. Singapore's army, security and defence systems in the early days were built with Israeli support and advice. Our national trade union follows the pattern of the Israeli Histadrut. My church taught that the modern Israel was the fulfilment of Scriptural prophecy. We all rejoiced and celebrated at the victory of Israel against the Arab States during the Six Day War in 1967.

Years later, I was completely shocked when I saw on British television the ten week long ruthless Israeli aerial bombardment of Lebanon in 1982. Schools, factories, homes, hospitals, clinics and even cemeteries were blanket bombed. It was sold to the world as Operation Peace for Galilee, an anti-terrorist campaign against the Palestine Liberation Organisation, and that in order to make an omelette, Israel had to crack eggs. Yet the people killed and wounded were children, women, elderly and civilian men. I could only do one thing in my power. I resigned from my job in a London teaching hospital, said good-bye to my husband Francis and left for Lebanon to help the wounded.

I arrived in Sabra Shatilla Palestinian refugee camp in West Beirut in August 1982. West Beirut was as devastated as the news bulletin in London reported. Blocks of high rise buildings were reduced to rubble. There was no running water and electricity. People were hungry and the field hospitals had run out of supplies. The western press, especially the BBC, continued to run news bulletins on this human suffering as Israel's necessary campaign against the Palestinian terrorists.

But what did I find in Sabra Shatilla Palestinian Refugee Camp? I found no PLO terrorists. I found a patient, gentle and generous people who were deliberately forgotten by the world. They had suffered long, being pushed around from refugee camp to refugee camp when they were robbed of their homeland Palestine in 1948. They were maligned as terrorists when they were the victims of terror, persecution and injustice. Their humanity despite the persecution and injustice committed against them struck hard into my heart and soul. Their courage and steadfastness continue to inspire me daily. Many of them were already third generation refugees, a part of the 750,000 Palestinians thrown out of British Mandate Palestine to make room for the new Israel in 1948. At that time the population of Palestine was 1.5 million, so half of the population of 1948 Palestine were driven out, never to return to their ancestral homes.

The people of Sabra Shatilla taught me Palestine history. The women shared with me their beautiful embroidery. I listened to Palestinian songs, tried to learn the Dapke dance, tasted Palestinian Zatar and Arabic coffee. Palestinian generosity meant that I was immediately accepted as one of the family. It was in one bombed out home that I drank my first cup of Arabic coffee. Their families were decimated by the war – through death, disappearance and war wounds. It was also just after fourteen thousand PLO members were evacuated in exchange for a ceasefire. Families had lost fathers, husbands and brothers through the evacuation, leaving behind vulnerable women, children and old people. The western powers of USA, France and Italy promised to protect the refugee camps which were totally disarmed and defenceless. A few weeks later more than 3,000 of my friends in Sabra Shatilla were massacred.

I continued to work in Sabra Shatilla in Gaza Hospital after the massacre, and continued to witness more brutality committed against the Palestinians. The brutality meted out to the Palestinians was transcended at every stage by their courage and resilience. In 1988 I left Lebanon for Occupied Gaza to look after the wounded of the First Palestinian Uprising – the First Intifada, until Israel prevented me from continuing to work in Gaza in 1989.

From then on I was exiled from Palestine and could only support the Palestinians from abroad. It was only after the Oslo Accords that I was allowed to visit Occupied Palestine again through the special invitation of President Yasser Arafat in 1996.

In 2014, at the beginning of Operation Protective Edge, some of us who had lived and worked in Gaza before feared the worse for Gaza. We were concerned that this could be another Cast Lead which destroyed half of Gaza in 2009. I visited Gaza immediately after Cast Lead and what I found was in the chapter "The Wounds of Gaza". We wrote an open letter for Gaza which the Lancet published online on 23 July 2014: The open letter is as follows:

AN OPEN LETTER FOR THE PEOPLE IN GAZA

Paola Manduca, Iain Chalmers,
Derek Summerfield, Mads Gilbert,
Swee Ang, on behalf of 24 signatories

We are doctors and scientists, who spend our lives developing means to care and protect health and lives. We are also informed people; we teach the ethics of our professions, together with the knowledge and practice of it. We all have worked in and known the situation of Gaza for years.

On the basis of our ethics and practice, we are denouncing what we witness in the aggression of Gaza by Israel.

We ask our colleagues, old and young professionals, to denounce this Israeli aggression. We challenge the perversity of a propaganda that justifies the creation of an emergency to masquerade a massacre, a so-called "defensive aggression". In reality it is a ruthless assault of unlimited duration, extent, and intensity. We wish to report the facts as we see them and their implications on the lives of the people.

We are appalled by the military onslaught on civilians in Gaza under the guise of punishing terrorists. This is the third large scale military assault on Gaza since 2008. Each time the death toll is borne mainly by innocent people in Gaza, especially women and children under the unacceptable pretext of Israel eradicating political parties and resistance to the occupation and siege they impose.

This action also terrifies those who are not directly hit, and wounds the soul, mind, and resilience of the young generation. Our condemnation and disgust are further compounded by the denial and prohibition for Gaza to receive external help and supplies to alleviate the dire circumstances.

The blockade on Gaza has tightened further since last year and this has worsened the toll on Gaza's population. In Gaza, people suffer from hunger, thirst, pollution, shortage of medicines, electricity, and any means to get an income, not only by being bombed and shelled. Power crisis, gasoline shortage, water and food scarcity, sewage outflow and ever decreasing resources are disasters caused directly and indirectly by the siege.

People in Gaza are resisting this aggression because they want a better and normal life and, even while crying in sorrow, pain, and terror, they reject a temporary truce that does not provide a real chance for a better future. A voice under the attacks in Gaza is that of Um Al Ramlawi who speaks for all in Gaza: "They are killing us all anyway – either a slow death by the siege, or a fast one by military attacks. We have nothing left to lose – we must fight for our rights, or die trying."

Gaza has been blockaded by sea and land since 2006. Any individual of Gaza, including fishermen venturing beyond 3 nautical miles of the coast of

Gaza, face being shot by the Israeli Navy. No one
from Gaza can leave from the only two checkpoints,
Erez or Rafah, without special permission from the
Israelis and the Egyptians, which is hard to come by
for many, if not impossible. People in Gaza are
unable to go abroad to study, work, visit families, or
do business. Wounded and sick people cannot leave
easily to get specialised treatment outside Gaza.
Entries of food and medicines into Gaza have been
restricted and many essential items for survival are
prohibited. Before the present assault, medical stock
items in Gaza were already at an all time low because
of the blockade. They have run out now. Likewise,
Gaza is unable to export its produce. Agriculture has
been severely impaired by the imposition of a buffer
zone, and agricultural products cannot be exported
due to the blockade. 80% of Gaza's population is
dependent on food rations from the UN.

Much of Gaza's buildings and infrastructure had
been destroyed during Operation Cast Lead, 2008 –
09, and building materials have been blockaded
so that schools, homes, and institutions cannot
be properly rebuilt. Factories destroyed by
bombardment have rarely been rebuilt adding
unemployment to destitution.

Despite the difficult conditions, the people of Gaza
and their political leaders have recently moved to
resolve their conflicts "without arms and harm"
through the process of reconciliation between
factions, their leadership renouncing titles and
positions, so that a unity government can be formed
abolishing the divisive factional politics operating
since 2007. This reconciliation, although accepted by
many in the international community, was rejected by
Israel. The present Israeli attacks stop this chance of
political unity between Gaza and the West Bank and

single out a part of the Palestinian society by destroying the lives of people of Gaza. Under the pretext of eliminating terrorism, Israel is trying to destroy the growing Palestinian unity. Among other lies, it is stated that civilians in Gaza are hostages of Hamas whereas the truth is that the Gaza Strip is sealed by the Israelis and Egyptians.

Gaza has been bombed continuously for the past 14 days followed now by invasion on land by tanks and thousands of Israeli troops. More than 60 000 civilians from Northern Gaza were ordered to leave their homes. These internally displaced people have nowhere to go since Central and Southern Gaza are also subjected to heavy artillery bombardment. The whole of Gaza is under attack. The only shelters in Gaza are the schools of the UN Relief and Works Agency for Palestine Refugees in the Near East (UNRWA), uncertain shelters already targeted during Cast Lead, killing many.

According to Gaza Ministry of Health and UN Office for the Coordination of Humanitarian Affairs (OCHA), as of July 21, 149 of the 558 killed in Gaza and 1100 of the 3504 wounded are children. Those buried under the rubble are not counted yet. As we write, the BBC reports of the bombing of another hospital, hitting the intensive care unit and operating theatres, with deaths of patients and staff. There are now fears for the main hospital Al Shifa. Moreover, most people are psychologically traumatised in Gaza. Anyone older than 6 years has already lived through their third military assault by Israel.

The massacre in Gaza spares no one, and includes the disabled and sick in hospitals, children playing on the beach or on the roof top, with a large majority of non-combatants. Hospitals, clinics, ambulances, mosques, schools, and press buildings have all been attacked, with thousands of private homes bombed, clearly directing fire to target whole families killing them within their homes, depriving families of their homes by chasing them out a few minutes before destruction. An entire area was destroyed on July 20, leaving thousands of displaced people homeless, beside wounding hundreds and killing at least 70 – this is way beyond the purpose of finding tunnels. None of these are military objectives. These attacks aim to terrorise, wound the soul and the body of the people, and make their life impossible in the future, as well as also demolishing their homes and prohibiting the means to rebuild.

Weaponry known to cause long-term damages on health of the whole population are used; particularly non fragmentation weaponry and hard-head bombs. We witnessed targeted weaponry used indiscriminately and on children and we constantly see that so-called intelligent weapons fail to be precise, unless they are deliberately used to destroy innocent lives.

We denounce the myth propagated by Israel that the aggression is done caring about saving civilian lives and children's wellbeing.

Israel's behaviour has insulted our humanity, intelligence, and dignity as well as our professional ethics and efforts. Even those of us who want to go and help are unable to reach Gaza due to the blockade.

This "defensive aggression" of unlimited duration, extent, and intensity must be stopped.

Additionally, should the use of gas be further confirmed, this is unequivocally a war crime for which, before anything else, high sanctions will have to be taken immediately on Israel with cessation of any trade and collaborative agreements with Europe.

As we write, other massacres and threats to the medical personnel in emergency services and denial of entry for international humanitarian convoys are reported. We as scientists and doctors cannot keep silent while this crime against humanity continues. We urge readers not to be silent too. Gaza trapped under siege, is being killed by one of the world's largest and most sophisticated modern military machines. The land is poisoned by weapon debris, with consequences for future generations. If those of us capable of speaking up fail to do so and take a stand against this war crime, we are also complicit in the destruction of the lives and homes of 1·8 million people in Gaza.

We register with dismay that only 5% of our Israeli academic colleagues signed an appeal to their government to stop the military operation against Gaza. We are tempted to conclude that with the exception of this 5%, the rest of the Israeli academics are complicit in the massacre and destruction of Gaza. We also see the complicity of our countries in Europe and North America in this massacre and the impotence once again of the international institutions and organisations to stop this massacre.

This letter received 20,000 positive endorsements within less than a week of publication. Of course it also invited a host of hostile emails from Israeli supporters. Some of the authors received personal threats. Even I, a four foot ten inch woman refugee of ethnic Chinese origin, became the target of a massive smear campaign alleging that I "was a White Supremacist and sympathiser of the Ku Klux Klan". Two thousand five hundred Israelis and their supporters petitioned for the dismissal of Dr Richard Horton, the editor-in-chief of Lancet, to punish him for publishing our letter. When they failed to get Dr Horton fired they went on to campaign against Elsevier, the scientific publisher of Lancet. Dr Horton is a man of great integrity and took the position that events following the publication of the letter, in particular the mounting casualties, civilian death toll and the escalating destruction of homes and medical institutions vindicated his decision to publish the letter, and if he did not undertake this publication, he would not be able to live with his conscience.

Since I was denied entry into Gaza, I cannot write a firsthand eye-witness account about Gaza, but the account from Dr Mona El-Farra from Gaza below sums it all. Her article was published widely and the contents continue to haunt me. Eleven members of Dr El-Farra's family, including five children were killed in the recent assault, though she did not dwell much on this in the following article.

"GAZA: WHOLE VILLAGES HAVE BEEN WIPED OFF THE MAP

Posted by Editor
on August 15, 2014 in News & Analysis, Palestine

"The smell and the sights we saw were shocking. The moment we parked and I got out, a very strange smell hit us – the smell of dead bodies. That smell will never leave me; it is still stuck in my nose. We saw totally flattened houses and other houses partially destroyed. It reminded me of pictures from war-torn areas where years of fighting erased a village"

by Dr. MONA EL-FARRA

I'm writing now from my home, but I still feel dizzy from shock and nauseated by the sights and smells on my visit to Khan Younis and Khuza'a.

Yesterday I decided to use the opportunity of the ceasefire to visit my family in Khan Younis. I especially wanted to see my sister who had open heart surgery before Israel's assault. I hadn't seen her for 36 days. I'm lucky that I have enough fuel in my car to drive 24 kilometers (15 miles) so I struck out towards the south.

I drove down Salaheddin Road and passed rubble from mosques, houses, and factories. Some buildings were destroyed completely and some partially. Later on in my drive, I saw dozens of big trees uprooted and smashed, fruit trees destroyed and farms and gardens decimated and ruined. The Israeli bombs were aimed to destroy the infrastructure, to destroy Gaza's economy. Even the main cookie factory was targeted and destroyed.

I passed UN trucks distributing food to people in long lines. This siege and assault by the Israelis has made everyone in the Gaza Strip live as a refugee, missing basic needs and struggling to survive.

When I drove up to my family's place in Khan Younis, it was a very emotional moment. We've lost many family members and, excuse me, my friends; I'm not going to talk about this meeting because every family in Gaza is going through the same thing.

My sister and relatives decided they wanted to go to see Khuza'a, a village located east of Khan Younis. At first I didn't want to go to Khuza'a. I didn't want to be reminded of the massacre, to witness more horrors. But I decided to go so I could give you, my friends from the Middle East Children's Alliance (MECA), and others living outside of Gaza my first-hand account. I know you are following the news closely but I also know the news might not tell you what has gone on and is going on in Gaza.

As we set out to the east, my niece pointed out the devastation, "You can see where the Israeli tanks were – here and here." When we came to the village Abbasan, there was an Israeli military vehicle destroyed. Palestinian flags were flying from it and Palestinian children were playing on it while their families stood watching them.

We continued toward Khuza'a. It was a model Palestinian agricultural village with open fields and green everywhere. They had fruit trees and vegetable fields. But there was nothing left of the village I remembered.

Suspected IDF mass execution in Khuza'a

The smell and the sights we saw were shocking. The moment we parked and I got out, a very strange smell hit us—the smell of dead bodies. That smell will never leave me; it is still stuck in my nose. We saw totally flattened houses and other houses partially destroyed. It reminded me of pictures from war-torn areas where years of fighting erased a village. I could tell that something huge and terrible had happened here, the rubble and the destruction were extreme. Some villagers told us they had found two bodies in the rubble a couple of hours before we arrived. Still people were searching the ruins for their relative's remains. Many times I had to stop myself from vomiting because the smell was so strong.

This Israeli assault has hit the Palestinian people more deeply than the last two military attacks. This one is even more deadly and destructive. Whole neighborhoods and villages have been wiped off the map.

I ask myself now how can we start again?

Dr. Mona El-Farra, Director of Gaza Projects, is a physician by training and a human rights and women's rights activist by practice in the occupied Gaza Strip.

She is also Middle East Children Alliance Director–Gaza

Deputy and Health Chair of the Red Crescent society for Gaza Strip founded by the late Dr. Haidar Abdel Shafi)"

But I know the Palestinians WILL start again. Through my 32 years with the Palestinians I have known them to be extra-ordinarily strong and resilient. When I used to despair over the situation of the Palestinians and especially Gaza, my friend Alia Showa always said "Swee, be strong. Don't worry about us. We will never give up. Humdullelah we are a strong people!" With that I always became comforted. I remember the words of Yasser Arafat: "To be a Palestinian you not only have to be builder, but also rebuilder". This I know to be true of all Palestinians of any political shade, whether living under Occupation or in the Diaspora in the refugee camps all over the Middle East. I am a witness to, and survivor of, the Sabra Shatilla Massacre of 1982. I not only witnessed death and carnage, but I went on to witness the resurrection of Shatilla, of how the survivors rebuilt their homes and lives, only to be destroyed and to be rebuilt again and again, each time with greater resilience. Today Shatilla still stands. I have every confidence that Gaza will be rebuilt. The Palestinian people will never be crushed by injustice. My thirty two year journey with the Palestinians is the basis of this confidence.

As I write, Gaza is still being blockaded by sea and on land. Her 1.8 million people are still mourning those slaughtered and crying from the pain of their wounds. The rebuilding of homes, hospitals, clinics and factories is prohibited. Mixed in the ruin and rubble are also toxic contaminants from the shells and bomb debris. No one can accurately estimate how much depleted uranium is left in Gaza. Their deadly radioactive rays will continue to affect Gaza for generations to come. Tents are pitched over this nuclear wasteland. The homeless have only these tents to shelter in the bitter winter. There are floods and no electricity. Sewage overflows, and the hospitals have run out of essential supplies. Apart from emergency UN rations, food is scarce.

Children who survived the recent military assault are still having nightmares.

In the midst of this, I suddenly received an invite from the doctors of Gaza to participate in the First Gaza Surgical Conference in March 2015. This invitation is a great honour, but with great sadness I replied that the Israelis and the Egyptians have refused me permission to enter Gaza. I have been arrested in Israel and also a deportee. They wrote back to invite me to speak through Skype. They encouraged me to be strong in doing good deeds, and not be beaten down by my deportation. I have so much to learn from my Gaza colleagues. I too have to learn resilience.

Gaza is not defeated. Gaza – I salute you.

Dr Ang Swee Chai, February 2015

POSTSCRIPTS

TWENTY YEARS AFTER SABRA-SHATILA, 2002

From Beirut to Jerusalem is the enduring dream of every Palestinian exile. Uprooted and driven into exile since their native Palestine became Israel in 1948, the millions languishing in refugee camps throughout the Lebanon, Syria, Jordan and elsewhere in the region have never given up that hope of return and the right to go home. If not this year, then, next year in Jerusalem.

For friends and families left behind in Gaza and the West Bank and under occupation since 1967, Palestine is also an idea that will not die. All are painfully aware of their history and the call for yet more sacrifices to bring about a free, peaceful Palestine. Since childhood, each can recite the injustices — the massacres, expulsions, invasions, occupations, the death and destruction.

Twenty years ago, the *Sabra-Shatila* massacre happened. I was working in the camps, having arrived a month ago as a volunteer surgeon to look after those wounded during the Israeli invasion of Lebanon.

The slaughter of unarmed children, women, the aged and the infirm was shocking. For me, I was doubly

373

outraged that I had to discover the truth about a brave and generous people only through their deaths. Until then, I never knew Palestinian refugees existed. As a fundamentalist Christian, I had been a supporter of Israel, hated Arabs and saw the Palestine Liberation Organisation as terrorists to be loathed and feared.

Sabra-Shatila humanised all Palestinians. The powerful forces conspiring to demonise them had been undermined. How could they be villains if they are victims of a grave injustice? Like others, I had to face the painful truth, I had to repent — my own ignorance and prejudice had blinded me against the suffering of the Palestinians.

The survivors encouraged me to testify before the Israeli Kahan Commission of inquiry. And, in so heading south across the Lebanese border to Jerusalem, I realised I was tracing a journey all refugees hope to make one day. I was inadvertently making a pilgrimage to their homeland and was 'going home'.

"*From Beirut to Jerusalem*" is my testimony. In the intervening years, I have returned many times to the Lebanon and the Occupied Territories to continue my work as a surgeon treating the injured. Through charities like Medical Aid for Palestinians which some of us helped form, we would appeal to ordinary British and other people to render material medical support for the beleaguered Palestinian health institutions. I have never said 'no' to any chance to speak about them, for those who perished and those who survived, at countless meetings throughout much of the world.

Anniversaries are important. They allow us to commemorate tragedies; they are also occasions to hope. Never forgetting them is the prelude to redemption. We remember their crucifixion, and we affirm our faith in their resurrection.

<u>On the first anniversary</u>, some of us doctors and nurses went to the United States to speak to the American people. People in the west were forced to confront the truth of the massacre — for the first time, they had to acknowledge the Palestinians as victims of a grave injustice.

<u>On the tenth anniversary</u>, we brought together imams, rabbis and priests in a service of peace in a London church to honour the dead of *Sabra-Shatila*. It was a sober gathering but 1992 was a year of quiet optimism, with the peace negotiations on the way.

The first Palestinian *Intifada* — uprising — in Gaza and the West Bank had been raging on since 1987. Media coverage of the event showed thousands of unarmed Palestinian children confronting the ferocious might of the Israeli Army. It was a war of stones against tanks — little Daud (David) against the mighty Goliath. The cost was high: hundreds of Palestinians dead, more thousands injured, mass arrests, house arrests and 'curfews' of entire populations, the ruthless destruction of homes, closure of schools, harassment of hospitals. The ferocity of crushing the resistance broke international law in an occupation which was itself illegal.

During the first Intifada, I was attached to Gaza's *Al-Ahli* hospital as a United Nations consultant surgeon and had treated many of those injured. My hospital grounds were often raided by troops hunting for young people they were after; maternity wards were invaded by fully armed Israeli soldiers, scornful of women in labour. Patients lying on my operating table were threatened. A *BBC TV* crew filmed '*Life Under Occupation*', featuring some of us working under those intolerable conditions. My male nurse spent two years in prison following the documentary. The military made my continued stay in Gaza untenable, and it took several years before I could return.

The resistance against the 1982 Israeli invasion of the Lebanon inspired the *Intifada.* Without *Sabra-Shatila*, there would not have been the international sympathy for the *Intifada. Sabra-Shatila,* in short, was pre-cursor and catalyst for the *Intifada.*

In 1992, a peace process begun in Madrid stalled; by 1993, secret Oslo talks offered some Palestinian autonomy. Despite grave doubts over this fledgling entity, many were hopeful this was a helpful step forward in the return to nationhood. At the very least, they were offered a pause to allow schools, hospitals, social institutions to be rebuilt. Some kind of normalcy could possibly return. The tanks would hopefully leave, and the curfews would be lifted to allow the children to come out into the sunshine to play again.

This was simply too optimistic. Settlements, illegal under international law, were accelerated. No one could move between Gaza and the West Bank, and within towns inside West Bank without the approval of the Israelis. East Jerusalem remained annexed. There was still no right of return for the millions of exiles.

In October 2000, a provocative march by Ariel Sharon through the *Al-Aqsa* Mosque with 2,000 Israeli soldiers sparked off the second *Intifada.* The repression that followed was even more severe than those encountered during the first *Intifada.*

There are far more deaths and destruction and the numbers are mounting. In November, 2002, *Amnesty International* published its findings, accusing Israel of unlawful killings, torture and the use of Palestinians as human shields. Among other "grave breaches" of international law were ill-treatment of prisoners, wanton destruction of homes, sometimes with the residents still inside, and the blocking of medical aid to the wounded. It called upon Britain and other signatories to the Geneva conventions to put on trial Israeli soldiers "responsible for war crimes in *Jenin* and *Nablus*".

2002 is the twentieth-anniversary of *Sabra-Shatila*. I made twin trips to the Lebanon and the Occupied Palestine. In May, I saw the same wholesale destruction of Palestinian society in Gaza and the West Bank described in the *Amnesty* report. Homes were shelled and bulldozed, ambulances carrying critically ill patients were shot up. schools were shelled. By the time I was there nearly 40 women in labour had to give birth at Israeli checkpoints when access to hospitals was blocked. Several mothers and infants died as a result. Both Gaza and the West Bank were cut up into tiny cantons under siege by the tanks; curfews were routine and prolonged. Yet the Palestinians remained steadfast.

The *BBC* wanted me to re-visit the refugee camps of Sabra and Shatila in Lebanon to invite survivors to speak about those traumatic days in September 1982. After the depressing visit to the occupied territories, I was fearful of what Beirut would offer. I knew their physical conditions have deteriorated. Has the world forgotten? Much has happened elsewhere, but has anything changed for the refugees? Do they still aspire to return to Palestine?

Yet, Beirut revived me once again. In their limbo world, in the Shatila which was nothing more than just heaps of rubble, I met youngsters born after the massacre. A whole new generation has grown up. The children who survived the Sabra and Shatila massacre now have children of their own. Parents are now grand-parents. These exiled Palestinians are now four generations away from home, yet their little ones can rehearse the same stories of their parents about places like *Ramallah, Hebron, Akka, Haifa, Gaza, Al-Quds*. Many have journeyed to South Lebanon to look over the border into Galilee, where their families were forced to evacuate in 1948. Despite uncertainties for the future, they know they will one day return. And deep within me, I pray with them — from Beirut to Jerusalem, next year in Palestine.

Dr Ang Swee Chai
November 2002

Reflections on the 25th anniversary
of the Sabra-Shatila massacre, 2007

The Yad Vashem Holocaust museum in Israel has an engraving on the wall, saying: "Forgetfulness leads to exile, while remembrance is the secret to redemption". Having worked and lived with those in exile and under occupation, I know Palestinians never allow themselves to forget the pain, death and suffering they have endured over the decades.

Every September, survivors and witnesses commemorate the massacre of thousands of innocent Palestinians in Beirut's Sabra and Shatila camps. It is now a quarter of a century later and many of us have since died while the rest are a lot older. Sabra's Palestinian refugee camp no longer exists, while Shatila is a shell of its former self. The initial international outcry has long faded and the current media focus has shifted from those in exile to those living under occupation in Gaza and West Bank.

For those in exile, they see the prospect of ever returning home torn apart by the turmoil in the Occupied Territories. Gaza starves and is under military siege for months in an effort by Israel to topple a democratically-elected Palestinian government. The West Bank is cut up into pieces by a long serpentine Wall suffocating it like a boa constrictor. In 2006, Lebanon was savagely attacked by Israel in its war against Hizbullah. At least a million cluster bombs litter the southern half of the country. These were wickedly left at the moment ceasefire talks were being negotiated. Unless cleared, no one can return to the land to rebuild their homes and livelihood.

I mourn all who perished. On a personal level, I especially mourn the passing of Dr Fathi Arafat, brother of the late President Yasser Arafat. Both brothers died within days of each other, not knowing the fate of each. With their passing, Palestinians entered a new uncertain phase in their history. Dr Fathi was the founder of the Palestine Red Crescent Society. The PRCS served as a ministry of health with hospitals and clinics and treated all in need in the Lebanon. Dr Fathi had been my mentor and friend. Always an optimist, he had been inspiring to work with, and like my friends of the PRCS, I miss him.

Factionalism, military siege, starvation, arrests, bombs both conventional and unconventional, deportation and massacres are not new. They are weapons regularly deployed since 1948 to intimidate, terrorise and demoralise the Palestinians. Those who use these tactics aimed to crush them into giving up their aspiration to nationhood and to surrender their claim to membership of the human family.

But I remain optimistic and have reason to be so. Since I began my journey with the Palestinians in 1982, I have learnt that all the above repressive measures have failed to wipe the Palestinians out. I have seen strength and resilience in the face of untold hardships and persecution. I still have with me my picture of destitute Palestinian children of Shatila camp standing amid the ruin and rubble. They survived the massacre but lost their parents and homes. We thought all was lost. But they raised their hands making the victory sign and said to me: "We are not afraid, let Israel come". I have returned many times to the camp but never been able to find those children again. They must have perished since. But they live forever in my heart. Whenever the situation becomes unbearable, I revisit this picture for strength. With each tragedy, the Palestinians' resolve strengthens. Having been witness to this I can reassure my Palestinian friends in Occupied Palestine that they will overcome, because I have seen how the Palestinians in Lebanon overcame.

I have always felt it a great privilege and honour to be able to be a part of these events. It is a special gift from God that I am given the honour to join them on their journey in pursuit of justice. *From Beirut to Jerusalem* is my testimony of this journey. It is also my prayer for the Palestinians in exile that they too will make the journey one day. From exile they will surely return home

On 18 September 1982, the last day of the massacre, I emerged from the basement operating theatre of Gaza Hospital in Sabra and Shatila camp. I had been operating for 72 hours to save a handful of people only to see piles of mutilated bodies in the camp alleys. I emerged from the hospital to see the body of an old man whose eyes were dug out. A terrified mother tried to hand me her baby to keep in safety. She failed in her attempt – and both were killed. The world was initially outraged, but forgot very quickly. The survivors of that massacre lived on through yet more violent events.

On that morning I felt trampled on and life became meaningless. As a doctor, I could do nothing to save the dead. As a human being my whole world had collapsed. Where was God, where was world conscience? I was alive, yet I felt dead.

I recall how I first came to Sabra and Shatila a bigoted, self-righteous fundamentalist Christian. I believed in the goodness of the Western "Christian" countries and the righteousness of Israel. I thought I knew the Bible, and God was on *our* side. My favourite stories in the Old Testament at that time were how Joshua captured Jericho and the story of David and Goliath. I rejoiced in the military triumph of Israel. Just like my Christian friends, I celebrated the great Israeli military victory of the Six Day war of 1967, with the subjugation of Gaza and West Bank. I greeted the Foundation Day of the State of Israel as a day to rejoice.

On that morning in Sabra and Shatila God destroyed that self-righteousness. I was made to confront the broken bodies in the camp alleys. Through them I met the crucified Christ. Sin was no longer an intellectual business. In a split second the sins of hatred, of murder, of militarism, of greed, of anger, of cruelty were all translated into wounds inflicted on the bodies of the victims. The Palestinians were collectively crucified. I felt crucified with them and would have remained so until I remembered as a Christian that crucifixion was not the end. Deep in my Christian consciousness crucifixion is only the prelude to resurrection.

Jesus was crucified 2,000 years ago. Both Jesus and the massacred Palestinians were innocent and did not deserve to be tortured and killed. But there is one difference. Jesus chose to suffer and die for our sins, to take on the punishment which we deserved. He is our Messiah. The will of God is always justice and that would mean the perpetrators of crimes have to be punished. Jesus had borne the punishment for us. We are all therefore on a level-playing field before God our judge and redeemer. And I am just as guilty as those who committed the massacre. To some, war crimes are sins committed by others; and so they are. But that morning in the full glare of the blazing

Beirut sun, I understood. Palestinians could only have died because collectively we have condoned it. Like the crucifixion, some Christians blame the Jewish leaders in Jesus' time; others blame Pontius Pilate and the Romans. Others blame the crowd which shouted: "Crucify Him". But He was crucified on our behalf. In the same way I ask myself again and again – who has got the Palestinians' blood on their hands?

After going through much soul-searching, I came to the conclusion that I, too, had blood on my hands. Up to that time I was bigoted and prejudiced. I cannot excuse myself by claiming ignorance. For the weeks preceding the massacre, I was too prejudiced to believe the stories told to me by the camp people. I rejoiced in the evacuation of the PLO from Beirut and failed to see the pain of the Palestinian families being split up. I was naïve to trust the Western countries which guaranteed the safety of those left behind. I was self-righteous, still thinking of Palestinians as terrorists. I cannot blame others if I who had eaten with them, stayed in their homes, enjoyed their kindness and hospitality, refused to understand until they were murdered. My prejudice had blinded me.

When I saw those broken bodies, I was stunned and emotionally numb. I asked God to forgive me and remembered praying, "Lord Jesus, I have spent more than 30 years denying the Palestinian people their existence. I have hated Arabs. I was blinded by prejudice. Please forgive me. Please let me make amends. Grant that I may spend the next 30 years serving the Palestinians and help me be their friend". I repented. God forgave me, and the Palestinians embraced me. Suddenly I am no longer the living dead. God had breathed into my withered soul and filled my heart with love for Him and for the Palestinians.

He has brought me back to life. Step by step He brought me back to His side.

Many of my Zionist Christian friends have since shunned me. They refuse to talk to me for I have fallen for the "Philistines". But I am no longer intimidated by all this. I have seen a different face of God – that of love, compassion and grace. I believe He will heal the broken bodies of the Palestinian people and give them strength to carry their burden. Just as He raised Jesus on the third day, He will bring salvation to the Palestinian people. From their crucifixion will come their resurrection!

For a long time after the massacres I could not bring myself round to read the Old Testament, thinking it was full of prejudiced passages supporting Israel. I finally plucked up courage to read it and feared it would be the last time before giving it up. I was pleasantly surprised. I went no further than the first book Genesis when I found out how God, after driving Adam and Eve from the Garden of Eden, followed them out. I learnt God never abandoned them. He made clothes of animal skins for them to keep them warm. I broke down when I read how God saved Ishmael and his mother Hagar in the desert. Abraham was ordered by his jealous wife, Sarah, the mother of Isaac, to abandon them in the desert to die. Hagar placed Ishmael under a bush when their water ran out. She went into the desert and cried out to God. God heard her and a fountain was opened for them to drink. He promised Ishmael would be a father of many nations. Palestinians are the children of Ishmael and the children of Abraham.

So on this 25th anniversary of the massacre I would want you, my dear friends, to open your hearts so that God can fill you with His love and compassion. May He also grant you the honour of joining the Palestinians in their journey from "Beirut to Jerusalem". As we journey on, may we always have faith that God who made us is compassionate and just and there will be room in His heart for all His children, and His grace and justice will always sustain us as we submit ourselves to Him. May we be able to be like the grieving old grandmother from Shatila, who lost 27 loved ones that morning. Yet she could still say: "the will of God be done". She still called God holy and committed her dead children to His care. May we draw strength from our faith that He will heal the deep wounds. He will restore the broken lives. He will bring His justice, He will pour His grace and love on His children, He will mend the broken hearts, He will bring peace to the tormented souls. He will wipe away all tears. And bring us home, to the city He has built and bears His name. Al Quds... Next year in Jerusalem.

Dr Ang Swee Chai
September 2007

DEPORTATION TIMELINE

On Monday 18 August 2014, Dr Swee Chai Ang, Consultant Orthopaedic Surgeon and Patron of Medical Aid for Palestinians was accompanied by Dr Asif Chaudry, an Oesophagogastric/Upper GI Surgeon working at Royal Marsden Cancer Hospital and Chelsea & Westminster Hospitals, to leave for Israel. Both had responded to the call for surgeons to go to Gaza to help treat the wounded a few weeks earlier on behalf of a MAP initiative. At the time of their departure, fifteen London consultants had already applied to work in Gaza. This initiative was broadly in line though not directly accepted as part of a broader platform supported by DFID and the UK Government in terms of the humanitarian disaster in Gaza. The overall initiative also had the personal support of the Prime Minister, David Cameron as reported by the national media. Whilst applications for Gaza entry permits had been made prior to governmental support, confirmation of approval had not been forthcoming. As both surgeons had arranged for leave from their NHS commitments as the first team, they left as scheduled with the intention of supporting the humanitarian needs of the people of Gaza either through direct clinical work or the support of medical training of the doctors in Gaza. Both doctors are Specialist fellows of the Royal College of Surgeons of England.

As there have been widespread reports of the Immigration authorities at Ben Gurion airport obstructing the entry of humanitarian workers to the occupied territories in general and Gaza in particular, and driven by the overwhelming imperative to assist the people of Gaza, the doctors proceeded to Tel Aviv with the intention of travelling to Jerusalem and remaining on standby to enter Gaza through the Erez checkpoint as soon as the permits were made available. The two doctors agreed among themselves that if permits were granted prior to arrival they would declare this at immigration, expecting this to trigger a thorough interrogation; on the other hand If there were no permits granted, they would simply ask for entry to Jerusalem and spend their week's leave as "tourists" while on standby. The logic was there should be no point complicating the issue at the airport border control and inviting a prolonged interrogation, denial of entry to Israel, the borders of which they must cross to get to Gaza and potential deportation at the mention of intent to get to Gaza. If upon arriving and during the time of stay in Jerusalem their permits came through they would leave for Gaza and face the interrogation at Erez Crossing. Meanwhile they should just stay in Jerusalem as tourists

As the doctors boarded an Easyjet flight from London, Luton Airport bound for Tel Aviv, Israel, it was confirmed by Medical Aid for Palestinians that entry permits for Gaza had still not been granted, but the field staff of Medical Aid for Palestinians in Gaza were in negotiation with the Israeli Authorities. The flight departed at 11:10 am. The atmosphere on the plane was very pleasant and jovial, many of the doctors' fellow passengers on-board were from Jewish families from north London, Eruv areas,

and most had children and were in a holiday mood to
spend the summer break in Israel.

1. The plane landed 17:40 18 August 2014 at Ben
   Gurion International Airport, Tel Aviv.

2. Dr Asif Chaudry and Dr Swee Chai Ang approached
   the Israeli passport control, a large open area with a
   high 'modern terminal' ceiling. Asif proceeded to the
   desk prior to Swee arriving at the border/passport
   control before 18:00.

3. From behind him in the queue, Swee could see that
   Asif was asked almost immediately to go to the
   security waiting hall for further assessment.

4. The officer at the first security desk, was young,
   presumably in her early 20s, she was polite, smiling
   throughout with an engaging manner: a little chatty.
   Her questions covered preliminary background
   information and the intended purpose of the visit:
   Name, Father's, Grandfather's name. Where are you
   going to go, which places will you visit? Asif
   mentioned various historical sites in Jerusalem and
   Tel Aviv/ Jaffa. Where are you staying? All questions
   were fairly brief and polite. Who are you travelling
   with? The officer seemed to scroll through details on a
   computer terminal and entered additional details.
   After a short period she asked Asif to go to a security
   waiting area/hall and he was told his name would be
   called. The waiting area was at the rear of the
   immigration hall, a small secluded enclosure with a
   few seats and a couple of drinks machines, this felt
   relatively open but had three uniformed security
   officers hovering around the entry point, all were
   relatively young possibly of Yemenite Sephardic
   background, all also wore IDF identity toggles. There
   were three offices along an adjoining open corridor.
   The one to the right had the most junior officers with
   the seniority of interrogators increasing as one

sequentially progressed to the left. The general attitude also became somewhat more aggressive and restrictive as the person progresses towards the left office. There were bathroom facilities around the corner, with a water fountain, at the initial stage of the interrogation process it was possible to access this without any impedance, as matters progressed this was restricted.

5. Swee followed Asif in the queue and travelling as Mrs Khoo was given a B2 visa on a separate piece of paper in under 3 minutes. Swee then asked the passport officer for permission to join Asif in the security waiting hall since both were travelling together. It was granted by the passport officer who remained polite and friendly.

6. Asif returned to the waiting area to join Swee. Whilst waiting they both met two young American TEFL teachers who had intended to travel to teach in Nablus (African American man and White woman, both were subsequently deported). They also met two Italian young men who were questioned for over 4 hours as they had a single UAE stamp. There was also a Palestinian man originally from East Jerusalem who now resides with his Dutch family in the Netherlands. He had travelled to Tel Aviv with a Dutch passport and was desperate to visit his elder brother in his 80s who had recently been hospitalised in Jerusalem with a brain haemorrhage and had a terminal outlook. He had been held for 4 hours, and sobbing at his predicament that despite being in his own land, possessing a Jerusalem ID and a EU passport from the Netherlands he could not enter Jerusalem for just an hour to say farewell to his brother who had raised him. He had not visited Jerusalem for 12 years, and he just wanted to hold his 85 year old brother before he died. Asif later met him again in detention as he

replaced him in his bunk later that night. He was being deported back to the Netherlands and had been told by the Israeli authorities he could try fly out to Amman from the Netherlands and cross the Allenby Bridge to get to Jerusalem. This alternative exercise would take at least 24 hours and his brother might have died by the time he made it.

7. After waiting for around an hour Asif was called in for a second interview: On this occasion he was asked to enter the first room on the right where he was met by a stocky young woman in her mid-20s, somewhat dishevelled, who essentially re-entered the same data he had been asked at the first Immigration counter. In addition he was asked to write his email address and mobile phone number in capitals on a pro-forma. This was all fairly brief, less engaging and matter of fact with no real cross examination. He was asked to write down the name of his 'colleague'. Interestingly, no mention had hitherto been made about a professional connection between the two.

8. Asif returned to Swee in the waiting area. The two waited together for another hour.

9. Asif was asked to enter the third room from the right. He was met by a male security officer, in his early 30s, accompanied by a younger man in his early 20s, both looked tired, were in plain clothes wearing Chinos and casual shirts left untucked. The room looked a little rough, with a principle desk and a smaller desk in the back left corner for the younger officer. There were two separate desktop computers, both looking fairly old. On the wall to the right of the main desk there was a large picture bearing the official emblem of the State of Israel between a photo of 'Bibi' Netanyahu and Shimon Peres. The approach in this room was much more akin to a Police interview/ interrogation. The younger assistant took

notes, subsequently looked through devices and cross referenced points on the internet.

10. Asif was questioned: So what's this all about? Why are you here? Why now? Just tourism to Jerusalem? Which places are you going to visit? Why? What interest do you have in them? Are you married? Do you have children? Who are you travelling with? Write her name in capitals on this sheet of paper. Call her in, call her in now! Get out! Get out of this room!

11. Asif asked Swee to enter the interrogation room. The male officer repeated his questions about where the two doctors had intended to go. He knew that Swee already had a B2 visa. He referred to both as colleagues assuming that they were not friends. Asif mentioned that it was his colleague in the previous room who had used the term 'colleague', this made him somewhat irate shouting 'I don't give a damn about the woman in the other room!'.

12. The focus moved almost entirely to Swee and her activities during her last visit in May. Swee told them that she was mainly in Jerusalem visiting Christian churches, but she also visited the al-Makassed Hospital and a handicapped children's school. This became a major thread that they probed extensively. He continued to question why Swee had become interested in Makassed, why should a tourist visit a hospital. She told them that she had stayed at the Meridien hotel during the last visit and bumped into some Doctors in the lobby who had suggested she might want to visit their hospital in the Old City, in any case her visit had only been for an hour or so and she had not conducted any clinical work. The interrogator appeared to get increasingly irate and said this was not 'normal' tourism, visiting a hospital. The presumption was that a one hour visit to Makassed hospital disqualified Swee as a tourist. Asif tried to

explain that as doctors we often like to see hospitals and explore healthcare in countries we visit out of professional curiosity. They became suspicious and asked if the two wanted to volunteer to work Israel. Swee denied this by saying that she had no work visa, and Asif would really like to see the Old City and Jerusalem, this being his first visit. At this point Swee also remembered that she had attended a Thalassemia Conference in Ramallah and met the orthodox Archbishop then but they were not interested. At this point they were angry and shouted that we should make up our minds whether we were colleagues or friends. We tried to explain that we are colleagues but also friends. At this point they got really loud and angry and asked Asif to get out, and Swee asked them if they wanted her out too, and they said yes. They thought people who do not know the difference between friends and colleagues are liars.

13. Asif and Swee sat in the waiting hall, not knowing what to expect. Swee decided to go back in to the interrogators and apologise to them for making them so angry. They told Swee curiously at this point that Asif "will have to calm down".

14. Swee came out to the security waiting hall and told Asif that they wanted him to calm down though she did not think Asif was wound up at all. After some time and following discussion Asif suggested it might be worthwhile returning to apologise to the interrogator, he approached the office and asked if he could enter the response was 'no!' he suggested he just wanted to apologise, the Officer said 'nothing happened, we are all fine!'

15. Asif was called in again. As soon as he went in he was asked to place his phone and wallet on the table. He was then asked in detail about the places they intended to visit, he suggested he was very keen to

visit the old city, Aqsa Mosque, the Dome of the Rock, the quarters, the Church of the Holy Sepulchre, Hebron for the Tomb of the Patriarchs, Masada and if time permitted Tel Aviv itself. They repeated the same question a number of times and sought further elaboration. They asked which hotel the two were going to stay in and whether he knew anyone in Israel, the West Bank or Gaza. He told them that he did not know anyone but his friend Mrs Khoo (Swee Ang) had made the arrangements as she knew Israel and Jerusalem in particular very well. They asked briefly about his previous visit in 2009 to Syria and family visit to Pakistan 4 years earlier, they didn't seem particularly interested in this. The focus seemed to be on potential Humanitarian activities. Asif was told to 'get out' once again.

16. Swee was called in and they asked the name of her father and grandfather, and how did she book the flight ticket and how are they going to St George's Hostel. She said they had a taxi and she knew the St George's from before and it was not difficult to find it. The two of them told Swee that they needed to verify a few things and that everything would be alright. She was told to go out to take a seat.

17. Whilst waiting for the next phase of questioning, Swee received a text from Mark McGuiness (a MAP fieldworker) who asked about progress through immigration. Swee replied with a text saying there had been some security delays and while pressing send, she was called back in and asked abruptly who she was she texting. The officers demanded her phone and her wallet. They were upset that she only had one visa debit card in her wallet. The next question was shocking as they asked if Swee had been imprisoned and detained before. This took Swee by surprise and she replied, 'definitely not!' as she assumed they were

referring to Israel. The next question was if she ever worked in Beirut, Swee said 'yes a long time ago'. They then called her a liar and turned the computer over with 2 pictures of her with a caption below saying "I was arrested, and detained without trial". Swee recognised that immediately and realised that it referred to her arrest and detention in Singapore in 1977. Amidst accusations of lying and insults Swee explained that her late husband was a Singapore human rights lawyer and they wanted to detain him, he escaped and a few weeks later they detained her for questioning about him and his whereabouts, and that episode was 37 years ago in Singapore and nothing to do with Israel. They then examined Swee's phone and found Mark's text and two missed calls from the driver waiting outside and asked who these people were. Swee said Mark works for MAP and they can call him to verify the fact. Instead they spoke to the driver in Hebrew. Swee does not understand Hebrew but picked up the words St George's. Swee understood from this that they had figured out that Swee Khoo is Swee Ang and had googled her, finding a plethora of information on the internet about her. They also asked about the cash she was carrying for the children of Gaza and asked where the cash was since it was not in her wallet. Swee insisted that she would not allow them to confiscate the money for the children and if she cannot get into Gaza, she will give the money to MAP. They then asked Swee, where was the third doctor? Swee told them there were only the two doctors. Swee told them she understood on the morning of departure that they had still not received formal confirmation for permits to enter Gaza, but since they had taken their leave to go to work in Gaza, they would still leave and since Swee had previously been to Jerusalem she could guide Asif and they should allow them entry to visit Jerusalem. At this part of the interrogation they were joined by a third person: a female who seemed to be their senior and they reported to her in Hebrew. The only question she asked Swee was her age. They then told Swee to get out and it was then Asif's turn to be interrogated again.

18. Asif returned to the room, he encountered the original two male interrogators and a senior female officer who he had not seen before. After repeating the preliminary questions about his father's name, grandfather's name and the places he wanted to visit they asked about where he intended to stay, who owned the St George's hotel, did Asif know anyone in the West Bank, Gaza, Lebanon, Iran, and Pakistan? He said no to the first four and said he knew many people in Pakistan; they didn't seem very interested in that per se.

19. The female interrogator asked 'how much money are you carrying' Asif said £1240' she responded 'just for a few days?' Why are you travelling to Israel now? Why with Ms Khoo, there is a large age gap, are you married, do you have children? Asif said he was divorced and had children who lived predominantly with their mother but he had a week off from work and wanted to spend his annual leave exploring Jerusalem as he knew a lot about it from reading and friends, Roman, Byzantine history and Islamic history but had never visited and Swee would be a great guide. They asked who Mark is. Asif was surprised by this question and said that he had never met him and he was someone Swee knew. Asif was told to fill out another pro-forma listing all of his email addresses, home and mobile phone numbers. As this was happening, the younger male interrogator started to flick through Asif's smartphone; He looked up and

said 'who is Ayub?' Asif said it was his younger brother, 'why is his WhatsApp profile picture a Palestinian flag?!' he shook his head with disdain! There was then a series of question, referring to anyone in the WhatsApp contacts who might have a connection with activities in support of the Palestinians, 'who is Monir': a friend involved with a Muslim Professional Organisation called City Circle. 'Who is Nizar?': a friend who is the CEO of Kuwait Petroleum Company. They then interjected, 'you know, we love good doctors who help, but we hate liars! Mark has already told us you have a permit for Gaza and that is where you are going tomorrow! We have no problem at all with that! Many Israeli doctors are there now, you would have been very welcome but you 'fucked it up' if you need any help knowing why you are here look at these messages to your work colleagues in London!' Asif said that whilst there had been an interest in going to Gaza for humanitarian purposes and an application had been made for a Gaza permit, as this had not been granted and he had a week off work what he wanted to do now was to visit Jerusalem, something he had wanted to do for a long time. The summary response was: 'You cannot enter Israel!'

20. Asif returned to Swee and told her of the decision to deny entry, but also that the Gaza permits had apparently been granted. Swee was called in yet again and was told by both interrogators that had she not lied they would have happily supported the two doctors to help children. Swee reiterated that she had not lied and as they had not received confirmation for permits the intention was to visit Jerusalem. One of the interrogators then said they have their permits. Swee told him it was not possible and she would check with Mark immediately. She picked up her

mobile phone where it was positioned in front of the interrogator and dialled Mark and thankfully he picked up immediately. Swee told Mark they were being deported, and asked whether he actually got their permits. Mark said 'not yet but he was pushing hard' and 'they might come through tomorrow (Tuesday) or the day after (Wednesday)", At this point the interrogator became infuriated and told Swee to stop the call. Swee felt that she may have provoked him when she said Mark had denied the permits had been granted but might hopefully be available in a day or two and therefore she did not lie. By implication the interrogator was lying about the permits being granted. Of course he would also be angry that Mark was informed of the intended deportation. If Mark had not been informed there would be anxiety and confusion for the entire period until the doctors arrived back at UK and could call him. He then switched the subject and told her to provide personal details: home phone, mobile, and all of her email addresses. By this time Swee asked why she should do this since they were going to deport her anyway. He told Swee in no uncertain terms that if she did not comply he was empowered to put her in jail indefinitely until she changed her mind!. Swee complied thinking to herself, how futile since they already knew everything. They then asked about Lebanon, and she told them about the Sabra and Shatilla massacres of 1982 which took place before they were born. She also explained that the Israeli government of that era was somewhat different to the present time and had set up commission of enquiry into the behaviour of the Israeli Defence Force during massacre for which Swee was a witness. The interrogators suggested that they were good people and would happily facilitate doctors going to Gaza to help children, but they demanded people be upfront about their intentions. They accused Swee of humiliating and insulting the chief interrogator by making him spend "more than two hours" finding out about her. Swee asked, 'if other doctors arrived should they simply announce their intention to proceed to assist Palestinians in Gaza at the passport counter? Would they be granted entry?'. He said 'yes' and if it was his shift he would definitely help. "Israelis are good people, and we want to help children". Swee explained that she was not in a position to have said that since she had not received a permit, and would have been deported immediately. He then said that she could have said she was going to Jerusalem to wait for her permit but it is too late now because the deportation order cannot be cancelled and that she should return to London and ask MAP to speak with the Israeli Embassy. His last sentence to Swee was – "I think you still do not trust me!" Swee nearly said 'of course I don't! Why should I?' She was glad she kept her mouth shut.

DETENTION

The two were then asked to return to the waiting area again where they were now guarded more closely and had to be escorted to the bathrooms and to access the water fountain. The exact nature of the deportation was never clarified, for instance it remained unclear at that point as to whether they had been given an exclusion order rather than a simple denial of entry. Both Asif and Swee repeatedly asked the junior security staff (all were in a simple civilian uniform but wore IDF army metal tags around their necks, under their shirts) to see the interrogators for clarification but this was denied. Their passports remained with those officers throughout. At around 22:00 they were asked to provide their boarding cards for the outbound flight. Nobody clarified when their return flight would be or if they were at liberty to book a flight with an alternative airline or to another port to avoid a prolonged stay in detention. They were told that they would soon go to the 'Motel' where they would have a place to sleep, be provided with food and be able to shower. They were repeatedly told "We are Israelis, we are nice to people".

After a very long wait, at about 23:00 they were escorted to an enclosed security room occupied by 5 security officers. All were relatively polite but it was clear that they were entirely under guard with no freedom of movement. They were not allowed to sit next to each other or talk to each other. The terminal was largely deserted at this time. Their luggage was taken away for some time. All of their personal items in their checked in luggage and hand baggage were removed, smears were taken for a mass spectrometer and passed through an X-ray machine. Asif was taken to a separate room and strip searched and both were frisked with a hand held detector. The two doctors were then returned to the waiting area again. Whilst in the waiting area they met a 23 year old TEFL teacher of Dutch origin from Washington also facing deportation. She had told the interrogators very clearly that she intended to go to Nablus to teach English, to the same school as the Americans mentioned previously. They insisted on flying her to Istanbul and she could sort herself out from there. The young lady was really upset since she lives in Washington and had no friends in Turkey and how would she find her way home from Turkey! They also met a British Pakistani Christian girl who had been held apart from her Christian pilgrimage group. She was very tearful as she saw no reason for what she described as a humiliating interrogation. She said that they made her feel degraded and treated her like an animal. One of the security guards sat with her and looked through her Bible.

After a further wait under guard they were told they were going to the 'Motel'. They were escorted to a side exit of the Terminal by two guards in police type uniforms who had arrived from elsewhere. They were led to a heavily armoured van, the back door had been left open, and they were asked to leave their luggage including hand baggage in the rear hold that also had two seats. Additionally, they were told to remove their telephones and cameras and to place them with their baggage. They then found themselves being forced into a fully secure central holding area of a vehicle with two layers of heavy black steel armour plating completely encaging the area in which they were forced to sit. There was no lighting in the vehicle and as dark in the caged area of the van as outside. The atmosphere felt somewhat intimidating. Asif thought that they might now face further 'enhanced' questioning, long term detention, rendition or even torture ran through his mind.

After around 15 minutes of being driven away from the airport on Tel Aviv roads they arrived at a place they called the facility. In retrospect they found out that this was the detention centre in Ramle. This was a shabby two storey compound surrounded by high metal fencing, cameras and barbed wires. The area was also patrolled by dogs. They were led to a holding area where they could see lots of luggage. They were stripped of all their personal belongings. Asif insisted they should be allowed to take overnight clothes and reading material. A request to take any writing material was flatly rejected. They were told to take any money they have with them, lockers were available for other items of value such as mobile phones. Swee was not allowed her handbag and told toiletries such as toothbrushes will be supplied. Having been stripped of their belongings they were taken to a waiting area, a more senior guard was behind a glass screen in a room watching 'American Jihadi' on youtube and 'Suits' on a flat screen TV on the wall. Next to this there was another LED panel with a listing of each of the individuals detained, name, destination etc in Hebrew and some English. The guard had their passports with multiple inserts that looked like notes from the interrogators. They were asked if they wanted to eat and were each handed a cold salami roll and given tepid water in an old worn plastic cup. Swee was told 'your embassy representative is on the phone'. An on duty Consular Officer who manned the appropriate desk in London was on the phone, she identified herself as Joanne and asked if they were being treated well and said that she could not do anything for them, and told Swee to phone Mark. Swee then explained to her that they were detained in some kind of facility and all their belongings including mobile phones were taken away, and asked her to please call Mark to let him know. Swee told her that they would be likely to be on the next Easyjet flight back to London hopefully the following day. They were told that they would be in separate parts of the building until the end of their detention.

They were then escorted to their respective areas.

The male section had 4 cells, each with 2 metal double-decker bunk beds, with the bed poles screwed into the wall. This was covered with a thin, hard pad with used sheets and a used blanket, no pillow. Each individual was given a toothbrush and toothpaste but no soap on entry. Upon entry the heavy steel cell door was slammed shut and it was clear that the two of them were formally under detention and they were not in a 'motel'! The cells had a small window with two layers of heavy steel protection to prevent escape. There was a small toilet, shower and sink area that also functioned as the place where meal packages were placed. There was toilet paper in the toilet but no soap. There were three Georgian men in their mid to late

20s in Asif's cell. Each had been there for two to three days and clad in the same outdoor clothes in which they entered. One of them was a professional footballer who had played for Israel. All seemed to spend most of their time lying in their bunks asleep. The sink area was covered in food detritus. There was no drinking water in the cell. The armoured lights were kept on until around 1AM and then switched off centrally. Asif performed his prayers and slept. There was no way of communicating with the captors and getting their attention other than banging on the glass portal in the heavy steel cell door. The back of the toothbrush proved to be useful for this. Unfortunately a request for soap and drinking water was met by an angry response from the middle aged, portly guard who shouted through the glass portal that 'this is not a hotel' and he better not bang on the door again!

The women's cell had 5 double-decker beds screwed into the wall. Each bed had a thin pad, and an unwashed sheet. Swee had no blanket and it was very cold. Lights were controlled by the guards outside and on until 1 am. There was one toilet permanently lit and the window had security glass, heavy metal guards, no curtains so that that the security camera could see everyone sitting on the loo clearly all hours. The shower room was separate and also permanently lit but thankfully there were no windows for the cameras to watch. The toilet and the shower doors could not close and also had no locks. There was a separate sink with one mixer tap. The area around the sink was wet and food and half eaten sandwiches were around the sink, some soaking with water. Heavy steel cell doors ensured confinement.

Asif and Swee were held in this detention centre for 14 hours overnight while waiting for the next flight. The women's side saw 7 Ukrainian women and Swee detained and deported. There were more from the men's side.

The items Swee desperately needed but not there were ear-plugs since her lady fellow inmates snored loudly. They all slept in their outdoor clothes and from the odour had probably been there for some days. They probably could not shower since there were no towels, despite a few bits of dried half used bars of soap lying next to the sink! But the group were well dressed and polite though they spoke no English. They were taken out of the cell separately throughout the night and possibly deported on different flights? After the Ukrainian women left Swee was in solitary confinement. Interestingly, following the departure of the Ukrainians she looked around and noticed the names and messages written by many previous detainees, with messages of solidarity. Some of the messages were written in tooth-paste, others with regular biro and there was one particular message that stood out as it was written in marker pen. It said "You are in good company. Signed Cynthia McKinney, US Congresswoman, 29-30 June 2009; Mairead Maquire, Nobel Peace Prize winner, 29-30 June 2009 Free Gaza 21." Swee thought if only she had her camera to photograph these writings. Swee had met Cynthia McKinney on several occasions and would like to send her a picture of her cell. There was also a heart wrenching message from another "You can prevent me crossing your borders, but you cannot prevent me loving and marrying a Palestinian ... signature illegible". Did she try to enter to marry him? It must have been so painful for the doomed couple. Swee thought of what the woman security officer told her "we are Israelis, we are nice people".

Food was in the form of cold sandwiches and a single ready meal. Swee recalled her detention in 1977 in Singapore, and agreed with the female Israeli guard that the current detention facility in Israel was definitely an improvement. She felt the ordeal must be a sanitised, "five star" version for foreign nationals, compared to the detention for ordinary Palestinians that would certainly include physical abuse and torture.

Swee and Asif were woken at 07:30, salami rolls and black tea in the same old plastic jugs was left in the sink area. After 2 hours a shabby, ill-kempt female guard in her 30s opened the door and saw Asif pacing, she shouted some commands in Arabic and seemed surprised when he responded in English asking if she would repeat that in English! She said 'you, all of you must leave so we can clean!' Asif and his cellmates were escorted out to exercise in the yard area. He encountered the other detainees, 8 Georgians and 6 Ethiopians, the Ethiopians had been detained for some time. Both groups sat in separate areas and smoked, as did the 5 security guards lounging and chatting, looking fairly bored next to the fence that enclosed the area, separating the yard from a cluster of old Palestinian date palms, their height declaring they predate the State of Israel and its war of 'independence', Asif wondered if the area might have been the site of a razed Palestinian village, perhaps one of the many mapped out for transfer (Palestinian ethnic cleansing) under the orders of David Ben Gurion.

Following the return to their cells after an hour or so Swee and Asif were called out to be examined by a Doctor, a man in his late 50s wearing a white coat in a small room next to the counter with the detainees information screen. The doctor was uninterested, had a vagueness about him, he asked if Asif had any allergies and how he was feeling. Asif said 'thirsty' as his previous requests for water had been rejected. The doctor replied, 'oh, sign here!' Asif refused to sign the Hebrew form. Swee signed hers.

DEPORTATION

Asif and Swee were removed from their cells at 14:10 on 19 August, encaged in the same armoured vehicle to Ben Gurion airport. The vehicle stopped at the plane and they were escorted directly on to the Easyjet A320 to Luton. They were asked to move their luggage that was put into the aircraft hold by the security guards which at this point also allowed them to take possession of their hand luggage. The security guards entered the plane with Asif and Swee and handed their passports to the pilot to be held on the flight deck. All of this was in front of a cabin load of Israeli passengers, many of whom took careful note of the humiliation. They were told their passports would only be returned on arrival. The Israeli security guards waited with their armoured deportation vehicle at the side of the plane until it took off. The cabin crew seemed blasé about the manner of deportation suggesting deportation is probably a routine procedure at Tel Aviv airport.

They arrived at Luton Airport to overhear one of their fellow passengers saying loudly "Oh they are firing rockets again. How I wish I had stayed another day in Ashkelon to experience the sirens, the bomb shelters and watch the rockets being intercepted". They were to learn subsequently that 22 Palestinians were killed in Gaza while they were on the Easyjet plane, with 50 wounded. There were no Israeli casualties.